35 TECHNIQUES
EVERY COUNSELOR SHOULD KNOW

Bradley T. Erford

Susan H. Eaves

Emily M. Bryant

and

Katherine A. Young

Merrill

Upper Saddle River, New Jersey
Columbus, Ohio

Library of Congress Cataloging in Publication Data

35 techniques every counselor should know / Bradley T. Erford . . . [et al.].
   p. cm.
Includes bibliographical references and index.
ISBN-13: 978-0-13-170282-0
ISBN-10: 0-13-170282-3
1. Counseling.   2. Counseling psychology.   I. Erford, Bradley T.
II. Title: Thirty-five techniques
   every counselor should know.
BF636.6.A18 2010
158'.3—dc22

2008055854

Vice President and Executive Publisher: Jeffery W. Johnston
Acquisitions Editor: Meredith D. Fossel
Editorial Assistant: Nancy Holstein
Cover Design: Candace Rowley
Cover Image: © Gabriela Medina/SuperStock
Operations Manager: Renata Butera
Director of Marketing: Quinn Perkson
Marketing Manager: Amanda L. Stedke
Marketing Coordinator: Brian Mounts

This book was set in 10/12 Minion by GGS Higher Education Resources, A division of PreMedia Global, Inc. It was printed and bound by RR Donnelley. The cover was printed by RR Donnelley.

Pearson Education Ltd., London
Pearson Education Singapore Pte. Ltd.
Pearson Education Canada, Ltd.
Pearson Education—Japan
Pearson Education Australia, Limited

Pearson Education North Asia, Ltd., Hong Kong
Pearson Educación de Mexico, S.A. de C.V.
Pearson Education Malaysia Pte. Ltd.
Pearson Education Upper Saddle River, New Jersey

Merrill
is an imprint of

www.pearsonhighered.com

10 9 8 7 6 5 4 3 2 1
ISBN-13: 978-0-13170282-0
ISBN-10:   0-13-170282-3

This effort is dedicated to
The One: the Giver of energy, passion, and understanding;
Who makes life worth living and endeavors worth pursuing and accomplishing;
the Teacher of love and forgiveness.

CONTENTS

INTRODUCTION

To some, a book specifically featuring counseling techniques is anathema, an abomination even. From their perspective, counseling is a process and an art; a relationship built between client and professional counselor that is undergirded by the core conditions of genuineness, empathy, and respect as espoused by Carl Rogers, best conducted using effective communication skills, such as those delineated by Ivey and Ivey's Microskills approach, and facilitated using theoretical counseling processes, such as those championed by Glasser, Ellis, Adler, or Perls. We, the authors, couldn't agree more! Counselor education programs all over the world do an excellent job preparing counselors to do all of the above to a high degree of skill.

But what led us to compose this book was the pragmatic realization that even professional counselors who are highly skilled communicators, grounded in a rich theoretical approach, and truly living the core facilitative conditions, sometimes have difficulty moving the client toward the objectives of the counseling experience. Counselors-in-training experience these difficulties very frequently and often desire specific, direct guidance on what to do in these situations to create movement. Specialized techniques, arising from important counseling theories, can provide this movement, when judiciously applied.

This specific training need is the true motivation behind this book. While the techniques in this book are presented one at a time in a deconstructed manner, each has a theoretical genesis and a rich, extant literature base that informs professional counselors about its appropriate and effective use. The techniques presented in this book are clustered within the theoretical domain with which it is most closely associated as outlined in Table 1. Admittedly, categorizing techniques in this manner is imprecise, primarily because several techniques are claimed by multiple theoretical camps. But publishers require a table of contents and formal structure for

TABLE 1 The Techniques Described in this Book, Categorized by Primary Theoretical Approach.

Theoretical Approach	Techniques
Section I: Brief Counseling	Scaling; Exceptions; Problem-Free Talk; Miracle Question; Flagging the Minefield/Mind Mapping
Section II: Adlerian or Psychodynamic	I-Position/I-Messages; Acting As If; Spitting in the Soup; Mutual Storytelling; Paradoxical Intention
Section III: Gestalt	Empty Chair; Body Movement and Exaggeration; Role Reversal
Section IV: Social Learning	Modeling; Behavioral Rehearsal; Role Play
Section V: Cognitive	Self-Talk; Visual/Guided Imagery; Reframing; Thought Stopping; Cognitive Restructuring
Section VI: Behavioral—Positive Reinforcement	Premack Principle; Behavior Chart; Token Economy; Behavioral Contract
Section VII: Behavioral—Punishment	Extinction; Time out; Response Cost; Overcorrection/Positive Practice
Section VIII: Cognitive-Behavioral	Rational-Emotive Behavior Therapy; Bibliotherapy; Deep Breathing; Progressive Muscle Relaxation Training; Systematic Desensitization; Stress Inoculation Training

presentation, so we appreciate the reader's flexibility and gracious forgiveness for categorizing the chapters of this book in such a manner. In truth, we believe that all techniques are integrative in nature and will eventually be categorized as such, because the future of counseling will entail becoming more integrative. But for the time being, various theoretical camps claim certain procedures and techniques within their domains, and Table 1 was constructed to basically demonstrate this artificial partitioning.

Each technique in this book will be presented in a standardized manner. First, the origins of the technique will be presented. Some have a rich history steeped in a single theoretical orientation. Others are more integrated or claimed by several theoretical approaches. Next, each chapter covers the basic steps or procedures for how to implement each technique, followed by common variations of these procedures documented in the literature. In order to demonstrate real life applications of how each technique can be used in counseling, a case example is presented, most including actual transcripts from an actual session. Yes, the transcripts were edited for brevity, clarity, and to remove those distracting affectations clients and professional counselors present in real life (e.g., um's, ah's, divergent thoughts, digressions)! Finally, each technique is evaluated for usefulness and effectiveness using sources from the extant literature. The literature provides a rich source of ideas regarding what each technique has been, or could be, used to address, and how effective it was in addressing those issues. This allows the reader to make empirically based decisions to maximally benefit clients and maximize client outcomes.

Each of the techniques in this book has been selected because of its usefulness and effectiveness in creating client movement toward agreed upon objectives. Of course, writing a measurable behavioral objective is an important issue in itself and will be addressed here at the outset.

MULTICULTURAL COUNSELING AND TECHNIQUES

It has been said that all counseling is multicultural counseling. Each client comes to a session with a unique worldview shaped by various cultural experiences, such as through race, ethnicity, gender, sexual orientation, socioeconomic status, age, and spirituality, among others. Such client worldviews will affect a client's receptiveness to certain theoretical approaches and the resulting techniques or interventions. Multiculturally competent counselors recognize that theories are used in counseling in order to answer "why" questions (e.g., Why is the client seeking counseling? Why is the difficulty occurring? And why now?). Interrelated with this realization, multiculturally competent counselors realize that while the experience of a human being may have some finite limitations, the perceptions and interpretations of these experiences is infinite. Explained another way (Orr, in press), "There is a specific range of emotions that humans are capable of expressing; however, the meaning that is a assigned to those emotions is dynamic and based on the ever-evolving variables of culture and context." Orr proposed that counselors must constantly strive to adapt counseling theory to meet the diverse client needs stemming from this dynamic interplay, all the while realizing that, where culture is involved, within group differences are almost always larger than between group differences. Adapting theories to the individual client context allows counselors to frame client problems in unique ways, creating new challenges—and opportunities—for the application of techniques to problem resolution. In this way, counselors can choose to stay grounded in a primary theoretical orientation while simultaneously integrating techniques into that approach which help to create movement for clients of diverse backgrounds.

So how does a multiculturally competent counselor adapt a theory to fit the unique worldview of a client? While the detailed answer to this question is rooted to the context of each client's dynamic situation, four general guidelines were offered by Orr (in press):

1. *Illuminate Assumptions:* All theories are predicated on certain assumptions about mental health and worldview. Before using your chosen theory with any client you need to familiarize yourself with the associated underlying assumptions.

2. *Identify Limitations:* All theories do not fit all people, so explore the limitations of your chosen theory even before you begin working with clients. Pinpoint the gaps or gray areas in your theoretical orientation and strategize ways to compensate for them.
3. *Simplify Concepts:* Theories are notorious contributors to jargon. Quite often various theories will use multiple terms to refer to similar phenomena. Consider the concept of the therapeutic alliance as first described by Freud. Subsequent theorists have used any number of terms such as partnering, rapport building, etc. to describe the same process. Develop a layman's explanation for your chosen theory that contains easily recognizable concepts in the place of jargon.
4. *Diversify Interventions:* Many theories are accompanied by a particular set of interventions. These interventions may be primary to the theory, but they are by no means the only way to apply that theory. Consider the commonly recognized empty chair technique that involves clients imagining and role-playing a conversation with someone whom they are in conflict with as if that person is actually present. This technique is typically attributed to Gestalt theory but it can be adapted for use with a wide range of theoretical orientations. This technique can be especially useful with clients who have a more collectivist worldview regardless of counselors' primary theoretical orientation. In those situations the empty chair can be occupied by imagined family or community members, elders, or other supporters who might be needed to endorse the particular treatment.

COUNSELING OBJECTIVES

Erford (2007, 2008a, 2008b) provided an easy to implement nuts-and-bolts procedure for how to write measurable objectives using the ABCD model: (A) Audience, (B) Behavior, (C) Conditions, and (D) Description of the expected performance criterion. In individual counseling, audience (A) refers to the individual client. In other types of counseling the audience could be a couple, family, group, or some other system or configuration. Behavior (B) usually refers to what the client and counselor will observe to change as a result of the intervention; that is, the actual behaviors, thoughts or feelings that one will observe to be altered. Conditions (C) refer to the specific contextual applications or actions that will occur. In counseling sessions, this usually refers to the intervention that will be implemented and the context or circumstances surrounding its implementation. The description of the expected performance criterion (D) is usually the quantitative portion of the objective; how much the behavior will increase or decrease.

Counseling goals are differentiated from counseling objectives by the degree of specificity and measurability. A counseling goal is broad and not amenable to direct measurement. A counseling objective, on the other hand, is both specific and measurable. A reasonable goal of counseling may be "to increase a client's ability to manage stress and anxiety." Notice how the wording of a goal is nebulous and not amenable to measurement as stated. In developing a counseling objective related to this goal, particular emphasis is given to specific actions that are measurable. For example, a possible objective stemming from this goal could be, "After learning thought stopping procedures, the client will experience a 50% reduction in episodes of obsessive thinking over a 1-week period." Another possible objective might be, "After learning deep breathing procedures, the client will practice deep breathing for at least 5 minutes, three times a day every day of the week." As a third example, "After implementing time-out with contingency delay procedures, Leroy's display of noncompliant behaviors will decrease from the current average of 25 episodes per week to no more than 5 episodes per week." Notice how the objectives designate the audience, the stated behavior, how the behavior will be addressed, and the level of expected performance (Erford, 2007a, 2008a, 2008b).

Establishing counseling objectives early on in a counseling relationship is important for at least five reasons. First, there is an emerging consensus in the research literature that about half of the progress in counseling occurs within the first eight sessions (Budman & Gurman, 1988; Howard, Kopta, Krause, & Orlinsky, 1986) and one of the best indicators of counseling outcome is whether the counselor and client were able to gain immediate agreement on counseling goals (Tracey, 1986), ordinarily defined as occurring during the first session.

As one can easily see, establishing counseling objectives early in the counseling relationship is the key to successful client outcomes. This doesn't mean that clients will always immediately know or understand the true nature of the problems that bring them to counseling. But it does mean that those clients who can immediately establish counseling objectives are more likely to experience successful outcomes. By extension, it also means that professional counselors skilled at getting clients to develop counseling objectives quickly will be more successful in helping clients reach desired outcomes. It also does not assume that the "real problem" will be identified early on in counseling. Many times, making progress toward obvious, surface-level problems will facilitate the client-counselor trust needed to tackle those deeper psychological issues the client is less likely to reveal early on in a counseling relationship.

Second, counseling objectives provide a concrete, operationalized target of where the counseling process is headed and how both the client and professional counselor will know that progress is being made. As such, objectives allow periodic updates of progress and concrete displays of whether the counseling interventions are having the desired outcomes. In program evaluation we refer to this as formative evaluation, because periodic checks reveal whether the professional counselor should stay the course and continue the current counseling approach, or modify their approach to improve client outcomes.

Third, objectives present targets that initiate movement. Targets are essential in counseling because they motivate clients and, thus, create movement. Indeed, at its core, counseling is all about motivating clients to move in the direction of counseling goals and objectives in a way that empowers clients to be able to continue making progress toward life goals independently after counseling has ended.

Fourth, a well-crafted objective allows the professional counselor to glean effective approaches, interventions, and techniques from the extant counseling literature shown to be useful in helping the client. Counseling has a rich outcomes research literature and this literature informs professional counselors of best practices for resolving client issues. Each technique featured in this text includes a section entitled "Usefulness and Evaluation of . . ." which features outcome research from the counseling literature to guide professional counselors in the effective application of each technique, including the issues each technique has been demonstrated to address and its effectiveness in doing so. Such information informs professional counselors of the appropriate use of each counseling technique.

Finally, a measurable objective lets the client and professional counselor know when counseling has been successful, new objectives can be crafted and pursued, or termination can occur. Objectives serve as the target for success in counseling. It is important to note that each of these five purposes of objectives serve to motivate both the client and counselor, and energize the counseling process. Having gained an understanding of this book's purpose and having discussed the development and effective use of counseling objectives, the reader is now ready to begin a whirlwind tour of "35 Techniques Every Counselor Should Know!" Enjoy!

ACKNOWLEDGMENTS

We thank Megan Earl and Lacey Wallace, graduate assistants extraordinaire, for their tireless assistance in the preparation of the original manuscript. As always, Meredith Fossel, Kevin Davis, and Nancy Holstein of Pearson Merrill Prentice Hall have been wonderfully responsive and supportive. Their production staff included: Mary Irvin and Renata Butera. Finally, special thanks go to the outside reviewers whose comments helped to provide substantive improvement to the original manuscript: Mary Andres, University of Southern California; Sheri Anna Atwater, California State University, Los Angeles; William J. Casile, Duquesne University; Laura Choate, Louisiana State University; Kimberly Nicole Frazier, Clemson University; and Heather C. Trepal, University of Texas at San Antonio.

ABOUT THE AUTHORS

Bradley T. Erford, Ph.D., NCC, LCPC, LPC, received his doctorate in counselor education from The University of Virginia and currently is a professor in the School Counseling Program and Education Specialties Department at Loyola College in Maryland. He is an American Counseling Association (ACA) Fellow and the recipient of ACA's Research Award, Professional Development Award, and Carl Perkins Government Relations Award. He has received the Association for Counselor Education and Supervision's (ACES) Robert O. Stripling Award for Excellence in Standards and the Maryland Association for Counseling and Development's (MACD) Maryland Counselor of the Year, Professional Development, Counselor Visibility, and Counselor Advocacy Awards. His research specialization falls primarily in development and technical analysis of psycho-educational tests. He has published eight books, numerous journal articles and book chapters, and eight psycho-educational tests. He is an ACA – Governing Council Representative; Past Chair of the ACA - Southern (US) Region; Past President of the Association for Assessment in Counseling and Education (AACE); Past President of the Maryland Association for Counseling and Development (MACD); Past President of the MD Association for Counselor Education and Supervision (MACES), Past President of the MD Association for Mental Health Counselors (MAMHC), and Past President of the MD Association for Measurement and Evaluation (MAME). Dr. Erford is the Past Chair of ACA's Task Force on High Stakes Testing, Past Chair of ACA's Task Force on Standards for Test Users, Past Chair of ACA's Public Awareness and Support Committee, Past Chair of ACA's Interprofessional Committee and member of the ACA 20/20 Vision Task Force. Dr. Erford is a Licensed Clinical Professional Counselor, Licensed Professional Counselor, Nationally Certified Counselor, Licensed Psychologist and Licensed School Psychologist. He teaches courses primarily in the areas of assessment, human development, research and evaluation in counseling, school counseling, and stress management (not that he needs it, of course).

Susan H. Eaves, Ph.D., NCC, LPC, received her doctorate in Counselor Education from Mississippi State University. She is the recipient of ACA's Glen E. Hubele National Graduate Student Award, the International Association of Marriage and Family Graduate Research Award, SACES' Emerging Leader Award, Mississippi's Janie G. Rugg Award, Mississippi State University's Faculty and Professional Women's Association Award, Mississippi State University's Women's Award, and Chi Sigma Iota, Mu Sigma Upsilon's Presidential Excellence Award. Dr. Eaves has conducted research and published journal articles and book chapters primarily in the areas of empirically based counseling, personality disorders, research methodology, and sexual relationship behaviors as they relate to gender, attachment, and self-worth. Both nationally certified and state licensed, Dr. Eaves has nearly 10 years of counseling experience working with children, adolescents, and adults. She is currently employed as a behavioral specialist at Weems Children and Youth and serves as graduate adjunct faculty with experience teaching courses in Sexuality, Human Development, Group Techniques, and Personality.

Emily M. Bryant, M.Ed., NCC, is a professional school counselor at Amity Primary Center in Douglassville, Pennsylvania. She earned her school counseling degree at Loyola College in Maryland. She is currently working on a post-master's certificate in counseling at Villanova University.

Katherine A. Young, M.Ed., NCC, is a professional school counselor working in Pennsylvania at the Montgomery County Intermediate Unit. She earned her master's degree in school counseling at Loyola College in Maryland. She holds the NCC credential and plans on pursuing a post-graduate program in the very near future.

Techniques Based Upon Brief Counseling Approaches

Brief counseling approaches have become increasingly popular since the 1980s due to managed care and other accountability initiatives. Brief counseling approaches go by many names, but currently the most prominent orientation is called solution-focused brief counseling (SFBC). SFBC is a social constructivist model underlain by the observation that clients derive personal meaning from the events of their lives as explained through personal narratives. SFB counselors value a therapeutic alliance that stresses empathy, collaboration, curiosity, and respectful understanding, but not expertness. deShazer (1988; 1991) and O'Hanlon and Weiner-Davis (1989) are often credited as scholarly and theoretical forces behind the prominence of SFBC, which de-emphasizes the traditional therapeutic focus on a client's problems, and instead focuses on what works for the client (i.e., successes and solutions) and exceptions in the client's life during which the problems are not occurring. Berg and Miller (1992, p. 17) summed up the SFBC approach very nicely by proposing three basic rules upon which SFB counselors operate: (1) "If it ain't broke, don't fix it," (2) "Once you know what works, do more of it," and (3) "If it doesn't work, don't do it again." It is easy to see the basic appeal of this common sense approach to counseling.

Walter and Peller (1992) proposed five assumptions that expand upon these three basic rules: (1) Concentrating on successes leads to constructive change; (2) Clients can realize that for every problem that exists, exceptions can be found during which the problem does not exist, effectively giving clients the solutions to their problems; (3) Small, positive changes lead to bigger, positive changes; (4) All clients can solve their own problems by exposing, detailing, and replicating successes during exceptions; and (5) Goals need to be stated in positive, measurable, active terms. Sklare (2005) successfully applied SFBC to children and adolescents using the rules and assumptions above to focus on changing client actions rather than insights. Sklare concluded that insights do not lead to solutions; successful actions lead to solutions.

The five techniques covered in this section include scaling, exceptions, problem-free talk, miracle question, and flagging the minefield. Scaling is a very commonly used technique when counseling individuals of nearly any age and from any theoretical perspective. Basically, scaling presents clients with a 10-point (or 100-point) continuum and asks clients to rate where they currently are with regard to, for example, sadness (1) or happiness (10); calm (1) or irate (10); hate (1) or love (10); totally unmotivated (1) or motivated (10). Scaling is helpful in gauging a client's current status on a wide range of issues. It is even more helpful when it is reused periodically to gauge the progress of a client. Scaling is a very quick and helpful assessment technique with wide applicability in counseling.

Exceptions are essential to the SFBC approach because exceptions provide the solutions to the clients "problems." Counselors probe and question the client's background for times when the problem wasn't a problem, determining exceptions and providing the client with alternative solutions to act upon. Problem-free talk is the technique that allows the counselor to turn the counseling intervention from a problem-focused environment to a solution-focused environment. SFB counselors hold the core belief that when clients focus on problems they become discouraged and disempowered, and any insight they might gain into the origin and sustenance of the problem is not therapeutically valuable. A complementary belief is that finding exceptions/solutions to problematic circumstances encourages and empowers clients, leading to actions and successes. The miracle question helps to reconstruct the way a client perceives a problematic circumstance into a vision for success that motivates the client to pursue the actions that will lead to successes.

The final technique is a treatment adherence technique called flagging the minefield. Treatment adherence is critical in any field in which clients or patients seek and receive help. Many, even most, receive the help they seek but then do not follow the treatment regimen, for whatever reason, basically guaranteeing the treatment will not be effective. For example, a patient may go to a doctor to address a medical condition but then not follow the doctor's advice. If medication is prescribed, the patient may not have the prescription filled or may not take the medication according to the doctor's directions. Flagging the minefield is a technique ordinarily implemented during termination that facilitates clients' thinking about situations during which the positive outcomes and strategies learned during counseling may not work, and gets clients thinking ahead of time about what should be done in those circumstances to persevere and succeed. Treatment adherence is a critical issue in counseling; what good is all that hard work and effort to alter problematic thoughts, feelings, and behaviors if the client will return to problematic functioning shortly after termination?

MULTICULTURAL IMPLICATIONS

SFBC is an incredibly culturally respectful approach to working with clients of diverse backgrounds because it discourages diagnoses and focuses on the client's personal frame of reference and encourages clients to integrate and increase actions that have already been shown to be a successful fit for that personal frame of reference. The SFBC approach proposes that the client is the leading expert on what works for the client and the counselor's role is to help the client recognize what the client knows to already work. The counselor then encourages the client to alter his actions and cheerlead the client's successes. SFBC approaches are particularly appreciated by clients who prefer action-oriented, directive interventions and concrete goals (e.g., men, Arab Americans, Asian Americans, Latinos/as). SFBC is one of the more effective cross-cultural approaches because it empowers clients' personal values, beliefs, and behaviors, and does not try to dispute or alter these.

CHAPTER 1

Scaling

ORIGINS OF THE SCALING TECHNIQUE

Scaling is a technique that helps both counselors and clients make complex problems seem more concrete and tangible (De Jong & Miller, 1995). Scaling originated within behavioral approaches to counseling and today also is largely used in solution-focused brief counseling, which was started by de Shazer and arose out of Strategic Family Therapy (Lethem, 2002).

Because client thoughts, feelings, and behaviors are not always realistic or concrete, scaling questions provide a way to move from these more abstract concepts toward an achievable goal (Lethem, 2002). For instance, the counselor can say, "On a scale of 1 to 10, where 1 represents the worst things could be and 10 represents the best things could be, where are you today?" Scaling questions can also help clients to set tasks that will allow them to move to the next rank-order number (Corcoran, 1999). In this way, scaling can help measure client progress over time. Scaling techniques give clients a sense of control and responsibility over their therapy because scaling techniques help the clients specify goals for change as well as measure their progress toward those goals (Corcoran, 1997).

HOW TO IMPLEMENT THE SCALING TECHNIQUE

Scaling questions usually involve asking the client to give a number between 1 and 10 that indicates where the client is at some specified point (De Jong & Miller, 1995). The counselor designates 10 as the more positive end of the scale, such that higher numbers equal a more positive outcome or experience. Scaling can be used to identify goals or to help the client progress towards an already established goal. Clients can identify goals by identifying specific behavioral indicators that signify they have reached a 10 on the scale (Corcoran, 1999).

Once a goal has been established, scaling techniques can be used to help the client move towards reaching the goal. After the client has identified where he is on the scale with 10 being that he has reached the goal, the counselor can ask questions to discover what small steps the client could take to reach the next rank-order number (Corcoran, 1999). Questions include: What would you take as an indication that you have moved to a number 6? What would you be doing then? (Lethem, 2002). Scaling also provides an opportunity for counselors to compliment client's progress by using questions such as, "How did you get from a 1 to a 5?"

VARIATIONS OF THE SCALING TECHNIQUE

Instead of using a 1 to 10 scale, scaling can be shown pictorially for small children (Lethem, 2002). For instance, professional counselors can use a range of facial expressions from frowning to smiling or numbered steps leading to the desired change. When using scaling in a group, it is important to ask each person for a rating (Lethem, 2002). Differences should be explored to discover the reasons behind these differences. In addition, relationship scaling questions can be used to help clients identify the perspectives of other people in their lives (Corcoran, 1999). Clients can be asked, "How do you think your parents (or teachers) would rank you?" These answers can then be compared to the client's self-rating, which often forces clients to realize what actions they need to take in order show others the improvements they've made (Corcoran, 1997).

EXAMPLES OF THE SCALING TECHNIQUE

Following are several short scenarios for which scaling would be appropriate and useful to assist both the client and professional counselor in viewing or assessing the problem in a more tangible way.

EXAMPLE 1: Scaling used to reduce catastrophic thinking

Mary (M):   I'm completely panicked. Thinking about my first day of school, and not as a student, but actually as a teacher . . . me, a teacher . . . is sending me right over the edge.

Counselor (C):   Right over the edge?

M: (Speaking rapidly) Right over the edge. Like, just thinking about it makes me want to throw up. I really don't think I can do it.

C: I can see how nervous you seem even now, just from talking about it.

M: I am! Thinking about it, talking about it . . . if I can't handle that, how am I going to handle it when I actually get to that moment? You know? I'm a basket case.

C: Okay. All right, I'd like to try something with you for a moment. I'd like you to go ahead and close your eyes for a second and picture your first day of school, okay? You're in front of your class. (Pause) You're getting ready to teach a new lesson that you've never taught before. (Pause) Your new classroom is full of your new students. (Pause) They are sitting in their seats, looking at you. (Pause) Now, go ahead and feel the emotions that come up. Don't try to prevent them or hold them back. (Speaking very slowly) Feel the anxiety, and the fear, and the dread. Feel any emotion that may come up. Okay, now can you describe to me how you're feeling?

M: Um, I have this nauseous feeling in my stomach. Um, my palms are kind of sticky or sweaty or something. Um, I'm kind of concerned about the students and what they're thinking and making sure that um, you know, they're gonna like my lesson. There's a lot of thoughts going through my head about what's gonna happen in the next few minutes or whenever I get started. I'm just really anxious . . . my feelings and thoughts.

C: Okay, on a scale from 1 to 10, with 10 being really, really extremely anxious—like you probably wouldn't even be able to stand up there—and 1 being very confident and comfortable, where do you think you'd be on that scale?

M: Um . . . I guess maybe like a 6.

C: Okay, so that doesn't sound quite so terrible. You could probably get through the lesson at a 6, yeah?

M: Yeah, I guess I could. It wouldn't be the most comfortable or enjoyable experience, but you're right, I could definitely get through it. It just feels so much worse sometimes though . . . like the dreading it is the worst part maybe.

C: Uh-huh. That could be true.

M: I just feel like something will go terribly wrong, and I get myself so worked up.

C: All right, then. Let's try this. Tell me, and I bet you've already thought about it, tell me what the worst thing is that could realistically happen on that first day of you being the teacher.

M: Hmm. (Laughs slightly) I have actually thought about it . . . Sometimes I visualize that the students, just a few at first, lose interest in the lesson. More and more they become disinterested and a few of them begin talking to one another. Then more students begin to follow their lead, and they begin to giggle and talk louder so that it is very obvious they are not paying attention to me. Pretty soon, the entire class is chaotic and doing what they please and not one student is attending to the lesson.

C: Okay, so you have thought about that! On a scale of 1 to 10 again, with a 10 being a catastrophic, career-ending, mortifying event that you absolutely could not get through, and a 1 being no big deal at all, where would this scenario that you've visualized fall?

M: A 5.

C: Now, not to say that your anxiety is not justified, but to help you view it more objectively, let's scale it against another event. Okay, so thinking about the worst thing that could ever happen to you in life in general . . . the very worst thing in life . . . someone you love being murdered, your child being kidnapped, something that horrific . . . with that in mind, now rescale the visualized classroom event. With 10 being catastrophic and 1 being no big deal, where would you place the classroom event?

M: Like a 1 or 2. In the big scheme of things, it's not a big deal at all. It would be a little embarrassing if the other teachers saw I couldn't handle my own class, but other than that, really not that big a deal after all.

C: Okay. And if the worst case scenario of that day is actually only a 1 or 2, then how will that change where your anxiety level would be on that scale of 1 to 10?

M: Way lower. Way, way lower. Really nothing beyond a few first day jitters.

Counselor (C):   So Amy, so far Mollie has been sort of reporting on her progress and how she's doing in moving toward her goals . . . which is a necessary condition to her living with you . . . that she make movement toward her goals and keep her life, you know, going in a positive direction.

Amy (A):   Yes, she is making some progress.

C: Okay. You know, to really make sure and to monitor your sister's progress, let's set up some kind of monitoring system to help you make sure that she's following through—that she wants to, so that your confidence will increase as well as your seeing her meet these goals.

A: Okay.

C: So thinking about your perception of Mollie's motivation to change and follow through with her goals, currently, in comparison to when you two first came in to see me, on a scale from 0 to 100, with 100 being extremely confident that Mollie is moving in a positive direction and definitely going to follow though with and accomplish her goals, and 0 meaning you have no confidence at all and see no real progress being made, or even any effort on her part—where do you think you lie on that scale?

A: Um, (Thinking) I would say probably about a 65.

C: 65?

A: Yeah.

C: Okay, well that's 35%, you know, 35 points to go before we get to 100. That's not bad at all! What is it about the 65? Tell me a little bit about that 65.

A: Um, well, the reason I'm not higher than 65 is that she hasn't started saving any money for the courses that are starting really soon and I don't know that she's going to have much financial help so that kind of worries me. But at the same time, um, this past weekend she was studying for her GED. So I think she's serious about that. She's registered for her classes at this college so that's why it's a little bit higher, but the money thing kind of worries me.

C: Okay, so the 65 comes from the studying for the GED and the registering for classes. But the other 35 points comes from the lack of money or effort towards saving?

A: Yes. And I think that sounds fair (looking over at Mollie).

C: Mollie, what do you think about this 65? Is this where you would place your progress and motivation?

Mollie (M):   Well, when you were first asking Amy that question, I was thinking around 80 or 85 even. But then listening to her explain how she came up with that number . . . well, I guess a 65 makes sense. (Thinking) I don't know, maybe a little higher than a 65 just because I know my motivation for change is high, but I can't expect anybody else to know that because it's inside of me.

C: Yes. Everyone else can gauge your motivation only by looking at your actions.

EXAMPLE 3: Scaling in personal relationships

Counselor (C):   Well, what I believe I'm hearing from both of you is that you "can't" talk to the other. Kevin, you said Tamara "can't have a conversation without picking a fight" and, Tamara, you said that Kevin "ignores me and says almost nothing" when you try to talk to him. (Pauses) But you both feel that you are the better communicator in the relationship?

Kevin (K):   Yes.

Tamara (T):   I at least try. He doesn't even bother. And I don't see how we are going to get through some of our issues if we can't even communicate with each other about them.

C: I agree that communication is going to be very important to working through these other dilemmas and feelings. So perhaps we should focus some of our attention on improving communication. Kevin, what are your thoughts on this?

K: We've never been really good at talking things through. But everything just seemed to work itself out anyway—until now. So, I'd love for you to help Tamara have a conversation without making it into something more.

C: Well, what I'd like to do is help you both improve *yourselves* and the way *you* communicate. Okay. Here is a sheet of paper for each of you. On the bottom half of the paper, I'd like you to give yourself a score from 1 to 10 based on how well you think you communicate, with 1 being a terrible communicator and 10 being a great communicator. (Both Kevin and Tamara were able to do this very quickly with little thought.) Now, on the other half of the paper, on the top half, I want you to each think for a moment about the way your spouse communicates with you. After this, we will change the focus to yourselves, but for this last moment, you get to focus on your spouse and their shortcomings. All right, so for now, thinking about how your spouse communicates with you, I want you to give them a score from 1 to 10, with 1 being the worst communicator ever . . . everything they do leads to problems and miscommunications rather than effective communication. Now a 10 would indicate that you find your spouse to be a very effective communicator and find that the end result of a conversation is satisfying and the reason it was begun was accomplished. (Gives them both a few moments to write down a number) Okay, I would like to hear what each of you has.

T: I'll go first. Do you want to know what we put for ourselves or just for the other person?

C: Um, however you want to do it is fine.

T: Okay. Well, I gave myself an 8 because there are probably one or two minor things I could do a little better, but for the most part, I am an effective communicator, just based on what I do.

C: Ummhmm.

T: Okay, and so I gave Kevin a 4 . . .

K: (Interrupting) A 4???!!!

T: Yes, a 4, because if he's involved, it's just bound to go badly.

C: And what about you, Kevin, what did you write down?

K: Well, I gave myself a 9 because I'm not the problem here. And I gave Tamara a 6.

C: The great news is neither of you scored the other as a 1 so you both agree that the other does some things right with regards to communication. Okay. I want to ask you both if you would now be willing to completely scratch out the score you gave for yourself.

T: Why?

C: Well, if we assumed, Tamara, that you really were an 8 on a scale of 1 to 10, and you, Kevin, really were a 9, we wouldn't have a lot to work on. You would both be nearly perfect communicators. Instead, I'd like to help you both to let go of your self-perceived communication skills and to focus on how your partner perceives you. If we are going to improve, we have to really consider how our partner sees us. Tamara, the way Kevin perceives you is as important as the way you perceive him. And the same is true for you, Kevin. And as long as we feel we are near-perfect at this, we won't improve. So, if you're willing, I'd like for you to each scribble over the number you gave yourself and trade papers, and now let's operate from the assumption that you, Tamara, are a 6, and you, Kevin. are a 4.

T: I'll change his to a 5.

C: Okay, Kevin, you are a 5.

K: Can I change hers to a 5 so we're the same?

T: No! (Laughing somewhat) (Kevin laughs.)

C: Now, with your new numbers, I'd like you to both consider what's keeping you from being a 10.

K: (After some thought) Well, I can be pretty defensive sometimes when she tries to talk to me, and I'm bad about tuning her out.

C: That's certainly a good start. Tamara? What about your new score? What do you suppose keeps it from being a 10?

T: Well, I suppose I don't always pick the best time to start a discussion and, um, I tend to dominate the conversation and get angry . . .

EXAMPLE 4: Scaling to recognize old baggage and personal reactions

Dorothy (D): I just get so angry. I really lose my cool and I don't even know why I get that mad. She just makes me so . . . I could just . . . scream . . . well, I do, I mean, I do scream. Not at her of course. But as soon as I hang up the phone, I just scream as loud as I can to get it all out. Like, the other day, she called to tell me happy birthday, and it wasn't my birthday, it was my sister's. And I just kidded with her about getting older and forgetful, but then I couldn't wait to get off the phone because I was just boiling inside. And as soon as I hung up, I screamed . . . and cried. I really don't get it . . . why I let her push my buttons like that . . . over something so silly that she probably really can't even help, because she really is getting older.

Counselor (C): This phone call with your mother is a good example for us to work with to maybe help you gain some insight into your reactions.

D: Okay. How?

C: Your reaction the other day, after you hung up the phone, on a scale of 1 to 100, with 1 being no reaction at all, no emotional reaction whatsoever, and 100 being this huge, overwhelming, uncontrollable emotional reaction, what would you say your reaction the other day was on this scale?

D: (Looking down and fidgeting) Um, well, let's see . . . I guess it would have been about a 90. It felt very uncontrollable and overwhelming . . . it just swallowed me.

C: Okay. Now, realistically, what your mom said on the phone, about the birthday when it wasn't your birthday, but your sister's, on a scale of 1 to 100, with 1 being no big deal and 100 being just this terrible thing for a person to do to you, what was your mother's comment?

D: Give her comment a number too?

C: Yes, from 1 to 100 if you can.

D: Well, because I know she didn't do it intentionally, I would say like a 15, I guess.

C: Okay, Dorothy. We have a comment at a 15 and a reaction at a 90.

D: Yeah, yeah, we, uh, we do, don't we? How does that happen?

C: Let's think for a moment about what 16 through 89 represent. Usually when we get a 15 and we react with a 90, there is much more there that accounts for our reaction. What are all those other numbers about do you suppose? What button did your mother's comment push?

D: (Thinks for a moment while still looking down and begins to cry) I feel so bad for even saying this, and I know I should be past it by now, and I try so hard to be grateful for her *pathetic* attempts at being a mother now, but she *still* can't get it right and I just want to *scream* because every time I talk to her its this *ridiculous* reminder that she still sucks! (Crying harder) She walked out on us when we were kids because her boyfriend was more important and he didn't like kids, so she chose him over us and we didn't for the life of us understand why she had left us or what we had done wrong, and God that was so long ago and she's apologized a hundred times, but she still is not . . . she'll *never* be the mother I need her to be. I'll *never* get over what she did to us. (Angrily) We weren't important enough for her to stay with us then and we're not important enough for her to know when our damn birthdays are now!

EXAMPLE 5: Scaling in suicide assessments

Counselor (C): So, John, your life right now, how you feel about your life, on a scale of 1 to 10, with a 1 being satisfying and relatively happy and a 10 being unbearable, where would you say your life falls on this continuum?

John (J): Like a 9 or something.

C: Okay, and the likelihood of you harming yourself, even killing yourself as you've been considering lately, on a scale of 1 to 10, with 1 being totally no intention to hurt yourself and a 10 being definitely going to commit suicide, where would you say you are right now?

J: Probably an 8 or maybe even 9 again.

C: (Pauses for a moment) John, I don't know if this is true for you, but I've noticed that when I've worked with others that feel as you do at this moment, I've noticed something very interesting. I've noticed that almost always, they don't *really* want to die necessarily . . . they just don't want to keep living at a 9. (Pauses) Might that be true for you also, John?

J: I never thought about it like that. I mean, (thinking out loud) "I don't really want to die, I just don't want to keep living at a 9." (Thinking again) You know, I can see where that fits . . . but if I don't know how *not* to live at a 9, then I feel like I only have one choice.

C: Yes, yes, I can see that. So if you'd be willing, I'd like for us to work together right now to consider how we can get you from a 9 to a . . . .

J: Anything would be better than a 9.

C: Okay, then, let's work together to see how we can get you to anything better than a 9. What are some things that you need to be different in order for life to be better than a 9?

USEFULNESS AND EVALUATION OF THE SCALING TECHNIQUE

Scaling techniques tend to measure progress towards concrete goals; consequently, they lend themselves to outcomes research (Lethem, 2002).

SAVE YOUR RECEIPT !!!

LYNCHBURG COLLEGE BOOKSTORE

Book Return Refund Policy
- Fall 2009 -

No returns on textbooks unless you drop the class

- ➤ Refunds for used textbooks available until September 11.
- ➤ Refunds for new (unmarked) textbooks available until September 25.
- ➤ Textbooks for Fall classes may not be available after September 25, so be sure to purchase all textbooks and course materials before September 25.

- ➤ You MUST have your sales receipt.
- ➤ New books must be in NEW UNMARKED condition.
- ➤ NO REFUNDS on textbooks or software if shrinkwrap has been removed.
- ➤ NO REFUNDS on optional purchase (recommended) textbook (note shelf tag).

<u>STORE HOURS</u>: 9 a.m.-4 p.m. Weekdays

Visit our web site at
www.lynchburg.edu/Bookstore
for special hours, announcements,
selling used books,
student accounts and more !!

SAVE YOUR RECEIPT !!!

A Guide to Selling Used Books

You don't have to sell your books at the buyback! If you value your book more than you are offered for it, just say you would rather keep it.

If an instructor has placed an order for your book to use next semester, we can buy it back for half of the new price, whether you bought it new or used. Once the bookstore has bought back all it needs, the book is bought 'wholesale'. Wholesale means you will be paid at best, 25% of the retail price, if it is a current edition. You may be offered less or nothing if there is no demand for the book nationally or if there is a new edition.

If you have any specific questions about selling books, stop by the bookstore or email us at mccombie@lynchburg.edu

TEXTBOOK BUYBACKS
Aug 27-28: 10 a.m.-4 p.m
December 14-18: 8:30 a.m. -3:30p.m.
December 19: 11 a.m. – 1 p.m.

Scaling can be used in a wide variety of situations. Some examples include assessment of progress toward a solution, confidence about finding a solution, motivation, severity of a problem, the likelihood of hurting self or others, and self-esteem (De Jong & Miller, 1995). Scaling has also been used with youth involved with the juvenile justice system and their families (Corcoran, 1997) as well as with families involved with child welfare services (Corcoran, 1999). Juveniles from multiproblem families, low socio-economic status (SES), or from diverse backgrounds improved on their treatment goals.

CHAPTER 2

Exceptions

ORIGINS OF THE EXCEPTIONS TECHNIQUE

According to Presbury, Echterling, and McKee (2002, p. 75), "Finding exceptions is the quintessential technique of resolution counseling. The exception—a time when the problem is not happening—is a resolution that the client has already achieved, however temporarily." The origin of the exceptions technique lies in the assumption that all problems have exclusions that can be used to facilitate solutions. Typically, as humans, we view our problems as having always occurred, as constant, and as unrelenting even for brief moments. If we do recognize exceptions to the problem, we tend to deny their significance. This is most likely due to the way the brain filters, processes, and stores information. However, most every situation has a time period, however brief, where the problem was not a problem at all. Professional counselors must listen closely for these exceptions, point them out, and use them to facilitate solutions. In this way, clients gain hope and are empowered by their own ability to affect their environment.

HOW TO IMPLEMENT THE EXCEPTIONS TECHNIQUE

The exceptions technique can be used in a nondirective way where the professional counselor is constantly listening for an instance of when the problem was either improved, even if only slightly, or did not exist at all (e.g., "She never listens. The only person who can get through to her is her grandmother"). This complaint, or description of the problem, contains an exception that is going unnoticed and unutilized.

"Problems never always happen. Exceptions always do" (Presbury et al., 2002, p. 74). But because clients often do not recognize their own exceptions or give credence to them, the professional counselor must notice them and use them effectively. After all, it is rare to find clients who seek counseling to communicate about the times they were trouble free. Likewise, professional counselors have been trained historically to listen for the details of the problem. In order for the exceptions technique to be of use, counselors must retrain their ears to listen for the potential solution, sources of strengths, and personal resources.

For example, consider the case in which a 16-year-old female complains weekly of the conflict in her home. She and her twin brother in particular have vicious battles on a daily basis, almost unable to tolerate each other's presence in the same room. One week she comes in for her session and briefly mentions the past week's happenings and in so doing states, "Me and Tony went to the mall. He drove us there so I could hang out with my friends while he shopped for a present for his girlfriend." This is an exception and one that could easily go unnoticed by the counselor! Instead, it should be pursued and elaborated upon in a way that enables the client to identify what was different about this day that she and her brother not only refrained from fighting but actually had a positive collaborative encounter. When pointed out, if the client's response is similar to, "I guess he just decided to stop being such a jerk for a day," continue to facilitate a personal focus. The counselor might respond, "Perhaps. But let's pretend that it was more than that . . . that maybe there was something *you* did differently that helped lead to that exception."

The exceptions technique can also be used directly by asking questions like, "Tell me about a time when . . ." or "How close have you come . . ." These questions are also helpful after the answer to the miracle question (see chapter 4) is formulated. The professional counselor can ask if any part of the miracle is already occurring or if the client can recall a time when it did occur. The counselor will then want to listen for what the client did differently that led to the absence or improvement of the problem.

VARIATIONS OF THE EXCEPTIONS TECHNIQUE

Exceptions can be listened for and pointed out. They can be asked for directly. As a technique it can be combined with the miracle question (see chapter 4). It can also be combined with scaling. When expected exceptions do not immediately make themselves known, the client can be given a task designed to illuminate exceptions to the problem. The task variation entails giving the client an assignment between sessions that generally takes the form: "Between now and our next session, pay attention to (take note of, list times) when you experience part of the miracle (notice less of the problem, respond in a way that is helpful). . . . "

When directly asking for exceptions, the professional counselor must use caution as certain phrasing of the technique could lead a client to feel patronized or his concern trivialized. Make certain that pointing out exceptions heard through the telling of the problem is done in a way that is hopeful and reminiscent of cheerleading (i.e., "Wow, how'd you manage to get through that? Most people couldn't have done it!")

(Sklare, 2005). When directly asking for exceptions, make sure to validate client concerns and perspectives before respectfully inquiring "Your situation seems especially difficult. Can you recall a time when you remember feeling better than you do right now?"

In addition to delicate phrasing, the exceptions question can also be asked in a way that focuses on the circumstances or environment (i.e., "What is going on around you at that time that is different than at other times?" or "Who is around during the times the problem seems less noticeable?") or with follow-up questions that emphasize client resources (i.e. "What are you doing differently that could be leading to this exception in the problem?" or "What have you been able to do since our last session to cause an exception to occur?"). Regardless of the variation or follow-up, always ask in a way that presumes there are in fact exceptions, and always have the client elaborate on the exception with enough detail to assist in formulating a solution.

EXAMPLE OF THE EXCEPTIONS TECHNIQUE

Stan is a 12-year-old boy who has been missing school more and more frequently, stating physical illness as his most common reason for his absences. After a thorough physical examination by his medical doctor, it was recommended to Stan's mother that she seek counseling services for Stan, as the root of his somatic complaints were presumed to be something other than medical in nature. Upon meeting Stan, he comes across as both emotionally mature and intelligent, though lacking in social skills and confidence. He immediately begins talking about his strong dislike of his new school and the difficulty he has had making friends and getting through the day without being teased relentlessly.

Stan (S): I wish I never had to go back there. I just don't seem to fit in. It's real clique-ish. It's like if you didn't grow up here or you don't have lots of money . . . they just . . . they're just brutal.

Counselor (C): The other students?

S: Yeah, it's bad. Really bad. It's like they targeted me from day one and haven't let up since.

C: Really bad how?

S: Really bad as in there's nothing about me that seems to please anybody around there. They find fault with everything about me. And it's constant. It's like I can't get a moment of peace around there. It starts as soon as I set foot on campus and doesn't let up until I leave. It's never-ending.

C: I can see why you don't like going.

S: Seriously, right? Who wants to go through that every single day of their life? They invaded my locker the first week of school. I don't know how they got in it . . . I can't even get in it half the time . . . which is something else I get made fun of for. Anyway, they went through it and found some song lyrics I had written in one of my notebooks and xeroxed them and posted them all over the place. That's when it began, and it hasn't stopped.

C: Wow. That would feel like an invasion of privacy.

S: Yeah. Those were personal to me. You know? A lot of it was about how I missed my old girlfriend and my old home town and stuff. I got labeled a cry baby because of it. That's where the nicknames came from—"Stan's Not the Man", "Stan the Man . . . Not!", "Stanny Wanny Wants to be a Manny." It's ridiculous. It's awful is what it is. And nothing I do will change it. I swear some days I think I'm gonna lose it. For real.

Up to this point, the professional counselor has facilitated Stan's telling of the story and has provided support and validation. The counselor will now ask a form of the exceptions question in a supportive way to avoid the client feeling trivialized.

C: It really does sound like a very difficult situation for you. And yet you've almost made it through the entire school year. Most people would've already "lost it." Yet you haven't. How have you been so strong?

S: I don't think I have. I've obviously not been able to stop it from happening. And I keep missing school to avoid it.

C: But you've not "lost it," so you're doing something right.

S: I try to tell myself that it doesn't matter . . . that these people don't matter to me . . . or won't in the future . . . that this is all temporary and it will be different one day.

C: So you try to put it into perspective, realize that it's just a small part of your life and that it won't feel this terrible down the road, not as terrible as it feels now when you're in the middle of it.

S: Yeah. I try. It helps. I also think about how, when I get real down on myself and feel like I'm worthless, I also think about how many friends I had at my old school and that people really did like me. That helps too . . . helps me feel less like a loser.

C: Good. So putting it in perspective and thinking about a time when you were well liked and treated fairly help you keep from "losing it."

S: Exactly. But it doesn't make the problem go away. It just keeps me from making it a lot worse.

C: Fair enough. So tell me, Stan, can you think of a time since you started your new school when the problem didn't seem quite so bad?

S: It always seems bad.

C: I bet. I bet. (Pauses) But maybe there was a break in the teasing or an incident where they were nice to you?

S: They've never been nice, but sometimes I do get a break . . . usually around fourth period.

C: What's fourth period?

S: History. They don't seem to be as bad around the time of my history class.

C: What so different about history class?

The counselor wants to assess for situational or environmental exceptions.

S: Oh, it's just because of Jason being around at that time.

C: Who's Jason?

S: He's this really cool guy. Everybody respects him and he's nice to me so none of those jerks give me a hard time when he's around.

C: Good! That's great news! Right? That one of the well-respected cool guys likes you and takes up for you?

S: Yeah. Thank goodness for him, or it would really be unbearable!

C: Okay, so we're really glad about Jason. But tell me, Stan, how are you different when Jason's around?

Now the counselor wants to bring the exception back to being influenced by something Stan is doing.

S: What do you mean?

C: Well, I'd be willing to bet that you come across a little differently around time for fourth period. What do you think?

S: I'm probably breathing a sigh of relief, that's for sure.

C: I bet you're right. What does that look like?

S: I'm probably a little calmer, more relaxed, less nervous and tense. I know I'm about to have some positive interaction instead of all the negative.

C: Good. What else?

S: You mean what else am I like?

C: Yes. What else are you doing differently around fourth period?

S: Well, I probably don't look so down and out. Probably don't walk with my head down, staring at my feet.

C: Good. So that would mean you look and walk how?

S: Well . . . hmm, I've never thought about this . . . I mean, I guess I would have to say that if I'm not looking down and out and I'm not staring at the ground then I'm probably looking a little more upbeat and holding my head up.

C: Exactly. Do you think you might look a little more confident around fourth period?

S: Sure.

C: Less like a target of bullying?

S: Definitely.

C: Do you think that has anything to do with why they leave you alone around that time? Not just because of Jason?

S: I never thought about it that way . . . maybe I guess . . . yeah, maybe . . . sure.

C: Do you think you could do more of that? Even when Jason is not around? Just try it . . . oh let's say, during second period each day this week and see what happens?

S: Definitely worth a try!

Stan is now enthused because he's been validated, he's realized there is an exception to his misery, and even more importantly, he's realized he may play some part in that exception, meaning he may have some control over this situation.

USEFULNESS AND EVALUATION OF THE EXCEPTIONS TECHNIQUE

In general, finding exceptions to problems is a basic tenet of solution-focused brief counseling approaches and is beneficial for identifying strengths and resources within the client that are already being used to create instances where the problem is no longer a problem. In this way clients begin to view their situations with an internal locus of control, thereby increasing their responsibility for events. The exceptions technique is also useful in helping clients view brief moments of relief as keys to solving problems.

The literature showed beneficial results with various populations and settings when utilizing solution-focused methods, including the exceptions technique. In 1998, Corcoran described effectively using a solution-focused approach to work with middle and high school at-risk youths. A year later, in 1999, she continued by demonstrating the utility of exceptions and other solution-focused methods while working with Child Protective Services clients. Both of these populations are noted as resistant to treatment and oftentimes involve involuntary treatment. Additional studies have documented the effectiveness of the exceptions technique in combination with other solution-focused approaches in working to produce positive change with behavioral problems in an inclusive classroom (Quigney & Studer, 1999), violence in a psychiatric inpatient facility (Oxman & Chambliss, 2003), with families (Reiter, 2004), and with juvenile offenders (Corcoran, 1997).

CHAPTER 3

Problem-Free Talk

ORIGINS OF THE PROBLEM-FREE TALK TECHNIQUE

George, Iveson, and Ratner (1990) established problem-free talk as an important solution-focused technique useful for establishing a connection with clients. Through this tool, the professional counselor engages the client and/or the client's family in discussion of the positives in life and what is currently going well and working for them, getting to know them as people first. As with other solution-focused techniques, problem-free talk is a purposeful tool to illicit conversation that will reveal strengths and resources. It has been realized that the presence of abilities, interests, resources, and strengths is as important as the absence of complaints, illness, stress, and symptoms.

Problem-free talk serves several purposes. First, it is useful in the beginning of a helping relationship to develop rapport with the individual, couple, or family seeking counseling services as it demonstrates that you are interested in them as a person. Second, it is helpful in abating nervousness about the counseling process, which many people new to counseling services can feel is mysterious. Third, it can undo the power imbalance that is assumed by many clients to exist, so that the professional counselor seems like a person rather than an all-knowing expert. Most importantly to solution-focused brief counseling however, engaging in problem-free talk can provide an opportunity for the counselor to see the client defined by something other than the presenting problem, and in doing so, allows for identification of strengths and resources that should be noted for future use in solutions.

HOW TO IMPLEMENT THE PROBLEM-FREE TALK TECHNIQUE

More than simple chit-chat (Sharry, 2004), problem-free talk is to be used intentionally both at the beginning of the counseling process, at any time throughout the session or range of services, and anytime a new family member is introduced into the counseling setting (Rhones & Ajmal, 1995). Problem-free talk oftentimes occurs naturally at the onset of the first session and at the beginning of subsequent sessions as a result of socialization. However, as naturally as it may come, the professional counselor should be intentionally listening during this time specifically for the client's competencies and potential. These should then be noted and used later as exceptions to problems, as material for the preferred future, and as part of the solution.

When problem-free talk does not occur naturally at the beginning of counseling, the professional counselor can ask specific questions to elicit it. Typically, these questions take the form of, "Before discussing your problem further, I'd like to hear more about you. What is it you enjoy doing and feel especially good at?" Other tag-on questions could include, "What do you feel you have handled well?" and "How have you coped in the past?" and "What good things might others say about you?" Another version of this could be, "Tell me what your life was like before all this began. What were you like as a person?" The professional counselor should join into this conversation so that it has a light and natural feel to it. During this two-way conversation, the counselor should listen for times when the client has had better experiences and for positive attributes the client possesses.

The professional counselor must be careful to engage in this talk either at the beginning, prior to the discussion of client concerns, or wait until a respectful amount of time has passed and the client has been given the opportunity to discuss the problem as fully as necessary. Otherwise, to switch the focus to problem-free talk may appear insensitive, disrespectful, annoying, or patronizing (Lowe, 2004; Rhones & Ajmal, 1995). Lowe further warns that clients may not benefit from lengthy problem-free talk, may simply want to discuss the problem at hand, or may be hostile so that talking about positives would be counterproductive.

VARIATIONS OF THE PROBLEM-FREE TALK TECHNIQUE

Problem-free talk can be initiated at the beginning of counseling to get to know the client, at any time during the counseling session to take a break from heavy problematic story-telling, or throughout the course of therapy to specifically elicit resources for a solution. When new members enter the counseling relationship, it is important to engage in problem-free talk to put the new member at ease and also to catch a glimpse of the interactions and relationships between members outside of the problem situation. Questions or statements used to facilitate this talk can range from "Tell me more about yourself as a person" to "What positive things do you have going on for you in your life at this time?" Essentially, the timing, intention, and form of problem-free talk can vary.

Sharry (2004) also suggested variations of this technique by using it as a game or exercise in family counseling where the members of the family pretend to be one another and state their greatest asset, name their favorite family trip or times together, or develop and draw pictures of their family motto.

EXAMPLE OF THE PROBLEM-FREE TALK TECHNIQUE

Jaylen, age 17 years, and her mom, age 35 years, frequently engage in extremely volatile conflicts where they scream obscenities at one another, throw items occasionally, and make threats such as, "maybe I'll just die and then you'll be sorry." Jaylen is what most would define as a "good kid," working part-time at the same job for over a year, staying out of trouble in school, obeying most rules at home with the exception of curfew violation from time to time, and maintaining well above passing grades. However, she and her mom are very similar in their conflict style and "do battle," as they call it, far too often. Up to this point in counseling, Mom has been in only one time and Jaylen has insisted on coming to counseling alone to work on issues unrelated to Mom. Today, Mom is coming in with Jaylen as requested to begin focusing on their relationship now that other concerns have abated. Upon first entering the counselor's office, the following takes place.

Counselor (C):   Hi, Mom! So glad you're with us today!

Mom (M):   Yeah, I didn't think Jaylen was ever going to ask me to come. I was just trying to give her space . . . you know how she is . . . all particular and stuff!

Jaylen (J):   Whatever! (Playfully said)

C: So what good things have been happening for you two this week?

M: God, we've had a crazy week! I was so proud of Jaylen. This other mom came in the mall where she works and started going off on her because she and her daughter are in an argument over a boy right now. Normally, I wouldn't put it past Jaylen to go off on some woman that came up to her like that. I mean, Lord, her daughter isn't four! She can take up for herself! But Jaylen didn't. She just smiled and nodded.

The counselor notes this as an exception and praises Jaylen.

C: Wow, Jaylen. Impressive. How'd you manage to hold your tongue so well?

The counselor is briefly cheerleading and asking for details to this exception.

J: I didn't want to get in trouble at work. I really respect my boss.

This is important information to use to decrease conflicts between mom and Jaylen: respect for another equals ability to respond appropriately and avoid conflict.

C: Good, good. What else? What else has been good this week . . . what about with you two?

M: Jaylen stayed home Friday night with me and we ordered pizza and watched a movie. I couldn't believe she actually ditched her plans to hang out with me!

J: Oh, Mom . . . I'm gonna get all emotional! (Stated in a playful manner, grabbing Mom's arm and leaning over to her at the same time)

The counselor is a bit surprised to see Jaylen and her mom interacting in such a playful manner as previous information about their relationship has centered only on the destructiveness of it. This interaction has provided the counselor with important information for preferred future details as well as exceptions. Most helpful, however, has been the observation of their loving and playful interaction, which helps the counselor consider this mother/daughter pair as perhaps having a very distinct interaction pattern that works

for them, though not typical and in need of some modification.

USEFULNESS AND EVALUATION OF THE PROBLEM-FREE TALK TECHNIQUE

As with other solution-focused techniques, problem-free talk is useful in providing information about client strengths and abilities that may have gone unnoticed or undervalued in importance. Realization of these hidden strengths, times of coping, and potential resources can serve to decrease hopelessness and instead increase motivation. Some have worried that it may interfere with engagement; however, it has instead been found to be a relief for clients and informative for counselors (Hogg & Wheeler, 2004).

In addition to this, Bowles, Mackintosh, and Torn (2001) found it to be a useful tool for nurses to use consistently at the beginning of an interaction with a patient in order for the nurses to show they were interested in the patient and not simply the medical condition. Smith (2005, p. 103) discussed a client situation in which problem-free talk was helpful. "Dave was seen at his request together with his support worker. He appeared deeply ashamed of his behavior and reluctant to discuss it when we first met. Much of our first two sessions were spent in *problem-free talk.*" In this example Smith went on to say that because of this tool being used, positive attributes about Dave were discovered. It also seems fair to surmise that this technique is helpful when working with clients who are ashamed, reluctant to talk, noncompliant, or involuntary.

This technique has also been incorporated into a number of studies evaluating the usefulness of solution-focused methods. Among them, Bucknell (2000) cited the incorporation of problem-free talk when training future teachers in the classroom. Similarly, Lynch (2006) documented its use with drug offenders, stating "Instead problem-free talk is encouraged illustrating how the drug user does in fact cope with many aspects of their life successfully" (p. 42).

CHAPTER 4

Miracle Question

ORIGINS OF THE MIRACLE QUESTION TECHNIQUE

Erickson's crystal ball technique encourages clients to imagine a future with no problems and then to identify how they resolved the problems to create such a future. It is this technique that originally served as the foundation for the miracle question, as knowledge of the crystal ball technique, coupled with deShazer's frustration with clients' inability to formulate goals, resulted in what has now become known as a key strategy in solution-focused therapy.

Historically, counseling has entailed a problem-focused direction. The miracle question forces clients to consider what it is they really want, rather than simply what they do not want, thereby shifting from a problem-focused perspective to one that is generating solutions. It is obvious that a client wants to stop feeling depressed, that a parent wants their child to stop misbehaving, or that a spouse wants their husband or wife to stop taking them for granted. What this question requires, however, is the consideration of what that looks like. If these things were to stop, what would that entail? What would be different? How would you know?

In exploring this idea, clients often find their own solutions, or at least brainstorm possibilities that had previously gone unrecognized. Oftentimes progress is made in counseling unbeknownst to, or at least unacknowledged by, the client. In other words, if a client never considers what "better" looks like, how will he recognize it once he is there? By detailing tangible evidence of the absence of the problem, the miracle question sets criteria for evaluating improvement. In addition to putting a face to what improvement is, the miracle question in its very process achieves a solution-focused course, emphasizes the hope of a better future, places responsibility on the client, and triggers the client's inner resources in an effort to define what it is he wants.

HOW TO IMPLEMENT THE MIRACLE QUESTION TECHNIQUE

The miracle question is especially helpful in goal setting, though it can be used at any time throughout therapy. When used for goal setting, it can help to develop clear and concrete descriptions of what the client hopes to gain from counseling. In addition, it emphasizes the presence of, rather than the absence of something, thereby helping to create a positive goal rather than a negative one.

Asking the miracle question typically takes the form of: "Suppose that one night, while you were asleep, there was a miracle and this problem was solved. How would you know? What would be different?" (de Shazer, 1988, p. 5). It is important, however, for the professional counselor to assist clients in making their proposed solutions tangible, reasonable, and focused on themselves. If a client were to say that she would know a miracle had occurred because she would wake to find her husband cleaning the house and bringing her breakfast in bed, the professional counselor would need to refocus the client to examine how she (the client) would be different, not necessarily how others would be different unless that other person is also in counseling.

For instance, in the case of a parent and child, it is perfectly acceptable and quite useful to ask the parent the miracle question regarding her child. However, in the instance that a client states her miracle would entail a behavior change in others, help her understand reciprocity and the ripple effect of our own behavior by asking, "If your husband were cleaning the house and bringing you breakfast in bed, how would you be behaving differently toward him?" Helping a client understand that even small changes in her behavior can illicit more changes in other's behavior is empowering.

Other useful ways to ask the miracle question include:

If this problem suddenly vanished, what would you be doing tomorrow at school that would be different than what you usually do? What would be the very first sign of this miracle? Then what? (Murphy, 1997, p. 76)

Pretend there are two movies about your life. Movie #1 is about your life with this problem, and Movie #2 is about your life without the problem. I already know a lot about Movie #1. Tell me what Movie #2 would look like. Who would be in it? What would they be doing? What would you be doing differently in Movie #2? (Murphy, 1997, p. 76)

If someone waved a magic wand and made this problem disappear, how would you be able to tell things were different? (Murphy, 1997, p. 76)

Magic wand, magic pill, and magic lamp questions seem best used with children who oftentimes have difficulty understanding the concept of a miracle. Regardless of how it is asked, it is important to facilitate the client in expanding on the solution, following up in a way that explores deeper the idea of resolution and a problem-free future. It is also useful to ask for imagined third-party observations in a way that will further clarify what the change looks like.

VARIATIONS OF THE MIRACLE QUESTION TECHNIQUE

The miracle question can be used to identify and examine exceptions to the problem. After a client answers the miracle question he can then be probed to consider if any of those signs of improvement are currently occurring or have at various times. If so, what was different, or better yet, what was he doing that was different and can he do more of it? This technique essentially emphasizes the need for behavioral changes rather than cognitive or affective changes. It is assumed that if one acts differently, one will subsequently feel and think differently.

The miracle question can be combined with the scaling technique (see chapter 1) so that the client, after describing a symptom free scenario, can be asked to then consider how a small improvement might look? Or a moderate improvement? For example, the counselor might ask, "If that is how your optimal outcome would look, life without this problem, how might it look with some improvement? In other words, if the scenario you just described is a 10 on a scale of 1 to 10, 10 being the best outcome, how might a 5 look?" The miracle question can also be combined with the "acting as if" technique (see chapter 7), resulting in a challenge to the client to begin behaving as if the miracle has already occurred.

EXAMPLE OF THE MIRACLE QUESTION TECHNIQUE

Jesse is a 14-year-old male who has been referred because of his "bad attitude" that often results in disagreements with his parents and disruption of the home environment. Over the past six months he has had many disagreements with his parents, conflicts with his siblings, noncompliance with chores and other requests, and dropping grades. He takes no responsibility for these issues and is sick and tired of everyone else blaming him.

Jesse (J):   Seriously, I don't see what the big deal is. I'm tired of everybody being in my business.

Counselor (C):   So you don't know what all the fuss is about?

J: Nope. If everybody would just leave me the hell alone . . .

C: You'd be fine.

J: Totally fine. But that don't seem to be happening now does it?

C: Doesn't seem to be, no. (Pauses) So what do you think everybody else sees as such a big deal?

J: My "bad attitude." Whatever. God they get on my nerves.

C: Your bad attitude?

J: Yeah, everybody says I have a chip on my shoulder or something.

C: You disagree.

J: Yeah. I disagree. I don't need to be here.

C: So what could we do to prove that?

J: What do you mean?

C: Well, how can you and I show them that you don't need to be here in counseling?

J: Just tell them I don't need it.

C: Let's suppose it's not that simple . . . me just saying so. Let's assume that it will also take us *showing* them that you don't need to be here. How might we do that?

J: No ideas here.

C: Well, let's pretend for a minute that you can travel in time. And let's say that you travel into the future a few months from now, and during that time we had worked together to solve your problem . . . the one that brings you here today. So you travel in time to a few months from now, and you wake and everything is better. What would you notice that

would be different in your life that would let you know you no longer needed counseling?

J: Well, I'd notice that everybody wouldn't be on my case anymore.

The client gives a negative goal (e.g., the absence of something) as well as a goal that is focused on others. The professional counselor's task is to move the client in the direction of a positive goal focused on himself.

C: What would they be doing instead?

J: They'd be nice to me.

C: Okay. And if they were being nice to you, what would you be doing?

J: I'd be happy.

The client gives an emotional state. The counselor's job is again to attempt to move the client toward behavioral and action-oriented goals.

C: Okay. And if they were being nice to you and that made you happy, what would you be *doing*?

J: I'd be smiling. And being nice.

C: Okay. And what does "being nice" look like?

J: I'd probably be playing with my brother, getting along with him, and letting him hang out with me.

C: Okay. So you'd be getting along well with your brother and letting him hang out with you. What else?

J: I wouldn't be arguing with my parents.

C: What would you be doing instead? Instead of arguing with your parents?

Again, attempts are being made to change the absence of something into the presence of something.

J: I'd be saying "yes ma'am" and "no ma'am" and being respectful. I'd probably be telling them about my day and stuff.

C: So you'd be getting along well with them and using respectful language with them and telling them things about yourself and your life.

J: Yeah. And if we were getting along like that I'd be doing my chores too, and they'd be all proud of me and junk.

C: How would you know they were proud of you?

J: 'Cause they'd tell me so. They'd be all shocked and happy.

C: And if they told you they were proud and were happy, what would that look like for you?

J: That'd just make me want to do more. Probably even my school work.

C: So you see how you doing something differently causes them to do something differently, which then makes you want to do even more things differently?

It is important to help clients see that by focusing on their own behavior, rather than insisting others change, they can create changes in others through the ripple effect.

J: Yeah, I see that.

C: And you see that if you traveled in time and this problem were solved, it might look something like you getting along well with your brother, being respectful to your parents, telling them things about yourself, doing your chores, them being proud of you, all of you being happier, and you maybe even doing more of your school work?

J: Yeah, I can see that too. Guess we have some things to work on, huh?

USEFULNESS AND EVALUATION OF THE MIRACLE QUESTION TECHNIQUE

Not only is the miracle question technique especially useful in identifying solutions and forming concrete goals, it is also beneficial for use with clients who seem to have lost optimism or hope for a better future. Oftentimes clients become emotionally hardened and resigned to their current way of feeling, thinking, and behaving. By using this technique, the professional counselor is tapping into and reviving the client's sense of hope and promise for improvement. This inspiration and motivation is necessary for effective change to occur.

The miracle question also forces the focus to shift from problem oriented to solution oriented. It identifies what specifically will be different, often leading to improved goal setting in that it is more concrete and tangible. Finally, it serves as a tool to measure progress in counseling as it gives very specific things that need to be achieved rather than vague and overgeneralized complaints.

To date, the literature does not show the effectiveness of the miracle question technique as an independent tool used alone. However, the effectiveness of solution-focused tools, including the use of the miracle question specifically has been documented, and with a variety of populations and issues. In particular, the miracle question has been used in combination with other SFBC techniques to produce favorable results. For instance, Atkinson (2007) utilized the technique along with other solution-focused tools to assess the motivation level of those who used tobacco, alcohol, and other drugs. Burwell and Chen (2006) used these same tools with clients seeking career counseling to assist them in becoming their own change agents and problem solvers. In 2007, Franklin, Streeter, Kim, and Tripodi evaluated the effectiveness of an alternative school incorporating solution-focused techniques and found it to be useful in reducing dropout rates for at-risk teens. Additional studies focused on the effectiveness of the miracle question and solution-focused tools when working with couples (Treyger, Ehlers, Zajicek, & Trepper, 2008) and addictions (Emlyn-Jones, 2007).

CHAPTER | **5**

Flagging the Minefield

ORIGINS OF THE FLAGGING THE MINEFIELD TECHNIQUE

Flagging the minefield (Sklare, 2005) is a technique that is a form of treatment adherence created to help clients generalize what they learned in counseling to future situations that they may encounter. Many clients go through numerous counseling sessions and have difficulty applying what they learned in the sessions to their real life experiences. Using the flagging the minefield technique at various therapeutic transition points, and especially upon termination, helps clients identify situations in which they may encounter difficulties coping or adjusting, times when what was learned in counseling sessions may not seem helpful enough. By considering these potential problem situations in the safety of the counseling relationship, the counselor can help the client consider how to cope and adapt in the real world. In other words, flagging the minefield is a generalization technique; it helps the client transfer counseling insights and compensatory behaviors, thoughts, and feelings into the world the client encounters everyday.

HOW TO IMPLEMENT THE FLAGGING THE MINEFIELD TECHNIQUE

Flagging the minefield is typically used at the end of the counseling process. This technique got its name because the counselor and client mark future situations in which the client can use what has been learned to avoid setbacks just like miners mark mines in the fields when they are working to avoid explosions. The counselor and client create situations that may occur in the future that have not yet been discussed. The counselor asks the client to problem solve the situation using what the client has learned in previous sessions and then to predict what he or she would do in the given situation. Once the client has given a prediction, the counselor helps the client process the situation drawing on what they have discussed throughout the counseling process. In this way, the counselor helps the client transfer learning to the external world and future events.

EXAMPLE OF THE FLAGGING THE MINEFIELD TECHNIQUE

In order for the changes made in counseling to generalize to future issues, it is imperative that potential pitfalls and obstacles to optimal functioning be identified. Many professional counselors worry that discussion of such things will cause the client to place less value on counseling by feeling that its effectiveness can easily be undermined. However, identification of such issues is a necessary part of the counseling process and can be viewed as underlining empowering the client to address future concerns independently. Increasing client confidence is part of empowerment and it is therefore especially important for the professional counselor to praise the progress made and to encourage the continuation of meaningful gains. In flagging the minefield, the importance of recognizing warning signs and potential pitfalls is crucial. Being proactive through potential problem identification and plan development are critical components to lasting changes as well.

Counselor (C):   The important thing is to not need a system. The important thing is to behave responsibly and respectfully without needing to have all of this intervention. Right? And you'll be good at it—you've already shown that. Look at all the progress that's been made. Okay, so now we're ready to do the culminating activity called flagging the minefield, which is basically kind of looking into the future and preparing yourself for situations that will really test the progress you've made as a family. Flagging the minefield is a way for you to identify obstacles to success and ways to overcome those obstacles. You know that Damon has been challenging—well, that might be an understatement. There are times when that gets very frustrating, and that may be the case for some time into the future. So we need to think into the future about these times that are bound to happen, no matter how good you are with the techniques and skills that you have learned. You know, no matter how well they've worked in the past, whether it's time out or a token economy or these response-cost systems or overcorrection or positive reinforcement procedures, there are going to be times when they're just not working. There are going to be times where he's going to be what we call "emotionally labile" and really kind of upset and emotional and it just seems like nothing is going to work. So it can help for us to know that up front, and discuss them together, and perhaps consider when those moments are most likely and how

we might handle them. Okay? So, when are some of those times when you know he's going to be particularly challenging?

Mom (M):   There are times where we are there with the whole family and we're doing things that are not particularly interesting to him but he needs to be with us because it's a family situation. There are moments when he is not happy about doing something and he will make sure he lets us know that he isn't happy.

C: Yeah, so, family events that must include him, but that he doesn't necessarily want to be a part of.

M: Yes. And it can be a very difficult situation because a lot of times you might be out at a restaurant or you're in a place where you really . . .

C: Public places, right.

M: Public places are very difficult.

C: Okay, so you've already identified two situations that are naturally going to occur in the future, and you realize even now that these are going to be more difficult times than others. And by difficult I mean that not only will he be more likely to act out but also that you may find it more difficult to follow through with the skills you've learned in counseling . . . mainly due to the scenario and the surrounding circumstances of being forced to go along with a family event or being in a public place.

M: I agree with that. Definitely those are going to be the more difficult situations.

C: Right, so imagining yourself in either of these situations, how might you deal with it?

Dad (D):   Well, the first thing that comes to mind for me when I think of a family event is that Damon is often expected to support his older siblings in their activities, because we as a family support them and Damon is part of that. Um, for instance, his older brother plays golf and we, as a family, often watch his golf matches. Anticipating and being realistic in my expectations for Damon would probably help. I think we have to be realistic enough to know that he can only take so much of a certain thing.

C: Exactly. Okay, so, reminding yourself ahead of time that Damon will only want to watch his older brother golf for so long, and being realistic with your expectations for his attention span . . .

D: Yes, and you know, it's even difficult for some adults to want to watch an entire game of golf. And, of course, some matches are particularly painful to watch! And then I think back to this one day that we were all out shopping for like 4 hours or something, and this was quite enjoyable for my wife and daughter, and Damon did really well for 3 hours, but then that was it. He reached his limit. And I think we can be very conscious of that and take that into consideration when planning our day, rather than assuming that since he's done well for 3 hours, we can continue on for 3 more. That's not rewarding his good behavior at all. In fact, he might view it as punishment. I think we must respect his opinion and feelings to a certain degree and be able to separate "taking his feelings into consideration" from "giving in to his demands."

C: Okay, so what I'm hearing you say so far is that being realistic in your expectations of his behavior and feelings can certainly help these potential minefields. Also, knowing what his limits are and trying, within reason, not to push beyond those limits. And then also anticipating which family events are going to pose a problem for Damon would be beneficial.

M: Right. Also, it might help to talk to him ahead of time, instead of simply hoping he doesn't notice he is spending all day doing something he doesn't want to do. Maybe instead, I could tell him up front that for this amount of time today, we are all going to do this certain activity as a family, and that you know everybody gets their time. Perhaps I could even use the Premack Principle with the delayed rewards to help with these situations. For instance, saying ahead of time, "Damon, we are going to watch your brother's golf game this morning, but as soon as it is over, you can spend the afternoon playing with your remote control cars."

C: Absolutely. Seems you two are both strategizing a good offense. Let me ask, what are some things you have tried in the past and have these things worked?

M: Sometimes what we do works and sometimes it doesn't. And a lot of it has to do with something you said earlier about his emotional . . . what did you call it?

C: Lability.

M: Ummmhmmm, and sometimes you can't predict it.

C: Yes, and just knowing that can be helpful.

D: Well, I think the main thing that we've done in a lot of those instances where we want to do something that we know he doesn't want to do is to find an alternative something for him to do. For instance, when we know he's not going to like the plans that day we may work something out with another parent or friend to say "So and so has a lacrosse game and we know he doesn't want to sit through another one of those" and so he may go to a friend's house and play and then we'll pick him up when the game is over. The problem I think we both have with this is that we sometimes feel like we are giving in to him and he is training us rather than the other way around.

C: Right. I understand that. Certainly there will be events that do not require his presence and that any child his age would have difficulty sitting through and in these cases I certainly see where finding another option for what he does during that time frame would be appropriate.

M: I like that you sort of qualify it as certain instances that neither require his presence nor are easy for any child to enjoy. That feels more like we are making an informed and intentional decision that makes sense, rather than giving in to him to make it easier on us.

C: Good. Good. So, while these family events are probably more often than not public events let's talk about public places as a potential minefield in general. Let's think of ways to be proactive with Damon's behavior in public

places. What do you find difficult for yourselves or for Damon in these circumstances?

D: I think he knows he is more likely to get his
way when he misbehaves in public because
we are more likely to give in to make it easier
on us just for that brief moment.

C: Ah, good point. So if he knows this ahead of
time, I'm willing to bet that public places are
more often the setting for his misbehavior.

M: These days, yes. He has gotten so much better
at home and in private. But in public, he's
still, um, he is still the old Damon.

C: Hmm, could this in any way be a result of
Damon's parents being the "old mom and
dad" in public? Children catch on very quickly.

M: You know, I hadn't thought about that, but
absolutely. We are very much the way we
always were when others are staring or whispering or giving that judgmental glance.

C: Uhhuhh. And what is it about those judgmental glances that make you more likely to
be the old mom and dad?

D: Well, we live in a society where we care what
others think of us. And if it comes down to a
stranger thinking I have a spoiled child or
I am a mean parent, well, I'd just rather them
think Damon is spoiled.

C: Okay, so are there any exceptions to this general example?

M: Well, I can remember one time that all the
glances in the world didn't matter and I followed through with my instructions to
Damon even though he proceeded to have a
very embarrassing temper tantrum in the
middle of a store.

C: And what made this time different?

M: Well, um, I remember we were out of town
and I remember thinking that I didn't really
care what those people thought of me or my
child because none of them knew me and
I would never see any of them again.

C: Ah, yes, I see. So perhaps we could apply that
same thinking to situations that are not out
of town. Okay, what are some other things

that you can do, what are some resources that
you can bring to bear on the situation to
make it a lot easier, without having to abandon the skills you have already shown work?

The professional counselor moves on to identify two
to three more specific potential mines and problem
solve general solutions and identify resources to use to
address these issues should they occur. Interestingly,
this type of intervention makes it more likely that
clients will think creatively when problem situations
do occur. Rather than giving up, clients are more likely to demonstrate <u>treatment adherence,</u> persevering
through challenging situations.

USEFULNESS AND EVALUATION OF THE FLAGGING THE MINEFIELD TECHNIQUE

Flagging the minefield is used to help clients understand how they can use what they learned in counseling to overcome problems they may have in the
future. This technique can be used with clients who
were brought to counseling for a variety of different
reasons, including "smoking cessation, dietary
change, increasing physical activity, stress reduction, and alcohol use reduction" (Ockene, 2001, p. 43),
cocaine dependency (Barber, Liese, & Abrams, 2003),
social skills training (Piccinin, 1992), depression
(Akerblad, Bengtsson, von Knorring, & Ekselius,
2006) and mood disorders and medication (Byrne,
Regan, & Livingston, 2006).

There are several factors that contribute to the
efficacy of flagging the minefield. Miller et al. (2001)
suggest that the counselor should expect that there
will be some noncompliance on the part of the client
and throughout the counseling process should
explain to the client the importance of the client's
actions. If the client has a positive perception of the
alliance with the counselor, the client will be more
likely to adhere to the treatment (Patton & Kivlighan,
1997). The client's beliefs about the issues and
whether or not the client thinks she needs treatment
also contribute to the efficacy of this technique
(Davidson & Fristad, 2006). When working with
children, this technique is more effective when the
parents play a role in the child's participation and
adherence (Nock & Kazdin, 2005).

Techniques Based Upon Adlerian or Psychodynamic Approaches

Section 2 represents a grouping of techniques that have psychodynamic origins, and several were specifically introduced by Alfred Adler, a colleague of Freud and the originator of Individual Psychology. Adler was a highly respected theorist; Albert Ellis (1993, p. 11) stated that, "Albert Ellis, more than even Freud, is probably the true father of modern psychotherapy." Adler was an early "constructivist" who believed that clients construct and narrate the realities to which they respond, which he called "fictions," and then take these fictions as truth or fact. Adler contributed several theoretical constructs including: life style (a person's unique goals, beliefs, and ideas for coping with the challenges life brings); birth order (psychological reactions to the order one is born into a family, which shapes perceptions and experiences); feelings of superiority/inferiority, sometimes leading to a superiority complex or an inferiority complex; and early recollections, which place an importance on memories from early childhood events. The primary goal of Adlerian counseling is to recognize and assimilate explanations for events and occurrences that may vary from the client's fictions in order to experience growth and develop alternative ways of compensating for challenging episodes in life.

Adlerian counselors use a variety of experiential, behavioral, and cognitive techniques in order to enhance interpersonal relationships and intrapersonal understanding. The techniques expounded upon in this section include I-messages, acting as if, spitting in the soup, mutual storytelling, and paradoxical intention. I-messages help clients take responsibilities for their own thoughts, feelings, and behaviors while encouraging others to do the same. Clients can be taught a simple way to structure their comments so that the clients communicate their needs and desires to others without blaming or criticizing. Acting as if is a technique that allows the client to either purposely act according to their fiction or alter an assumed fiction by behaving in a different manner (e.g., assuming an alternative to the fiction). Spitting in the soup is an expression used to name a commonly used paradoxical technique in Adlerian counseling. In this technique, the professional counselor encourages the client to increase the use of the problematic thought, feeling, or behavior in order to help the client learn that they are actually in control of the symptom, empowering him to change.

Mutual storytelling is primarily a psychodynamic technique, and was developed by Dr. Richard A. Gardner to help elicit therapeutic content from children and adolescents who are not able or willing to address therapeutic content through direct verbal discussion. Clients tell a story, which the counselor analyzes for themes and metaphors. Then the counselor retells the story using the same or similar characters, but with a more pro-therapeutic message, often including various alternative scenarios for the characters to resolve conflicts they encounter.

Paradoxical intention is also claimed by numerous theoretical orientations and should be undertaken with caution. Paradox ordinarily involves reframing the client's problem behavior and asking the client to engage in the behavior she is trying to stop, but restraining the expression of that behavior to certain circumstances (e.g., place, time). Paradox is quite effective in eliminating problematic behaviors because clients realize they actually have control over when they do and do not display the behaviors, thus breaking the cycle of expression.

MULTICULTURAL IMPLICATIONS

The Adlerian approach focuses upon social interest and is quite respectful of individual clients, their worldviews, and various cultural heritages. Primarily, this is because Adlerian counselors understand the importance of feelings of inferiority and superiority, and directly relate to feelings and issues presented by clients from disenfranchised groups who may feel discouraged or alienated. Adlerian views of egalitarianism help to counteract feelings of inferiority and stigmatization and may be particularly useful with clients from diverse cultures, ethnicities, genders, and sexual orientation. Adlerians offer a cooperative approach, rather than the competitive approach common in the American society.

The Adlerian approach may be particularly appropriate for clients of African descent because of the inherent principles of collectivism, social interest, collaborative goal setting and intervention development, and exploration of multigenerational family issues. These emphases on family and community building are appealing to individuals from many cultures.

Clients from some cultures (e.g., Latino/a, Native American) may feel particularly comfortable with storytelling techniques, and psychodynamic approaches have been particularly effective with Latinos/as. The emotive aspects of psychodynamic approaches may be particularly appealing to women more so than men. Conversely, emotionally laden psychodynamic approaches, particularly interactions that are highly intense and require self-disclosure of feelings and personal/family information, may not be appropriate for individuals of Arab or Asian descent because individuals from these cultures may not feel comfortable expressing strong emotions. On the other hand, the authoritative style of some psychodynamic therapists may be appealing to these same individuals. In addition, analysts tend to ask probing questions, which may be interpreted as insensitive. Thus, counselors using this approach must take additional care to gauge a client's comfort level with commonly used techniques.

There are some potential additional limitations of psychodynamic approaches when used across cultures. For example, not all cultures emphasize or even acknowledge the unconscious processes that analysts assume underlies motivation and behavior, and psychodynamic approaches tend to diagnose and view some culture-specific behaviors as pathological (e.g., child-rearing practices that foster dependence over independence; perceived unequal treatment of genders). In addition, the speed of these approaches may be problematic for some individuals, especially those who may be unable to afford a long-term therapeutic approach. Finally, these approaches often do not pursue concrete outcomes, making some clients uncomfortable expending the investment of time required for changes to occur.

CHAPTER 6

I-Messages

ORIGINS OF THE I-MESSAGES TECHNIQUE

The use of personal pronouns is important in a number of theoretical counseling orientations, including Adlerian and Gestalt (Dinkmeyer, McKay, & Dinkmeyer, 1997), person-centered, and existential therapy (Parrott, 1997). For example, Perls and other Gestalt therapists encouraged clients to use "I" instead of "it," "you," or "we" when talking about themselves (George & Christiani, 1995; Hansen, Warner, & Smith, 1980). Using I-messages, sometimes called I-statements, forces the client to take responsibility for his feelings, behaviors, or attitudes (Doyle, 1998) without placing blame on another (Smead, 1995). I-messages also help the client to realize that he is required to take action in order to change the situation.

In 1970, Thomas Gordon introduced the idea of I-statements to the area of family studies (Burr, 1990). Gordon, who focused on the individualistic and autonomous aspects of relationships, believed that I-statements were an effective way of relating to others. I-messages contain minimal negative evaluation, usually promote a willingness to change, and do not harm the relationship between the speaker and the receiver of the message (Gordon, 1974).

I-messages express feelings in a way that minimizes counterattacks (Hewes, 1975) and is less likely to cause resistance or rebellion (Burr, 1990). Unlike you-statements, which are often judgmental and accusing, I-messages convey neither judgment nor directives (Peterson et al., 1979). Instead, I-messages identify feelings inside the speaker and communicate the speaker's recognition that his view of the situation is subjective (Burr, 1990). This acknowledgement leaves room for other perspectives to be expressed, thus initiating dialogue between the two people in conflict, helping to solve problems through open, respectful communication (Dinkmeyer et al., 1997; Hopp, Horn, McGraw & Meyer, 2000; Meeks & Heit, 1999; Remer, 1984; Warnemuende, 2000).

I-messages are sometimes called responsibility messages (Gordon, 1974). People are often unaware of the impact their behavior has on others (Gordon, 1970). However, when using an I-message, the speaker takes responsibility for his feelings and shares them with the receiver (Gordon, 1974). The speaker also communicates the impact of the problematic behavior, leaving the recipient aware and therefore responsible for modifying his behavior.

HOW TO IMPLEMENT THE I-MESSAGES TECHNIQUE

Individuals can be encouraged to substitute personal pronouns in any situation where they are avoiding responsibility for their actions or feelings (Doyle, 1998). For example, if the individual says, "It will not happen again," he can be asked to change this statement to, "I will not let that happen again."

Simple I-messages acknowledge the existence of a problem, feeling, or idea (Burr, 1990). They involve only the person making the statement, and therefore are relatively nonthreatening. Simple I-messages can be used when a person wants to identify a problem but fears that others will become defensive.

On the other hand, compound I-messages are helpful when simple changes in behavior will solve a problem or when the speaker wishes to start a dialogue about a more complex problem (Burr, 1990; Remer, 1984). Compound I-messages involve three parts: a description of the problem (usually a behavior), the effect the problem or behavior has on the speaker, and the feeling experienced by the speaker (Burr). Gordon recommends that I-messages follow the sequence: behavior, effect, then feeling (Gordon, 1974). This sequence communicates that the feeling is caused by the effect, not the person's behavior.

More recently, professional counselors using I-messages have been taught to follow the structure: I feel _____ (feeling) when you _____ (behavior) because _____ (consequence) (Burr, 1990). I-messages should be specific and focus on behaviors rather than personalities. The consequence part of the I-message can be either consequential or interpretive (Remer, 1984). Whereas consequential confrontations focus on concrete results, interpretive confrontations deal with the reasons for the behavior. For example, an interpretive confrontation would be: "When you leave dirty dishes in the sink, I feel angry because I think you're doing it to irritate me" (p. 58).

When working with children or adolescents, or even adults with low cognitive ability, it is important to remember that some may confuse emotions with behaviors (Kammerer, 1998). It can be helpful to discuss emotions and act out a few example emotions before teaching about I-messages. Also, demonstrating the difference between I-messages and you-messages can be especially useful (Phillips-Hershey & Kanagy, 1996). After the demonstration, children can process the different reactions the two produce and why I-messages are more effective.

VARIATIONS OF THE I-MESSAGES TECHNIQUE

Sometimes I-messages contain a fourth part, in which the speaker communicates what he would like to happen (Frey & Doyle, 2001; Phillips-Hershey & Kanagy, 1996). After the traditional I-message, the speaker adds: "And I want _____." The speaker is therefore responsible for taking a proactive role in finding a solution to the problem.

Another variation is the use of we-statements, which communicate that the speaker thinks a group or relationship has a problem (Burr, 1990). For example, a group leader may comment, "We seem to be more interested in staying on the surface of this issue." Unlike I-messages, we-statements do not identify the source of the problem nor do they imply or suggest individual responsibility or solutions. Consequently, we-statements identify a problem in a way that does not create defensiveness or resistance. They suggest that the people involved are connected and need to work together to find a solution. We-statements are useful in situations where someone wants to emphasize the togetherness of the group and initiate a problem-solving process in the group. However, we-statements are inappropriate when the speaker is trying to avoid taking responsibility for an individual problem by defining it as a group problem or when the speaker is using the message to coerce or control others.

EXAMPLE OF THE I-MESSAGES TECHNIQUE

As you will recall, an excerpt from a counseling session with Tamara and Kevin was incorporated into the chapter on scaling. In their example dialogue, they both agreed to accept the other's scaled perspective of themselves and their communication abilities. They also agreed that the ability to effectively communicate would influence the course of their marriage as they attempted to cope together with more difficult issues. Building upon their previous progress, the professional counselor now begins educating Tamara and Kevin about the importance of I-messages and begins teaching them to use these messages in place of less productive means of communication.

Counselor (C):   So we all agree that there are some needed improvements in the way we communicate. And that it is necessary and important to make these improvements for the well-being of your relationship.

Tamara (T):   Yes, and I like that we both agree now that neither of us talks to the other in a productive and healthy way.

C: That's right. What I've gathered is that Kevin feels like you are picking fights with him and so he tunes you out and becomes defensive. And, Tamara, it seems you feel that Kevin ignores you and so you dominate the conversation and become angry.

Kevin (K):   That sounds like a cycle.

C: A cycle is exactly what it is.

T: It's like I'm thinking, "If he would pay attention to me I wouldn't have to keep on and get angry!" but he is probably thinking, "If she would talk less and lower, I wouldn't have to tune her out or feel the need to defend myself!"

C: Exactly. Now that you know that, is that enough for you to communicate differently?

(Pause)

T: Umm . . . well, hmm . . . I don't know.

K: It helps. But when we are in that moment, I don't know that that is going to be enough.

C: Okay. So I know I've heard one of you say in the past that a common source of tension is the division of household and family responsibilities . . .

(The professional counselor intentionally brings up a topic that will likely lead Tamara and Kevin to initiate a heated discussion so that he can observe their typical style of communication.)

K: That's a nice way to put it . . . not exactly how I would say it.

C: And how would you put it?

K: Um, let's see . . . nothing is ever enough to satisfy her. She is never happy with what I do.

T: That's because you don't do enough. You think that just because you lift a finger that I should be *so* grateful and appreciative when your "exceptional contribution" to the running of our household is just one of a hundred things I do every day!

K: (Takes a deep breath and contorts his face.)

T: Do you not have anything to say to that?

K: What good would it do?

T: None. That's because you know you have no defense. Because what I'm saying is the truth.

C: Okay, if you don't mind, I am going to interrupt now, simply because you have provided me with an excellent example of how you typically communicate and that will help us know where to begin. What I am hearing as I listened to you just now is a lot of focus on the other person, which tends to set the stage for an argument. When we do this, we are avoiding responsibility for our own feelings and behaviors, and instead putting the other person on the defense . . . hence their need to either defend themself or attack and blame the other person. What I want us to begin with then, is a very basic communication skill that stresses your own personal feelings, behaviors, and attitudes, rather than pointing the finger at the other person. Staying with the same topic that you two just discussed, I want you to complete the statement, "I feel" . . . Tamara, would you like to start? "*I feel* . . ."

T: I feel . . . taken for granted.

C: Good. "I feel taken for granted *when you* . . ."

T: I feel taken for granted when you expect me to take on most of the household responsibility.

C: Good, and a little more. "I feel taken for granted when you expect me to take on most of the household responsibility *because* . . ."

T: Okay. Let's see . . . I feel taken for granted when you expect me to take on most of the household responsibility because I think you are capable of doing more to help me.

C: Great, Tamara. And now, Kevin, I would like for you to respond to Tamara with "I feel . . ."

K: Ugh . . . okay . . . I feel . . . I don't know . . . I feel irritated.

C: Uhhuhh. "I feel irritated when you . . ."

K: I feel irritated when you point out everything that I don't do.

C: Good, and "I feel irritated when you point out everything that I don't do because . . ."

K: Because . . .

C: Start at the beginning if you don't mind, since we are learning this. "I feel irritated . . ."

K: I feel irritated when you point out everything that I don't do because it's like the times I do help are completely overlooked.

C: All right. What are each of your reactions to the statements you just heard from your spouse?

K: I'm feeling all mature and respectful for saying it like that. I'm pretty proud of myself.

T: (Laughs) Yeah, I'm kind of feeling bad for not complimenting him more for what he does do to help.

C: Ahh, both good points. What you'll find with this style of communication—it's called a I-message—I think is that not only will you feel better about yourself for communicating this way but you'll also be more likely to see your partner's point of view, understand where they are coming from, and in turn, feel empathy for their position.

T: I can see that.

C: Good. Okay, I want you to continue with your conversation now, and I will interject to help you practice until you get very good at it.

T: So just keep talking?

C: Sure. Keep expressing yourselves with the "I feel . . . when you . . . because . . ." We'll keep it very specific like this until you feel it comes more naturally.

T: Okay. I guess it's my turn, unless you want to go, Kevin?

K: You can go ahead.

T: Well, I'll respond to your last statement. I tend to overlook the good you do because I feel so angry because . . .

C: "When you."

T: Oh yeah. Kevin, I tend to overlook the good you do because I feel so angry when you don't do more because I think you don't care that I'm already overwhelmed with responsibilities as it is. It's hard to be appreciative when you're pissed, you know?

K: Believe me, I know. Okay, okay, my turn. Hmmm, honestly, I sometimes don't care that you have more responsibilities when you are fussing because I feel like whatever I do, it's not enough and it won't be noticed anyway . . .

USEFULNESS AND EVALUATION OF THE I-MESSAGES TECHNIQUE

I-messages can be used in many situations. Gordon (1970, 1974) believed that I-messages work especially well with children, both in parenting and in school disciplinary situations. I-messages are commonly used in a variety of conflict situations and may help those involved to reach an effective resolution (Kammerer, 1998). I-messages are frequently taught to help people manage their anger in positive, nonviolent ways (Phillips-Hershey & Kanagy, 1996), and applied in assertiveness training to help those who are overly aggressive or too passive (Hollandsworth, 1977). Martinez (1986) found I-messages to be effective in handling general classroom behavior problems, as did Cohen & Fish (1993), who found the technique useful with specific problem behaviors such as laughing, arguing, burping, and other off-task behaviors.

There has been considerable research on the effectiveness of I-messages, in both disciplinary and conflict situations. In a study examining the use of I-statements to influence student behavior in the classroom, Peterson et al. (1979) found that using I-messages produced a decrease in disruptions, although not in all subjects. Remer (1984) studied subjects' reactions to I-messages in video taped confrontation situations. He found that in response to I-messages containing all three components, behavior-feeling-consequence, participants rated themselves as more willing to change their behavior and more likely to be open to negotiation. They also rated this method of confrontation as more effective than any one component alone or any combination of two components.

Two other studies explored the effectiveness of I-messages in conflict situations. Both examined the difference in self-reported reactions produced by assertive and aggressive/accusatory statements. Assertive statements were defined as I-messages, and aggressive/accusatory statements were composed of you-messages (Kubany & Richard, 1992). Kubany, Richard, Bauer, and Muraoka (1992) found that female participants rated assertive statements as less aversive, less likely to evoke antagonistic emotions, more likely to evoke compassion, less likely to evoke antagonistic behaviors, and more likely to

evoke conciliatory behaviors. They concluded that using accusatory statements to express anger in close personal relationships may antagonize, alienate or impede conflict resolution. When Kubany and Richard (1992) extended this research to the adolescent population, they found nearly identical results. Both male and female adolescents rated themselves as more likely to express anger and respond antagonistically to you-statements than to I-messages. Although much of this research is based on self-reports, not actual behavioral observations, the results suggested that I-messages were more effective at promoting conflict resolution than you-messages or other methods of dealing with conflict.

Finally, cultural sensitivity and specificity is required when using I-messages. For example, Cheung & Kwok (2003) concluded that in Chinese culture, parents avoided and actively resisted using I-messages when communicating feelings of anger, but readily used the techniques to convey feelings of worry and frustration.

CHAPTER 7

Acting As If

ORIGINS OF THE ACTING AS IF TECHNIQUE

"Acting as if" is a technique based on the Adlerian approach. The goal of Adlerian therapy is to increase clients' social interest and community feelings (Carlson, Watts, & Maniacci, 2005), as measured according to four criteria: (1) decreasing symptoms, (2) increasing functioning, (3) increasing the client's sense of humor, and (4) producing a change in the client's perspective. Acting as if helps the client change not only his perspective but also his behavior, which in turn leads to increased functioning. It is not enough for clients to see things differently; they must also act differently.

Adler (Carlson et al., 2005) believed that all people created cognitive maps of their lives and that these maps served as a guide for how to lead their lives. These cognitive maps were fictitious. However, Adler believed that people act "as if" these maps were real and therefore live accordingly. But Adler also believed that these maps could be changed to help the client behave in a more productive manner. The acting as if technique has clients assume roles and behave as though they can accomplish what they believe they cannot accomplish.

HOW TO IMPLEMENT THE ACTING AS IF TECHNIQUE

Acting as if is a technique in which the professional counselor asks the client to act as if he had the skills to handle a difficult situation effectively (Seligman, 2001). Many clients use the excuse, "If only I could . . . " (Gilliland & James, 1998). At this point, the counselor instructs the client to act out the role as if she could do whatever she was hoping. The client may find it useful to think of someone who has these skills and then envision how this person would handle the situation at hand (Carlson et al., 2005). By trying out a new role, clients often learn that they can not only carry out the part, but also become a new person in the process (Gilliland & James, 1998).

Acting as if one is the person one wants to be can challenge self-limiting assumptions that a person holds (Corey, 2007). Clients are asked to try and catch themselves repeating their old patterns of behavior. Commitment is a very important part of the acting as if technique. If clients truly wish to change, they must be willing to do something about their problems.

VARIATIONS OF THE ACTING AS IF TECHNIQUE

Some professional counselors segue into the actual implementation of the acting as if technique by using a reflective questioning process. The counselor asks the client questions meant to get the client thinking about what he would do differently (thoughts, feelings, and actions) if he were actually in the situation and already behaving differently. This allows the client to imagine how he would act before he is actually asked to do it in real life, preparing the client ahead of time. It also allows the professional counselor to "flag the minefield" (see chapter 5) by exploring times when "acting as if" in real life might be challenging.

EXAMPLE OF THE ACTING AS IF TECHNIQUE

Laney is a 16-year-old girl whose boyfriend of one year broke up with her 8 months ago. She was so distraught at that time that she refused to return to school where he also attended. Mom, who is emotionally reactive and inconsistent but also overly indulgent with poor parental boundaries, allowed Laney to withdraw from public school to be "home-schooled." After 4 months at home, Laney had yet to complete any of her school work. In addition, other troublesome behaviors had developed and at the onset of counseling 4 months ago, she was engaging in starvation, self-injury, and was described as emotionally erratic and destructive. After 4 months of weekly sessions, she exhibits no self-injury or starvation and has begun to catch up on her school work. She has improved emotional stability, with reduced destructiveness and explosiveness, but continues to struggle with becoming overly somatic and distraught. She has recently made the decision to return to school when the new academic year begins in a few weeks.

Laney (L):   I just want to be normal. I just want to be like other girls my age.

Counselor (C):   And that would mean returning to school?

L: Yeah. I'm tired of being at home all the time . . . like some hermit . . . what if I'm a hermit . . .

you know my dad has schizo-something . . . he's like that. He's a hermit. Oh, God, what if I'm like him? What if that's why I quit school? What if I'm crazy? (Becomes physically affected by her thinking, pulls her knees up to her chest, places her head between her knees and begins running her hands through her hair too harshly)

C: Laney, we've worked on this. You know how to stop that.

L: (Stops moving her arms but stays with her head between her knees. Takes a deep breath and is silent for several moments) I am not a hermit. I am not like my dad. I do not have to be like my mom. I am my own person. I'm not a freak. I'm not crazy. I'm really not crazy. I'm getting better. I'm okay. I am okay. I am okay. (Another deep breath, raises her head, gives a half-hearted smile with eyebrows raised)

C: You are okay.

L: Yeah. I'm gonna be.

C: Good. You were wanting to be "normal" like other girls your age?

L: Yes. Normal. Like, not crazy. My old friends think I'm a freak for staying home. They know I'm not really being home-schooled. I shouldn't be home anymore. I should be a normal 16 year old.

C: And what do you think that would that look like?

L: For one, I'd be in school. I would be at the mall. I would be at the pool this summer. I've been avoiding all these places because of Matthew. I really lost it when he broke up with me. Really lost it. I know I'll lose it again if I see him and all this progress I've made will be for nothing.

C: So you believe that if you're put back in the same old situation, you'll go back to being the same old Laney.

L: That's what I'm afraid of, yeah, pretty much. I can't go back to that. I mean, I know I still have a ways to go even now, and I'm okay with that. But I really can't go back to that.

But he just has that effect on me, you know? I mean, not as much as he did. It killed me when he broke up with me though. It felt like my life was over. I didn't know who I was anymore. I had been Matthew's girlfriend. I didn't know who Laney was anymore. And I totally lost it. I felt like everyone was staring at me . . . talking about me. And he was talking to other girls. I felt so abandoned . . . so alone. And I freaked out. I lost it. I cut his tires. I threatened to kill myself. Then I cried my eyes out, refused to leave his house, begged him back. Was on the ground crying. It was ridiculous. I just couldn't go back to school and face that. I refused to go back for 2 straight weeks, but I just kept getting worse instead of better so Mom didn't make me go back. She said it would be too much for me. (Pause) But I want to go back now. I don't want it to control my life anymore. I'm just terrified it will.

C: You control that, you know.

L: How? I don't know how I'll react. What if I can't control it?

C: If you script it ahead of time, learn the art of pretense . . . charades . . . make-believe . . .

L: What do you mean? (Looks very interested and amused . . . eager even)

C: Well, you've talked before about wanting to be an actress and you certainly have a flare for the dramatics (both grin). Have you ever seen the movie *Mean Girls*?

L: Yeah. I love that movie.

C: Remember Lohan's character? She was intelligent and conscientious and therefore not as popular as the superficial girls. So she decides to fake being "a plastic." She's really nothing like that in the beginning. But she creates a character for herself and before you know it, she really is a plastic. Or Drew Barrymore in *Never Been Kissed*. She is by nature a klutz and a social disgrace. But she too creates a new persona and acts as if she's someone she's not. Or Julia Roberts in *Pretty Woman*.

L: I like the way this sounds.

C: What do you wish you could be like when you return to school?

L: Wow . . . (thinks seriously, showing how invested she is in this idea) . . . I want to be normal . . . and healthy . . . I want to be the epitome of cool, calm, and collected. I want to appear confident, unaffected by ridiculous high school drama. I want to be happy, with myself, but not in a giddy immature way, but in a mature, self-assured way. I want to be the girl that would never be so ridiculously emotional that she would grovel in the dirt, slice up tires, or cut herself. I want to be poised. I want to be unaffected. Because it won't just be facing Matthew that will be difficult. Everyone will be whispering about where I've been and why I'm back. I've got to be able to handle all of that. But that's not me. I'm not that together and strong.

C: Then let's develop your new character.

L: Like a movie character?

C: Exactly like a movie character. And you can base it on one you already know of. If you can think of a character in a movie that exhibits these traits and skills you are talking about . . .

L: (Suddenly her enthusiasm is deflated.) But isn't that like asking me to be something that I'm not?

C: Or, maybe I'm just asking you to be different than you were. Because it wasn't working too well for you. But you aren't quite sure how to be different yet. But you do know what you want to be like. So you act as if you are . . . what it is you want to be. Because sometimes the easiest way to change, is to act like you already have.

L: I love it. I can totally do this. (Enthusiasm obviously returning) Okay, so don't laugh, but the person that comes to mind is Scarlett O'Hara. Honestly, she is exactly what I'm describing. Nothing got to her. Nothing.

C: Well, maybe she had one or two weak moments. Remember when Ashley left for war? And what about at the end when Rhett left her? Let's think about how she handled rejection and losing the two men she loved the most.

L: You know she did have a few moments where she groveled too. But she dusted herself off way quicker than I did. It was like it never happened.

C: Exactly.

L: And usually, she would wait until after the storm was over to fall apart . . . and she would usually do it in private. It was rare that anyone saw her weaknesses.

C: How could you tell she was strong?

L: The way she walked in a room. The expression on her face. The calmness in her voice. The way she handled situations.

C: And even when she fell apart, she got it together quickly. Scarlett was a master at "resetting" herself. It's like she herself was playing a character and she had a restart button that she would press if she ever came

out of character. Could you act as if you were Scarlett when you return to school? Could you give more thought this week to how she would handle various situations that you might face when you return?

L: Absolutely. I think I'll watch the movie again this week and pay very close attention to the traits she has that I want to possess.

USEFULNESS AND EVALUATION OF THE ACTING AS IF TECHNIQUE

Acting as if can be used in a variety of situations where the client does not believe he possesses the necessary skills to confront a challenging situation. A man struggling with shyness can "act as if" he is assertive (Carlson et al., 2005). A woman who is scared of her verbally abusive husband can act as if she were brave enough to stand up to him (Seligman, 2001). In addition, children undergoing medical treatments have handled the treatments more successfully when they have pretended to be their favorite superhero.

CHAPTER 8

Spitting in the Soup

ORIGINS OF THE SPITTING IN THE SOUP TECHNIQUE

Stemming from an old German proverb (Adler & Brett, 1998) and credited to Ansbacher and Ansbacher (1956), "spitting in the soup" is a paradoxical Adlerian technique that is used to decrease client symptoms by first determining the underlying purpose for them, and then pointing this purpose out to the client. In this way, Adler believed that even if the client chose to maintain their symptomatic behavior, he could only do so with the realization that he was somehow benefiting from it. For most, this knowledge renders the symptoms less attractive, or to continue the metaphor, less palatable. If symptoms are less attractive and seen as beneficial in some way, clients are typically less likely to continue them.

While the professional counselor does not necessarily encourage the continuation of symptoms, he does not request that they stop either. Instead, the counselor acknowledges that behavior has a purpose. The purpose is validated as useful and the counselor works with the client to develop the skills needed to meet this purpose in a different, more pro-social way. According to Rasmussen and Dover (2006, p. 387), "By understanding that it is the client's desire to feel as good as possible, the therapist can work with the client to find better ways to obtain that sought-after goal." If newer more adaptive ways of obtaining the goal are not taught, the client will engage in symptom substitution rather than adopt a behavior replacement (Kopp & Kivel, 1990). Adler believed that in order to maintain symptoms, clients must fight against them. Paradoxical techniques demonstrate how clients create their own symptoms, unconsciously, but for a purpose.

HOW TO IMPLEMENT THE SPITTING IN THE SOUP TECHNIQUE

Prior to using this technique, an established rapport and trusting relationship must be in place. Otherwise, the client's likelihood of rejecting the technique's use is increased. In addition to this, professional counselors should also have conducted a thorough lifestyle assessment in order to increase insight into the underlying motivations of the client. Prior to spitting in the soup of the client, useful questions the counselor might ask to formulate a hypothesis about the purpose of symptoms might include, "How do you gain from this behavior/emotion?"; "Does anything positive come as a result of your behavior/emotion?"; "If you were to give this behavior/emotion up tomorrow, what would you be losing?"

In order to use this technique effectively, it is important to understand its full purpose and capacity to bring about change. When implementing this technique, it may be useful to keep in mind that Adler believed most maladaptive behavior to be a result of poor social interest, feelings of inferiority, or relational issues. Oberst and Stewart (2003) maintained that unhealthy behaviors or symptoms typically result from avoidance of life's demands and tasks, or in an effort to gain power, attention, or love.

According to Rasmussen and Dover (2006, p. 387), "a client has developed a way of life that enables him or her to reach a desired goal, but his or her methods are flawed." Typical motivations and maladaptive symptoms may include: the use of anger outbursts to gain power, respect, and control; depressive symptoms to gain nurturing and support from others; feigned helplessness to avoid responsibilities and tasks; or lack of self-care to gain displays of love and affection from significant others. Just as a 3 year old will use a maladaptive behavior, such as a temper tantrum, to gain a tangible item or avoid a task, older children, adolescents, and even adults continuously engage in similar versions of this same age-old behavior.

By "spitting in the soup," the professional counselor shows the client what he is gaining from his symptoms (Carlson et al., 2005). Then the counselor acknowledges that the client may continue using his symptoms, though now he will have increased knowledge of why. Although the client may continue to display symptoms, they have now lost their good "taste." In other words, the counselor identifies the motives behind the client's self-defeating behaviors and ruins the client's supposed payoff by making it unappealing (Seligman, 2001). The client may still try to "eat the soup" (i.e., continue the behavior), but it is no longer enjoyable (Gilliland & James, 1998). The counselor has spoiled the soup (i.e., the game) of the client.

When encountering resistance to change despite use of this technique, the professional counselor must examine the reasons for the resistance. Typically, when clients resist change despite having their soup spoiled it may be because they have different goals than the counselor, feel the counselor is not sympathetic, understanding, or supportive enough, find the counselor disagreeable, too direct, or unlikable, or lack the necessary motivation for change (Rasmussen, 2002). In each of these instances, the counselor would do well to redefine goals, employ methods to increase client motivation, and focus efforts on establishing a deeper level of rapport.

VARIATIONS OF THE SPITTING IN THE SOUP TECHNIQUE

No variations of this technique were identified in the extant literature, though it certainly takes various forms depending on the counselor, client, presenting symptoms, and identified motivators.

EXAMPLE OF THE SPITTING IN THE SOUP TECHNIQUE

Dianne is a 46-year-old female who has been referred from a medical clinic designed to treat chronic pain. Dianne describes symptoms consistent with depression and emphasizes her complaints of physical pain that leave her feeling unable to function regularly. To date, these physical complaints have no medical explanation, therefore resulting in her referral for counseling.

Counselor (C):   So you've felt this way for some time now, though you're not sure exactly when it began. Can you recall what life was like before? (Exception)

Dianne (D):   I come from a large family, and I'm the oldest out of my other four siblings. My mom died when I was really young . . . I was eleven . . . Dad started drinking a lot after she died. He really never was the same. So it was almost like we lost both our parents at the same time, just in different ways.

C: That must have been extremely hard for you.

D: I almost didn't notice at the time how hard it was. I was too busy picking up the extra slack. With Mom gone and Dad passed out all the time, there was no one to take care of the others. It all fell on me. I was the one who had to take care of everyone else, including Dad. I don't remember stopping long enough to feel sad. (Long pause as she still thinks about this. Short deep breath) And then one day, I decided to get married. Part of it was just so I could get out of the house and pass the responsibilities on to my younger sister. But soon I got pregnant and had my first daughter . . . then another . . . and I was at it again . . . taking care of everybody else. I just got so tired. So . . . so very tired.

C: Sounds like you never really had a break.

D: Never. And then Charles left . . . that was my husband . . . that was years ago. We're still married, I guess. He calls every now and then. He moved up state somewhere . . . sends money every so often. My girls were angry at me for him leaving. They started running all over me, too. And my younger brothers still need taking care of, even as grown men. One stays in and out of jail. He's always needing help getting back on his feet. One is alcoholic and is always needing to be rescued. My sister is on disability, and I have to keep her kids sometimes. And my dad . . . his health is really bad now. I've tried my best to take care of him as well. I would go get his groceries every week and try to keep his house clean. (She's drifted off into her thoughts and begins to shake her head back and forth and puts her forehead down into her hand) And now to top it all off, I'm having all this physical pain that the doctors can't seem to find a reason for.

C: Seems to never end.

D: Exactly. And why is this happening to me of all people?

C: Doesn't seem fair.

(Thus far, the counselor has only made supportive statements used to validate the client's feelings and experience. This is especially important because her physical complaints have not been validated from a medical perspective thus far, and because the counselor is soon going to ask her a difficult question that has the potential to create defensiveness. This is less likely if the client feels validated beforehand.)

D: Not fair at all. My life has been hard enough. Filled with unfairness already . . . enough to last a lifetime. I'm sick of it.

C: Exactly. Sick of it indeed. Sick of your life. Because of your life.

D: What do you mean?

C: Is there any part of you that wants to be sick?

D: No! I don't want to feel this way! Why would I want to be sick? I'm the victim in all of this.

C: Let me ask it differently. Do you benefit . . . at all . . . in any small way . . . from being sick?

D: No.

C: So if suddenly you were well tomorrow, you wouldn't be giving anything up?

D: Well, yes, (speaking very rapidly) I'd lose this wonderful break I'm currently getting . . . my family would expect me to take care of all of them again . . . my brothers would constantly want money . . . my sister needing constant help . . . my daughters angry and hateful to me all the time . . . (stops) . . . oh, dear . . . um . . . seems that maybe I do benefit some from being sick.

C: It seems that the only way you've figured out to give yourself a break from taking care of everyone else is to be the one that needs taking care of. It's okay. It's okay to continue being sick. If it makes you feel better. If it gets your needs met. It's okay for now.

(The client may continue to eat the same soup, but it will not taste as good now that she knows what the ingredients are. In other words, the client may continue not feeling well, being a victim, but it will not have the same effect for her and so she will be motivated to find alternative ways, more healthy ways, to get her needs met.)

USEFULNESS AND EVALUATION OF THE SPITTING IN THE SOUP TECHNIQUE

No empirical evidence was located to validate the effectiveness of the spitting in the soup technique independently, although it has been used with other Adlerian techniques in several studies. In 1989, Doyle and Bauer suggested the use of this technique while treating children with post-traumatic stress in order to help them alter their distorted view of them-selves. In 1994, Herring and Runion used Adlerian techniques, including spitting in the soup, with eth-nic children and youth to increase social interest and improve lifestyles. Harrison (2001) advocated the use of this technique and other Adlerian principles

to work specifically with survivors of sexual abuse, who so often present with resulting symptoms of self-injury, depression, and eating disorders. For additional empirical evidence of the effectiveness of paradoxical techniques used to address a wide range of presenting problems, see chapter 10.

CHAPTER 9

The Mutual Storytelling

ORIGINS OF THE MUTUAL STORYTELLING TECHNIQUE

Storytelling has a rich tradition among humans and these stories, including the Bible, fables, and fairy tales, influence human behavior. Stories reflect cultural laws, ethics, and the day-to-day rules that govern behavior and guide decision making. As such, it stands to reason that storytelling can play a helpful role in counseling.

The early roots of the mutual storytelling technique can be found in play therapy, which included the use of stories and was first used with children by Hug-Hellmuth in 1913 (Gardner, 1986). In the 1920s, Anna Freud and Melanie Klein, both influenced by Hug-Hellmuth, incorporated play therapy into their analytic sessions with children (Knell, 1993). Anna Freud used play as a means to develop a therapeutic alliance with her clients before moving into verbalizations. In contrast, Melanie Klein believed that play was a child's primary means of communication. Beginning in the 1930s, Conn and Solomon began to notice that many children were unable to analyze self-created stories (Gardner, 1986). Conn and Solomon discussed the story on a symbolic level with the child and used this communication to bring about therapeutic change. It was from the work of Conn and Solomon that Richard A. Gardner, a psychodynamic therapist, developed his technique, which he called mutual storytelling, in the early 1960s.

Due to his experience with children's resistance to analysis, Gardner disagreed with the psychodynamic idea that the unconscious needed to be brought into conscious awareness (Allanson, 2002) for therapeutic progress to be made. He believed instead that allegories or metaphors could bypass the conscious and be directly received by the unconscious (Gardner, 1974). He also thought that children's resistance to hearing about their wrongdoings could be avoided by discussing the inappropriate behavior of others (e.g., fictional characters) and the lessons they learned as a result of these mistakes (Gardner, 1986). By using a story that is individually relevant to a specific person at a particular time, the lessons conveyed in the mutual storytelling technique are more likely to be received and incorporated into the listener's psychic structure. Importantly, Gardner used the child's level of engagement and the anxiety experienced while listening to his story to determine how accurate his interpretation had been and how well his lesson was understood (Allanson, 2002; Gardner, 1986).

HOW TO IMPLEMENT THE MUTUAL STORYTELLING TECHNIQUE

Before using the mutual storytelling technique, it is important to develop a therapeutic relationship with the child (Kottman & Stiles, 1990) and understand as much about the child's background and current issues as possible. This will help the counselor understand the child's metaphors and use them effectively in the retelling of the child's story.

The first step in the mutual storytelling technique is to elicit a fictional self-created story from the child (Gardner, 1986). The child is given broad range to create the story, but as with any good story, it must contain a beginning, middle, and end, with interesting characters and some action (Arad, 2004). Although this can be done in many ways, Gardner preferred to tell the child that she was the guest of honor on a make-believe television program. The program involved inviting children on the show to see how good they were at making up stories. The story needed to be from their own imagination, and it was against the rules to tell a story about anything that really happened, anything they read or heard about, or anything they saw on television or in a movie (Smith & Celano, 2000). The story must also include a moral or lesson.

Most children have little difficulty telling a good story, and even get better and more expansive with repeated attempts. However, if the child has difficulty beginning a story, offer to help the child. For example, say very slowly and with substantial pauses, "Once upon a time . . . a long time ago . . . in a very distant land . . . far, far away . . . far beyond the mountains . . . far beyond the deserts . . . far beyond the oceans . . . there lived a . . . " (Gardner, 1986, p. 411). Gardner would periodically point his finger at the child, indicating that the child should say whatever was on his mind at the time. Continue to prompt the child with "And then . . . " or "The next thing that happened was . . . " until the child is able to continue the story on his own. This method of prompting is successful in eliciting a story from nearly all children, except the overly resistive.

While the child tells his story, the counselor should take notes to help analyze the story content as well as formulate the counselor's own story variation

(Gardner, 1986). When the child has finished telling a story, it is important for the counselor to ask about the moral or lesson of the story. The counselor may also ask for a title to the story or which characters the child relates to, even who the child would or would not like to be (Gitlin-Weiner, Sandgrund, & Schaefer, 2000).

While silently interpreting the child's story, Gardner suggested considering the following guidelines:

1. Identify which figure or figures represent the child and which figures symbolize significant people in her life. Keep in mind that two or more figures may represent different parts of the same person.
2. Gain an overall sense of the atmosphere and setting for the story.
   a. Was it pleasant, neutral, horrifying, aggressive?
   b. There is a big difference in the interpretation of a story when the setting is one's home, school, neighborhood, the jungle, or desolate landscape.
   c. What feeling words were expressed by the child?
   d. What were the child's emotions/expressions while telling the story (e.g., animated, aggressive, depressed, stoic)?
   e. Separate typical from stereotypical content.
3. While numerous interpretations may be possible, select the one that is most pertinent at this point in time, often cued by the content of the child's moral or lesson.
4. Ask yourself, "What would be a healthier, more mature adaptation than the one provided by the child?"
   a. Sometimes presenting several options provides the child with future alternatives in resolving difficulties. Counseling should open up new avenues of thoughts, feelings, and behaviors not typically considered.
   b. Offer multiple, empowering options, rather than narrow, self-defeating options.
   c. The counselor's moral or lesson should reflect the healthier resolution.

5. Watch the child's reaction as you retell the story. Intense interest or marked anxiety, among other responses, may indicate that you are close to the mark.

Kottman (1990) added that counselors should also focus on how the child views self, others, and the world, as well as what patterns and themes emerged. Because the story may be subject to several different interpretations, it is important for the counselor to consider the child's own moral or lesson (Gardner, 1986). This will aid in selecting a theme that is most applicable to the child at that moment in time. Based on this information, the counselor should ask himself, "What is the primary inappropriate resolution to the conflicts presented here?" (p. 414).

After identifying a more mature or healthier mode of adaptation, the counselor uses the child's characters, setting, and initial situation to tell a somewhat different story, usually incorporating many similar characters and actions, but offering a healthier resolution to the conflict presented in the child's story (Prout & Brown, 1999). The goal is to provide the child with more and better alternatives to solve problems, gain insight into problems, and develop an awareness of new perspectives and possibilities. After the counselor finishes telling a story, the child is asked to identify the lesson or moral of the counselor's story (Gardner, 1986). It is preferable that the child figure out the lesson on his own. However, if the child cannot do so, the counselor may present the moral for him. Note that stories often present more than one lesson and each lesson should emphasize a healthier resolution to the problem.

Gardner (1974) encouraged recording (e.g., audio, video) the child while telling the story. Unlike other objects around which stories can be formed, such as drawings, dolls, or puppets, a tape recorder does not restrict or channel the child's story. In addition, taping allows the child to view stories (e.g., both child and counselor versions) a number of times in order to provide multiple exposures to the messages the counselor is trying to express (Gardner, 1986). Listening to or viewing the tape is often assigned as homework.

VARIATIONS OF THE MUTUAL STORYTELLING TECHNIQUE

The mutual storytelling technique can be helpful for addressing many situations involving unconscious or subconscious processes, and it is particularly helpful for engaging children or adolescents who are resistant to "talk therapy." As with many projective techniques, the clients unknowingly provide important information to the counselor.

The mutual storytelling technique has been used as a basis for several ancillary games or modes of presentation. Gardner developed a game called *The Story Telling Card Game*, published by his company, Creative Therapeutics, which allows clients to choose cut out characters and background scenes that act to stimulate storytelling. Erford (2000) developed a PC CD-ROM called *The Mutual Storytelling Game*, which provides background and character graphics (human and animal) to stimulate storytelling. The CD-ROM has the advantage of allowing the printing of hard copies of the scenes for the note taking, tracking, and evaluating process. It also provides multicultural (i.e., White, African American, Asian American, Hispanic American) and animal character sets.

Gardner developed another set of games that can be useful with children who are less receptive to telling stories on their own (Schaeffer & O'Connor, 1983). The *Pick-and-Tell Game* allows the child to pick a toy, a word, or a picture of a person from The Bag of Toys, The Bag of Words, or The Bag of Faces, respectively (Shapiro, 1994). The child then uses the object he has picked to create a story and tell the moral or lesson of that story. In addition, Winnicott developed the scribble game, in which storytelling is based on drawings (Scorzelli & Gold, 1999). The counselor begins by closing his eyes and drawing on a piece of paper. The child then turns the scribble into something and tells a story about it. The game continues as the child then draws something for the counselor to complete and interpret.

Other variations on the mutual storytelling technique include doll play, the use of puppets, and writing a story. Webb (1999) described combining storytelling with doll play in order to encourage children to act out family situations. Gitlin-Weiner et al. (2000) believed that puppets could be interviewed to allow the child to convey the motivation of the characters and hence discover solutions to problems. After interviewing the puppets, the therapist can talk directly to the child about the story in order to assess the child's defenses, coping styles, and capacity for self-observation.

Finally, the mutual storytelling writing game, developed by Scorzelli and Gold (1999), involves the counselor and child creating a story together. The counselor begins the story with "Once upon a time . . ." and asks the child to complete the statement. The story continues back and forth between the counselor and child until the child ends the story. Depending on the child's preference or limitations, either the child or the counselor can write down the story. Webb (1999) suggested writing down all of the stories told by the child and creating a journal.

EXAMPLE OF THE MUTUAL STORYTELLING TECHNIQUE

Justin, age 7 years and in grade 2, was referred for anger control issues and mild to moderate classroom disruption. He frequently became angry in peer interactions. Other students' parents had complained to the teacher and principal. The general goal of counseling was to help him to express his anger in a more prosocial manner and develop alternative reactions to frustrating and stressful interpersonal interactions. Justin composed a picture using the *Mutual Storytelling Game CD-ROM* (Erford, 2000) of a forest background, a fox, turtle, owl, and tiger cub.

Counselor (C):   All right, Justin. I want you to tell a really good story about this picture that you just did on the computer, and we printed out—and it's a beautiful picture. What I want you to do is to tell a great story, have the characters talking with each other any way you want them to. You want to tell what they're thinking and what they're feeling and certainly what they're doing. And if they want to talk to each, they can talk to each other. Remember that every great story has a beginning and lots of good details and also has a really good ending. And at the end of it, I'm going to ask you to tell a lesson or a moral for the story, kind of what did some of the characters learn when they're in the story. Then I will get my chance to tell a story, because it's only fair, right, if you tell a story then I should get my chance. I'll retell your story, and I might tell it a little bit differently the second time. But your job right now is to tell really good story about that picture. You ready?

Justin (J):   Mmmhmm. One day a baby tiger got lost in the woods, and um, and um, a fox was in the woods and was hungry. He kept on eating, eating all the animals in the forest. And the tiger didn't know about that. But one day the owl, the owl told him that and then he looked over to where the fox was at prowl and saw a um, turtle and the fox ate him. And, um, the fox liked it. Okay and then the tiger, um, went up the tree to live with the owl. And that's the end.

C: That's the end?

J: Mmmhmm.

C: Okay so the tiger is living up in the tree with the owl?

J: Mmmhmm.

C: Okay, and what is the lesson of the story or the moral of the story?

J: How to warn, warn people.

C: Okay. Tell me more. How would you warn people?

J: By telling them about danger and finding a safe place to hide.

Intermission

Justin's story was unusually short, lacking details, thoughts, and feelings. It also presented with some content related to his presenting problem, aggression. The counselor's response could address many issues, but the primary purposes of the retelling that follows were to: 1. Model more extensive, detailed storytelling, 2. Give alternative solutions to anger and aggression, and 3. Reinforce several themes applicable to his presenting problem. In addition the metaphorical use of the owl and turtle were irresistible, so the retelling cast the owl in a wise, friendly role while the protective features of the turtle were revealed.

C: Okay. Alrighty. OK, Justin, I'm going to go ahead and retell the story and I might add some details and I might subtract some details. But that was a really good story. That had a lot of exciting adventure in it. I'm going to be really hard pressed to tell a better story, but I'll try my best, OK.

J: (Nods and laughs)

C: One day there was a tiger, it was actually a tiger cub, a small tiger, a little baby tiger, and it got lost in the woods. And it was kind of walking through the woods, kind of looking around, going, "Wow, this doesn't look familiar, I'm lost and I don't know where my mom is, I don't know where my dad is, and I'm just kind of walking around trying to find my way home." And he was all alone because, as you can imagine, tigers don't have a whole lot of friends, because they're the kind of folks that kind of run around eating people. A lot of people wouldn't want to be a tiger's friend and that goes for tiger cubs, too; because they're afraid, you know, if I get too close to him, he might eat me.

J: Yeah. (Laughs)

C: So he was feeling kind of lonely and a little bit depressed because nobody will, you know, will talk to him, you know, kind of give advice. He goes by a chimpanzee and he says, "Hey, can you help me find my mom?" The chimpanzee, you know, heads for the tree because he doesn't want to get too close to the tiger. The baby chimpanzee said to the mother chimpanzee, "Hey why can't we help the little tiger cub out?" And his mom said, "Because he'll eat you. You just stay away from people like that 'cause he's a tiger and tigers are mean and eat people." So he's feeling kind of lonely and upset because no one will help him find his way back to his parents. But up in the tree, kinda watching all the action is this owl. That's kind of what owls do, sit way up high and check out what's going on, and they kind of see a lot of things the other people might not notice. That's why owls are often looked at as being very wise creatures, you know. Owls are kind of all knowing and very wise.

J: (Nods and laughs)

C: So, the owl's kind of checking things out, looking at the situation, and the owl has a pretty big heart. So the owl says, you know, maybe I should help the tiger cub out. He's not really hurting anybody and he's probably getting pretty hungry, but he's really in need of a friend right now to help him find his way back to his parents. So he swoops down and says, "Hey, what's going on little tiger cub?" The tiger cub is crying by this time and if you've ever seen a tiger cub cry, it's really kind of a sad thing because his fur and what not gets all matted and messed up—really a sad sight.

J: Sure is (laughing).

C: So the owl, of course, sees that the tiger cub crying, "Boohoo, I'm lost, I can't find my mom, I can't find my dad. I don't know what to do." Um, the owl says "Hey, maybe I can help you out." "Oh, could you please, sir. I'd appreciate it so much." And he thinks—hey, the tiger cub has some pretty good manners, and if the tiger cub has pretty good manners then maybe I'll take him under my wing so to speak, kind of help him along, help him find his parents. So while he's talking to the tiger cub—you know, owls have extraordinarily good hearing and eyesight—he spotted a fox, uh, coming along and this fox is actually kind of hungry, he's out looking for a meal. So the owl says, "I'll tell you what, let's go up into the tree over here because this fox is coming along and you don't want to be around when the fox comes through because he'll eat little tiger cubs like you."

J: (Laughs)

C: So the tiger cub climbs the tree, because tigers can do that, and they sit on the branch together. Then the owl says, "Oh my goodness, watch this," and sees that fox spying on the little turtle. And the turtle, um, of course has this nice hard shell on, and the fox is going to go and have turtle soup, without the soup if you know what I mean?

J: Yeah (laughing). He's gonna eat him up!

C: Right. He's going to eat this turtle, clean him right out of his shell and have him for dinner. So he goes over to the turtle, and of course the turtle sees the fox coming and so what does the turtle do, immediately?

J: Umm, hides in his shell?

C: That's right, he hides in his shell. And there's a reason why he hides in his shell; he's protected in there. And turtles, any time they feel threatened or scared, they will often times pull their feet and all four legs into their shell, and their head into the shell and inside they can think, you know, what should I do? And a lot of the times the best thing to do is just to wait and to think until the fox gives up. The fox comes over and moves the shell around, and you know, is trying to get in there, trying to get at some of that good old turtle meat, 'cause he's trying to make a good dinner. And eventually the fox, after about 15 minutes, gives up. He says, "This is just ridiculous. I can't get any dinner from this turtle, I'm just wasting my energy. I'm gonna go find something a little bit easier, or maybe a littler bit

tastier. I don't even like turtle meat to begin with. They're a little bit tough, they're not real tender like tiger cubs and stuff like that."

J: (Roaring with laughter)

C: So off he goes. He walks under the tree and doesn't even notice the owl and tiger up there watching this whole thing. He just kind of goes off to find something else to eat for dinner. They keep watching the turtle and see the turtle kind of poke his head out and look around real careful to see if the fox is still there. And then eventually when he feels it's safe, he goes walking along to find some water or someplace where he can relax a little bit, because he's done his job, he's protected himself, he's lived to see another day. The turtle is going on to see his family and friends, to see what they're doing. And so the tiger cub looks at the turtle and goes, "Wow, that was really great. I mean, here was the mean old fox that was gonna make him his dinner and all he did was just protect himself, go in his shell, he didn't seem to be scared or nothing at all." And the owl says, "Well that's the way it is, you know, when you're a turtle and you carry your home around on your back like that and if something threatens and you go right in and figure out what it is you should do and you wait for a safer time." And then the cub said, "You know, that's really what we did, wasn't it?" The owl said, "Absolutely, we saw the fox coming because we had good hearing and vision and we went ahead and climbed up into the tree to a safer place, to a place where we wouldn't get hurt." And the tiger cub said, "Wow, what a really important lesson." "Oh really," you know, the owl said, "What kind of lessons did you learn?" "Well, I learned first of all the one thing you do whenever you feel threatened and scared is to go find a safe place so that you don't get hurt and to think about what you should be doing." "Oh really, and what have you been thinking about?" asked the owl. "Well, I've been thinking about how to find my mom and dad." And the owl said, "Oh really? How would you find your mom and dad?"

"Well, you have such great vision and such great hearing, would you mind flying up above the canopy of the forest here and find, and see if you can locate my mother and my father?" And the owl said, "You know, because you've been so good and such a good friend to me today, I think I'll do just that." So the owl took off way above the trees and flew just a couple miles and already heard the tiger calling, because his mom was just worried sick because the little tiger cub wasn't anywhere to be found. And so he swooped down onto the tree and said, "Hey, mama tiger, I know where your little boy is, he's right up the road, you can go ahead right up the trail and just follow me."

C: So the mama tiger said, "Thank you so much, I've been worried to death about my little tiger cub." And the owl just flew away and the tiger kept running along, you know, as fast as she could and let out a big tiger roar. The father tiger heard this too and so they basically came at the same time and found the little baby tiger still safe up in the tree branch where the owl left him. The owl landed right beside him and the mommy and daddy looked up and saw the little tiger cub meowing, sitting right there on the tree branch. And the tiger club was so excited, he just climbed down the tree, went over, and, of course, his mom, you know how moms are, started licking him and stuff like that, "Oh I missed you so much, I love you," kissy, kissy, kissy, and having such a good time. But that's how tiger moms show how much they love their little tiger cub, you know.

J: (Laughing hysterically)

C: And so the little tiger cub looked up and said, "Thank you so much for helping me out today. I've learned so much today with you, would you mind if I came back sometime and we can play again?" And the owl said, "Sure, any time, that's fantastic." And, of course, the mommy and the daddy tiger said "Oh, thank you so much! If there's anything that we can do for you, you just let us know and we'll be there to help you out because you are a fantastic owl, and you did this very nice thing for us." The end.

J: Wow. That was way better than mine.

C: Sometimes longer stories are more entertaining. So, there are a couple of lessons they actually learned, the one the tiger cub already shared about finding a safe place to think and calm down when you feel scared or threatened. But both of them also learned some lessons too, didn't they? Can you think of any of the other lessons that the owl and tiger cub might have learned?

J: (Thinks for about 15 seconds and then shakes his head no)

C: Well, the tiger cub also learned that if people think you are mean or nasty—even if on the inside you really are not—then they will avoid you, or even not help you if you really need it. He also learned that friendliness and good manners are a great way to get people to like and help you, right?

J: He sure did!

C: Now the owl learned that if you show kindness to someone, you are oftentimes rewarded and so now his best friends in the whole jungle are who?

J: Uh, the tigers.

C: Right, the tiger family. And they are a good group of folks to have on your side, because if anyone's ever picking on you, all you have to do is go get your tiger family friends. Okay, so the tiger cub learned some really good lessons about how you go inside your shell, you relax, you try to figure out what to do and so forth. And the tiger cub and owl learned some good lessons about what it's like to be a good friend, okay?

J: That was a great story—I like tigers!

C: Great. Now I want you to take this video tape home with you and watch this story again every night until the next time I see you. OK?

J: No problemo! Can my mom and little brother watch it too?

Brief Analysis

In this retelling, the counselor sought to reveal several helpful alternative coping strategies that people (or tiger cubs) can use in anxiety producing situations— alternatives that do not involve aggression. The counselor also sought to reinforce a couple of themes that were applicable to his presenting problem: 1) Alienation occurs when you are mean to people, or even if they just think you are mean and 2) good manners impress people and make it more likely that they will want to be friendly or helpful toward you. Finally, because this was Justin's first time telling a story, the counselor wanted to model more extensive, detailed storytelling so that Justin would be more expansive the next time the technique was used in the following session.

USEFULNESS AND EVALUATION OF THE MUTUAL STORYTELLING TECHNIQUE

Originally developed to overcome children's resistance to analysis of unconscious material, the mutual storytelling technique can be used both as a diagnostic tool and a therapeutic technique (Shapiro, 1994). When used diagnostically, the therapist does not respond with a story of his own, but instead prompts the child to provide more stories in order to develop an idea of the child's unconscious drives, needs, or conflicts. To allow sufficient themes to emerge the child should provide at least a dozen different stories before the counselor forms a diagnostic opinion. When the technique is used therapeutically, the counselor responds with a story involving an appropriate resolution to the conflict in the story, as described above.

The mutual storytelling technique can be used to facilitate the development of a therapeutic relationship with children who have difficulty talking about themselves or who are resistant to counseling. It is not recommended for use with individuals with poor verbal skills or subaverage cognitive abilities. It can also be applied to the group counseling context (e.g., group members take turns contributing to a story).

According to Gardner (1986), the mutual storytelling technique is most useful with children between the ages of 5 and 11 years. Children younger than 5 are usually incapable of telling an organized

story, and children older than 11 begin to realize that they are revealing themselves in their stories and may become resistant to this technique. Alternatively, Stiles and Kottman (1990) suggested the prime ages of use were 9 to 14 years because of older children's more advanced verbal skill, imaginations, and life experiences. Gardner used the technique with children with posttraumatic stress, hyperactivity and distractibility, learning disabilities, disinterest in school, withdrawal from peers, shyness, acting-out behavior, and manifestations of the Oedipus complex (Gardner, 1974, 1986; Schaeffer & O'Connor, 1983).

O'Brien (1992) described the use of this technique for children with AD/HD in order to transmit insight, values, and standards of behavior. For example, the counselor can use a metaphor of trains and motors to explain to the child that his brain is like a motor that is going too fast. The people on the train cannot see anything out of the windows when the train is traveling very fast. But if the train could slow down, the people would be able to see the scenery. Likewise, Kottman and Stiles (1990) believed that the mutual storytelling technique could be used to help correct children's misbehavior. By listening to a child's story, the professional counselor can discover the child's motivation to misbehave: attention, power, revenge, or inadequacy. The counselor can then use a story to help the child to redirect his mistaken goal or faulty beliefs or to develop the child's social interest. Finally, the mutual storytelling technique can be used with children who are depressed or suicidal (Stiles & Kottman, 1990). Telling stories can help children come to terms with their sense of loss, desire for rescue, or feelings of helplessness or hopelessness. Likewise, the counselor can use stories to teach children new ways to express anger or cope with the world.

Little empirical research has been conducted on the efficacy of the mutual storytelling technique (Stiles & Kottman, 1990). Anecdotally, Schaeffer & O'Connor (1983) reported that Gardner successfully treated a child with posttraumatic stress disorder by repeated use of the technique (a sort of storytelling desensitization). Gardner cautions that the technique should be used only by counselors adequately trained in psychodynamics, dream analysis, and the interpretation of projective material (Gardner, 1974), although when using the technique simply for pointing out and increasing problem resolution strategies and choices, psychodynamic training becomes far less consequential. Gardner (1986) also mentioned that it is unrealistic to expect a single story or confrontation to bring about permanent change in a child. Some counselors will engage the child in one or two stories per counseling session for multiple sessions, devoting the remainder of the session time to other counseling strategies and processes. In this way, the mutual storytelling technique is used in conjunction with several other methods of treatment (Gardner, 1974).

CHAPTER 10

Paradoxical Intention

ORIGINS OF THE PARADOXICAL INTENTION TECHNIQUE

In paradoxical intention, the professional counselor directs the client to perform in a way that seems incompatible with the therapeutic goal (Dattilio, 2001). Victor Frankl, credited with developing this technique, described paradoxical intention as encouraging clients to seek what they are avoiding, to embrace what they have been fighting, and to replace their fears with a wish (Young, 1992). Milton Erickson and Jay Haley are also widely credited with development and applications of paradox, particularly as used in strategic family therapy. With this technique, clients are told to exaggerate their symptoms (Lamb, 1980). For instance, a client who experiences panic attacks and fears that he may die suddenly might be told to "go ahead and die" (Dattilio, 1987, p. 102). Instead of being told to try to get better, clients are encouraged to try to get worse (Lamb, 1980). When people consciously try to get better, their symptoms sometimes increase. Often, however, the harder clients try to produce their symptoms intentionally, the more they find they are unable to do so. As such, the "wind is taken out of the sails of anticipatory anxiety" (Frankl, 1946, p. 83).

Paradoxical intention is a truly eclectic technique because it is not tied to any one theoretical approach. It is used by a variety of theoretical orientations, including systemic family therapy, existential therapy, reality therapy, transactional analysis, and individual or Adlerian psychology (DeBord, 1989; Young, 1992).

There are several different types of paradoxical intentions, including symptom prescription (or symptom scheduling), restraining, and reframing. *Symptom prescription* involves a therapeutic directive for the client to continue his symptomatic behavior (DeBord, 1989). Sometimes the client is also given specific instructions on when to perform the symptom; this is called *symptom scheduling* (Kraft, Claiborn, & Dowd, 1985). In *restraining*, the professional counselor directs the client to prevent change or to stop trying to change the symptoms (Swoboda, Dowd, & Wise, 1990). Essentially, the client is given the message that in order to change, they must stay the same. The professional counselor may point out the negative consequences of change in order to encourage the client to resist feeling better. An example of a paradoxical restraining directive is "if your depression lifted, people would react to you more favorably and would put greater demands upon you" (Swoboda et al., 1990, p. 256). In *reframing*, the problem is explained in such a way that alters the client's point of view and therefore the meaning of the situation (see chapter 19 on reframing).

The rationale behind paradoxical intention is that most problems are more emotional than logical (Hackney & Cormier, 2005). Clients become involved in a cycle with fears evoking symptoms which in turn increase the fears (Seligman, 2001). By encouraging the client to do or wish for the thing they fear most, the client may undergo a change of attitude toward the symptom (Lamb, 1980). For instance, when a client who struggled with stuttering was encouraged to try to stutter, the client was attempting a task that he did well (Nystul & Muszynska, 1976). Therefore, the client no longer feared failure, and he was free of anxiety. Consequently, relaxed speech was able to proceed. On the other hand, another client, who was afraid to leave her house because she feared that she might faint, was instructed to try to make herself faint (Seligman, 2001). Despite her best effort, she was unable to do so. Thus, the client had to change her attitude about fainting, and her fear of fainting diminished.

Paradoxical intention helps clients become aware of how they are behaving in certain situations and their responsibility for their behavior (Corey, 2007). Paradoxical techniques often put the client in a double bind situation when asked to exaggerate the problematic behavior. If the client accepts the professional counselor's directive, he demonstrates control over the symptom. On the other hand, if the client chooses to resist the directive and decrease the symptomatic behavior, it is not merely under control but eliminated. The goal of paradoxical intention is to help clients reach a point where they no longer fight their symptoms but instead exaggerate them (George & Christiani, 1995). As a result, the symptoms will continue to decrease until clients are no longer bothered by them.

HOW TO IMPLEMENT THE PARADOXICAL INTENTION TECHNIQUE

Paradoxical intention is not usually used until more conventional methods of therapy have been tried (Corey, 2007). The paradoxical intention technique's illogical nature and novelty can be used to create motivation in a discouraged client (Young, 1992). Before using a paradoxical directive, the professional counselor should ask herself the following questions to determine if the technique is appropriate:

1. Have I established a strong bond of trust between myself and the client?
2. Might the use of paradox have a boomerang effect, so that the client feels tricked and thus becomes even more resistant?
3. How has the client responded to the use of other techniques?
4. Am I clear on what I expect to accomplish, and do I have an educated sense of how my client might react to this procedure (Corey, 2007, p. 386)?

After determining that paradoxical intention may be used, the professional counselor should ensure that the specific inappropriate behavior is identified (Doyle, 1998). Then the professional counselor should persuade the client to produce the behavior in an exaggerated manner. Finally, the professional counselor may inject humor into the situation as the client engages in the behavior. This allows the client to detach from the problem by laughing at it. These steps should be repeated until the inappropriate behavior in minimized. In addition, it is sometimes helpful to restrain the expression of the symptom to certain days, times, or situations.

Jay Haley (as cited in Lamb, 1980, p. 218) outlined eight specific facets of paradoxical intention:

(1) establish a relationship with the client, (2) define the problem, (3) establish goals, (4) offer a plan, (5) disqualify the current authority on the problem, (6) give a paradoxical intention directive, (7) observe the client's response to the directive and continue encouragement, and (8) avoid taking credit for the improvement.

VARIATIONS OF THE PARADOXICAL INTENTION TECHNIQUE

The *relapse technique* is similar to another paradoxical intention, symptom prescription. In this variation of the technique, the professional counselor asks the client to return to his former behavior after the problem is solved (Corsini, 1982). The relapse technique can help clients realize the inefficiency or silliness of their prior behavior. It also prevents against unintentional relapse because the clients are often unable to recreate their old behavior without laughing or feeling silly.

EXAMPLE OF THE PARADOXICAL INTENTION TECHNIQUE

The following case illustrates several principles of paradoxical intention. First, the problematic symptoms are reframed as positive behavior. They are not only defined as positive, but positive in a way that is contradictory to the client's value system and view of himself. Second, the will of the professional counselor is reversed as soon as it is discovered that this very will for the client to improve may be a predominant part of the problem, preventing a full recovery from symptoms and a completely healthy level of functioning. Third, the symptom that had recently shown vast improvement is prescribed. This symptom is prescribed in a way that bounds the client to make progress regardless of prescription outcome.

Michael is a 19-year-old male with a long history of social anxiety and a more recent history of panic disorder with agoraphobia. Upon graduation from high school, Michael accepted a scholarship to a university at a neighboring state where he experienced his first panic attack prior to an examination during his second semester. He found himself unable to complete the semester as the panic attacks worsened and he returned home to live with his family, dropping out of college and losing his scholarship. Once home, he returned to the part-time job he held while in high school, but soon found he was unable to maintain this position due to the panic attacks and the mounting fears of leaving the family house. Soon these fears generalized to any activity outside of the home, with the exception of church-related functions and counseling sessions. In general, Michael had a fear of fear, with church, home, and counseling being the only three places he found safe.

At the outset of counseling, which began approximately 7 weeks prior to the current session, Michael was "unable" to drive and insisted that his mother drive him to church and counseling. He experienced panic attacks several times daily, most notably in his mother's presence. When this was pointed out to Michael, he stated it was because "she makes me so anxious and upsets me with her constant nagging." Though it soon became clear to the professional counselor that Michael's behavior was beneficial to him in a number of ways, he sincerely had no awareness of this and found it impossible to take any responsibility for his symptoms. Various cognitive and behavioral interventions were employed (e.g., progressive muscle relaxation training, deep breathing, thought stopping, cognitive restructuring, positive reinforcement, role playing) during the course of the last 7 weeks of counseling, resulting in vast improvement.

Up to this point, Michael had made great strides toward improving his quality of life and level of functioning. He had maintained a very positive and determined attitude and always complied with work outside of counseling sessions. First, Michael began *allowing* his mother to drive him places other than church and counseling, as long as it was within a 5 mile radius of the home. He had also begun to venture from the car and stand outside the supermarket while his mother picked up an item or two inside. In addition, he even began driving himself at times, though he required a passenger "just in case." He was now able to go as far as 10 miles away from home. Finally, he had begun to ride and train his horses again and felt a great sense of accomplishment from this. Overall, he had experienced a reduction in panic attacks from approximately two to four a day to only one to two a week.

Quite unexpectedly, the improvements stopped. Over the course of the last two sessions, no improvements were made. Michael seemed unable to progress any further, or reluctant to. He continued to find it impossible to accept any responsibility for his remaining symptoms. He did admit to enjoying the sympathy and attention he received, and in general, was still able to control the lives of family members by his special needs. It was then that the professional counselor realized that this very control Michael wished to maintain and exert over his family was also being generalized to the therapeutic relationship. Suddenly, the resistance to improve became clear. The pressure to completely abandon the symptomatic behavior became the very reason it continued.

(Following is an attempt by the professional counselor to alter the way the client perceives the problem. This is termed Paradoxical Reframe. The counselor is redefining the problematic behavior as positive. This is especially useful if the professional counselor is planning to prescribe the symptomatic behavior.)

Michael (M):   I just can't seem to be the way they want me to be. I just can't seem to be completely healthy.

Counselor (C):   Then don't be.

M: I don't understand.

C: I can see how you are reluctant to give this last bit up.

M: What do you mean?

C: Well, I can understand how you can think you have no other means for getting your needs met, or having any power in your family. It probably just seems easier to remain needy and sick than to be strong and assertive. It's actually quite smart of you. And really you aren't doing all that poorly anymore. In fact, the initial reasons that brought you here aren't all that troublesome anymore. Sure, they're still there, but they're not really that bothersome and if they continue to get your needs met, well then, why not? In fact, you may even want to step it up a bit.

(Paradoxes are actually quite logical when considering the family system in which they are to function. With that in mind, the professional counselor offers the following.)

M: I'm confused.

C: Well, you mentioned earlier that Mom is so pleased with your progress that she's beginning to require more of you again. Even though you are not 100% better, you are certainly improved. Apparently that improvement is enough to convince her that you are a healthy adult again. It also seems to me, that since you and I have worked very hard together and have used every method proven to work with these situations, yet you still

have a few lingering symptoms . . . well . . . it seems to me that they may very well be a part of who you are. We may as well embrace them. And while we're at it, perhaps even increase them to get Mom off your back.

M: How will I do that?

C: Just do exactly opposite of everything we've been doing. When you initially came in, you were having anywhere from two to four panic episodes a day. Now, you are down to one or two a week. Is that right?

M: Yes.

C: Well, perhaps we moved too quickly. Yes, now that I think of it . . . yes, I think it might be best to have at least one panic attack a day.

M: But how?

C: Oh, easy enough. You are still having difficulty driving yourself further than 10 miles beyond your house . . . and with crossing bridges . . . you are still taking alternate routes to avoid bridges, aren't you?

M: Yes.

C: Well, just push the envelope a bit and when you hit that 10 mile mark, keep driving a little further than 10 miles and pull over to the side of the road, turn the ignition off, and then tell yourself, "I can't do this. I can't breathe. If I go further I will surely die!" Repeat that until you have an episode, complete with hyperventilation and heart palpitations.

(The pressure that is likely leading Michael to be resistant is now gone. He is no longer being pressured to be completely healthy.)

M: But this seems so different from what we've been doing.

C: This is a new situation we have here. A new situation calls for a new plan. Before, we wanted to make you as healthy as possible. Now we realize that you should embrace your fearfulness, because not only is this a part of who you are, it also gets your mom to ease up.

Either way, Michael will see an improvement. If he is able to have a panic attack as prescribed, he will see that he is able to cause them. And if he is able to cause them, then he is able to prevent them. If the symptom prescription is not successful, and Michael resists the professional counselor's attempts in order to maintain control of counseling, he will have driven beyond the 10-mile mark without a panic episode, thus still making progress. Michael has also now been given a paradoxical reframe that goes against his view of himself. The professional counselor has now painted the picture that his symptoms are manipulative, or are useful for getting what he wants. This is generally disagreeable to Michael's value set and presents him with a choice. He will either refuse to continue his symptomatic behavior to manipulate his family, or he will continue his behavior but refuse the inherent benefits of control and sympathy. If he refuses the benefits of his behavior, he will eventually give up the behavior as well, as his behavior is in fact motivated by this benefit.

USEFULNESS AND EVALUATION OF THE PARADOXICAL INTENTION TECHNIQUE

Paradoxical intention can be used with a variety of presenting problems. It may be especially useful with clients who are involved in repetitive behavior patterns that seem involuntary or automatic (Young, 1992). Paradoxical intention may also be useful with clients whose problematic behavior is a means of getting attention from others (Doyle, 1998). Paradoxical intention has been used to treat anxiety disorders, agoraphobia, insomnia, juvenile delinquency, stress,

depression, procrastination, disruptive behavior, temper tantrums, obsessions, compulsions, phobic reactions, behavioral tics, urinary retention, and stammering (Corey, 2007; DeBord, 1989; Frankl, 1946; Lamb, 1980; Kraft et al., 1985).

Paradoxical intention has been credited with inducing rapid reduction and frequent elimination of symptoms (Lamb, 1980). Most clients will respond within 4 to 12 sessions. According to a literature review conducted by DeBord (1989), paradoxical intention is an effective treatment strategy for agoraphobia, insomnia, and problem blushing. Indeed, 92% of studies on paradoxical intention reviewed by DeBord resulted in positive outcomes. DeBord also found that symptom prescription resulted in at least some degree of improvement in 14 out of the 15 studies reviewed. Finally, DeBord discovered that in all 4 studies examined, reframing was more effective in treating negative emotions than other forms of treatment. Likewise, Swoboda et al. (1990) looked at the effectiveness of restraining, reframing, and a pseudo therapy control in treating depression and determined that reframing was the most effective treatment, followed by restraining. In contrast, Kraft et al. (1985) noted that paradoxical directives were no more effective than nonparadoxical directives in treating negative emotions. Also, Greenberg and Pies (1983) concluded that outcomes research on paradoxical intention lacked adequate rigor and relied primarily on client self-report. Importantly, paradoxical intention should not be used when exaggerating the symptom may cause a real danger to the client, such as suicidal symptoms.

Techniques Based Upon Gestalt Principles

The word Gestalt means "a structured, meaningful unity that stands out against a background in the organism/environment field" (Wolfert & Cook, 1999, pp. 3–4). Gestalt therapists focus on the organism being whole and believe that people find and make meaning of their experiences by forming gestalts. Gestalt therapy provides an interesting combination of existential, phenomenological and behavioral approaches that relies heavily on present moment experiences, existential meaning, interpersonal relationships, and holistic integration.

While some other approaches to counseling may appear reductionistic, Gestalt therapy helps clients construct meaning and purpose through heightening their awareness and perceptions of what is happening in the present moment. Change is viewed as a perpetual state, and counselors using a Gestalt approach frequently attempt to discern environmental, interpersonal and intrapersonal challenges and barriers to change, thus helping the client to adapt and accommodate to internal and external environments. Counselors help clients complete "unfinished business" that prevents healthy contact and adaptation to the environment and satisfy needs through development of clear and flexible relational boundaries. Gestalt techniques tend to create intense emotions and can be viewed as contrived or silly by some clients expecting a more traditional talk therapy approach.

Three classic Gestaltian techniques are presented in the following chapters: empty chair, body movement and exaggeration, and role reversal. The empty chair is used to elicit powerful emotion-laden dialogue with important, albeit absent, individuals in the client's life, or two sides or dimensions of a single client, such as when a client is conflicted about how to deal with an issue and could benefit from acting out and discussing the internal dialogue in an externalized manner with a supportive counselor. Body movement and exaggeration are used to help clients understand meanings underlying their nonverbal communications, often bringing hidden meanings and communications to the conscious level. For example, a client who shakes a finger to emphasize a point, or says something that the counselor thinks is more meaningful that the client perceives, will be asked to repeat the action or the phrase, sometimes a half dozen times while the counselor and client discuss possible implications and hidden meanings in those actions. Role reversal is a technique that has the client take on the opposite perspective, argument, or role in order to explore meanings from various perspective. For example, a teenage client who believes her autonomy is being quashed by a controlling father will be encouraged to take on the father role and process her feelings and complaints from that perspective. All of these techniques aim to expand the client's awareness of their circumstances and create and construct new or revised meanings, in order to better adapt and accommodate to his environment.

MULTICULTURAL IMPLICATIONS

An advantage of the Gestaltian approach is the importance of the therapeutic relationship and underlying philosophy that each client should be approached openly and without preconception in order to help understand their present moment perceptions. It stands to reason that Gestalt therapy could be particularly effective in helping bicultural clients reconcile and integrate conflicting or confusing culturally based values and beliefs presented by the cultural contexts within which one exists. For example, many individuals whose culture of origin values collectivistic practices struggle in a competitive, individualistic American business world. Gestaltian approaches are made to address such conflicts.

Gestalt techniques often create intense emotional reactions in clients, and clients from some cultures may be unaccustomed to expressing strong emotions to others or just to nonfamily members. (e.g., Arab Americans, Asian Americans). Alternatively, some clients may be more emotive (e.g., some women) and appreciate the insights and existential orientation of a Gestalt approach. For example, women may appreciate the encouragement to express suppressed or even denied emotions, and discus-

sions of healthy boundaries in interpersonal relationships. At any rate, professional counselors must exercise caution and good judgment when using techniques based upon the Gestalt approach because interventions must always be timed appropriately and implemented with sensitivity to individuals with diverse cultural characteristics, especially those who are emotionally reserved, as these clients may resist such approaches and terminate counseling prematurely.

Some clients are more comfortable at expressing themselves nonverbally than verbally, or may say one thing but communicate conflicting information through nonverbal means. A Gestalt counselor's focus upon facial expressions and gestures can help these clients understand internal conflicts and construct a more integrated environmental connection. It is almost common sense, but it is essential to remember to focus upon the client and the client's needs, rather than the use of a Gestaltian technique in a mechanistic manner.

Gestalt techniques empower both men and women by emphasizing self-awareness, the legitimacy of feelings, and autonomy of action, and by integrating sometimes disconnected elements of thoughts, feelings, values, and behaviors. But it is important to understand that some clients from diverse racial, ethnic, or socioeconomic cultures may resist a Gestaltian approach because of emotional intensity or perceived artificiality (e.g., talking to your hand or an empty chair, repeatedly sticking out your tongue), which may make the therapy appear contrived and silly. In addition, some clients from non-Western cultures may perceive Gestalt counselors to be confrontational because of the nature of the directed physical interventions employed, feel threatened, and terminate prematurely.

CHAPTER 11

Empty Chair

ORIGINS OF THE EMPTY CHAIR TECHNIQUE

The empty chair technique originated from Fritz Perls' Gestalt theory. Gestalt theory aims to prevent the dichotomy that leads to a disconnect between the individual and his environment (Frew, 1992). Perls first used the empty chair to help individuals role play what they would like to say to, or how they would like to act toward, another person (George & Christiani, 1995). By definition, Gestalt includes both the creation and deconstruction of the whole (Crose, 1990), and the empty chair technique reflects the integration of polarities; that is, by expressing both sides of the issue at once, a person can work out conflicts between values, thoughts, feelings, and actions (Young, 1992).

To promote an understanding of this theory, and in turn the empty chair technique, the basic concepts of Gestalt therapy follow (Coker, 2004).

1. A person exists within his or her environmental context; no individual person is completely self supporting.
2. People either have contact with their environment or withdraw from it.
3. If a person has contact with the environment, she connects with people and things that are reinforcing or desired.
4. If a person withdraws from the environment, she tries to eliminate people and things that are believed to cause harm.
5. It is not always healthy to have contact, and is not always unhealthy to withdraw.
6. The main purposes of the personality are the contacts and withdrawals one has with the environment.
7. A person is both an individual and a function of the environmental context.
8. In Gestalt counseling the focal point is how (not why) the person perceives her troubles in the here and now.
9. The goal is for the professional counselor to provide the individual with what is needed to solve present and future issues.
10. Gestalt therapy places great importance on the experiential aspect of the here and now.
11. By becoming aware of the here and now, as well as contact and withdrawal attempts and interpretations, one can gain insight into living effectively in her environment.

HOW TO IMPLEMENT THE EMPTY CHAIR TECHNIQUE

After establishing the therapeutic relationship and building trust with the client, the professional counselor can use the empty chair technique during a session with the client. There are six steps in implementing this method (Young, 1992). To warm up, the professional counselor should request that the client think about the polarity and a specific example in which the client has felt both ways. In the first step, the professional counselor explains why he will be using this technique in an effort to quell any resistance the client may have. The professional counselor should set up two chairs directly facing each other; the chairs represent either side of the polarity. For the client, becoming aware of his feelings surrounding this polarity is important before moving on to the next step. In the steps that follow, the client will sit in one chair representing one side of the polarity facing an empty chair representing the other side. As the client expresses his feelings surrounding either side of the polarity, he switches to the corresponding chair.

In the second step, the professional counselor works with the client to "deepen the experience" (Young, 1992, p. 223). The professional counselor begins by having the client choose the side of the polarity for which she has the strongest feelings. The client is then given time to become familiar with and even more aware of how she is feeling. The professional counselor needs to help the client stay in the here and now by asking questions that bring the client back to the present. For example, if a client says, "I really could have punched him," the counselor can question, "Are you aware of that anger now?"

In the third step, the goal for the client is to express the most prominent side of the polarity (Young, 1992). During the expression, the professional counselor cannot be judgmental. By staying in the here and now, the client should act out his experience rather than describe it. The professional counselor can do this by instructing the client to use exaggerated gestures or vocal expressions. To deepen the experience, the counselor can request that the client repeat phrases or words several times. In this step, the professional counselor can also take time to summarize what she sees as the client's situation. The professional counselor should ask *what* and *how* questions rather than *why* questions to continue deepening the experience. Once the client has come to a point which the professional counselor sees as an appropriate place to stop, the counselor asks the client to switch chairs. A stopping point can be determined only by the professional counselor and occurs when the client has gotten stuck or seems to have fully expressed himself.

The fourth step in using the empty chair technique is counter expression. As the client sits in the opposite chair, she replies to the first expression. Once more, the professional counselor helps deepen the experience for the client by encouraging her to express the reverse argument and by evoking an emotional response (Young, 1992).

In the fifth step, the professional counselor has the client switch roles until it is determined (by the professional counselor or the client) that each side of the pole has been completely articulated. This allows the client to become aware of both sides of the polarity. Sometimes during this step, a resolution between the poles occurs, but a solution is not always an outcome of this technique (Young, 1992).

The sixth and final step of the empty chair technique focuses on getting the client to agree to an action plan. The professional counselor may assign homework as a way to get the client to investigate both sides of the dichotomy (Young, 1992).

VARIATIONS OF THE EMPTY CHAIR TECHNIQUE

Vernon (1993) illustrated a less involved variation of this technique for use with children. In this method, the professional counselor asks the child to play his side of the conflict. If the conflict is intrapersonal, the professional counselor asks the child to choose one side to begin. After the child expresses himself, the professional counselor should request that the child move to the empty chair and express the other side of the issue. Have the child switch chairs as necessary until both sides are adequately expressed. If the child has difficulty talking to a chair, Vernon suggests using a tape recorder instead of a chair.

Another variation of the empty chair is the fantasy dialogue. For example, if a client has many somatic complaints, the professional counselor can ask the client to have a conversation with the body part in an effort to find out if the ailment has any benefits for the client. By becoming aware of the benefits, the client may be able to resolve the issue (Young, 1992).

Forced catastrophes is an additional variation of the empty chair technique, but should be used cautiously, especially if working with anxious individuals. This variation can be used with clients who are always expecting the worst. The professional counselor works with the client and insists that the client face the worst scenario possible, even if it is unlikely to occur. The professional counselor helps the client express the emotions that go along with the nightmare situation (Young, 1992).

EXAMPLE OF THE EMPTY CHAIR TECHNIQUE

Sasha is a 19-year-old college student who has been in individual counseling for approximately 7 weeks. She first sought services due to relationship issues with her current on-again/off-again boyfriend. It quickly became evident that these issues were a pattern in nearly all relationships with Sasha, who oscillated between damaging, anger-driven strength and fear-based helpless dependency. Establishing a trusting relationship with Sasha proved especially difficult, though once established seemed particularly strong. Soon, issues of past sexual and physical abuse were brought to the forefront and Sasha felt confused by the dichotomy that she seemed to experience, represent, and express session after session.

Sasha (S): (Slightly lethargic) Sometimes, I just . . . I just get so tired, you know? It wears me out to be me sometimes. And that sounds so ridiculous. I mean, if being me is so tiresome, on me and everybody else, why not just be different? I mean really . . . why not? Why not just be different?

Counselor (C): If being the way you are now is so tiring . . .

S: Yeah. If this is so bad, change it! And now I feel irritable. I feel aggravated and I don't even know why.

C: Sasha, I see you experiencing just now, what it is that has been sort of happening all along . . . your emotions . . . the way you are feeling . . . it shifts suddenly . . . which leaves you feeling drained and bewildered.

S: And angry.

C: And angry.

S: You know, part of me wants so badly to be like, I don't know, like Scarlett O'Hara's sister-in-law in *Gone With the Wind* . . . what's her name?

C: Melanie wasn't it? Ms. Melanie.

S: Yes! Melanie. Sometimes I want to be like Melanie.

(It can oftentimes be very helpful to identify with a character in an effort to recognize intrapersonal characteristics, discuss complex feelings more easily, or as a figure to strive toward.)

C: And other times?

S: Oh, well, other times, like Scarlett of course.

C: And what do these two characters represent to you?

S: Well, Scarlett is obvious. She is strong. She doesn't let anything stop her from getting what she wants. She can be hurtful to others. But it keeps others from hurting her, you know? And I really respect her. And, well, Melanie . . . well, I could never be Melanie. She was so self-sacrificing, soft-spoken, and kind, but sometimes she seemed so sad. Scarlett walked all over her because she was weak compared to Scarlett. Very weak.

C: And it seems like I've heard you express a wish to be like Melanie, but then also say that you could never be like her?

(The professional counselor offers a very tentative confrontation to help Sasha see a very concrete example of the dichotomy she presents.)

S: See? It makes no sense. I don't think I know what I want. Or who I am. Or why I'm one way one minute and another way the next.

C: Sasha, I think that you, like most of us, have several selves that make up who you are. The difference with you is that you haven't always been very aware of these selves or their usefulness or purpose. Because of this, they often oppose one another rather than work together. Does that make sense to you?

S: Yeah. I think so.

C: I'd like to try something with you now to help you express both of these aspects of yourself.

S: Okay.

C: And it may feel silly at first, but because I believe in your ability to get past that and because I believe in the effectiveness of this technique, I think it will prove very beneficial.

S: I trust that.

C: Okay. What I want to do is called an empty chair technique, and it will actually involve the use of two chairs. (Pulls another chair up to directly face Sasha's)

S: (Laughs nervously)

C: It's okay to feel nervous or unsure at first. But I really think you can do this. Okay, so previous relationships have shown, and I've observed, and you've begun to realize that you seem to act and feel in completely opposing ways sometimes. In fact, just now, you related your opposing sides to the characters of Melanie and Scarlett, who are very opposite one another. (Pauses) If you could, Sasha, what emotional labels might you give these opposing selves?

S: Well, one is the obvious angry part of me. The other, umm, hmm, well the other part of me would be the scared part.

C: Okay. And which of these two do you feel most now?

S: Actually I'm feeling more scared and vulnerable today.

C: Okay. So imagine for a moment if I were able to actually pull two separate persons from you . . . one angry and the other scared. And

think about how they might look different . . . one of them might have her shoulders raised and squared off, with a glare in her eyes and a tightly clenched jaw. The other, well, she might have her shoulders slightly sunken, her hands clasped together, maybe looking downward to avoid others' gazes. Imagine that they are both able to sit in these chairs now, and speak to one another. But you are the only one who can give them a voice.

(The professional counselor is empowering Sasha.)

Only you know what they need to say to one another. So starting with the vulnerable you, what I'd like to have you do is express that part of yourself that feels vulnerable and afraid. And tell the "angry you" what the "vulnerable you" feels. Don't be "strong Sasha" right now. Just concentrate on feeling what "afraid Sasha" feels.

S: Right now?

C: Yes, whenever you are ready. You can do this, and I will help you if you need me.

S: (Takes a long deep breath and clasps hands in lap; looks down at her hands and speaks softly, almost in a whisper) I feel afraid—all of the time. All of the time, I feel afraid. And it is a miserable feeling. (Pauses for several moments, but is still looking down at her hands which are still clasped) I feel so helpless (pauses) and weak (pauses) and pathetic. (Takes another deep breath) I let others trample all over me. I let others get away with anything because I want them to love me. Or just like me. Just be nice to me. And I know it's so pathetic. (Whispers) It's so pathetic. (A little louder) But I also feel kind . . . and trusting. And that feels nice. It feels good to be good. I don't like not being good. You aren't supposed to hurt others just because they hurt you and you should be ashamed of yourself. (Looking up from her hands and looking directly at the empty chair) You hurting others is no better than what he was. You remind me so much of him sometimes. No, I shouldn't say that. God, sometimes I hate him.

C: What about right now?

S: Right now . . . right now I wish he liked me enough to . . . to not hurt me. I still wish he liked me. He so obviously didn't like me. And I don't know why. (Silence)

C: Okay Sasha, I'd like for you to move to angry Sasha's chair and give her a voice.

S: (Moving to the other chair) Yeah, now I'm feeling more comfortable! You *are* pathetic! (In a whining voice) "I want them to love me. Or just like me. Just be nice to me." Good Lord! Can you get any more disgusting? You make me sick. You do. You make me sick. If you'd been stronger to begin with, *we* wouldn't be here! You need me. You can just admit that. If it wasn't for me, you wouldn't have made it. And you can be "ashamed" of me all you want. But don't you dare say I'm just like him. I am what I have to be to get you through your pathetic life. You, my dear, are a liability. (Stops to take a breath)

C: Repeat that please. "You are a liability."

S: You are a liability.

C: Again.

S: You are a liability.

C: Again.

S: You are a liability!

C: And what you're feeling right now.

S: I'm exhausted and yet I cannot *afford* to be any different than what I am or she will cost us our life. We won't make it if I'm not strong. And I am so tired of being strong.

C: Because being strong is the same as being angry for you.

S: Anger is what makes me strong. But it is also so tiring.

C: Tell her.

S: If you would be a little stronger, I wouldn't have to be so angry. If you could be a little less pathetic, I could be a little less cruel. I don't want to be cruel or angry. It's too much work and I'm tired. I want to be more like you. But not exactly like you. You are just still far too weak. (Sasha seems to have exhausted this side of herself and seems to be at a stopping point.)

C: I'd like you to switch chairs once more and express anything that vulnerable Sasha has left to say.

S: (Switches chairs and clasps her hands in her lap once more, but doesn't stare down at them) I am sorry that you have to be a part of me. It is a constant reminder of what we've been through. I do not like you or what you do or how you feel or how you treat others. But for now, you are a necessary part of me. (Sasha pauses for several moments and then looks over to the professional counselor, indicating she is done.)

C: Excellent! (Turns unoccupied chair back forward and Sasha follows the same)

S: It helps . . . thinking of them like that . . . it helps me to see that I do have opposing selves but that they are both part of me. I feel more accepting of that.

C: And both necessary parts of you . . . maybe just to a lesser degree than you think.

S: So maybe if they could become a little less intense or learn to blend or compromise a little.

C: Exactly. There are positives to each of them you know. They both represent incredible characteristics that you have and show how you have coped in the past. I tell you what. I'd like for you to continue to think on this over the next week and I'd like for you to make a list of the positives associated with each of these parts of you, as well as circumstances where each of these aspects of yourself might prove very helpful. In other words, let's get an idea of their strengths and their usefulness, at least when used appropriately and in moderation.

USEFULNESS AND EVALUATION OF THE EMPTY CHAIR TECHNIQUE

The empty chair technique gets individuals to externalize the dichotomies of their feelings (Corey, 2007). The technique can be used with both interpersonal and intrapersonal issues. Professional counselors can use this technique to help individuals become aware of feelings that are below the surface, but still have an effect on the client's well-being (Hackney & Cormier, 2005).

Crose (1990) found the empty chair technique useful in working with clients who have unfinished business. By bringing the past into the here and now, professional counselors can help clients resolve issues they may have with people who are deceased or no longer a part of their lives. The professional counselor presents a safe and comfortable place for the client to express feelings of love or anger for the chosen person or people.

Coker (2004) supported the use of the empty chair technique by professional school counselors. If the professional school counselor wishes to use this technique with a student having a conflict with another person, she first asks the child to give a vivid description of the person. The child sits in one of the chairs and needs to imagine that person in the empty chair. The professional counselor then asks the child to describe the conflict and to say whatever he would like to the person with whom he is having the conflict. The professional counselor can use the previously mentioned steps to continue with the session. The professional school counselor can also use the empty chair technique when a student is having a conflict within himself. Coker suggested this technique is very useful with adolescents and, in particular, those who feel one thing in their head and another in their heart.

Clance, Thompson, Simerly, and Weiss (1993) used the empty chair technique in working with individuals with body image issues. The client has the opportunity to confront the polarities surrounding his or her attitudes and views of body image.

Although there is little empirical evidence supporting the empty chair technique, studies that do exist provide support for this strategy. In their work, Clance et al. (1993) conducted a research study investigating whether Gestalt techniques were effective in changing the participant's body image views. Of the 30 participants, 15 each were in the control group and the experimental group exposed to the Gestalt techniques. Clance et al. concluded that, "Gestalt therapy and awareness training do effect measurable and significant change in group participants' attitudes toward body and self" (p. 108). Additionally, they found that the Gestalt techniques were more effective with male than female participants.

Greenberg and Higgins (1980) compared the effects of two treatments, focusing and empty chair, when clients experienced a dichotomy. They measured the clients' depth of experience and reported change of awareness. The study had 42 participants, with an equal number in the empty chair, focusing, and control groups. Results of the study showed that the participants in the empty chair group made significant gains in awareness and depth of experience when compared with the focusing and control groups.

Paivio and Greenberg (1995) conducted a study investigating the efficacy of the empty chair technique in resolving unfinished business. Thirty-four participants were divided into two groups: the psycho-educational group and the empty chair group. Each group received 12 weeks of therapy and at post treatment, 81% of the empty chair group participants reported unfinished business resolution compared to 29% of the psycho-educational group participants. The researchers concluded that at the one year follow-up, empty chair therapy "was significantly more effective in reducing symptom and interpersonal distress, reducing discomfort and increasing change on target complaints, and achieving unfinished business resolution" (p. 425).

Young (1992) also provided a critique of the empty chair technique. He cautioned that clients may be resistant to engage in this strategy out of fear of appearing foolish. Also, he believed that some professional counselors are too quick in moving their clients from chair to chair, before either polarity is fully expressed. He warned professional counselors not to use this technique with clients who have problems controlling their emotions, as this technique can bring out a person's extremely strong feelings. As a result of the strong emotional response, professional counselors need to make sure to follow-up with clients soon after using this technique. Young also suggested that professional counselors who are inexperienced with this technique be under the supervision of a more experienced and knowledgeable professional counselor. Lastly, Young cautioned against using this technique with individuals experiencing serious emotional distress, such as those with a psychotic disorder.

CHAPTER 12

Body Movement and Exaggeration

ORIGINS OF THE BODY MOVEMENT AND EXAGGERATION TECHNIQUE

Body movement and exaggeration is a technique that emerged from Gestalt therapy. In Gestalt therapy, the therapist uses a holistic approach and utilizes an assortment of techniques intended to increase the client's awareness of himself. Professional counselors typically use body movement and exaggeration with clients who need to become aware of the nonverbal signals that they are sending to others (Corey, 2007).

HOW TO IMPLEMENT THE BODY MOVEMENT AND EXAGGERATION TECHNIQUE

When implementing body movement and exaggeration, the counselor first needs to observe the client's verbal and nonverbal cues. Paying close attention to the client's nonverbal behavior, the professional counselor should pick out what may seem like an unimportant gesture (Harman, 1974). This gesture could be "trembling (shaking hands, legs), slouched posture and bent shoulders, clenched fists, tight frowning, facial grimacing, crossed arms" (Corey, 2007, p. 212). Once the counselor identifies this gesture, he asks the client to exaggerate it with the hope that the meaning of the gesture may become apparent (Harman, 1974). As the client is exaggerating the movement, the client is asked to give a voice to the movement (Corey).

VARIATIONS OF THE BODY MOVEMENT AND EXAGGERATION TECHNIQUE

Exaggeration can be used in counseling sessions where the client says something important but does not realize that the statement is important. In this case, the counselor would ask the client to repeat the statement, increasing the emotional intensity each time the statement is said, until the client is able to realize the full impact of the statement (Harman, 1974).

EXAMPLE OF THE BODY MOVEMENT AND EXAGGERATION TECHNIQUE

Thomas is a 56-year-old man who has no prior history of receiving any type of counseling services. He experienced the passing of his 81-year-old mother just over a year ago but has been unable to deal with her death and feels stuck. He has requested help with sorting out his resulting emotions related to her and stemming from her death.

Thomas (T):   I don't understand. I just don't quite understand why I'm having such difficulty . . . feeling what I know I feel.

Counselor (C):   The sadness . . . loss . . .

T: Yes. It's there. It won't go away. Yet it won't come out either.

C: It's seems stuck?

T: Trapped. I feel stuck because it feels trapped.

C: Ummhmm.

T: I want to stop being so preoccupied by her. By her death. Her life. I want to move forward. It's like she's still got hold of me.

(The counselor notices the subtle yet important use of the word "still," implying that this is not new, and that in life, she also had hold of him.)

C: Still?

T: (Thomas looks up now, raising his head, and giving full eye contact.) Yes, *still*.

C: She still has hold of you.

T: She still has hold of me.

C: Can you say that again?

T: She *still* has hold of me.

C: And again, a little louder.

T: She *STILL* has hold of me.

C: Again.

T: She *STILL* has hold of me! She *STILL* has hold of *ME*!!! She won't let me *GO*!!!

(Pause, purposeful silence)

T: I don't know where that came from. Or what that was . . . (pauses as he thinks)

C: What did it feel like?

T: Panic. Anger.

C: Ummhmm. Yes, to me, too.

T: But I'm not angry.

C: Maybe not all of you . . .

(The counselor now notices a clenched fist Thomas almost seems to be hiding between his knees. It is very common to notice a discrepancy between verbal words and nonverbal behaviors when someone is denying their real emotion.)

C: Your fist seems angry.

T: My fist? (He looks down, notices his clenched fist, and immediately unclenches it and moves it to the side.)

C: I'd like for you to clench it again. This time harder. And place it back between your knees.

T: (Clenches his fist, places it between his knees and begins shaking his legs now)

C: Your legs are shaking. Make them shake more.

T: (Begins moving legs more rapidly)

C: Give your legs a voice. What would they say now if they could talk?

T: They're nervous.

C: Nervous?

T: Yeah, they don't like what the fist is doing.

C: What is the fist doing?

T: Getting angry.

C: And that makes the legs nervous.

T: Yes.

C: Clench your fist a little harder and keep it pinned down with your knees . . .

T: Very angry.

C: So part of you is very angry. And the legs want to hide it . . . the fist. But the fist wants to . . .

T: Hit something.

C: Which is why the legs want to pin it down . . . to keep it from hitting.

T: Anger is no good. It just makes a mess. It should be contained.

C: Trapped?

T: (There is a pause in body movement as Thomas looks back up, realizing the connection between denying his anger and feeling stuck.)

In this dialogue, body movement and exaggeration was used to highlight an important keyword that held meaning and then to acknowledge a denied emotion. It could also be used to further express that emotion and pinpoint its root.

USEFULNESS AND EVALUATION OF THE BODY MOVEMENT AND EXAGGERATION TECHNIQUE

Flexibility is one of the reasons why Gestalt techniques are popular among counselors. Because there are no rigid guidelines for utilizing these techniques, they can be altered and modified for many different issues (Harman, 1974). While the techniques from Gestalt therapy can be modified to work with many different clients and presenting problems, there are some clients who will most likely not benefit from the Gestalt approach (Harman, 1974; Wolfert & Cook, 1999). For example, professional counselors should consider using techniques from other theoretical approaches when working with clients who are severely disturbed or who are not aware of their own experiences (Harman, 1974). Another limitation of using Gestalt therapy is that some clients may feel "small, belittled, unimportant, and confused" while others may feel "attacked and resentful" (Dolliver, Williams, & Gold, 1980, p. 141). Still, Strumpfel and Goldman (2002) reviewed the research on Gestalt techniques and found that techniques such as body movement and exaggeration can be used with a variety of emotional disturbances, such as depression, phobias, personality disorders, psychosomatic disturbances, and substance abuse issues.

CHAPTER 13

Role Reversal

ORIGINS OF THE ROLE REVERSAL TECHNIQUE

Role reversal is a technique derived from Gestalt theory. Gestalt therapists view existence as interconnected and use a holistic counseling approach. Role reversal is typically used when a professional counselor believes that the behavior that the client is displaying is the reversal of some underlying feeling (Harman, 1974), thus, behaving in a disconnected manner.

HOW TO IMPLEMENT THE ROLE REVERSAL TECHNIQUE

Professional counselors can use role reversal with clients who are experiencing a conflict, or a split, within themselves. The counselor takes an active role when using this technique, identifying the different roles that the client is undergoing in the paradoxical situation (Hackney & Cormier, 2005). Then the client is asked to take on the role that is causing the anxiety and to "contact those parts of themselves that have been submerged and denied" (Corey, 2007, p. 212). The counselor assists the client in a paradoxical examination of his views, attitudes, or beliefs. By playing the other role and examining both sides of the conflict, clients may heighten their awareness of the situation and work out the underlying issues.

VARIATIONS OF THE ROLE REVERSAL TECHNIQUE

In one variation of the role reversal technique, clients were asked to play another person who was involved in the situation. By taking on someone else's role, clients have the opportunity to view themselves and the situation from a different perspective and gain further awareness (Doyle, 1998).

EXAMPLE OF THE ROLE REVERSAL TECHNIQUE

The following is a variation of the role reversal technique where the counselor asks the client to play the part of another person, considering the position of another, rather than role-playing a different aspect of self. However, some might say that even though Krista is technically viewing her daughter's position, in some ways, she is role-playing an internal struggle as she views her daughter as representative of her child within, and has transferred her hatred for herself onto her daughter.

Krista is a 34-year-old female who has had years of therapy with various providers throughout her childhood, adolescence, and adulthood. Severely abused as a child, sexually, physically, and emotionally, she tried for years to be the perfect daughter. As a young teen however, she stopped trying to be perfect and instead began to rebel. She recalls being filled with hatred for herself and for others and began using alcohol and drugs, stealing and vandalizing, running away repeatedly, and engaging in sexually deviant behavior. She spent much of her adolescence in various mental health hospitals and upon each release would return to the same behaviors and chaotic lifestyle. She eventually had two children and later married and continues to have episodes every few years where she runs away from her husband and children and returns to this former lifestyle. Currently, she is employed and free of drug use for 2 years. She shows no physical indications of her former life and presents as a very attractive, well-groomed, stylish, and well-spoken young lady. Her chief complaint upon entering counseling 6 weeks ago primarily centered on relational concerns with her mother, husband, and children. She also complains of an explosive temper and bouts of depression. She states she doesn't understand what is wrong with her and feels she is pushing her husband away and emotionally damaging her daughter. To this point, much time has been spent developing a trusting relationship, gaining insight and knowledge into her previous and current diagnoses, medication evaluation, and various therapeutic techniques aimed at improving emotion regulation and reactivity, from mindfulness to identification and rebuttal of illogical beliefs.

Krista (K):   I feel so hopeless again. I mean, I knew I wouldn't be instantly cured . . . but I was amazed at how quickly I was beginning to improve. I mean, I went 6 entire days without any major chaos . . . Six days!!! . . . I don't know that that's ever happened! I wasn't letting stuff at work, or the kids, or Josh get to me or anything. I was so proud of myself.

Counselor (C):   And hopeful?

K: Definitely hopeful. Hopeful that maybe I could start feeling normal for the first time in my life. I'm so tired of feeling this way.

C: This way . . .

K: Like a crazy evil monster. I got so angry yesterday at Kaley. I just get so damn angry . . . (Krista balls up both fists and grits her teeth.) . . . I could just pinch her head off. I'm still mad. *So* mad. I don't know why she gets to me the way she does but boy does she. She knows *exactly* how to push my buttons, and she does it on purpose. Just to spite me. Why would she *want* me to get that mad with her? Surely she doesn't *enjoy* that! God . . . but she knows exactly what she's doing . . . little *brat*.

C: (Tentatively) You feel like her behavior is on purpose.

K: I know it is. Hell, you would have to be *stupid* to continue to act the way she does, *knowing* I'm going to go off on you.

C: Can you put yourself in Kaley's shoes for just a minute? I just want you to put yourself in her shoes for a moment . . . and respond to the statement you just made. If you were Kaley, how would you respond to "Your behavior is on purpose, Kaley . . . that or you must be stupid to act the way you do." How do you respond . . . as Kaley?

K: (Without hesitation) Maybe I do. Maybe I am. Maybe I do it on purpose. And maybe I *am* stupid. Maybe I *hate* you. Maybe *you're* stupid. If you're going to act like a lunatic, I'm not going to stop you. I'm sick and tired of trying to tip-toe around your precious feelings. We all are. I've learned to not give a *shit* about your stupid little feelings. It does . . . *no* . . . good! I tried for years to be what you wanted. Nothing was ever enough. I am *tired* of wasting my energy on you. I get nothing back! You are this vacuum . . . this black hole . . . you suck the life right out of me! I gave up on you. I gave up! (Pause) On you! (Pause; affect changes from anger to sarcasm) And now? . . . well, I might as well be entertained by the lunatic.

(Typically role reversal produces identification and empathy for the position of the other person. Krista is both angry and projecting her own feelings about

herself at age 14 years and transferring her feelings about her own mother at that age onto her daughter now. But there was another side to Krista at that age, and based on prior information she has given the counselor about her daughter and their interactions, this verbalization is not entirely representative of her daughter either. Krista is presented with this and asked to bring to therapy next week a diary entry written from the perspective of her daughter. Writing will oftentimes tap into material difficult to reach through verbal expression.)

C: Were you able to complete the diary entry we talked about last week?

K: I was, but it was really difficult.

C: Difficult how?

K: Upsetting, I guess.

C: Ummhmm. Okay, upsetting then.

K: Upsetting and difficult because it made me realize how she must feel. Kaley is a really good kid . . . Here, just read it. (Hands a folded paper to the counselor and the counselor reads it aloud)

C: "Dear Diary, tonight my mom and I argued . . . again. I don't understand why she gets so angry at me. She doesn't do that to my brother. It's like she hates me sometimes. I can see it in her eyes and hear it in her voice. I'm not even sure why. And she goes crazy. I'm scared of her sometimes. I don't know what she's going to do next. I never know what to expect with her. Sometimes things that were okay yesterday aren't okay today. It's like the rules change with her, and I just never know what is safe and what isn't. It makes me feel like giving up. And it really hurts. I swear I do my best to be a good daughter. I'm not perfect. But I do try. I know I can be sassy sometimes. But isn't that normal for my age? Aren't I a pretty good kid? My teachers like me. They tell me they're glad to have me in their class. But I don't think my mom is glad to have me as her daughter. And I think I'm starting to get

angry. I can feel myself sometimes talking back to her in my head. I can feel myself getting tired of trying. I can feel myself giving up on being a good daughter. It's not getting me anywhere. And it hurts too bad to keep trying only to feel like you're hated anyway." (The counselor looks up and Krista is crying.) What's upsetting you most now?

K: That I'm killing her. I'm emotionally killing her. I'm making her hate me. And she *is* such a great kid.

C: So last week you felt her behavior was purposeful and bratty and you were so angry at her, but today . . .

K: I understand her. And I hurt for her. I don't want to *hurt* her. I hurt *for* her. I've been so afraid that she had already crossed that line . . . the one I crossed at that age. And I hate myself for the things I did. And I think when I looked at her, I saw me at 14 and I hated what I saw. But I don't think she has yet . . . crossed that line. She's not me. She's not at all like I was at that age. She is still so good . . . she still has so much good in her. There's still a chance for her.

(The empathy that role reversal is so useful for creating has now been achieved and Krista is beginning to see her daughter separate from herself and with compassion rather than hatred.)

USEFULNESS AND EVALUATION OF THE ROLE REVERSAL TECHNIQUE

No empirical studies exploring effectiveness of the role reversal technique were located in the extant literature. When implementing this technique, professional counselors initially may experience resistance from clients because the client is being asked to take on what may be an uncomfortable role. In order for this technique to be effective under this circumstance, the counselor needs to provide extra encouragement in a safe environment to help the client participate with comfort (Hackney & Cormier, 2005).

Techniques Based Upon Social Learning Approaches

Albert Bandura's social learning theory proposes that much human learning occurs without the contingencies associated with reinforcement and punishment. Bandura broke away from traditional behavior therapy based on operant conditioning (see Section 7) because he viewed it as simplistic and lacking a cognitive component. Bandura noticed that human beings often did a lot of observation, preplanning, and thinking before engaging in behaviors, and behaviorism ignored all of these essential components. Bandura noticed that a reciprocal interaction between the person, behavior, and environment were at the core of most behaviors.

Bandura noticed that clients frequently learned to perform tasks and behaviors simply by watching others and imitating the observed behaviors. He referred to this process as vicarious learning, and he and subsequent counselors applying social learning theory to counseling developed a number of techniques helpful to clients, including modeling, behavioral rehearsal, and role playing. Modeling involves demonstrating a certain skill or sequence of skills to a client so that the client may imitate the modeled behavior. For example, a professional counselor may demonstrate the appropriate manner for a client to introduce himself to an adult, or how to assertively handle a conflict with a peer.

After a client understands how to perform a given task or interpersonal interaction, behavioral rehearsal usually ensues. Behavioral rehearsal is the actual practicing of social behaviors with constructive feedback from the professional counselor or other counseling participants. Finally, role play allows a free flowing, dynamic interchange between client and counselor (or another counseling participant) to try out new behaviors in mock situations with constructive feedback. A primary advantage of role play stems from the players' abilities to improvise and introduce real life twists and turns that clients may encounter when implementing the newly learned skills outside of the counselor's office. Techniques based on social learning theory can yield powerful learning opportunities.

MULTICULTURAL IMPLICATIONS

Techniques based upon social learning have wide applications across cultures because they allow clients and counselors to consider the essential interchanges of a client's cultural and social dimensions. Social learning approaches allow clients to conceptualize social difficulties within a cultural context, establish specific goals, plan therapeutic conditions to maximize successes, and use social interactions between the client and counselor or other individuals to accomplish these goals. Clients of some cultures (e.g., Latino, Arab American, Asian American men) prefer action-oriented, instructional strategies stemming from concrete goals and objectives, while avoiding emotional expression and catharsis.

In particular, counselors should be knowledgeable about what is considered normal and abnormal behavior within a client's multicultural context and how the client defines and conceptualizes the presenting problems. Behavioral approaches based upon social learning accommodate these culturally based preferences by focusing on specific behaviors and allowing clients to solve problems through social interaction. A final advantage of social learning approaches when used in a multicultural context is that traditional behavioral approaches have been criticized for viewing the problem as one internal to an individual. Ethnically diverse individuals often appreciate the more neutral and inclusive social learning approach for appropriately focusing on social interactions and skill enhancement in the sociocultural context.

CHAPTER 14

Modeling

ORIGINS OF THE MODELING TECHNIQUE

Modeling is the process by which individuals learn from watching others. Modeling is a component of the social learning theory developed by Albert Bandura (Bandura, 1971). Modeling has also been referred to as imitation, identification, observational learning, and vicarious learning (Bandura, Hackney & Cormier, 2005). Early research on modeling was conducted by Miller and Dollard (1941) who found that through reinforcement, participants could learn to imitate one model, learn not to imitate another model, learn to distinguish between these two models, and generalize this discrimination of whether or not to copy the behavior to other similar persons.

There are three basic types of modeling. *Overt modeling* (or live modeling) occurs when one or more persons demonstrate the behavior to be learned (Hackney & Cormier, 2005). Live models can include the professional counselor, a teacher, or the client's peers. Sometimes it can be helpful for clients to observe more than one model in order to draw on the strengths and styles of different people. *Symbolic modeling* involves illustrating the target behavior through video tapes, audiotapes, or films. Symbolic modeling allows the professional counselor to have more control over the accuracy of the behavioral demonstration. Also, once an appropriate symbolic model is developed, it can be easily stored for repeated use. Self-as-a-model activities involve recording the client performing the target behavior (Hansen et al., 1980). The client can then either observe the recording directly or use positive self-imagery to recall performing the skill successfully. Finally, *covert modeling* requires the client to imagine the target behavior being successfully completed, either by himself or by someone else (Hackney & Cormier).

Modeling can produce three different types of responses (Bandura, 1971). Clients may acquire new patterns of behavior by watching others, termed an *observation learning effect*. Modeling may strengthen or weaken the client's inhibition of already learned behaviors, referred to as *inhibitory effects* (when strengthened) or *disinhibitory effects* (when weakened). Finally, modeled behaviors may serve as social cues to signal the client to perform a certain known response, called *response facilitation effects*.

In order for clients to successfully learn a modeled behavior, four interrelated subprocesses must exist (Bandura, 1971). First, the client must be able to attend to the modeling demonstration (attention). Second, the client must be able to retain the observation of the modeled event (retention). Attention and retention phases are required to acquire the behavior. Third, the client needs to be motorically capable of reproducing the modeled behavior (reproduction). And finally, the client must be motivated, either internally (i.e., intrinsic motivation) or through external reinforcement, to perform the target behavior (motivation). Reproduction and motivation are required to perform the behavior. Bandura referred to the first two subprocesses as the acquisition phase, and the second two processes as the performance phase. Bandura distinguished between acquisition and performance phases primarily to underscore the reality that just because a client has acquired a behavior does not mean the client will be motivated to perform the behavior!

Several other factors influence of the success of observational learning. Research shows that modeling is more effective when the client perceives the model to be similar to himself (Hallenbeck & Kauffman, 1995). In addition, clients will more readily imitate a model who seems to be acquiring the modeled skills rather than those who are already highly skilled at the behavior. The characteristics of the observer also play a role in how willing the client will be to imitate modeled behavior. Gender, age, motivation, cognitive capacity, and prior social learning are all factors in the success of modeling. Moreover, successful social learning relies heavily on reinforcements (Bandura, 1971). Reinforcement can be directly applied to the client's external behavior, whether or not the client performs the target behavior. Or clients can observe vicarious reinforcement, where the model is either rewarded or punished for performing the target behavior. In general, imitative behavior is increased by observed rewards and decreased by observed punishment.

HOW TO IMPLEMENT THE MODELING TECHNIQUE

Before modeling can begin, the client and professional counselor must select an alternative behavior that will be taught to replace the undesirable behavior (Macht, 1990). The professional counselor should also provide the client with a rationale for the use of modeling (Hackney & Cormier, 2005). The modeling scenario should minimize the stress that the client might experience and should also break down complex behaviors into small, simple steps. As the target behavior is performed, either the model or the professional counselor should describe the steps

to carry out the modeled behavior. Once the target behavior has been demonstrated, the professional counselor should lead the client in a discussion of the behavior (Hansen et al., 1980). During this discussion, the professional counselor can verbally reinforce the client.

The client should be allowed many opportunities to practice the target behavior after the modeling has occurred (Macht, 1990). Frequent, short sessions, lasting no longer than 10 minutes, are more effective than longer sessions. The professional counselor can also assign homework for the client to practice the behavior outside of sessions (Hackney & Cormier, 2005). Self-guided practice can help the client apply the modeled behavior to real life situations. However, the professional counselor should be careful not to expect too much too soon; teaching new behaviors often creates resistance, especially if clients do not understand the reasoning behind the target behavior (Macht).

VARIATIONS OF THE MODELING TECHNIQUE

Cognitive modeling was developed to help clients avoid negative, self-defeating thoughts and behaviors by replacing them with positive statements (Gilliland & James, 1998). Cognitive modeling involves five steps. First the professional counselor models the behavior as if she were the client. Then the client performs the task while the professional counselor talks the client through each step. Next the client performs the task again, this time instructing himself aloud. Then the client performs the task a third time while whispering the instructions to himself. Finally the client performs the task while instructing himself covertly (i.e., in his head).

Skill training is a counseling intervention that is composed of many different techniques, including modeling (Hackney & Cormier, 2005). In skill training, the professional counselor and client determine the skills to be learned. Then the skills are arranged in order from least difficult to most difficult. The training proceeds by modeling the skills, having the client imitate the skills as modeled, providing feedback to the client, and repeating the sequence until skills are mastered.

EXAMPLE OF THE MODELING TECHNIQUE

The following transcript demonstrating modeling involves teaching a 17-year-old female client, Nicole, a deep breathing technique. The chapter that follows this one, behavioral rehearsal, provides a complementary transcript immediately following this one in the session to demonstrate the practice phase that frequently occurs in a modeling procedure. Prior to the moment the transcript begins, Nicole and the counselor agreed that an effective way to help her relax was to help her calm her breathing from shallow, quick breathing (which led to stress and hyperventilation) to long, deep, slow breathing; that is, they selected an alternative behavior. Next, the counselor discussed the rationale for the use of modeling and behavioral rehearsal. Finally, the counselor began to explain the steps of the deep breathing technique and the reason why deep breathing works.

Counselor (C):   When you slow your breathing you will slow down your whole central nervous system, just like Johnny did in the picture, making you calm and relaxed. Just inhale and exhale at a slow, yet comfortable pace . . . Don't hold your breath when you complete your inhale, but I want you to breathe in until you can't get any more air into your chest, okay, into your lungs. Then I want you to breathe right back out. I will model for you and then we can practice.

Nicole (N):   Okay.

C: Okay, I'm going to show you how to do it correctly. I'll show you when I'm finished inhaling and when I start to exhale . . . (Pause for inhale) . . . Okay, now I've got about as much air in me as I can, and now I'm going to purse my lips and exhale slowly . . . (Pause for exhale) . . . There, did you see how I did that? I can even exhale a bit longer if I need to. The interesting thing is your exhale usually is longer than your inhale.

N: Yeah, I noticed that.

C: Ordinarily, when I get to deeper levels of relaxation, I can get down to two breaths per minute, sometimes even about one and a half per minute. So I'm actually breathing in for about 10 or 15 seconds on my inhale.

N: Mmmhmm.

C: And you don't hold it, you immediately start your exhale and I can ordinarily exhale for about 15 to 25 seconds. So my whole breath might take, you know, 30 or 40 seconds from the time that I begin to inhale and then finish my exhale and then begin again. Now your lung capacity may not be as large, so try to slow down your breathing to a level that is comfortable for you.

(The counselor leads a guided discussion of the steps again, verbally reinforces her as Nicole performs the practice steps, and answers any questions Nicole has.)

C: . . . Do you want me to show you again or are you ready to try it?

N: I'm okay.

C: All right. I want you to slow your breathing down, again to about eight or six or even four breaths per minute so you can take your body into that relaxing state . . . So let's go ahead and I want you to concentrate again on breathing very slowly on your inhale and then very slowly again on your exhale . . .

(Note: This transcript continues in the next chapter to demonstrate how modeling is often followed by behavioral rehearsal.)

USEFULNESS AND EVALUATION OF THE MODELING TECHNIQUE

Modeling can be used to teach clients many different skills. In general, live modeling seems to be more effective in teaching personal and social skills, while symbolic modeling is helpful with more cognitive problems (Hansen et al., 1980). Self-as-a-model procedures are effective with self-acceptance problems, interpersonal skill development, and teaching or counseling skill development. Modeling can also be used to help teens deal with peer pressure, to help family members learn new communication patterns, or in any other situation where the client does not have an appropriate alternative response (Hackney & Cormier, 2005). Moreover, modeling has been used to teach autistic children to speak, coping skills to hospital patients, new behaviors to socially disturbed children, interpersonal skills to drug addicts and alcoholics, survival skills to mentally retarded individuals, and to treat phobias (Corey, 2007).

Elias (1983) investigated the effects of viewing social problem-solving videos on the behavior of socially disturbed boys. Elias observed that during the 5-week program, those children who participated in video discussions showed a decrease in social isolation and an increase in popularity. They were also noted to show an increase in self-control, an improved ability to delay gratification, a decrease in emotional detachment, and an overall decrease in personality problems. These results suggested that symbolic modeling, as observed through problem-solving videos, is effective in improving children's social skills.

Flowers (1991) studied the effects of modeling on self-confidence, measured by students' willingness to answer trivia questions. He found that low self-confidence students, who observed other previously low self-confidence students, increased in confidence and showed an increase in self-confidence when compared to a control group and a group that observed only high-confidence students. This study confirmed that modeling is most effective when clients perceive that models are similar to themselves. Likewise, Hallenbeck and Kauffman (1995) reported that students with emotional or behavioral disorders do not learn effectively from the modeling of well-adjusted peers due to the fact that they do not perceive themselves as similar to these peers. These observations suggested that emotionally or behaviorally disturbed students would benefit more from modeling by others with similar disorders who have acquired some success at overcoming their tendency to behave poorly.

CHAPTER 15

Behavioral Rehearsal

ORIGINS OF THE BEHAVIORAL REHEARSAL TECHNIQUE

Behavioral rehearsal is one of the many techniques stemming from behavior therapy (Thorpe & Olson, 1997), but has been adapted for use by counselors using a social learning approach. This technique, first labeled "behavioristic psychodrama," is a blend of "Salter's conditioned reflex therapy, Moreno's psychodrama technique, and Kelly's fixed role therapy" (Thorpe & Olson, 1997, p. 44). Professional counselors typically use behavior rehearsal with clients who need to become completely aware of themselves. It is a form of role play in which the client is learning a new type of behavior to use in response to certain situations and people outside of the counseling situation (Hansen et al., 1980). Behavioral rehearsal includes several key components: modeling the behavior, receiving feedback from the counselor, and frequently practicing the desired behavior (Bootzin, 1975).

HOW TO IMPLEMENT THE BEHAVIORAL REHEARSAL TECHNIQUE

When implementing behavioral rehearsal, events that occur in day to day life are role played by the client and professional counselor in an attempt to decrease any anxieties the client may have when expressing herself (Thorpe & Olson, 1997). The client acts as herself and the professional counselor plays the role of the person about whom the client has surrounding anxieties. The professional counselor instructs the client to communicate her feelings about the anxiety-producing person or circumstance. The client needs to use a strong voice and repeat a feelings statement or appropriate behavior while the professional counselor gives feedback to the client. The client continues rehearsing until the professional counselor indicates the statement or behavior was communicated effectively (Wolpe, 1990). Naugle and Maher (2003) suggested that the professional counselor and client should attempt and master simple skills first, and only then move on to more complex skills. Naugle and Maher (2003) provided the following steps for the professional counselor to use in implementing the behavioral rehearsal technique:

1. Prompt client practice of modeled behavior, 2. Reinforce client efforts to enhance motivation, 3. Provide specific and concrete verbal feedback regarding execution of the skill, [and] 4. Shape behavioral approximations to desired behavior using contingent reinforcement. (p. 242)

For behavioral rehearsal to be effective, Bootzin, (1975) suggested clients practice the following six rules: (a) express emotions verbally; (b) present feelings nonverbally using body language; (c) contradict others when one disagrees with them; (d) speak in the first person, using the word I regularly; (e) agree with the counselor's praise; and (f) "improvise, live for the moment" (p. 105).

VARIATIONS OF THE BEHAVIORAL REHEARSAL TECHNIQUE

Naugle and Maher (2003) claimed that *in vivo* rehearsal could make the treatment even more effective by helping the client engage in the desired behavior in a natural setting. Importantly, Naugle and Maher warned that the professional counselor must provide comments and feedback that are specific to the desired client behavior. Then, after initial successes, the behavioral tasks assigned by the professional counselor can become progressively more difficult and practiced outside of the counseling session.

Seligman (2001) suggested that professional counselors have clients practice behavioral rehearsal not only in counseling sessions but also in outside settings. She recommended that clients practice the tasks with friends in their day-to-day lives. Seligman also suggested that professional counselors tape record clients engaging in the behavioral rehearsal or encourage clients to practice in front of the mirror, allowing the client to monitor himself and provide his own feedback.

Smokowski (2003) incorporated technology into behavioral rehearsal sessions with clients by videotaping them and using computer simulations. In this variation, Smokowski used the video camera in a group session. He suggested having the camera represent the person who is working on a desired behavior and the group members role play the situations or people involved in the behavioral rehearsal. At the point in the role play when a response is needed from the camera, the tape is stopped and the member responds. Because the beginning part of the rehearsal is videotaped, the member can practice several different responses. Smokowski also suggested having a member play the role she is having trouble responding to. By playing the role of the antagonist, the member can work on building her own assertiveness.

EXAMPLE OF THE BEHAVIORAL REHEARSAL TECHNIQUE

The following transcript is an excerpt of instruction and behavioral rehearsal of a deep breathing procedure. This transcript picks up at the point that the transcript for chapter 14 [Modeling] left off.

Counselor (C):   All right. I want you want to slow your breathing down, again to about eight or six or even four breaths per minute so you can take your body into that relaxing state . . . So let's go ahead and I want you to concentrate again on breathing very slowly on your inhale and then very slowly again on your exhale . . .

Nicole (N):   (Pause to inhale)

C: Great. You breathed through your nose and your lungs are full, now exhale.

N: (Pause to exhale)

C: Your lips are pursed and I can barely feel your exhale. Very good. Now inhale . . .

N: (Pauses to inhale and exhale) . . . I feel a little light headed . . .

C: Okay, now you might feel a little bit light headed as you start to do that, you slow down, you slow your breathing down from the normal rate down to a slower and relaxed rate. Sometimes you feel a little bit light headed, but usually by the time you take your fourth or fifth breath the light headedness goes away.

N: Okay. (Continues to breathe several more cycles) . . . You were right. I'm not light headed anymore.

C: Keep going. Your mind told your body to adjust and the relaxation response kicked in, slowing down your entire central nervous system. Do you feel any anxiety or anything?

N: (Continues to breathe) . . . None at all. In fact, I am starting to feel . . . (Nicole yawns) . . . a little sleepy.

C: That's your body relaxing. Sometimes you get so relaxed you fall asleep. This is why a lot of people practice deep breathing and progressive muscle relaxation training before they go to sleep—it helps them fall asleep quicker and gives them a headstart on deep, relaxing sleep.

N: I can understand why! (Nicole practices a half dozen more times with feedback from the counselor, then breathes deeply on her own for 3 minutes.)

C: Okay, so you're already at four breaths per minute. Was that comfortable for you to breathe that way?

N: Wow, I didn't even know that. Four? Really? Yeah, that was comfortable.

C: You're a pretty quick learner. You learned this deep breathing technique like you've been doing it all your life

N: Well, I have (laughs).

C: All right, you know what I'm going to tell you to do next . . .

N: More homework?

C: Right, practice this deep breathing activity five times a day for at least 3 minutes each time—and preferably 5 to 10 minutes each time. I want you to take nice, long, deep, slow breaths in and out. For a couple of minutes, about 3 or more minutes . . . I want you to practice that first thing in the morning before you jump out of bed. I want you to practice this right after breakfast or so, before lunch, before dinner, and then again at bedtime . . .

USEFULNESS AND EVALUATION OF THE BEHAVIORAL REHEARSAL TECHNIQUE

Turner, Calhoun, and Adams (1981) indicated behavioral rehearsal has been successfully used with clients dealing with anger, frustration, anxiety, phobias, panic attacks, and depression. Professional counselors often use the behavioral rehearsal technique with clients experiencing difficulty interacting with others in specific, anticipated situations. This technique is frequently used to achieve catharsis, attitudinal change, or specific targeted behaviors (Hackney & Cormier, 2005).

Walsh (2002) found behavioral rehearsal useful when working with people who have social anxiety. The client first learns new ways of thinking or behaving and gets to practice these new responses in the counseling situation. Then the client practices the new behaviors in a naturalistic setting. By practicing first in a safe environment, clients are able to develop more confidence before having to act in the real life setting. The hope is that the client will master these altered ways of thinking and behaving, and eventually shed shy or inappropriate behavioral tendencies. Turner et al. (1981) found the behavioral rehearsal technique useful in working with heterosexual males who had anxiety surrounding dating, resulting in reduced anxiety and increased assertiveness and number of dates these men scheduled upon follow-up.

Although there is little empirical research focusing on the behavioral rehearsal technique, it is a method that is widely used among professional counselors for a variety of reasons. This technique is not dangerous for clients; it is not associated with any substantial risks. The behavioral rehearsal technique is efficient in terms of both time and money, and works with many populations, including those who are challenged cognitively, socially, and emotionally (Naugle & Maher, 2003). Implementation of this technique is fairly simple and change can be seen quickly, sometimes even in several sessions. Still, Naugle and Maher cautioned professional counselors to be careful when using this technique with clients who: (a) cannot take responsibility for their behaviors; (b) are scared of the consequences, whether or not they are real; (c) will not practice the rehearsal; (d) will not complete the out-of-session assignments; (e) have daily crises; or (f) "experience severe psychomotor agitation or retardation" (p. 241).

Finally, in a study conducted by Kantor and Schomer (1997), the researchers studied the effects of a stress management program on the participants' lifestyles. Behavioral rehearsal was one of the coping resources taught to the participants. While the program was effective in some of the areas evaluated, the difference in coping resources was not statistically significant. It appeared that the participants were not consistently using the techniques taught to them. The results of this study remind professional counselors of the necessity that clients repeat the behavioral rehearsal frequently and receive frequent and specific feedback.

CHAPTER | **16**

Role Play

ORIGINS OF THE ROLE PLAY TECHNIQUE

Role play is a technique used by counselors of different theoretical orientations with clients who need to develop a deeper understanding of, or change within, themselves (Gilliland & James, 1998). Within a role play, clients are able to perform a decided upon behavior in a safe, risk-free environment (Doyle, 1998). Role play is a blend of "Salter's conditioned reflex therapy, Moreno's psychodrama technique, and Kelly's fixed-role therapy" (Hackney & Cormier, 2005, p. 211). Moreno's psychodrama process involved three facets: (a) warm up, (b) enactment, and (c) reenactment. Hackney and Cormier described four aspects commonly found in role plays. In most role plays, a person reenacts oneself, another person, a set of circumstances surrounding a situation, or one's own reactions and receives feedback from the professional counselor, or group members when instituted in a group work context. Role plays occur in the present, not the past or the future; it is common to begin with scenes that are not difficult to reenact and to work progressively toward scenes that are more complex.

HOW TO IMPLEMENT THE ROLE PLAY TECHNIQUE

Before implementing this technique, it is helpful for professional counselors to understand the four elements and three phases found within role plays. The first element is called the encounter, which in this situation means being able to understand the perspective of another person. This is a necessary part of the role play, as the client will sometimes switch roles and play the part of another individual involved in the situation. The next element, the stage, is "any space with rudimentary props to increase the realism of the experience" (Young, 1992, p. 181). The soliloquy, the third aspect, is another term that professional counselors must know; it is a speech in which the client expresses his private thoughts and associated feelings. Professional counselors can learn more about their clients, including their irrational beliefs, through the soliloquy. The last element, doubling, leads to increased awareness on the part of the client and occurs when the professional counselor or another group member "stands behind the client during the acting out of the scene and expresses the unexpressed thoughts or feelings of the client" (Young, 1992, p. 181).

The three phases in a role play include warm-up, action, and sharing and analysis. There is a debate about splitting up the third phase and having four phases. The goal of the warm-up phase is to encourage the client to become connected with the situation, including the related emotions that she will be reenacting. The warm-up activity can either be performed mentally or physically. In the action phase, the professional counselor helps the client set the scene by going over the details of the situation. The professional counselor also has to guide the client from reality to the imagined situation and back to reality. In the sharing and analysis phase, the professional counselor and group members (if performed in a group setting) share what they experienced during the role play. The analysis often occurs in a follow-up session since the client is typically emotionally aroused at the end of the role play. In this session, the client has a chance to process information and receive feedback (Young, 1992).

Young (1992) provides a seven step process for professional counselors to follow when implementing this technique with a client:

1. *Warm-up:* The professional counselor explains the technique to the client and the client provides a detailed description of the behavior, attitude, or performance he would like to change (Doyle, 1998; Young, 1992). The client should be encouraged to discuss any reluctance he may have about the role play technique.
2. *Scene Setting:* The professional counselor assists the client in setting the stage. If necessary, furnishings can be rearranged.
3. *Selecting Roles:* The client names and describes the significant people involved in the scene.
4. *Enactment:* The client acts out the target behavior and if he has difficulty doing so, the professional counselor can model the behavior (Young, 1992). The client should begin with the scenes that are the least difficult and gradually move on to those that are more difficult (Doyle, 1998). During this step, the professional counselor can interrupt the client in order to show the client what he is doing that contributes to his disturbance (Corey, 2007).
5. *Sharing and Feedback:* The counselor gives the client "specific, simple, observable, and understandable" feedback (Young, 2006, p. 185).
6. *Reenactment:* The client repeatedly practices the targeted behavior in and out of the

counseling sessions until he and the professional counselor believe that the goal has been met.
7. *Follow-up:* The client informs the professional counselor of his practice results and progress.

VARIATIONS OF THE ROLE PLAY TECHNIQUE

Behavioral rehearsal is one of the most common variations of role-playing. When the client performs the target behaviors, he is reinforced and rewarded, first by the professional counselor and second by the client's own self-praise (Young, 1992). To learn more about this variation, read the chapter focused on behavioral rehearsal in this book (see chapter 15).

An alternative five-step process for implementing the role play technique is: (a) specify the behavior to be learned; (b) determine the context or environment of a particular event; (c) start with small scenes and then build to scenes with greater complexity; (d) in session, engage in role plays with minimum risk and work up to situations that involve higher risk; and (e) apply the role playing in real life situations, again starting with situations of minimum risk and working up to situations with higher risk. Importantly, video-taping the role plays can be extremely helpful in analyzing a client's strengths and struggles in a given role.

Young (1992) described another variation of the role play, called the mirror technique in group therapy. In this version, the member who is reenacting the scene "steps out of the drama at a moment when a crucial behavior occurs" (p. 186). Another group member takes this member's place and, sometimes exaggeratedly, reenacts the behavior or response of the original performer. The original performer is able to watch and evaluate her response. A new response can be discussed and the original performer can then practice it.

In a variation used commonly by Gestalt therapists, two chairs are used in place of other people who are involved in the scene. The chairs can symbolize a variety of different things including, "the client and another person; two parts of the person (i.e., intellect and body); parts of a person's dream or fantasy; physical symptoms, or conflicting emotions" (Seligman, 2001, p. 269). The client sits in each chair and needs to speak the point of view that each chair holds. Often feelings or thoughts that are truthful, but until that time unsaid, are expressed.

Another variation of this technique is useful when working with children. If possible, the child can put on different costumes when switching roles. This may help the child understand that he is not just acting like himself (Vernon, 1993). Children can role play by "imitating the actions or words of familiar people and objects," "using actions or words to represent real objects," "creating actions and situations that demonstrate his or her ability to use representational thought," and "developing play themes that relate to imaginary situations and preferred roles that are increasingly realistic."

Shepard (1992) described yet another variation of the role play technique he uses when training beginning counselors. Often, counselors-in-training are asked to role play with each other to gain experience using the different techniques that they are learning. Shepard taught students to role play using screenwriting techniques and commonly the result was more realistic role plays. The first step for the class was to create a character. They needed to describe the general characteristics of the character, including name, age, ethnicity, profession, relationship status, and family. A back story, which includes "personal history and key influences on a character's life," also needs to be created. The character's dreams, fantasies, goals, crises, conscious and unconscious desires, and societal influences should all be considered. Another important piece of the back story is deciding what the character's family life was like when growing up. Professional and personal forces faced by the client should be decided upon as should the event that triggered the character to seek counseling. The presenting problem needs to be realistic and have at least one of the following manifestations: affective, cognitive, somatic, or behavioral. After the example is created in class, the students create their own characters using this model. Throughout the semester, Shepard created plot turns (major events) in the lives of students' characters.

EXAMPLE OF THE ROLE PLAY TECHNIQUE

The counseling intervention below takes place in a group counseling setting for high school juniors and seniors who are working on improved emotional expression and social interactions with their peers and family members. Tina, the focus in this part of the session, is one such group member with a history of being passive in her relations with others, often ignoring her own needs in order to maintain friendships, peace, or a person's favor.

Counselor (C):   Okay, we've checked in with everyone but you, Tina. You seem to have something on your mind . . .

Tina (T):   Yeah, I guess I do. Umm . . . I guess I could tell you all about it? I mean if you want.

C: (Looking around group, seeing heads nod in favor) We'd like that, Tina.

T: Well, this might seem super shallow to some of you, but it's like a big deal to me and it's completely stuck in my head and I don't know what to do about it . . . (She looks around to check the facial expressions of the other group members before proceeding.) . . . Okay, so some of you are going to know who I'm talking about, and I just want to make sure that what we say in group stays in group.

C: I'm glad you brought that up. I think its good to remind everyone of that from time to time and just make sure that we all agree to keep this information between us . . . not talking about it to others that aren't here, and not talking to each other about it outside of here either, right? (Group members reassure Tina with their head nods again.)

Group member: Don't worry, Tina, we got your back. We ain't saying nothing to nobody.

T: I know. I just had to make sure. Okay. Umm . . . (deep breath) . . . so I heard that my best friend of like 4 years has been talking bad about me to some of our other friends. At first I didn't think it was true, but then I noticed she was acting funny towards me, like ignoring me when I was talking, or cutting me off when I was saying something.

I swear I think she even rolled her eyes at me yesterday. And then today, I felt like she was avoiding me 'cause I've hardly seen her and usually we meet up in the hallways between classes.

Group member: Man, I'm glad I'm not a girl. Guys don't play that mess. My heart goes out to you, Tina, 'cause you're a stronger person than I am for even caring.

Group member: I totally get it, Tina. Having your best friend mad at you, or whatever it is, is like the worst feeling in the world. It messes with your head and makes everything seem like drama.

T: Yeah, exactly.

C: So tell me, Tina, how has all of this affected you this week?

T: I've been super paranoid and paying way too much attention to every little thing. I've thought and thought about what I might have done to make her mad at me or tired of me or whatever. I swear I can't think of anything. I've even tried extra hard to be way nice to her and go along with whatever she wanted to do even if I didn't feel like it, just so she would be like normal to me again. I just really want this all straightened out. More than anything, I just need to know if it's for real or just in my head.

Group member: Why don't you just ask her?

Group member: Yeah, just talk to her about it. Just come out and be like, "Are you mad at me or tired of me or what is up with how you've been lately?"

C: Have you considered talking to her about it?

T: I want to. I know I need to and that is the only way for this to get resolved. But I don't do so well with that sort of thing.

C: You mean you've tried this sort of thing in the past and it's not gone well?

T: Yeah. Its like whatever I say just comes out wrong or I'm never prepared for what the other person is going to say and it just . . . I just . . . I'm not very good at it or

something . . . (pauses for a moment) . . . But I do know I'm going to have to do it. I kept thinking it would all just miraculously disappear, but obviously it isn't and I know I need to talk to her about it before I drive myself nuts. I'm just scared to . . . I don't know what I'd say.

C: Would you be willing to try it out here today?

T: What do you mean?

C: Well, this sort of issue, not being able to express yourself or confront uncomfortable situations, seems to be something you've dealt with before. I think role playing the conversation you want to have, actually having you try it out here with us, could help. I'd bet the other group members could learn from it as well. What do you say?

T: Well, I'd feel silly, but I guess if it would help me . . .

C: All right then. Is there anything else we should know about the situation before we begin?

T: Umm . . . like what?

C: Well, perhaps you could just reiterate what you want the goal of the conversation to be?

T: I just want to know if she's mad and why.

C: Okay, anything else?

T: Yeah, I guess I would like to be able to tell her how I've been feeling all week.

C: Okay. So with those goals in mind, to find out her feelings, and to express your own feelings, let's think about when you might want this conversation to really take place and where.

T: Umm, you mean like for real "where and when?"

C: Mmmhmm.

T: Well, we have basketball practice tomorrow after school. Usually we hang out afterwards, just us two. That would probably be the best time.

C: And you would be at the basketball gym?

T: Yeah, we'd be there shooting hoops.

C: Okay. Is there anything here in this room that we can move around or do differently to make it resemble where you'll be having this conversation tomorrow?

T: (Looks around . . . thinks for a moment) . . . Nah, not really. I mean we'll be standing up, so I should probably do that, but nothing else really. I'll have a basketball in my hand but I don't see one in here, so I can just stand up.

C: Okay. So we understand the problem you are having with your best friend and how much it is bothering you. We understand that you want and need to have an open and honest conversation with her but that it is difficult for you to do. We also heard you say that you want to know how she feels and you want her to know how you feel as a result of the conversation. And we know when and where the conversation is to take place. Now, the last thing I need you to do before we begin is to select a group member to play the part of your best friend.

(Up to this point, the professional counselor has guided the client through the warm-up phase, identification of a behavior in need of change, and scene selection and setting. As soon as roles are selected, enactment can begin.)

T: (Looks around the group, grins a little) . . . I pick Kenya.

C: Kenya? Okay, very well. (Looking towards Kenya) Would you be willing to play Tina's best friend?

Kenya (K):   Sure, I'll do it!

C: Thanks, Kenya. Do you have any questions for Tina before we begin?

K: Well, I was wondering if she could tell us a little more about what her best friend is like, so I'll know how to play my part better.

C: Good point, Kenya. Tina?

T: Well, umm, hmm. It's hard to say how she normally is with everything going so different this week. Let's see . . . she's loud, very outgoing, fun, everybody loves to be around her and she is definitely a leader. She always has cool ideas and usually makes the decisions for everyone else when it comes to social events

and get-togethers and stuff. But she can also be very defensive . . . and weird reactions sometimes . . . and she disses others, I guess. Yeah, that's all. Is that enough? K: I think so. That helps.

T: Oh, and don't go easy on me (speaking to Kenya) . . . I mean . . . make it a little bit hard for me so I'll be prepared if it really goes that way.

C: Okay, (standing up and motioning for Tina and Kenya, as the best friend, to stand as well) I'm going to ask everyone to push their chairs back just a bit so we have some more room . . . (pauses while chairs are moving) . . . Thanks, guys. And, Tina, if you don't mind, I'm going to stand behind you and to your right . . . like this . . . and there may be times during the role play when I feel you're stuck or struggling to get to the crux of the matter . . . and what I'm going to do is something we call *doubling*, and all that means is that I may speak on your behalf, say what it is I believe is going unsaid . . . to help you out. Is that okay?

T: Sure, that'd be helpful.

C: Good. And when I do that, I may put my hand on your shoulder if that's okay. (Tina nods, seemingly relieved to have the support.) And what I want you to do is either accept what I say as your own and repeat it aloud for yourself, or change it to better reflect how you feel and then state that aloud. Does that make sense?

T: I think I've got it, yes.

C: Okay. Now imagine tomorrow being much like today. You get through the day much the same as all week, assuming nothing has changed, and now basketball practice is coming to an end and everyone is leaving and the two of you stay behind to practice shooting.

(Remember, the professional counselor is responsible for moving the client from reality into the imagined situation.)

T: Yea, okay.

C: And now it's just you and your best friend . . . what's her name?

T: Stacy.

C: Okay, so now it's just you and Stacy in the gym shooting. And you have this important conversation that you need to have with her . . . whenever you're ready . . .

T: Okay . . . this is hard . . . I can do this . . .

C: You can do this . . . we're supporting you . . .

T: Okay. Stacy, I wanted to talk to you about something.

Kenya as Stacy (S): Yeah, okay, what's up?

T: Well, it seems like lately, this week mostly, that you've been acting different.

S: What do you mean? (Still shooting her baskets)

T: Umm . . . well . . . I mean you just haven't been yourself.

S: Sure I have. What are you talking about? (Taking somewhat of a defensive tone and still shooting)

T: I just feel like you've been treating me different and I was wondering . . .

S: *What* are you talking about? (obviously aggravated to be bothered with this)

T: (Turns to the counselor) I can't do this.

C: (Doubling with hand on Tina's shoulder) This is important to me. I'm talking about how *I* feel. And I feel like you've been ignoring me this week.

T: Yeah, this *is* important to me and I feel like you've been ignoring me this week.

S: So what if I have?

T: I was wondering if I did something wrong?

S: I don't know, maybe. Not really. I don't know. Why are you freaking out?

T: I don't know. I guess I shouldn't. (Looks down at floor, clearly feeling ashamed for bringing it up and ashamed of feeling the way she feels . . . long pause.)

C: (Doubling) Because you've been my best friend for a long time and it really hurts to think that might change. This week has been really hard feeling like you are mad at me.

T: I care about our friendship and I don't want to lose it. It *has* been really hard this week and I *have* been hurt by the way you've acted.

S: (With a change in demeanor, less flippant, and now taking Tina's concerns seriously) Okay, so let's talk . . . (thinking) . . . I don't want to hurt your feelings. Really I don't. It's just that sometimes you are right under me and you try too hard. You should know by now that we are the best of friends. You don't always have to try so hard. It's a little annoying at times. I guess I should have just talked to you about it instead of acting the way I did. I just didn't want to hurt your feelings. But now I see that I did anyway . . . and I'm sorry.

T: Really? I mean, so you still want to be my best friend? You just want me to give you some space sometimes?

S: Yeah.

T: I can do that. I can totally do that. As long as I know you're not mad at me or anything. (Tina looks relieved and there is a long silence.)

C: Okay. Tina, do you feel done with this?

T: (Breathing a sigh of relief) Yeah . . . yeah . . . I feel done. I think I can do this tomorrow.

C: Good! All right, we can sit back down now and I'd like to hear reactions, thoughts, or any other feedback from the group members, and of course we want to hear from you as well, Tina.

(The counselor continues to facilitate a discussion with feedback from the group and with reactions and feelings from Tina.)

USEFULNESS AND EVALUATION OF THE ROLE PLAY TECHNIQUE

A technique used by reality (Wubbolding & Brickell, 2004), rational-emotive, behavior (Gilliland & James, 1998), cognitive, Gestalt (Seligman, 2001), and social learning (Young, 1992) counselors, role play is commonly used with clients who would like to change something about themselves. The role play technique is effective when working with individuals and groups (Carroll, Bates, & Johnson, 1997). It can also be used with families in family counseling sessions (Hackney & Cormier, 2005). Through role play, clients can learn new skills as well as explore different behaviors and observe how these behaviors affect others. If a client has trouble setting goals for the counseling sessions, the professional counselor can have the client role play to figure out why she is having difficulty coming up with a goal (Hackney & Cormier, 2005). The role play technique has been used to teach research ethics to graduate school students (Strohmetz & Skleder, 1992) and counseling techniques to undergraduate students (Rabinowitz, 1997).

The technique of role play can also be used to help prepare teachers for parent-teacher conferences. This is particularly useful for beginning teachers who may be nervous about this type of conference. Teachers are given a list of situations, and they either role play the part of the teacher or the part of the parent. Each situation deals with a different type of difficult parent with whom the teacher may have contact. The practice that the teachers get by role playing may help them feel more comfortable once it is time for the meetings with the parents to occur (Johns, 1992).

Role play is a technique that is also useful when working with adolescents in school. Students can learn more about the beliefs and values that they hold and can gain a further understanding of those which others hold (Kottman, 1990). Role plays can help enhance a child's social skills, promote higher levels of thinking, and lead to better listening skills. Role play is exceptionally useful with adolescents because it is an active technique requiring the students to participate.

This technique can also be used to teach empathy to elementary school children. By introducing the children to moral dilemmas, the students may begin to understand a perspective different from their own. Upright (2002) described how a teacher could do this in the classroom. There are nine steps in the process:

1. The teacher needs to observe the students and evaluate their moral developmental level.
2. An appropriate story needs to be chosen; an obvious problem must exist.
3. The teacher describes the background of the story to the children and should make sure that the students understand any terms which may be found in the story.

4. While the teacher reads the story and presents the moral dilemma, she can have the children role play different parts of the story.
5. The teacher should ask questions to make sure the students understand the situation including the conflict.
6. The students work in groups and discuss the moral dilemma, role playing the different sides of it.
7. If needed, the teacher can add details to the story that could alter students' opinions.
8. To encourage students to think about the moral dilemma, the teacher can have them create alternate endings to the story.
9. By recording the responses of students, the teacher can "look for growth in both empathy and decision-making ability" throughout the school year (p. 19).

To increase the efficacy of this technique, it is important for clients to feel comfortable exposing their weaknesses in front of professional counselors and for professional counselors to be honest with their clients. Professional counselors need to remind themselves and their clients that this technique takes time to work, it is not a quick fix (Wubbolding & Brickell, 2004). Some theorists consider role play more effective if it is paired with cognitive restructuring (Corey, 2007).

While role play is considered an effective technique, there are some problems that may arise. Clients sometimes get stage fright and do not want to reenact the scenarios. Professional counselors need to make sure that they are allowing clients to have control over the direction of the role play. Sometimes, such strong emotion is expressed that it makes the client and professional counselor uncomfortable (Young, 1992). A study conducted by Thompson and Bundy (1996) found role play to be an ineffective method of measuring assertiveness in elementary school children.

Finally, Ivey and Ivey (2007) point out that role playing should not be used with a client until the client's problem is clearly understood. In addition, client performance should be "checked out" after implementation of the role play to bolster client efficacy.

Techniques Based Upon Cognitive Approaches

Early cognitive theorists had a very similar reaction to behaviorism as social learning theorists. Cognitive theorists believed the behavioral approaches were reductionistic and simplistic because behavioral approaches did not acknowledge a human being's propensity to plan and think before behaving. Cognitive psychologists and counselors noticed that clients could make progress in counseling by perceiving and thinking about problems and solutions through different contexts and lenses.

Research has shown a number of cognitive techniques are particularly effective in reducing stress. Several of these techniques are based on Wolpe's principle of reciprocal inhibition, which basically means that you can't do two opposite things at the same time. As applied to counseling, a client cannot: feel stressed and relaxed at the same time; think positive, reaffirming messages to oneself at the same time one is thinking negative, nasty thoughts; or visualize positive, empowering scenes at the same time one is visualizing disempowering, negative images. Thus, by using counseling techniques that engage in the positive dimension of these continua, the client effectively blocks out the negative dimension and the resulting stressful ramifications.

Self-talk empowers clients to monitor their internal dialogue, which most people are able to do by the time they are 8 years old, and alter that dialogue in order to think positive affirming self-messages (sometimes called a "positive spin cycle"), while simultaneously blocking self-defeating or negative self messages (sometimes called a "negative spin cycle"). Similarly, visual or guided imagery can help clients to block out intrusive visualizations by substituting a relaxing or empowering visualization or image. Additionally, guided imagery allows a counselor to "covertly" (i.e., through the use of visual imagery) expose clients to empowering or relaxing images, ordinarily by having a client close their eyes and imagine a scene or series of actions the counselor suggests. Guided imagery is used very frequently in therapeutic approaches to relaxation, such as when a client imagines taking a walk through the woods along a stream and imagines the sights and sounds one might encounter, all suggested by the counselor or a relaxation recording. Guided imagery can also be used for covert modeling or role playing, in which the client imagines himself perform a certain skill or behavior before trying it out in the real world.

Three other cognitive-based techniques covered in this section are reframing, thought stopping, and cognitive restructuring. Reframing requires a counselor to take a client-perceived problem situation and adapt (reframe) it in a more positive or productive manner; for example, the behavior of a defiant adolescent could be reframed as a need to develop independent or autonomous decision-making practices. As such, the problem is viewed not as maladaptive or pathological, but as developmental or even pro-social (e.g., she is telling you she is trying to become an adult). Reframing is often considered an Adlerian technique, but is covered here because of its strong cognitive component. (How's that for a reframe?!)

Thought stopping is particularly effective in ending repetitive thought cycles, sometimes even reaching the point of obsession, by physically breaking a cognitive "spin cycle" and substituting positive self-talk and statements. Cognitive restructuring helps clients systematically analyze, process, and resolve cognitively based issues by replacing negative thoughts and interpretations with more positive thoughts and interpretations.

MULTICULTURAL IMPLICATIONS

Like humanistic/phenomenological or psychodynamic approaches to counseling, cognitive approaches to counseling emphasize the importance of rapport and the therapeutic alliance. But unlike these other approaches, counselors using a cognitive approach do not require clients to reveal intimate details of their lives or past events or to focus on intense emotions. Cognitive approaches deal with the present and use a logical and clear process that appeals to clients who are systematic thinkers in a nonthreatening manner that many clients find empowering. As a result, cognitive approaches ordinarily appeal to clients from a wide array of cultural backgrounds, particularly those whose cultures may discourage the sharing of family-related issues (e.g., Latino culture) or exploration or exhibition of intense emotional displays (e.g., Asian culture).

The approach also lends itself to the use of numerous techniques that transfer meaningfully across numerous cultural contexts, including gender, racial, ethnic, socioeconomic, disability, and sexual orientation contexts (Beck & Weishaar, 1995; Douglas, 1989; Jacobson, 1987). Thomas (1992) found that cognitive approaches were particularly helpful in exploring negative expectations and creating more positive expectations among clients of African descent. Clients from lower socioeconomic strata often find that cognitive approaches help them discover that they can control the events and perceptions of events in their environment, empowering them to develop positive expectations and positive steps to change their lives.

Other clients may feel uncomfortable with a cognitive approach because it focuses on present moment events rather than self-awareness or insight derived from past experiences. Cognitive therapy is a time limited approach that requires clients to think clearly and logically, and many clients find the approach to be superficial or failing to meet their emotional needs or needs for self-awareness. Of course, like other approaches, some techniques based on cognitive approaches require more training and sophistication than other. Counselors using a cognitive approach with clients are, at their core, nonjudgmental, nonthreatening, and accepting of clients from diverse backgrounds and worldviews because they do not view clients or client problems/behaviors as bad or inferior; they view client issues as stemming from distorted thoughts that can be analyzed and modified to adjust to a complex and fluid sociocultural environment.

CHAPTER 17

Self-Talk

ORIGINS OF THE SELF-TALK TECHNIQUE

Seligman (2001) described self-talk as a positive pep-talk that a person gives to herself each day. When using self-talk, a person repeatedly states a helpful, supportive phrase when she is faced with a troubling issue. Self-talk is a technique that comes from rational-emotive behavior therapy (REBT) and other cognitive approaches to counseling (see chapter 30). REBT holds that "people make irrational demands on themselves" that lead to psychological disturbances (Ellis, 1993, p. 200). People's conversations with themselves are based on their beliefs about themselves. Self-talk is self-fulfilling, and it is important for a person to learn ways to challenge irrational beliefs (Schafer, 1998). Self-talk is a technique that can be used to dispute these irrational beliefs and develop healthier thoughts, which will lead to more positive self-talk. It is a way for people to deal with the negative messages that they send to themselves. An underlying principle of this technique is that people have the ability to control their emotions (Weikle, 1993).

There are two types of self-talk that a person may use, positive and negative (Egan, 1998). A person's self-talk can be influenced by what other people (e.g., parents, teachers, peers) say about the person (Burnett & McCrindle, 1999). Positive self-talk, as described above, is the type professional counselors will want to teach their clients to use (Egan, 1998). When people use positive self-talk, they are much more likely to remain motivated to reach their goals (Pearson, 2000). Negative self-talk is often self-defeating and prevents clients from improving and succeeding (Egan, 1998). It is dominated by "pessimism, guilt, fear, and anxiety" (Pearson, 2000, p. 3). Borton, Markowitz, and Dieterich (2005) conducted a study to examine the most common types of thoughts associated with negative self-talk. The top three concerns the researchers found to be related with negative self-talk include interpersonal concerns, physical appearance, and personality characteristics (Borton et al., 2005). Schafer (1998) identified at least 16 different types of negative self-talk: negativizing (i.e., focusing on the negative aspects), awfulizing (i.e., perceiving situations as awful), catastrophizing (i.e., perceiving situations to be catastrophes), overgeneralizing, minimizing, blaming, perfectionism, musterbation (i.e., perceiving that one "must" do something), personalizing, judging human worth, control fallacy (i.e., perception that everything is within one's control), polarized thinking (i.e., an all or none mentality), being right, fallacy of fairness (i.e., the belief that life should be fair), shoulding (i.e., perceiving that one "should" do something), and magnifying. By using self-talk to change their absolutist ways of thinking, clients can gain more control over situations (Corey, 2007). A person's negative self-talk is not always unhealthy as it sometimes helps a person recognize a risky situation; a balance between positive and negative self-talk is important (Weikle, 1993).

HOW TO IMPLEMENT THE SELF-TALK TECHNIQUE

Before teaching a client how to use this technique, it is helpful if the professional counselor first works with the client to develop a positive attitude about self-talk and herself. To do this, the professional counselor and client should evaluate the client's thoughts about herself to figure out which thoughts are helpful to the client's well-being. Later in the process of teaching the client to use self-talk, the professional counselor can have the client focus on these thoughts (Weikle, 1993).

A popular way to reduce negative self-talk is called the countering method (Young, 1992). There are four steps involved in this method. In the first step, the goal is to "identify and explore negative self-talk" (p. 156). In order to enhance effectiveness, it is necessary for the professional counselor to know in which type(s) of negative self-talk the client engages, how often negative self-talk occurs, and the types of situations that bring about negative self-talk. Young suggested having clients carry an index card so the clients can record any self-criticisms made. This card will provide the professional counselor with valuable information and may also assist the client to further understand the feelings that the self-criticisms produce.

After one full week of self-monitoring, the professional counselor and client are ready to begin step two of the countering method. In this second step, the goal is to examine what purpose is served by the client's negative self-talk. There are typically three or four common themes that emerge when the professional counselor and client review the index card. It is important for the professional counselor to help the client understand the basis of the beliefs. Most of the time, clients will not easily let go of their beliefs. The beliefs are difficult to let go of because of habit and self-protection (Young, 1992). To explore the function of the negative self-

talk, the professional counselor can ask the client questions such as, "What does this negative thought help me do or feel?" (p. 157). Not only will investigating this area help the client and professional counselor understand the basis for negative self-talk, but the client may also realize that there is something else he would like to work on during the counseling sessions.

Once the client is aware of the reason he uses negative self-talk, the professional counselor can help the client develop counters. McMullin developed this term in 1986 "to describe the production of a self-statement that is incompatible with the critical thought" (Young, 1992, p. 157). The most effective counters dispute the irrational belief and are consistent with the client's values. They also are in the same "mode" as the statement that is being challenged: images are countered with images, and thoughts are countered with thoughts (Young, 1992). Pearson (2000) suggested using words like "I" and "me" so that the counters are personalized. Counters also should be worded positively and in the present tense, realistic, easily memorized, and repeated often. If a professional counselor has a client who "musterbates" (e.g., simply must have everything he wants) an effective counter could be, "I never must have what I want, I only prefer it" (Ellis, 1997a, p. 97).

The goal of the last step of the countering method is for the client to review the counters after practicing them. The amount of time that clients need to practice their counters varies, but they frequently will need more than one week. The subjective units of distress scale (SUDS) (see chapter 34) can be used to evaluate the effectiveness of a counter. First the client identifies the negative self-statement and rates her discomfort on the 100-point SUDS scale. Then the client identifies one of the counters and again rates her discomfort on the SUDS scale. The effectiveness of the counter can be measured by subtracting the second rating from the first rating. If there is a reduction in the feelings of discomfort, the counter can be considered effective. Of course, the greater the drop of the second rating, the more effective the counter. Counters that are evaluated as ineffective need to be revised, practiced, and evaluated again until an effective counter is found (Young, 1992).

VARIATIONS OF THE SELF-TALK TECHNIQUE

A variation of this technique is the P and Q method. In this method, when negative self-talk begins, clients pause (P), breathe deeply, and question (Q) themselves to figure out what is upsetting about the situation. One of the questions should address an alternative way of interpreting what happened so that the client can deal with his feelings appropriately (Schafer, 1998).

Instant replay is another variation of self-talk. When a client notices herself responding to something in an unwanted way the client needs to "catch the negative self-talk, challenge it, and change it" (Schafer, 1998, p. 373). To challenge their negative self-talk, clients can evaluate whether it is factual or distorted, moderate or extreme, and helpful or harmful.

EXAMPLE OF THE SELF-TALK TECHNIQUE

Nicole is a 17-year-old rising high school senior with a test phobia. This transcript is the first in a series that will be followed over several chapters throughout the remainder of this book, covering self-talk, deep breathing, SUDS, and culminating in the implementation of systematic desensitization. This transcript provides some preliminary information regarding her symptoms and how they affect her, then ends with the implementation of a scaling technique. During her treatment, Nicole was also taught the techniques of visual imagery and progressive muscle relaxation. Nicole was initially referred for psycho-educational evaluation to rule out learning disorders and attention-deficit/hyperactivity disorder. During the evaluation, it became clear that a test phobia was the primary concern.

Counselor (C):   . . . About a month or two ago we talked about how you sometimes have some fears or anxieties that are related to testing, tests and taking tests and things like that. Tell me about this so I can understand more about what happens to you in these situations.

Nicole (N):   Umm, I get really nervous before I take an exam or SATs and it affects the way I perform on my tests because I'm so nervous.

C: When you say it affects your performance on the tests, what do you mean by that?

N: I bomb them 'cause I'm worrying.

C: And what kind of thoughts go through your mind whenever you're worrying and thinking that you're not going to do well?

N: "Oh my God! What if I don't do good?" Umm, what's going to happen if I do bad, the outcome, things like that.

C: Do you say things to yourself? Do you carry on a conversation in your mind?

N: I tell myself to calm down.

C: You tell yourself to calm down. Do you tell yourself other things, things that make you more anxious and nervous sometimes?

N: I'll tell myself, like, you gotta do good or else you're in big trouble.

C: Or else get in big trouble, what is big trouble?

N: Big trouble means like I won't get into a good college, I'll fail, stuff like that.

C: And whenever you say those things to yourself, how do you feel?

N: Bad.

C: Do you feel those things in your body, too?

N: My stomach, neck.

C: Any place else?

N: No.

C: So butterflies in the stomach and pain in the neck?

N: Yes.

C: . . . One of the assignments that I gave you before you came to session today was to write down a couple of things that you might be able to say to yourself when you are anxious and upset. We call that cognitive self-talk. It's whenever you think inside your own mind and say things to yourself. Because you can either think negative, nasty, hurtful things and spin yourself up into a frenzy where you get the butterflies in your stomach and start to feel the tension in your neck, or you can think positive and affirming types of things.

N: Right.

C: And if you're thinking the positive and affirming types of things, then it's impossible to think about . . .

N: The bad stuff.

C: The bad stuff, right, and we call that <u>recipro-cal inhibition, that basically means that you</u> <u>can't do two opposite things at the same</u> <u>time.</u> So if you're thinking the positive and uplifting thoughts, then it's impossible to think the negative and hurtful types of things.

N: Okay.

C: So one of the things that I'd like you to do is share with me a couple of things that you could be saying to yourself instead of, I better do good or I'm going to get into big trouble or not get into a good college. These types of thoughts can really get the anxiety and worry flowing. So what kinds of these could you say . . . . (At this moment, Nicole reaches into her pocket and pulled out a slip of paper with the self-talk phrases written on it.) . . . ah, you have them written down.

N: I have them written.

C: I can tell that you're very serious about these problems and really appreciate your efforts so far. What is on the paper?

N: Umm, I tell myself stuff like, don't worry because in the end everything's going to be all right so it's no use trying to stress over it.

C: (Counselor writes this down.) Don't worry, no use trying to stress. Anything else?

N: I tell myself to take a deep breath and relax.

C: Good, deep breath and relax. Have you ever taken a deep breath?

N: A couple of times. If I'm really losing it, I will.

C: How does that feel?

N: It's okay, it works . . .

C: Okay. Lean back in your chair and close your eyes. And say out loud the things that you used to say. Things like, "I gotta do good on this test," "I gotta get into a good college," and so forth and I want you to feel the tension inside your body . . . (Pause for about 15 seconds) Now I want you to go ahead and say these calming and relaxing things to yourself. I want you to say, "Don't worry because everything's going to be all right, don't stress over it, take a deep breath and relax." (Pause for a half minute) How was that?

N: Pretty good. I stopped feeling so nervous and felt more positive, like I could really do it without being scared. I wonder if it'll work in class . . .

C: Good. So what you're finding is that whenever you are thinking these bad, nasty things, about how life's gonna end if you don't get a good score on those SATs or something like that, then you're feeling really anxious and stressed out. Way up there on the scale. But whenever you think these calming and relaxing things, and I can see you actually taking a deep breath when you were saying that to yourself, then you start to relax and feel better.

N: Mmmhmm.

C: Great. That was called cognitive self-talk and that's based on that principal of reciprocal inhibition, which again means you can't think nasty things and calming and relaxing things at the same time, so you block all that nasty stuff that comes into your mind. All those hurtful and stressful types of things that you say to yourself, you block it with all these calming and relaxing phrases and that's one very helpful way to keep you from feeling stressed out. It's also a very helpful way for you to calm yourself back down so that you can focus and get the work done that you need to get done. . . For your homework I want you to practice positive self-talk five times a day for at least 1 minute each time, every day until I see you next week. Spread them out during the day so that you do one or two practices in each of the morning, afternoon and evening . . . .

USEFULNESS AND EVALUATION OF THE SELF-TALK TECHNIQUE

Self-talk is a technique that is commonly used to deal with issues of perfectionism, worry, self-esteem, and anger management (Corey, 2007). This technique can also be used with clients who need to develop motivation. For example, if a client wanted to motivate herself to exercise, she could list positive statements about exercising on index cards and pick several of them to recite each day. This helps to change the person's statements from negative to positive and in turn the person develops a better attitude about exercising (Schafer, 1998). Professional counselors can teach this technique to clients who need help managing stress. Because negative self-talk can result in stress, it makes sense that positive self-talk can result in less stress. By altering the effect that the stressful situation has on the client, stress can be reduced (Corey & Corey, 2006). Weikle (1993) suggested using self-talk with clients who have an internal locus of control and value health.

Smith (2002) described using self-talk as a part of a cognitive-behavioral intervention that teachers can use with students who have behavioral deficits. Vernon (1993) described using self-talk with high school students who have hostile reactions when confronted by an authority figure. When students find themselves in situations where they want to react with hostility, they can repeat, "I'm okay. I don't agree with the way _____ is treating me, but that's his/her problem. I'm okay." (Vernon, 1993). By focusing on their "okay-ness," the students feel less victimized and more in control of the situation and will typically react with less hostility.

There are many studies that provide support for the efficacy of self-talk in addressing issues of control (Thompson, Sobolew-Shubin, Galbraith, Scwankovsky, & Cruzen, 1993), self-regulating academic behavior (Wolters, 1999), and anxiety (Prins & Hanewald, 1999; Treadwell & Kendall, 1996). Importantly, Grainger (1991) cautioned that it is important for a person not to dismiss all of his or her negative thinking. Instead, professional counselors need to help their clients make a distinction between negative thinking that leads to negative self-talk and negative thinking that helps keep them safe. Negative thinking is necessary, especially when a person is in a high-risk situation. This type of thinking sometimes helps a person realize that he must create a plan to be able to live or work effectively.

CHAPTER 18

Visual/Guided Imagery

ORIGINS OF THE VISUAL IMAGERY TECHNIQUE

The origins of visual imagery techniques began with Freud's dream interpretations in the late 1890s and were heavily influenced by Jung's "active imagination" (Koziey & Andersen, 1990; Schoettle, 1980). Hypnagogic visions under deep relaxation were noted by Frank in 1913 and later in 1922 by Kretschmer, who named them "bildstreifendenken," which means thinking in the form of a movie (Schoettle). In the 1920s, Robert Desoille developed the "guided daydream" method as a therapeutic technique. He required the client to actively daydream, while in a state of muscular relaxation, about themes introduced by the psychotherapist. More modern influences for the technique are Leuner's "guided affective imagery" in the 1950s and Swartly's "initiated symbol projection" in 1965.

Today, visual imagery is used in many therapeutic approaches, including cognitive, behavioral, transpersonal, Gestalt, psychodynamic, and Ericksonian (Arbuthnott, Arbuthnott, & Rossiter, 2001; Seligman, 2001). For example, behavioral therapists use imagery in the treatment phobias and in relaxation and stress management training (Arbuthnott et al.). Cognitive therapists employ imagery to access a client's key beliefs and urge reinterpretations of experiences. Psychodynamic therapists use imagery to help clients process difficult memories or thoughts. Gestalt therapists draw on imagery to help clients work through internal conflicts or alleviate anxiety. Most recently, solution-focused counselors use imagery to implement the "miracle question" (Murdock, 2004) (see chapter 4).

There are several types of visual imagery. *Mental imagery* is the process through which a person focuses on a vivid mental picture of an experience. Mental imagery can help assess the relationship between the client's experiences and presenting symptoms and help determine how those experiences became intensified in the client's mind. *Positive imagery* is the visualization of any pleasant scene, real or imagined. Positive imagery can reduce tension, inhibit anxiety, or help a person cope with pain. *Goal-rehearsal imagery or coping imagery* requires the client to visualize himself successfully coping with each step of a process.

HOW TO IMPLEMENT THE VISUAL IMAGERY TECHNIQUE

Before beginning guided imagery, make sure that the room is quiet and the client is comfortable. Music may be used to create a soothing mood, but be aware that for some people music is a distraction (Myrick & Myrick, 1993). Help the client relax by suggesting he close his eyes and take slow, deep breaths

(Vernon, 1993). Once the client is relaxed, start the guided imagery experience. Speak in a soft, soothing voice. It is preferable to have a story scripted ahead of time to ensure that the words create the desired mood and direction (Myrick & Myrick). Guided imagery scripts do not need to be long, and it may take only a minute or two to lead a client through the experience, although some experiences may last more than 10 minutes. Keep the exercises simple at first (Vernon). Arbuthnott et al. (2001) provided the following example of how multi-sensory guided imagery might be used in a counseling session:

> Imagine that you are walking across a field of fresh green grass on a warm spring day. You feel the softness of the grass beneath your feet, the warmth of the air on your skin, and hear the sound of birds singing in the distance. You are moving toward a large tree that is near a creek. When you reach the tree, you sit down with your back supported by the trunk. Listening to the soft sound of the running water in the creek, you notice that you are filled with a sense of well-being. (p. 123)

Always allow the client to imagine something familiar and nonthreatening before moving onto scripts that pose serious dilemmas or require the client to confront specific issues (Myrick & Myrick, 1993; Vernon, 1993). Bring closure to the guided imagery experience by posing a final question, telling the client to let his mind go blank again, or by informing the client that the experience is ending and he should open his eyes on the count of three. Discuss the guided imagery experience afterwards (Myrick & Myrick). Ask the client how he felt about the activity and what he did or did not like about the activity.

VARIATIONS OF THE VISUAL IMAGERY TECHNIQUE

Guided imagery is a major subtype of visual imagery. Guided imagery can be used to help clients put emotional or interpersonal issues into words,

to help clients generate goals for change, to help clients rehearse new behaviors, or to help clients exert control over their emotions or stress levels (Arbuthnott et al., 2001). In guided imagery, a person is lead through a visualization process directed by stimulus words or sounds (Myrick & Myrick, 1993). Clients are encouraged to relax, imagine themselves in a situation, and then discuss and process the activity to gain insight. Therapists use three types of images in guided imagery (Vernon, 1993). *Spontaneous images* arise without conscious direction of content. *Directed images* involve the therapist suggesting a specific image on which the client should concentrate. *Guided images* combine the other two types by giving the client a starting point and allowing him to fill in the blanks. Guided imagery can be realistic or rely on fantasy or metaphors (Arbuthnott et al.). The timing, duration, and intensity of guided imagery should be modified to meet the needs of each individual (Seligman, 2001). Imagery is most powerful when it appeals to the person's dominant senses (i.e., visual, auditory, tactile, olfactory) and when it is practiced between sessions.

EXAMPLES OF THE VISUAL IMAGERY TECHNIQUE

EXAMPLE 1: The use of visual imagery in a reciprocal inhibition procedure

Nick is a 35-year-old male referred for symptoms of depression and anxiety. In the course of treatment he was introduced to the visualization insertion/blocking technique based on reciprocal inhibition.

Counselor (C): . . . Because you know when you close your eyes and you can still see things and you can play things, movies, inside your mind's eye; things that may have happened in the past or things that you might like to happen in the future. A lot of people call it fantasizing or daydreaming.

Nick (N): Yeah.

C: But, we actually call it visualization and visual imagery, and it's really important because, again taking you back to the term, reciprocal inhibition, it's actually impossible to run the negative nasty movies, the things you're worried about, while you're thinking about a calming and relaxing place that you might like to take yourself. One of the other assignments that I gave you before this session was to think about one or two calming and relaxing places you might like to take yourself whenever you're stressed out. What did you decide on?

N: Hawaii. Definitely Hawaii.

C: Oh, Hawaii, that's a good one.

N: The beach there was the calmest, most peaceful place I had ever been.

C: Great. What was so calm and relaxing?

N: I think it's just the environment, so beautiful.

C: Let's close our eyes, and you describe it to me so I can picture it in my head.

N: Umm, well I picture myself on the sand with the blue ocean right there, and the palm trees, and the sky, the warm weather.

C: Yeah, how did it make you feel when you were there? Were you lying on the beach or walking around?

N: I was lying on the beach and it was really calm and relaxing.

C: It sounds beautiful. Do you have pictures, videos, and things like that?

N: Yeah.

C: Some people are really good at visualizing it. It's almost like you close your eyes and you're there. And sometimes when you've not been there for quite some time, it starts to fade from memory and becomes more difficult to recall. And one of the things you can do is to look at the pictures or video of the beach with the surf and the waves and the sounds. And so whenever it doesn't seem as vivid, it doesn't seem like I'm right there when I close my eyes I can actually look at it on the TV and hear the sounds and it kinda brings that back. . . . What I want you to do right now is close your eyes and take yourself to Hawaii, on the beach. I want you to imagine that you're actually there and I want you to imagine the peacefulness and the calm. (Pause as Nick

closes his eyes and relaxes into his visual scene) And come on back to me whenever you're ready. There, feeling more relaxed? How did that feel?

N: Outstanding.

C: Sorry I had to bring you back. We still have some more work to do. Now I want you to close your eyes and visualize some of the unpleasant scenes that we were discussing earlier, your boss, ex-wife, that particularly nasty colleague. And when I tell you to, I want you to change the scene in your mind to Hawaii and relax; even do some deep breathing and some positive self-talk.

N: Got it. (Pause for a minute to let Nick visualize the stress-producing visualizations he presented with at counseling)

C: Now, Nick, I want you to take yourself to Hawaii.

N: With pleasure!!

C: That's the idea. . . When you think and visualize sad and stressful things, you become sad and stressed. When you think about and visualize relaxing things, you become relaxed. (Pause for about a minute as Nick relaxes in his Hawaii scene) Okay. It's time to open your eyes and come back to me. You can go back there anytime you want, as you already know. (Introduce scaling technique) Now, what I want you to tell me is, on that scale of 1 to 10, with 1 being total relaxation, "This is just so fantastic," and 10 being "Eeek! I'm completely stressed out," where are you whenever you're in Hawaii in your mind?

N: A 1. Definitely a 1!!

C: A 1. Great, that sure beats the 8 that you were at when we were discussing those challenging people in your life.

N: You got that right!...

EXAMPLE 2: Guided visual imagery

Numerous recordings of visual imagery exercises are available. Following is one of several excellent tracks available on *Stressbuster Relaxation Exercises*

(Volume 1) produced by Erford (2001) and available for purchase from the American Counseling Association Foundation (see www. counseling. org under publications).

TROPICAL HIDEAWAY

Today we are going to take a trip to a deserted tropical beach. Before we go, we are going to do a deep breathing activity to prepare us for our relaxing journey.

Get into a comfortable position and close your eyes. Now put one hand on your stomach. Breathe in so that you can feel your hand go up as it rests on your stomach. Imagine that your stomach has a beach ball inside. As you breathe in, fill the beach ball with air. As you exhale, let the air out of the beach ball.

Let's try it. Take a slow deep breath in through your nose.

(Pause)

Now breathe out slowly.

(Pause)

Again, take a slow deep breath in through your nose.

(Pause)

And breathe out slowly.

(Pause)

One more time, breathe in slowly and fill the beach ball with air.

(Pause)

And breathe out slowly. Let the air out of the beach ball. Continue to take long deep slow breaths as you journey to your tropical hideaway.

(Pause)

Take a moment to listen to your breathing. See how calm and relaxed it is. You are now ready to take your trip. Imagine that you are on a tropical island, you have left your traveling party in search of a relaxing hideaway.

(Pause)

You see a trail that leads into the jungle, feeling adventurous you enter the trail. In front of you, you see many lush green plants and several hanging vines. You also see brightly colored tropical flowers. You hear the chatter of tropical birds and other small animals. You smell the sweet fragrant flowers and plant life. You follow the trail enjoying the beautiful scenery. You eventually come to a clearing. In front of you, you see a white sandy beach surrounding a crystal clear turquoise colored lagoon. You notice that the beach is completely deserted. You can hardly believe that nobody is visiting this glorious place. You decide to walk toward the water. You feel the warmth of the sun on your body. You look up in the sky and see that it is completely clear. As you are walking, you hear the lapping of the waves against the sand. The closer you get to the water, the softer the sand becomes beneath your feet. Notice the feel of the warm grainy sand on your feet.

(Pause)

Finally, you have reached the lagoon. You see the gentle ebb and flow of the water. You stand for a moment and watch the water lap gentle little waves against the beautiful white sand.

(Pause)

You feel your worries and concerns wash away with every ebb and flow of the crystal clear water.

(Pause)

You decide to enjoy the cool, soothing, crystal-clear water. You submerge your feet in water. The tiny waves break gently against your lower legs. You stand alone in the lagoon acclimating to the temperature. The water is cool, yet refreshing. You decide to walk out a little further from the shore. You feel the refreshing water on your knees.

(Pause)

On your thighs.

(Pause)

On your buttocks.

(Pause)

And on your stomach.

(Pause)

You stand for a moment submerged to your waist in the cool, crystal-clear water. You feel as if you could just float away. Your entire body feels relaxed and refreshed. After enjoying the tranquil calm of the lagoon, you walk back toward the white, sandy beach

(Pause)

Once you reach the beach, you feel the warmth of the sand beneath your feet. You decide to get your beach blanket out of your back pack and put it down on the warm sand. You lie down on the blanket and look at the peaceful blue sky with puffy white clouds. You feel the sun warming your wet body. You close your eyes and listen to the lapping of the water. Take a moment and enjoy this peaceful relaxing sensation.

(Pause)

After lying there for awhile, you decide it is time to get back to your traveling party. Get up from your

blanket, enjoy the beautiful view of the water and the white, sandy beach. You gather up your belongings and head back toward the tropical jungle feeling relaxed, peaceful, and calm. You walk through the jungle enjoying the sound of the birds and the fragrant odor of the tropical flowers. You continue on the trail, thinking about your wonderful trip and how relaxed it has made you feel. You carry this positive experience with you the entire day, knowing that you can return to your tropical hideaway whenever you desire.

In order to learn the effects of the guided visualization on the client or to add additional meaning to the experience, the professional counselor should ask several follow-up questions before ending or transitioning to another topic or activity. Possible follow-up queries include:

➤ What did you like about this activity?
➤ What did you not like about this activity, etc.?

USEFULNESS AND EVALUATION OF THE VISUAL IMAGERY TECHNIQUE

Visual imagery can be used in many developmental and therapeutic situations. Imagery can reduce anxiety, facilitate relaxation, promote a sense of control, improve problem solving and decision making, alleviate pain, and help people develop new perspectives on their lives (Seligman, 2001). Imagery can also produce behavioral changes and enhance one's self-concept (Vernon, 1993). Guided imagery has been shown to effectively treat stress, posttraumatic stress disorder, panic attacks, bulimia nervosa, phobias, depression, and chronic pain (Arbuthnott et al., 2001). Visual and guided imagery are primarily used to enhance relaxation (Laselle & Russell, 1993), but are also helpful in addressing self-management (Penzien & Holroyd, 1994), pain management (Chaves, 1994; Cupal & Brewer, 2001; Gonsalkorale, 1996; Ross & Berger, 1996), and asthma (Peck, Bray, & Kehle, 2003). Guided imagery is also useful in treating enuresis and psychosomatic disorders (Myrick & Myrick, 1993).

Guided imagery can also allow clients to uncover and deal with highly complex emotions from experiences such as sexual abuse (Pearson, 1994), although Arbuthnott et al. (2001) cautioned professional counselors to be wary of a client's propensity to create "false memories" related to abuse or other traumatic events. Indeed, some individuals may visualize the occurrence of events that did not occur and convince themselves that the events really did occur. Imagery has shown minimal usefulness for clients with psychotic disorders and addictions (Schoettle, 1980). It is important to note that visual imagery may not be effective with young children who have difficulty separating fantasy from reality, who have trouble keeping their eyes closed and their body relaxed, or who repeat TV or movie plots rather than use their own imaginations (Schoettle, 1980).

CHAPTER 19

Reframing

ORIGINS OF THE REFRAMING TECHNIQUE

Reframing takes a problematic situation and presents it in a new way that allows the client to adopt a more positive, constructive perspective (Guterman, 1992). Reframing changes the conceptual or emotional viewpoint of a situation and changes its meaning by placing it in another context (frame) that also fits the same facts of the original situation (Watzalawick, Weakland, & Fisch, 1974). The goal of reframing is to help the client see the situation from another vantage point, making it seem less problematic, more normal, and, thus, more open to solution (Corey, 2007). When reframing, the professional counselor offers a new point of view to the client in hopes that he will see the situation differently and as a result, act more suitably (Eckstein, 1997). This alternative point of view must fit the situation as well as or even better than the client's original point of view in order to be convincing to the client (Kraft et al., 1985). If successful, reframing may result in the client seeing a previously unsolvable problem as solvable or seeing it as no longer a problem at all (Hackney & Cormier, 2005). Other times, reframing may allow the client to take a fresh approach to the presenting problem. At any rate, reframing is effective only when the alternative meaning is seen as totally credible.

Reframing is type of paradoxical strategy used in Adlerian therapy, strategic family therapy, and structural family therapy (Eckstein, 1997). The reframing technique actually evolved from Adlerian theory, but is addressed here due to its cognitive dimension. In addition, reframing is one of the six influencing skills included in Ivey and Ivey's (2007) counseling microskills approach. At its base, reframing operates on the premise that behavioral and emotional problems are caused not by events, but by how these events are viewed. Problems arise when events are perceived as blocking a client's goals, or interfering with client values, beliefs or purpose (Guterman, 1992). The reframing technique also involves the assumption that people have all the resources they need to make a desired change. Reframing also accepts the client's worldview and works within this framework to create a solution (Guterman, 1992). Reframing is especially useful when the situation involves redefining offensive motives or behaviors as problematic but well intended (Hackney & Cormier, 2005).

Since problematic behavior patterns often become ingrained, reframing works to reinterpret these behavior patterns. The assumption behind the reframing technique is that by altering perspectives on a behavior pattern, new behaviors will develop that accommodate this interpretation. Reframing can also move the client from blaming others to taking more responsibility for their behavior (Young, 1992) and can be used with both intrapersonal and interpersonal issues.

HOW TO IMPLEMENT THE REFRAMING TECHNIQUE

Reframing can be implemented using three simple steps. First, the professional counselor must use a nonjudgmental listening cycle to gain a complete understanding of the client's problem (Young, 1992). This is an essential starting point because reframing must be based on a firm knowledge of the client and the client's worldview so that the client can relate to the new frame of reference (i.e., the reframe). Second, once the professional counselor understands the problem, the professional counselor may then build a bridge from the client's point of view to a new way of looking at the problem. At this point it is important to include some aspect of the client's perspective while also suggesting the new one. Finally, the professional counselor must reinforce the bridge until a shift in perspective develops. One way of emphasizing the new perspective is to give the client homework that forces him to see the problem in the new way.

Kolko and Milan (1983) suggested a three-step procedure for extending and supporting implementation of the reframing technique: (a) reframing the behavior; (b) prescribing the behavior; and (c) maintaining the behavior through a contract.

VARIATIONS OF THE REFRAMING TECHNIQUE

There are several different varieties of reframing techniques. Reframing is also referred to as relabeling, positive interpretation, positive connotation, and reattribution (Eckstein, 1997). *Relabeling* is a specific type of reframing that consists of replacing a negative adjective with one that is more positive in connotation. For instance, if a woman describes her husband as "jealous," this label could be replaced with the description "caring." *Denominalizing* is the process of removing a diagnostic label and replacing it with a specific behavior that can be controlled. For example, a girl with anorexia may be seen as one who refused to eat. *Positive connotation* simply describes

the symptomatic behavior as being positively motivated. For instance, the statement "My mother never lets me do anything" can be reframed as "My mother loves me enough to set limits" (Vernon, 1993).

EXAMPLE OF THE REFRAMING TECHNIQUE

Lori is a 34-year-old female who is experiencing depressed mood, helplessness, and despair. She reports that prior to her current circumstances taking shape, she has never had any major episodes with depression and typically felt quite happy and in control of her life. She feels her current state of mind is in direct relation to her current situation.

Counselor (C): Well, from what I can tell, you seem like an insightful person. And you say this depressed mood you are feeling is related to your current situation? I'll certainly take your word for that. So tell me more about this current situation of yours.

Lori (L): Okay. Let's see. Up until about 6 months ago, life was good. I have a master's in accounting and am a CPA. Or *was* I should say.

C: You are no longer?

L: Well, technically I am. But it doesn't feel like it since I no longer work as one.

C: I see. Go on.

L: Okay, so anyway, life was good. I completed my master's before meeting my husband. I always knew I wanted to be an accountant, and I went straight through school and took a lot of pride in my abilities as a student, and later as an accountant. I went straight to work after graduation, landed an awesome job at a large medical corporation where I eventually worked my way up to a partial supervisory position. By that time I had met Terry, that's my husband, and then we married 3 years ago. I became pregnant fairly soon after we married and now have beautiful twin boys. We hired someone to care for the children in our home and I returned to work after maternity leave. Life continued to be good.

C: Okay. It sounds like life has been agreeable for you. You got your education out of the way and had time to focus on your career before meeting your husband. You had children, you hired a nanny, and you got to continue your career, which sounds very important to you.

L: Very. It's something I'm really good at. I feel valuable and appreciated. We all want to feel that, right? And its not that I don't get that from my family . . . it's just different, you know? It's like, how valuable can you feel changing dirty diapers? Not that I don't adore my children. They're great . . . really! But they don't say things like, "Wow, Lori, amazing work on the Bradford account! How about a pay raise?"

C: No, I don't suppose they do.

L: So, it's not that I'm pouting for ungrateful 1-year-olds. That's really not it. It's more that I really valued my career and the sense of worth that it gave me. I worked hard to get where I was. Even sacrificed being with my children to return to it . . . which was really hard . . . especially when they cried for me or were sick . . . Anyway, everything was still working out. I had it all . . . what every woman wants . . . and then . . . bam!

C: Bam?

L: Yeah, bam! All of a sudden, it's was all gone . . . taken from me! I can't believe how much I'm talking. I guess I'm just so relieved to be talking about this to someone without an agenda.

C: I'm very glad to hear that. Talking about it, being able to say out loud what it is you feel, can bring great relief. (Pause) So, it's gone . . . your career I assume?

L: Yep. All of that hard work just gone. Thanks to my husband. See, he's really close to his parents. And ever since the twins were born, they've been nagging at him and pulling at him and complaining that we lived too far away for them to see their grandchildren grow up. Becoming a father really changed his perspective on things too, and he began to

really question my drive to have a career and instead wanted me to focus more on being a parent. It's really not fair that women feel like they have to choose between the two or kill themselves doing both. Well, anyway, out of the blue, supposedly, he received a job offer back home that was just too good to be true . . . almost double the salary . . . which is important to him. He said it must be fate because he wasn't even on the market for a new job. I don't know if I believe him or not. But that's what he said and he said it was too great an offer to turn down. Looking back, I should have seen it coming. But at the time, I was completely blindsided. To make matters worse, he told his parents about the offer and they just took it to mean it was a done deal. They were so excited and talking as if we were already there and one big happy family again. Then I started to feel guilty like maybe my place should be at home with the kids. And then he felt obligated to his parents and didn't want to break his mother's heart. It was this huge mess and we ended up here before I could even absorb it all. He put our house on the market, he started his new position, I left my old one, and now the kids and I are at our new home.

C: So that's how everything unfolded to result in your current situation.

L: That's how it unfolded.

C: Can you tell me what exactly about the way things are now that is most troubling to you . . . that has your mood so depressed?

L: I feel like I'm talking too much. Am I talking too much?

C: Not at all. I want to get a very clear idea of what is important to you and what is troubling to you.

Recall that it is extremely important to get the full picture and to understand the client's perspective and worldview in order to more accurately present a reframe that will be acceptable to the client.

L: Okay, good. What is it about the way things are now . . . (Pauses for some time to really pinpoint what is most troubling) . . . umm, I guess . . . (really begins to slow her speech down) . . . that it feels so out of my control? . . . That it feels like a huge mistake? . . . That there's nothing I can do about it? . . . That he was so selfish? . . . And that I feel I have no meaning . . . no purpose . . . (begins to cry) . . . that all that hard work was wasted and I'll never have that kind of career again . . .

C: Ummhmm. Yes, I think I see now. What gave you the most meaning is now gone, through no fault of your own, and now you feel meaningless.

L: Completely.

C: I can see how sad this must make you feel.

L: I'm totally depressed.

C: I can also sense some anger.

L: Yeah, I haven't wanted to admit that, but it's definitely there.

C: That's not surprising you know. Anger and depression sometimes go hand in hand. Sometimes when we feel we can't do anything to change what we're angry about, we just give up and become depressed.

L: Makes sense. I would say that applies to me. Definitely applies.

There are many ways to arrive at the information you need to offer a reframe to a client and below is simply one such method, but certainly not the only one.

C: Okay, Lori, what I'd like to do for just a moment is brainstorm. I want us to work together to come up with a few possible options or exceptions to the current perspective we have on this situation.

L: Okay . . . I think.

C: Okay. Let's play *devil's* advocate for just a moment. I'm going to make a statement based on what you've told me here today, and I want you to make a statement in return, that argues against it. Make sense?

L: Sure.

C: Okay. I'll start with "I have *no* control over my daily life."

L: Ah . . . hmm . . . and I just say something back that goes against that?

C: Yes, but make it true to you.

L: Okay. "In some areas of my life, I have more freedom than I've ever had. I can schedule my day any way I like. I can stay up late. I don't have a boss telling me what to do." Like that?

C: Exactly like that. Okay, another one. "*Nothing* in my life gives me meaning."

L: (Talking to self) Nothing in my life gives me meaning . . . argue that . . . well . . . "I get meaning from being a mom, and a sister, and a friend. And I have a few hobbies that I'm really good at . . . they give me a sense of pride, I guess."

C: Okay. "There are *no* benefits to being home with my children."

L: "Oh, that's not true at all. They will never be 1-year-olds again. I never realized how much I was missing out on before. They'll never be exactly as they are right now."

C: Good. We've got just two more. "I will *never* have a career again."

L: "Well, that seems silly to say it like that. Of course I will eventually. It just seems impossible in this town to have the kind I want. But I don't suppose I have to stay here forever. So *eventually* I'll have a career again."

C: All right. Last one. "My husband is *completely* self-serving."

L: Oh dear. That's a hard one to argue. I mean, maybe he's not completely self-serving in everything he does, but in this situation, that's certainly hard to argue against. (Pauses and thinks for several moments) I can't come up with anything.

C: Okay, I think I can help with this one. Sometimes when we understand someone's position or motives, when we feel compassion or empathy for them and their choices, we find it impossible to be angry at them. That is, if you don't *want* to be angry with him anymore.

L: I don't want to be angry anymore. I don't want to be angry or depressed.

C: Okay then, what I mean is, understanding can negate anger. Assume, for instance, when someone cuts me off in traffic, that I immediately conjure up a reason or two why that person may be having the worst day of their life. I say to myself, "I bet they just got laid off from their job." Or, "I bet they just got dumped by their boyfriend." Something like that.

L: Okay. That's funny. I guess then it's hard to be mad at them for cutting you off.

C: Exactly. So, let's do that for your husband. Now you said earlier that this new job opportunity of his came with a large pay increase. Is that right?

L: Yes.

C: Could we possibly conjure up that he was worried about finances prior to that job offer?

L: Oh, we don't have to conjure. He has always worried about finances. And then when we had twins, he panicked. He was always afraid there wouldn't be enough to provide for all of us.

The counselor is about to offer a "relabeling" of the husband, from "selfish" to "provider." Recall that relabeling is a type of reframe, often used within a larger reframe. Also recall that it is especially helpful to redefine offensive motives as problematic but well intended.

C: Would it be possible then, to think of your husband as being motivated by the need to be a *provider* for his family, rather than having a purely selfish motive?

L: Yes, it would be possible for me to consider that.

C: (Standing up and walking to the window and opening the blinds) What do you see outside of my window?

L: (Somewhat puzzled) A dumpster! No wonder you keep the blinds closed!

C: Great view here on the backside of the building, isn't it? What else do you see?

L: I see a few small flowers. Oh, I see that beautiful dogwood tree behind the dumpster.

C: Yes, they grow wild here. Isn't it a sight?

L: Yeah, too bad that big green piece of metal is in front of it!

C: Yes, I don't suppose we can move that, can we?

L: Doubt it.

C: Probably can't change much of anything about what's already out there. (Pauses to let Lori think and returns to chair) From the view we have here, that dumpster is in front of that dogwood. See that building on the other side there?

L: Yes.

C: Suppose my office was in that building. Suppose we went over to that office and looked out that window instead of this one.

L: Okay.

C: The scenery wouldn't have changed would it have?

L: No. The dumpster would still be there.

C: That's right. But do you suppose it might look different from that angle?

L: Well, yes . . . it would . . . because from that window, the dogwood would be in front of the dumpster. You could still see the dumpster of course, but just barely because the dogwood would be the most obvious.

C: I believe you are exactly right. And I agree with you completely. Suppose that view out there is your life as you've described it early in this session. And suppose that I cannot for one minute change the situation that is your life. I cannot remove that dumpster. But I can lead you to that other window, with the different view. And even though that dumpster would still be there, it wouldn't be the focus of the view. Do you think that would be helpful for you at all?

L: I think that sounds like a fine idea.

C: Well, you've given me plenty of good material to work with. So here goes . . . When you arrived today, you were most troubled by your current situation. You felt both anger and sadness because you viewed your situation as out of your control, your life as meaningless, your career as over, and your husband as selfish. Now, I cannot change the *realities* of your situation, but I can offer you a new frame to view it out of. From this newly framed window, that very same scenery takes on new meaning. As it turns out, you have much control within your current situation. In fact, in some ways, you have more freedom than you've ever had. You have no boss to answer to. You set your daily schedule. You make many independent choices everyday . . . .Your life has meaning. You are a mother, and a sister, and a friend. You have hobbies that you are very skilled at and that you take pride in. These things give your life meaning and purpose . . . .Your salaried career is on hold for the moment, that is temporary. That does not mean that you will never have a career again. It only means that it will be just a little while longer. And in the meantime, you get to soak up every little morsel of joy those 1-year-olds have to offer. You don't have to miss one moment of their lives, which will never be as it is now . . . . Finally, it turns out that your husband may be more motivated by his need to provide for the financial welfare of his family than by purely selfish needs, and it is difficult to stay angry at that kind of motivation.

Pauses a few moments to let Lori take this all in

L: My gosh! If I could keep telling myself that, and really focusing on that part of the picture, I believe I could feel so much better, and maybe even actually *enjoy* my current situation.

Notice that the facts of the situation never changed. But with Lori's help in arguing her own points, a credible and alternative meaning was given.

USEFULNESS AND EVALUATION OF THE REFRAMING TECHNIQUE

Reframing can be used in many different situations and is especially valuable when redefining the problem situation changes the view of the problems so that it is more understandable, acceptable, or solvable (Gilliland & James, 1998). Davidson and Horvath (1997) indicated reframing was beneficial in couples counseling when addressing dyadic adjustment and marital conflict, while Robbins, Alexander, and Turner (2000) showed that reframing was effective in altering client attitudes toward counseling. Reframing can be used in family therapy to reduce the blame among family members by attributing negative consequences to situational causes rather than individual family members (Eckstein, 1997). For example, a child's curfew may be seen as a concern for safety rather than a lack of trust. Reframing can also be applied with those who are addicted to substances or those who are enablers or codependents.

Research on the reframing technique is limited (Robbins et al., 2000), but some studies have shown that positive reframing is effective in reducing negative emotions and mild to moderate depression (Swoboda et al., 1990). Kraft et al. (1985) evaluated the use of positive reframing against a control group for participants reporting negative emotions. Positive reframing produced greater improvement on outcome measures of depression and mood. Another study, conducted by Swoboda et al. (1990), compared the effectiveness of positive reframing, paradoxical restraining directives, and a pseudotherapy control for the treatment of depression. Statements such as "being alone and feeling down shows a great tolerance for solitude and basic self-satisfaction" and "feeling badly about yourself rather than taking grievances out on others shows a willingness to sacrifice for the good of others" (p. 256) were used with the positive reframing group. The participants in this reframing group showed the greatest improvement on several outcome measures, suggesting that reframing is a powerful technique for overcoming depression.

CHAPTER | **20**

Thought Stopping

ORIGINS OF THE THOUGHT STOPPING TECHNIQUE

Thought stopping involves teaching individuals to interrupt unwanted thoughts (Davis, Eshelman, & McKay, 1995), and was first used in 1875 to treat a man who was preoccupied with thoughts of nude women (Wolpe, 1990). However, many give credit to Alexander Bain for introducing thought stopping in his 1928 book *Thought Control in Everyday Life* (Davis et al., 1995). Thought stopping entered the behavior therapy domain after it was suggested by James G. Taylor and adapted by Joseph Wolpe for the treatment of obsessive and phobic thoughts (Davis et al.; Wolpe). Thought stopping trains the client to exclude, at the earliest moment possible, every undesirable thought (Wolpe), usually by invoking the command "stop" to interrupt unwanted thoughts (Davis et al.). Today, thought stopping is considered a helpful cognitive, or perhaps cognitive-behavioral, technique.

Thought stopping is successful for several reasons (Davis et al., 1995). First, the command "stop" serves as a punishment, thus decreasing the likelihood that the thought will reoccur. Also, the imperative "stop" acts as a distractor and is incompatible with the unwanted thought. Finally, the command "stop" can be followed by thought substitutions to help insure that the unwanted thoughts will not return. For instance, self-accepting statements may be substituted for undesired negative thoughts about the self, a process based on the principle of reciprocal inhibition.

HOW TO IMPLEMENT THE THOUGHT STOPPING TECHNIQUE

Thought stopping involves four steps. First, the client and professional counselor must decide together which thoughts are going to be targeted in the thought stopping procedure (Wolpe, 1990). Second, the client closes his eyes and imagines a situation in which the target thought is likely to occur (Davis et al., 1995). Third, the target thought is interrupted by the command "stop." The last step in thought stopping is to substitute a more positive thought for the unwanted thought. This step begins with the client's overt use of a thought substitution and then progresses to covert thought substitution (Horton & Johnson, 1977). A typical thought stopping session requires 15 to 20 minutes for client self-monitoring. The goal is to have the intrusive thoughts occur less frequently and bring their removal under the control of the client.

Thought interruption, the third step specified above, follows a four-stage process, shifting control from the professional counselor to the client (Horton & Johnson, 1977). First, the professional counselor interrupts the client's overt target thoughts until the client signals that the thoughts have subsided. As the client relays his thoughts aloud, the counselor yells "stop" anytime the client mentions the target thought. Second, the counselor attempts to stop the client's covert thoughts. When the client signals with a silent gesture that he is experiencing the target thought, the therapist yells "stop." Eventually by yelling "stop" aloud whenever he experiences the target thoughts, the client learns to overtly interrupt his own silent thoughts. And finally the client covertly interrupts his silent thoughts. In his head, the client commands himself to stop whenever he experiences the target thought.

VARIATIONS OF THE THOUGHT STOPPING TECHNIQUE

For some clients, the command "stop" is not sufficient to suppress unwanted thoughts. In these cases, other stronger methods of interruption may be used. Clients may keep a rubber band around their wrist and snap the rubber band when unwanted thoughts occur (Davis et al., 1995). They may also pinch themselves or press their fingernails into their palms in order to stop negative thoughts. In addition, pressing a loud buzzer when unwanted thoughts occur or accompanying the "stop" command with a slight faradic shock may successfully disrupt the negative thoughts (Wolpe, 1990). Some clients find it helpful to do something physical to break the thought cycle, like stand up and sit down, turn around several times, or simply cross their legs. Similar to the rubber band and pinching, the physical activity breaks the cognitive "spin cycle."

EXAMPLE OF THE THOUGHT STOPPING TECHNIQUE

Nancy is a 17-year-old high school senior with anxious-perfectionistic characteristics. She thinks constantly about maintaining high levels of school performance in order to meet future goals of attending a top-tier college. In the process, she creates a great deal of stress in her life and has sought counseling to help her to stop what she perceives to be constant, almost obsessional, thoughts.

Counselor (C): Okay. What kinds of things specifically do you say to yourself, that you think about all the time?

Nancy (N): I think that I have to do well in school, or my grades will go down. I have to do well so I can like accomplish my goals, you know, do well and succeed.

C: What'll happen if you don't?

N: Oh (nervous laughter), I'll feel bad about myself and like, my self-confidence will go down . . . . I won't feel like smart or anything.

C: Is that something you think about a lot?

N: Yeah, like all the time. I think about it *all* the time. (Pauses and begins to think)

C: You are worried about doing well in school and being smart?

N: What? Yeah, I guess I am.

C: What do you tell yourself specifically? I mean, to hear you tell it now, you're making it sound like an intellectual activity. "Oh, I just want to feel confident about myself." But what do you really say to yourself?

N: I'm dumb or I feel dumb, or I'm going to fail a test, or not get into a good college—stuff like that . . . sometimes, you know, I'm really down there.

C: What does that feel like, when you're really down there?

N: Bad, yeah, horrible.

C: On a scale of 1 to 10? (Scaling procedure)

N: Like a 1 or a 2—pretty bad.

C: And how often does that happen, when you think things like that to yourself?

N: Well, it usually happens if I'm really over loaded, which seems like all the time lately.

C: Okay, how often has that happened in the last week or 2, would you say?

N: Umm, all the time, especially at the end of like, a semester, or you know when teachers are cramming in all the. . . .

C: It's crunch time?

N: Yeah, end of the quarter, that's when it usually happens.

C: Would you like to learn something that can help with that?

N: Yep. That's why I'm here.

C: Right. Well, saying I'm dumb or I feel stupid or things like that are kind of self-disrespectful and even destructive things. Saying these things to yourself, you can understand why you might not feel good about yourself.

N: Right.

C: Because those are kind of nasty, negative things to think about yourself. What I'm going to show you is a technique called thought stopping.

N: Okay.

C: And this will work not just when you're saying things like I'm dumb or I'm stupid, but when you're saying any thing that's kind of nasty and self-destructive, whenever you tend to think about it over and over and over again. We call it obsessive thinking, when you're thinking about something over and over and you just can't get it out of your head. We talked last time about how that happens a lot at bedtime, where you're thinking about some things and you can't get to sleep. You keep thinking and thinking and thinking and just keep going and going and going. So thought stopping is a way of getting you to break the cycle of that obsessive thinking in order to think about something more positive. To start, I want you to think out loud, so I can hear you, the things you say to yourself. Go ahead and say it out loud.

N: I'm stupid and I feel dumb.

C: Oh, come on, say it like you really mean it.

N: I'm stupid and I feel dumb!

C: There you go, that's the way you say it in your own mind, right. You don't really go, "Oh well, gosh, gee, shucks, Dr. E., I feel stupid." You say, "Ugh, that was such a dumb thing to do, that was so stupid, I feel like an idiot!" Those are the types of things that you say, right?

N: Absolutely!

C: Okay, now whenever you start to say those things to yourself I want you shout out loud "Stop it!" Okay? Try it again out loud.

N: Okay. I'm such a stupid idiot for bombing that test. How dumb could I be . . . stop it!

C: Great. Now, doing something physical like saying "stop it" actually physically interrupts your negative thought cycle. You actually need to do something physical that will break that thought pattern and allow you to switch your thoughts to something that's a more positive thing to say to yourself, which is your self-talk message, which is what?

N: Everything's going to be okay.

C: Everything's going to be okay. Don't worry, everything's going to be okay. And then you can also use some visual imagery if you want, take yourself to some relaxing, calming place. So, again, you want to break that cycle by saying "stop it" out loud. You can scream it if you want, and then insert your positive self-talk phrase, "Everything is going to be okay," take a deep breath and go to a calming visual image, okay?

N: Okay.

C: Let's try it one more time.

N: I am stupid, I am dumb, I'm an idiot. Stop it! (Pauses for insertion of positive self-talk and breathing, and imagery)

C: Okay, how did that feel?

N: Relaxing.

C: On a scale of 1 to 10?

N: An 8—pretty relaxing, actually.

C: Excellent. All right, now whenever you're out in public, at school, shopping, at the gas station, and you start to think these things about yourself, immediately out in the middle of all these people, you're going to shout . . . . .

N: (Starts to laugh) Oh, my, would that ever be embarrassing! You'd have to change my diagnosis pretty quick, huh??!!

C: Oh, yeah. So when you are out in public we want to modify this technique somewhat. So, I have brought for you your very own rubber band for your wrist. (Counselor puts the rubber band on Nancy's wrist) Taadah!

N: Wow. Thank you. I'll treasure it always.

C: To be sure. Now instead of shouting out loud "stop it," instead you will say "stop it" to yourself inside your head, while at the same time reaching down to your rubber band and snapping yourself on your wrist. (Nancy does.) You feel that? How's that feel?

N: Stings a little, but not too bad.

C: Yeah, it's a little sting, some physical action to break the cognitive cycle. I want you to snap it once or, if you can't stop, do it twice while saying "stop it" inside your mind, and then I want you to switch to a more positive thought, take your deep breath and even begin a calming visualization if you like. Let's try it one more time—to yourself this time. Think the nasty, negative thoughts, snap the band as you say "stop it" to yourself, then take your deep breath, take yourself to your calm and relaxing spot, and change your thoughts to something that's more positive, something more productive.

N: (Engages in the thought stopping technique by herself)

C: How was that?

N: Great. I've got it.

C: Okay, so wear this rubber band all the time until I see you again and use it when the obsessive thoughts begin.

N: Yeah.

The professional counselor and Nancy then explore other times when thought stopping may be appropriate to help her generalize use of the technique.

C: (In conclusion) If you're starting to think these negative things, you just can't get your mind off of them, you know that you're just dragging yourself down. And you're just making your life more difficult and more miserable by telling yourself negative and nasty things. Go ahead and yell to yourself "stop it," snap your rubber band at the same time, and then substitute your positive self-talk, breath deeply, and take yourself to a more calming spot, just relax. Collect your thoughts and then in a short time, you're feeling calmer, and you can make a good decision.

USEFULNESS AND EVALUATION OF THE THOUGHT STOPPING TECHNIQUE

Although used with a variety of problems, thought stopping is most often used with episodic brooding, obsessions, and phobic thoughts, including sexual preoccupation, hypochondriasis, thoughts of failure, thoughts of sexual inadequacy, obsessive memories, and common fears (Davis et al., 1995). Leger (1979) conducted a case study on three individuals who experienced anxiety or obsessions. He found that thought stopping was successful in reducing the frequency of these ruminations for two out of the three individuals. Likewise, Horton and Johnson (1977) reported the use of thought stopping as a treatment procedure for a man with obsessions about killing his estranged wife. During the course of four sessions over a 27 day period, these obsessive thoughts decreased from a rate of once every 20 seconds to a rate of once every 2 hours while working and once every 30 minutes while not working.

Thought stopping has also been used to reduce negative self thoughts, smoking, and visual and auditory hallucinations (Horton & Johnson, 1977). Samaan (1975) reported a case study of a woman who experienced hallucinations, obsessions, and depressive spells. After 10 sessions of thought stopping, flooding, and reciprocal reinforcement treatment, the woman's disturbed behavior decreased from 22 hallucinations, 14 obsessions, and 8 depressive spells per week to an average of 1 or 2 of these events per week during the early part of treatment and eventually to an absence of any of these three disturbances. In addition, Peden, Rayens, Hall, and Beebe (2001) conducted an experiment using thought stopping as part of a multi-component cognitive-behavioral group intervention to treat college women with depression. They found that this intervention resulted in significantly lowered depressive symptoms, especially the symptom of negative thinking, and that these results lasted even through the 18-month follow-up.

Interestingly, some researchers (Wegner, Schneider, Carter, & White, 1987; Wenzlaff, Wegner, & Roper, 1988; Macrae, Bodenhausen, Milne, & Jetten, 1994) reported that attempts to suppress negative, obsessional thoughts may actually lead to greater expression of these thoughts, while other researchers reached the opposite conclusion (Purdon & Clark, 2001; Roemer & Borkovec, 1994; Rutledge, 1998). The technique also has been criticized because some proponents have advocated using mild shocks or skin pinching as the aversive stimulus; these stimuli should *not* be used.

CHAPTER 21

Cognitive Restructuring

ORIGINS OF THE COGNITIVE RESTRUCTURING TECHNIQUE

Cognitive restructuring is a technique that emerged from cognitive therapy and is usually credited to the work of Albert Ellis, Aaron Beck, and Don Meichenbaum (Beamish, Granello, & Belcastro, 2002). There are two basic assumptions of the cognitive restructuring strategy:

> . . . [S]elf defeating behaviors flow from either the development of defective cognitions or irrational thinking and/or self defeating self-statements and that a person's defective thinking or self-defeating self-statements can be changed by altering his or her cognitions or views about them. (Gilliland & James, 1998, p. 308)

Typically, professional counselors use cognitive restructuring with clients who need help replacing negative thoughts and interpretations with more positive thoughts and actions.

HOW TO IMPLEMENT THE COGNITIVE RESTRUCTURING TECHNIQUE

Doyle (1998) described a specific, seven step procedure for professional counselors to follow when using cognitive restructuring with their clients.

1. Gather background information to discover how the client handled past and current problems.
2. Assist the client in becoming aware of her thought process. Discuss real life examples that support the client's conclusions and discuss different interpretations of the evidence.
3. Examine the process of rational thinking, focusing on how the client's thoughts affect her well-being. The professional counselor can exaggerate irrational thinking to make the point more visible for the client.
4. Provide assistance to the client, so that she can evaluate her beliefs about self and others' "logical thought patterns" (p. 91).
5. Help the client learn to change her internal beliefs and assumptions.
6. Go over the rational thought process again, this time drilling the client on the important aspects using real life examples. Help the client form reasonable goals that she will be able to attain.
7. "Combine thought stopping with simulations, homework, and relaxation until logical patterns become set" (p. 92).

Meichenbaum (1994) described three goals of the cognitive restructuring strategy which can be met as the professional counselor and client go through the seven steps described by Doyle (1998) above.

1. Clients need to become aware of their thoughts; this goal can be worked on during Doyle's (1998) second step. To do this, Meichenbaum (1994) recommended asking the client questions that are directly related to his thoughts and feelings. The professional counselor can also help the client use imagery reconstruction to access specific thoughts. This process involves the client imagining a situation in "slow motion" so that the client can describe his thoughts and feelings surrounding the incident. It may be easier for the client if the professional counselor asks him to give advice to a person who experiences stress from a similar situation as the client. Meichenbaum also recommended that clients record their thoughts by self-monitoring. Any time the client becomes troubled he should describe, in a journal, the incident and any thoughts and feelings experienced.

2. Clients need to alter their thought processes. During Doyle's (1998) fourth step, the professional counselor can help the client meet this goal and learn to change the way he thinks. Professional counselors can assist clients in becoming aware of the thought process changes that need to be made by helping the clients to "evaluate their thoughts and beliefs, elicit predictions, explore alternatives, and question faulty logic" (Meichenbaum, 1994, p. 422). When evaluating the client's thoughts and beliefs, the professional counselor can ask questions that help the client define any labels he has given himself. By having the client make predictions, the professional counselor helps the client realize which thoughts are rational and which are self-defeating. For example, the professional counselor can ask, "What do you picture happening or think will happen when X occurs? How can we find out? How do you know that will indeed happen?" (p. 423). The point in exploring alternatives is for the client to take a different perspective. If the client can

generate an alternative that is rational instead of self-defeating, progress is being made. Throughout this step, the professional counselor should be sure to question the client's faulty logic including "dichotomous thinking, all or none thinking, overgeneralization, and personalization" (p. 424).

3. Clients need to experiment to explore and change their ideas about themselves and the world; this goal can be worked on during step five of Doyle's (1998) process. The professional counselor can start by having the client perform personal experiments in the therapeutic setting and move on to a real life situation when the client is ready. A scheme diary can also aid in altering a client's beliefs (Meichenbaum, 1994). The following is an excerpt from Meichenbaum (1994, p. 429) outlining how a client can set up a scheme diary:

Triggers: (What set off my reactions?)

Emotions: (What was I feeling?)

Thoughts: (What was I thinking?)

Behaviors: (What did I actually do?)

Lifetraps: (Which of my "buttons" got pushed? What early life experiences might be related?)

Coping: Realistic concerns (In what ways were my reactions justified? What did I do to cause or worsen the situation? Is there anyone I can check this out with?)

Overreactions: (In what ways did I exaggerate or misinterpret the situation?)

Problem-Solve: (In what ways could I cope better in the future or solve the problem?)

Learned: (What have I learned from this situation that I can apply in the future?)

VARIATIONS OF THE COGNITIVE RESTRUCTURING TECHNIQUE

One variation of this technique requires the client to be aware of and journal thoughts and feelings before, during, and after having a stressful incident. The professional counselor reads the client's journal and analyzes it, paying special attention to any self-defeating thoughts and specific instances that seem to cause the client stress. Once these things are identified, the professional counselor helps the client replace the self-defeating thoughts with coping thoughts.

Doyle (1998) described another variation that clients can use to analyze themselves. The client can use a three column method in which she learns more about her own thoughts. The client records the situations that cause anxiety in the first column. The client's thoughts about the situations are noted in the second column. In the last column, the client records the inaccuracies she can observe in the thought process.

Hackney and Cormier (2005) described how to use coping thoughts in cognitive restructuring. The professional counselor needs to work with the client to identify thoughts the client has that are self-defeating. After the client is aware of his negative thoughts, coping statements need to be formed. A coping statement is a positive thought that is a rational response to a self-defeating statement. For example, instead of thinking, "I am afraid of this airplane" (a self-defeating statement), a client can think, "This airplane has just been inspected by a specialist in aviation safety" (a coping thought) (p. 195).

Southam-Gerow and Kendall (2000) posed another variation of cognitive restructuring that they use with children. When a professional counselor and client are in step 2, attempting to identify the client's self-talk, the professional counselor can ask the child to imagine her thoughts as "thought bubbles." The child can picture these "thought bubbles" running through her head, just like in a comic strip. This alternative helps make the concept of self-talk more understandable for youth.

EXAMPLE OF THE COGNITIVE RESTRUCTURING

Kay is a 48-year-old female who initially presented for counseling for relationship issues. After a few counseling sessions, it became apparent that Kay became angry with family members several times daily, often resulting in spending an entire day feeling hostile, upset, and irritable.

Counselor (C):   I see you have several sheets of paper here with you today.

Kay (K):   Yep. I did what we talked about last time.

C: You wrote down each situation that made you angry this week?

K: Yeah. And I even jotted down why it made me so mad. Want to see?

C: I'd rather you tell me about a few of them if you don't mind.

K: Sure, okay. Umm, well I'll just start with the first one. Umm, so, as soon as I left here last week, my husband called me on the phone and asked where I was. Well, I had already told him I had a counseling appointment that afternoon and so first I got mad that he had forgotten and that he was calling me asking where I was. Then he said he was calling to tell me to pick up the ingredients I needed to make dinner because he forgot to get them earlier like I had asked him to do. Well, that really made me mad because he should have already done it.

C: I'd like to get a better idea of what "mad" in this situation means exactly. As a result of this phone call, how mad would you say you were on a scale of 1 to 10, with 1 being just slightly irritated and 10 being . . .

K: . . . Ready to smash windows?

C: Okay, 10 being ready to smash windows.

K: That's easy. I was a 10. By the time I got home I could have smashed every window in that house and on every one of those stupid cars he works on.

C: All right. I get the idea. And one more . . . thinking about your husband's behavior and comments during that phone call, on a scale of 1 to 10 again, with 1 being just a little thoughtless but probably not on purpose and a 10 being the worst thing a person could ever do to you . . .

K: I'd say a 10 again.

C: Okay, we'll come back to that a little later.

Following, the counselor uses a technique known as "laddering," which is helpful in uncovering the core beliefs behind a person's feelings and behaviors.

C: Now, thinking about this one situation, and I know you went to a lot of trouble this week to write down others and we will get to them after we talk this one through, but just thinking about the phone call right now, you said two things made you really mad about this call. One was that your husband didn't even remember you had told him you had a counseling session and was calling to ask where you were. Number two was that he asked you to pick up ingredients he was supposed to already have gotten. Is that right?

K: Exactly.

C: Your husband didn't remember you had a counseling session and called to ask where you were. What does this mean to you?

K: That he doesn't listen to what I tell him.

C: Okay, so your husband doesn't listen to what you tell him. What does this mean to you?

K: That he's not paying attention to me.

C: All right, and your husband doesn't pay attention to you. What does that mean to you?

K: That he doesn't care about me! (Head down, thinks for a few moments, looks up) . . . If he cared, he would pay attention. Right? Wouldn't he pay attention if he cared?

Kay has just discovered an underlying belief and is now questioning it herself.

C: Good, Kay. I know this is hard but let's keep going. And now, if he doesn't care about you, what does that mean to you?

K: That no one cares about me. I am unlovable. (She speaks this very softly and then gets loud and angry again.) Who would care about me if my own husband doesn't?

C: That's right, Kay. You believe that when he doesn't pay attention to you, or doesn't remember what you say, then he must not care for you. And if he does not care for you, then you are unlovable and no one can care for you.

K: Yes! You get it! That's exactly right!

The counselor suspects there is a theme to Kay's anger, and that "all roads will lead to the same destination," showing that her anger is predominantly tied to feeling unloved and uncared for.

C: Okay, let's go back to the phone call if you are ready. You said there was another part to that conversation that upset you. He asked you to pick up ingredients he was supposed to get himself. You said that he should have already done it.

K: Yes, he should have already done it! I'm the one that has to cook the meal to begin with, and I had a really bad week, you remember, I told you about it last week. I was so fed up with everything and everyone and he knew that! The least he could have done was get the ingredients from the store when he had plenty of time and little else to do! He knew how tired I was and yet he chose not to lift a finger to help me out! (Kay is angry again.)

C: Okay, this is going to sound familiar, but we are going to do the same thing we've just done to help us get to the heart of the matter. You are saying that he knew you were tired and that you had a bad week, and yet he "chose" not to help you. What does this mean to you?

K: Oh, I see where this is going. Well, okay. He knew I was tired and already sick of everything, yet he didn't do what I asked him to do anyway. Well, that means I'm not a priority to him, doesn't it?

C: Okay, so you are not a priority to him. What does that mean?

K: I guess it means I'm not too important.

C: Ummhmm. And if you're not too important to him, what does that mean to you?

K: Hell, I guess it means what I already know . . . that I'm not important period. I'm no damn good.

C: All right, Kay. Do you notice any similarities between this statement and the one you came to a few moments ago?

K: You mean when I said that no one cares about me?

C: Yes, that's what I mean.

There is silence for a few moments as Kay thinks this over. It is probably very difficult for her to acknowledge how her thoughts may be related to her anger at her husband as she much prefers to blame him.

K: And just now when I said that I'm not important . . . that I'm no good?

C: Yes, that's right.

K: Okay, I can see where those are similar. I'm unlovable . . . I'm no good. It's similar.

C: Kay, everybody has these sorts of beliefs, and we carry them around with us everyday. Sometimes we don't even know what they are or that they're there because they've been a part of us for so long that we don't even notice they exist. But believe me, they control how we interpret things, how we feel and what we do, because they are so strong and we believe in them so much. I would bet, Kay, that these beliefs that we just uncovered, these beliefs that you have, are at the heart of much of what you have on that paper there in your hand. I would bet that if we repeated this same process with every situation on that list, we might find a very similar belief for most of them. What do you think, Kay?

K: (Looks at list, thinks over several of the situations, is quiet for one or two minutes) I can see that, yes. I just sort of did that questioning thing in my head, and I can see that that is where it is going . . . to the same sort of thing, yes. But the way he acts sometimes is not fair to me. And I don't want to excuse all of the crappy things he does. I'm not taking responsibility for his behavior!

C: No, Kay, you're not. Not at all. We won't take responsibility for his behavior, and we can't necessarily change his behavior. But what we can do instead is focus on how it makes you feel, on your reaction and your angry feelings . . . those feelings that make you feel so awful about yourself.

K: Okay. We can do that.

C: I want to tackle this in two ways. First, I want us to think of alternative reasons for your husband's behavior. Then, I want us to rethink how others' behavior defines you. Okay?

K: Okay. Well, I can think of a few other reasons for his behavior.

C: Good. Good.

K: Well, when I told him about my counseling session, he was underneath the hood of a car and probably really had to pay attention to what he was doing and maybe I just picked a bad time to tell him.

C: Good, what else?

K: Umm . . . (thinks for a moment) . . . umm . . . well, he did sound worried when he called. Like when he couldn't find me he got worried or something. Probably not though. He was probably just worried about what he was going to eat for supper. I don't know, maybe.

C: It's possible then that he was so preoccupied with his work that he didn't really absorb your appointment time, and then it is also possible that he was worried about you when he couldn't find you.

K: Yes, it's possible.

C: Good. So remember earlier when I asked you to rate his behavior during that phone call on a scale of 1 to 10, with 1 being just a little thoughtless but probably not on purpose and a 10 being the worst thing a person could ever do to you?

K: Yep.

C: And you said a 10, absolutely a 10.

K: I did.

C: Now, just taking those possibilities that we just discussed into account, now how would you rate his behavior on that same 1 to 10 scale?

K: Mmm. Yeah. Well, that would have to be much lower, like a 2 or 3 maybe.

C: And is it entirely possible that these are more accurate reasons for his behavior?

K: Very possible now that I think about it rationally. Yes.

C: So given that this is possible, and you now rate his behavior a 2 or a 3, but your reaction was a "smashing windows" 10, what do you make of that?

K: It seems a little extreme. I have to admit that a lot of my reactions are that way. Sometimes I feel bad afterwards, but then I just get mad again and don't even have time to correct it or apologize for it. It's like as soon as I think maybe I overreacted, one of them makes me mad again.

C: Yes, it's easier for that to happen when every time a person forgets what you said, or forgets to do what you asked them to do, you interpret it to mean that you are no good and unlovable.

K: Makes a lot of sense. What am I going to do about it?

C: Good question. We've made so much progress already. You've worked very hard today. And I want you to know that these beliefs, they didn't develop overnight. They've been taking shape for well over 40 years now, and they are going to take some time to change.

K: Not 40 more years I hope!

C: No. Not 40 more years. But it will take some time and a lot of hard work like what we've been doing here today.

K: I can do that.

C: Well, then let's move on to the second way I wanted to tackle this. Remember I said I first wanted us to think of alternative reasons for your husband's behavior, and we did that just now. Then, I said I wanted us to rethink how other's behavior defines you. Remember?

K: I remember. Let's do that.

C: Okay. Then at the risk of you getting angry again, let's assume for just a moment that it is possible after all that your husband does not care about you, that you are not important to him. You said earlier that means you are unlovable and no good. But does it really? Does it really have to mean that, Kay?

K: Well, it's pretty bad when your own husband doesn't care. It must mean something.

C: Yes, it does. It does mean something. To me, it means your husband doesn't care. But does it have to mean anything else? Do his thoughts and feelings about you have to define you?

K: You mean does it have to mean that nobody thinks I'm important or good or lovable?

C: Exactly! Does it have to mean that?

K: No. I guess it doesn't. It just means that he doesn't.

C: And would that be terrible?

K: It would hurt.

C: Yes, it would hurt very much, but . . .

K: But it wouldn't be the most terrible thing ever. And it wouldn't mean that everybody feels the way he feels.

C: That's right, Kay!!! See? You're getting there. Doesn't that feel different?

K: It feels weird to say that.

C: It's very new for you to think this way, yes. But assume you were thinking this way during the phone conversation. A moment ago, we changed your perception and rating of his behavior. Now let's assume that you had had this perception during the phone call. Do you think your reaction would have been a "smashing windows" 10?

K: Not even close. I might have actually felt a little sad instead of angry. You know sad might be a nice change from being so damn mad all the time.

USEFULNESS AND EVALUATION OF THE COGNITIVE RESTRUCTURING TECHNIQUE

Cognitive restructuring is commonly used with individuals who are polarized thinkers, display fear and anxiety when in certain situations, and exhibit "extreme emotional reactions to normal life situations" (Doyle, 1998, p. 92). Velting, Setzer, and Albano (2004) suggested using cognitive restructuring with adolescents and children who have anxiety disorders. By identifying thoughts that lead to anxious feelings, children can learn to challenge their own self-defeating thoughts with coping thoughts.

Cognitive restructuring has been used successfully with clients with depression (Evans, Velsor, & Schumacher, 2002), panic disorder (Beamish et al., 2002; Beck, Berchick, Clark, Solkol, & Wright, 1992; Overhulser, 2000), self-esteem (Horan, 1996), stress (Hains & Szyjakowski, 1990), anxiety, social phobia, obsessive compulsive disorder, and substance abuse (Saltzberg & Dattilio, 1996).

Techniques Based Upon Behavioral Approaches Using Positive Reinforcement

This section begins with a brief introduction to behavior modification and the general classification of behavioral techniques based on positive reinforcement, negative reinforcement, and punishment. While no specific techniques based on negative reinforcement will be covered in this book, a number of techniques based on positive reinforcement strategies are presented to help clients increase display of the target behavior, including positive reinforcement, the Premack principle, behavior charts, token economy, and behavioral contracting. Likewise, a number of techniques based upon punishment will be presented in the next section (7).

A BRIEF INTRODUCTION TO PRINCIPLES UNDERLYING BEHAVIOR MODIFICATION

Behavior modification is the application of B. F. Skinner's theory of operant conditioning. The overriding tenet of operant conditioning theory is that true learning depends upon which behaviors are accompanied by reinforcement. Behavior that is rewarded increases in frequency, while behavior that is not rewarded decreases in frequency, and behavior that is actively punished ordinarily decreases in frequency as well. Applications of operant conditioning are defined by a juxtaposition of two dichotomous continua: Operation (i.e., whether a stimulus is added to or removed from the environment), and Effect (i.e., whether the goal is to increase or decrease the display of a behavior). This juxtaposition is presented in Figure 1 and yields four categories of behavioral intervention: positive reinforcement, negative reinforcement, punishment by stimulus application, and punishment by reinforcement removal.

POSITIVE REINFORCEMENT AND NEGATIVE REINFORCEMENT

Operant conditioning proposes three key terms that are helpful in categorizing applied interventions stemming from the theory: positive reinforcement, negative reinforcement, and punishment. (See the next section for a discussion of punishment.) Positive reinforcement is anything that strengthens and increases the likelihood of a desired behavior. A frequently used synonym for positive reinforcement is reward. Examples of positive reinforcers are favorite foods or snacks, preferred activities, stickers, money, attention, social praise, or other treats—virtually anything that a person is willing to work to earn (see Figure 1).

It is important to understand from the outset two essential points about applying positive reinforcement. First, the target behavior must be framed in a manner that indicates a desirable behavior to be increased. Clients, students, parents and teachers frequently have no problem telling the professional counselor what they would like the client to *stop* doing (e.g., stop getting out of his seat, calling out, cussing, talking back, refusing to do homework), but sometimes struggle with describing the positive behavior they wish the client to *start* doing or increase. In such circumstances, it is helpful to ask the client or other stakeholder (e.g., parent, teacher, spouse, client), "What would you like the client to do more of?" This helps the client or stakeholder to craft a positively framed target behavior that identifies the behavior to be increased; for example, "Stop getting out of his seat" becomes "Stays in his seat until permission is granted to get up," "Stop calling out" becomes "Raises her hand and waits to be called on before speaking," "Stop cussing" becomes

"Verbally expresses himself using appropriate language," "Stop talking back" becomes "Verbally addresses adults and peers appropriately," "Stop refusing to do homework" becomes "Completes homework 95% of the time." (Note that the term "appropriate" used in two of the examples above will require further defining and clarification.)

The second essential point related to positive reinforcement is that the reward must come just *after* the behavior! If the client gets the reward before displaying the behavior or in spite of failing to perform the required behavior to the agreed upon level, the contingency linking behavior and reward will not occur. Clients need to learn that rewards follow appropriate behaviors, or the system will not produce the desired results. Also, be sure not to wait too long after the client displays the behavior before providing the reward. One wants the client to make the connection between the behavior and reward in order to strengthen the display of the behavior. A long delay may weaken the association. Rewards serve as motivators of desirable behaviors and rewards must follow the occurrence of the behavior for initial learning to occur and for strengthening of previous learned connections to continue.

Negative reinforcement is anything that increases a desirable behavior by reducing or eliminating an aversive stimulus. Negative reinforcement

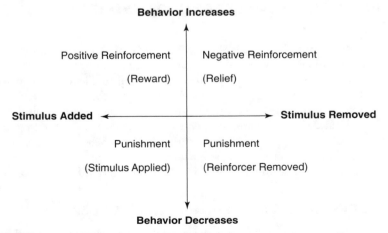

FIGURE 1   The juxtaposition of the Operation continuum and Effect continuum in operant conditioning, and resultant categories of behavioral intervention.

is synonymous with relief. Negative reinforcement is often confused with the term punishment, although it is true that many negative reinforcers are also viewed as punishing by clients. However, there is an essential difference between the two: the goal of negative reinforcement always is to increase a desirable behavior, while the goal of punishment always is to decrease an undesirable behavior. This distinction is critical to understanding the differences between these two important concepts. Negative reinforcement is a difficult concept to grasp and apply, so this book does not incorporate a chapter on its application. An example of negative reinforcement would be to increase verbalizations within group counseling interaction by removing a noxious noise (e.g., an annoying hum or buzz) when clients engage in verbal discussion, then reintroducing the noxious noise during periods of silence. A second example would be to increase a child's in-seat behavior (i.e., keeping Billy's bottom on the chair) by removing his chair for a 10-minute interval each time he leaves his seat without permission, forcing him to stand rather than sit at his desk. Again, having to listen to an annoying hum or stand rather than sit may appear to be punishments, but in these examples they are not so long as the counseling objectives are meant to increase the frequency of a desirable behavior.

ASSESSING PROBLEM BEHAVIORS

One final topic of importance before moving on to the individual behavioral techniques involves a brief discussion of problem behavior assessment. Ordinarily the assessment of problem behaviors is relatively quick, especially when the professional counselor focuses on the frequency, magnitude, and duration of the behavior. Frequency refers to how often a behavior occurs. Determining a behavior's frequency is important for at least two reasons. First, it is important to grasp how problematic a behavior really is and whether the display of a behavior is normal or not. Sometimes, clients and stakeholders expect perfection or have little context for understanding what a normal behavioral display might be, and professional counselors may help provide this context. Second, if professional

counselors are going to help modify a problematic behavior, it is critical to gather baseline data so that the client, counselor, and other stakeholders will be able to determine what a reasonable counseling objective might be and when progress is being made toward meeting that objective.

Magnitude refers to how problematic the behavior has become for the client and other stakeholders. If the magnitude is not substantial, perhaps intervention is unnecessary. After all, if clients or stakeholders are unrealistically expecting perfection or lack context for understanding whether the behavior is normal, professional counselors can be of help contextualizing or reframing the issue. The technique of scaling, discussed in chapter 1, is frequently helpful in determining the magnitude of a problem behavior.

Duration refers to two facets of assessing problem behaviors. First, professional counselors are interested in knowing how long the behavior has been occurring. The answer to this question, coupled with the response to the magnitude question above, often gives clients and counselors an idea of the seriousness of the problem, the likely resistance to treating the problem, and some impetus for building motivation to address and resolve the problem behaviors. The second facet of duration addresses the question "How long does the behavior last after it begins?" A behavior that lasts only a few seconds will require a different approach than the same behavior lasting hours.

Once the behavior frequency, magnitude, and duration have been assessed and the counseling goals and objectives developed, the client and professional counselor using a behavioral approach are ready to implement strategies and techniques to address the issue. The remainder of this section reviews 10 techniques professional counselors will find helpful when dealing with behavioral concerns. If the counseling objective aims to increase the frequency of a desirable behavior, the professional counselor may want to implement one of the techniques based upon positive reinforcement: positive reinforcement, Premack principle, behavior charts, token economy, or behavioral contracting. If the counseling objective aims to decrease or suppress the frequency of a desirable behavior, the professional counselor may want to implement one of the strategies based upon punishment: punishment, extinction, time-out, response cost, or overcorrection (positive practice). (See section 7 for behavioral approaches using punishment.)

MULTICULTURAL IMPLICATIONS

Clients from some cultures appreciate the directness, problem-centered, and action-orientated nature of behavior approaches to counseling (Hays & Erford, in press). For example, clients of Arab and Asian descent frequently expect advice and pursuit of concrete goals within the counseling relationship. Men, in general, appreciate the action-oriented, goal-focused directedness of behavioral approaches. Latinos prefer directive approaches, and parents of African descent frequently appreciate how behavioral approaches help them achieve obedience from children, an important intergenerational cultural value.

Behavioral counseling does not emphasize emotional expression and catharsis, or the sharing of personal difficulties or concerns, making it a more comfortable fit for individuals from some cultures (e.g., men, Asian Americans). Tanaka-Matsumi et al. (2002) pointed out that behavioral approaches value and focus upon the client's cultural and social dimensions by analyzing an individual's specific environmental situation and honing the interventions to address specific therapeutic goals and personalized outcomes. In the process, counselors help clients understand how personal life circumstances have contributed to the difficulties and whether desired changes are possible or how best to accomplish those changes in a way that helps the client adjust to the sociocultural, developmental, and environmental contexts. Behavioral counselors conduct a culturally sensitive functional behavioral analysis (Spiegler & Guevremont, 2003) to help the client understand cultural norms and client-based perceptions of the problem.

Counselors using behavioral approaches sometimes devalue the importance of the therapeutic relationship and this would be a mistake with individuals of diverse races, ethnicities, genders, and sexual orientations. Rapport and strength of the therapeutic alliance influence the therapeutic process and outcomes of counseling, so counselors using behavioral approaches with clients are well advised to attend to rapport and alliance issues throughout the counseling relationship. For example, it is well documented (Hays & Erford, in press; Ridley, 1995) that clients from some cultures are slow to trust European American counselors. Culturally sensitive counselors recognize and address these issues in the relationship early and often.

Finally, behavioral change affects not only the individual client but also those the client interacts with in the sociocultural environment. Counselors and clients need to discuss and anticipate the cultural as well as personal ramifications of behavioral changes desired by the client in order to predict the changes affect on not only the life of the client, but on the relationships among the client and other important people in the client's life. Changes in an individual often require adjustments by others in the client's environment; sometimes the changes, although viewed beforehand as positive, can lead to serious difficulties done the road. While all possible consequences can not be predicted with certainty, often, discussion ahead of time can lead to a heightened awareness of the possible ramifications of the considered changes. For example, if a man desires greater independence from his wife and family (e.g., more socializing time with friends, trips to "get away"), such behavioral changes can strain a relationship and create even more difficulties in the future (e.g., divorce, jealousy/suspicion, lower quality relationships with children). Behaviors have their consequences; sometimes the consequences lead to positive outcomes, sometime to undesirable, unanticipated, or mixed outcomes.

CHAPTER 22

Premack Principle

ORIGINS OF THE PREMACK PRINCIPLE TECHNIQUE

The Premack principle is based upon the operant conditioning theory concept of positive reinforcement, which states that higher probability behaviors may act as reinforcers for lower probability behaviors (Brown, Spencer, & Swift, 2002). In other words, individuals will be motivated to do an undesired task if it is followed by a desired one. The Premack principle is used often in everyday life. For instance, a parent might restrict a child from watching TV until he finishes his homework. In lay terms, this technique has been known informally as "Grandma's Rules," because Grandma made sure you finished your vegetables before you got a cookie.

The Premack principle was named after David Premack in the late 1950s to early 1970s, first used with laboratory animals, and then applied to human situations. The Premack principle contradicted the traditional theories of that time. Traditional reinforcement theories stated that activities are positive, negative, or neutral. Only neutral activities can serve as instrumental responses, and only positive activities function as reinforcers. Therefore, reinforcement occurs when a positive activity is made contingent upon the performance of a neutral activity. In contrast, Premack declared that the positive-neutral-negative trichotomy was irrelevant to reinforcement. Instead, he proposed that all activities are ordered on a preference or probability continuum and that only a difference in preference is necessary for reinforcement. In order for reinforcement to occur, the instrumental response must simply be less preferential than the reinforcing activity. To validate his theory, Premack (1962) set up a laboratory experiment with rats to show not only that running could be reinforced by drinking as evident in other earlier experiments, but also that if a situation were created in which running was more preferable than drinking, drinking could be reinforced by running.

In order to measure the probability of two or more behaviors, these behaviors should be compared in a paired-operant baseline in which both behaviors are simultaneously and freely available to the client. However, sometimes strict probability is difficult to measure. Therefore, other more readily available measures have often been used in place of probability. Preference may be measured simply by asking the individual what she would like to do in a given situation or by observing which activities seem to bring the individual pleasure. Preference seems to be quite compatible with Premack's original measure of probability. On the other hand, the use of frequency is somewhat problematic because it often relies on extrinsically maintained responses instead of allowing the subject free choice of activity. Similarly, imminent performance, or the likelihood that the activity will be done next, tends to measure merely a colloquial version of probability rather than the empirical probability that Premack intended. A good rule of thumb to follow when attempting to measure probability is to ensure that preference or relative value are being measured rather than frequency or imminent performance.

HOW TO IMPLEMENT THE PREMACK PRINCIPLE TECHNIQUE

In order to use the Premack principle, one must first assess the preferred activities of the client (Brown et al., 2002). Based on this assessment, a more preferred activity may be chosen to reinforce the target behavior. The client should be informed of the parameters of the Premack conditions. He should be told that in order to perform the preferred activity, he must first complete the target behavior. Once the target behavior is completed, the client may begin the preferred activity. It is essential to remember that if the target behavior is not finished in its entirety, then the preferred activity is not allowed. There is no "partial credit!"

VARIATIONS OF THE PREMACK PRINCIPLE TECHNIQUE

The Premack principle can easily be accompanied by a token economy (see chapter 24). Tokens may be issued upon completion of less-preferred activities and then traded in for the opportunity to perform more preferred activities. A reinforcement menu, or list of highly preferred activities, may be available for the subject to choose from.

EXAMPLE OF THE PREMACK PRINCIPLE TECHNIQUE

Veronica is an 18-year-old freshman psychology major in her second semester of college. In an effort to improve her academic habits, Veronica joined a study skills group near the beginning of the spring semester. This group consisted of her sorority sisters and took place in her sorority house. After catching up on much campus gossip but making no improvements in her study skills, Veronica decided

to explore the services offered through the university's counseling center instead. She opted to join an open support group offered for students adjusting to college life with the hope that she would encounter others having difficulty with the same stressors she was facing. Still attending, Veronica feels she benefits from this group in that it is helpful to talk about and hear others' similar issues. However, she has not made any changes in her daily lifestyle. Veronica describes herself as someone focused only on the moment with little thought to the eventual outcomes of her behavior. She states that in high school, she had little responsibility and focused most of her attention on her social life. Now in college, she finds her grades suffering, credit cards soaring, and weight increasing. The following is an excerpt of an individual session Veronica requested with the professional counselor.

Counselor (C):   So you describe yourself as lacking self-control . . . rather impulsive . . . interested in instant gratification.

Veronica (V):   That would be me.

C: And this is causing you some concern.

V: It really is. I hate this growing up and being responsible thing. It was so much more fun before. I could eat what I wanted without gaining weight. I could stay up on the phone all night and still ace my exams. That's just not the way it is anymore.

C: Things have changed?

V: I'll say. I'm totally getting fat, and my grades are embarrassing. I've got to do something different than what I'm doing before somebody notices!

C: Tell me specifically, Veronica, what you want to be different as a result of us working together.

V: Well, specifically, I want my grades to be different. I would also like to change some of my lifestyle habits, like being a total mouse potato . . .

C: Mouse potato?

V: Yeah, you know, like a couch potato, except someone who zones out in front of the computer and surfs the Internet all the time.

C: Okay, I'm with you now. So, you would like your grades to improve, I suppose . . .

V: Definitely.

C: And your lifestyle habits, like spending too much time on the Internet to change?

V: Pretty much. Umm, see, I shop online. I don't always buy, well usually I do, but I constantly surf for fashion ideas and trends, and I browse online catalogs relentlessly.

C: This doesn't leave much time for studying.

V: Or exercising, which I've also been meaning to do. Pretty much I just want to eat chocolate and shop.

C: Yes, I'm getting that general idea. But part of you also wants something different—something other than eating chocolate and shopping, like studying and exercising for example.

V: Yes, a big part of me wants something different like that. And the mirror and report card remind me of that. The last thing I want is to be unhealthy or to do poorly in school. I just have trouble sticking to that thought when I'm in that moment. You know? I'm just like whatever.

At this point, the professional counselor asks Veronica to complete a Reinforcement Hierarchy, listing the 10 activities she most prefers and least prefers to engage in. The hierarchy that resulted looked as follows:

Least Favorite	Studying/homework
	Exercising
	Cleaning/laundry
	Going to work at the coffee shop
	Going to class
	Watching television
	Talking on the phone
	Hanging out with friends
	Eating chocolate/sweets
Most Favorite	On-line shopping

C: Okay. Now that we have a good idea of the activities you most enjoy and least enjoy, I'd like to ask some specific questions concerning a few of these activities.

V: Sure, okay.

C: Okay, so, approximately how often would you say you exercise now?

V: Once a week, maybe.

C: And how often would you like to exercise in order to meet the criteria you have for this new and healthy self?

V: Ideally, I would exercise each morning during the week, Monday through Friday, for about 30 minutes. I'd like for it to become a part of my morning routine before I do anything else.

C: Very well, and how much time would you say you spend studying?

V: Some nights, not at all. I get on the computer to do school work, and then I decide to look something up online, and that's all I do the rest of the night. That's another reason I haven't been exercising. I spend so much time online at night that I'm too tired to get up an extra 30 minutes earlier in the morning.

C: Okay, good. So, how much time do you want to spend studying?

V: Well, again, I'd like to contain it to the week, you know, Monday through Friday again, unless there is a special reason to put more time in, like a big paper or exam or something. But for regular homework assignments and keeping up with reading assignments, I'd like to do that all during the week . . . so I'd say, at the most, about 3 hours per night for homework and reading assignments. Then I can put in extra time for larger projects if I need to.

C: Okay, so 3 hours per night then for studying. And 30 minutes per morning for exercise.

V: Sounds simple. But how am I going to make myself do that?

C: Would you work at the coffee shop if your boss stopped paying you?

V: Umm, no.

C: Well, would you expect your boss to continue paying you if you stopped working?

V: Umm, no again. That's just wrong.

C: Well, the way you're going about things now is similar to being paid without having worked.

On your reinforcement hierarchy that you completed, you listed your favorite activities as eating sweets and shopping. You admit to doing both of these things in abundance on a daily basis. Essentially, you are giving in to these indulgences without doing anything to earn them. Now, I'm going to set up a plan for you to begin incorporating physical activity into your morning routine and studying into your evening. But I'm not going to ask you to make all this effort without setting up a way for you to "pay yourself," because you wouldn't want to work for free. But this payment that you've been giving yourself up until now will have to be earned. And you will only pay or reward yourself with those activities you so enjoy if you've followed through with the activities that you don't prefer but know you need and want to do.

V: Hmm . . . so . . . okay, keep going.

C: Well, from now on, whenever you engage in physical exercise for 30 minutes, you are allowed one sweet treat, such as a small cookie. We don't want to go overboard on the sweets though or you'll be defeating the purpose. Now, if you don't exercise, you absolutely do not get the sweet. It is simply off limits because you did not work for that payment.

V: Okay. I like that.

C: Now regarding the studying, you said you want to study 3 hours each evening during the week. And you feel this is reasonable and possible.

V: Yes, it really is.

C: Okay then. For every 1 hour you spend studying, you may reward yourself with 30 minutes of Internet time. But you receive this Internet time only once you are completely finished studying for the night. So, when you put in your 3 hours of study tonight, you pay yourself with the privilege of 1.5 hours of Internet shopping time, to begin only after study time is complete.

V: That's not a whole lot of time to shop.

C: Much more than that will interfere with your ability to wake on time in the morning, right?

V: Well, that's true.

C: So, just as you said, you would never take payment from your boss if you had not done the work—"that's just wrong," you said—you also cannot allow yourself to engage in the rewarding activity unless you put in the required time.

V: And I just have to be very strict with myself. This is the new rule, and I am agreeing to it, right?

C: That's right. Keep your focus on the pay-off that comes with discipline. Not to mention how rewarding it will feel just to make these changes that you've known you wanted to make.

USEFULNESS AND EVALUATION OF THE PREMACK PRINCIPLE TECHNIQUE

The Premack principle is very helpful with classroom management. The Premack principle has been employed to abate chronic food refusal. Brown et al. (2002) used the Premack principle with a young boy who frequently refused to try new foods. He was required to eat small amounts of new foods before being allowed to eat his preferred foods. When the intervention began, the boy immediately ate the new foods that were presented to him in increasing quantities and flavors in order to be allowed to eat his preferred foods.

However, the Premack principle presents some limitations. Existing data have shown that lower probability behaviors can sometimes act as reinforcers for higher probability behaviors. For instance, Konarski, Johnson, Crowell, and Whitman (1981) reported that in an earlier study, they found that under certain conditions, children would increase coloring for access to math, considered a lower probability behavior. Likewise, experiments using the Premack principle do not always adequately control for the effects of a schedule. Therefore, it is difficult to determine if the reinforcement is the result of a probability difference between the actual responses or simply due to the unavailability of the reinforcing response for periods of time because of the response schedule. In other words, clients may be increasing the instrumental behavior because it is the only response available rather than because it allows them to then perform the contingent, or "reinforcing," response.

CHAPTER 23

Behavior Chart

ORIGINS OF THE BEHAVIOR CHART TECHNIQUE

Behavior charts target specific behaviors that are then evaluated at set points throughout the day (Henington & Doggett, 2004). The behavior is then reinforced on some sort of schedule. Behavior charts arise from behavioral theories that posit that behavior is shaped by reinforcement and punishment. Behavior charts include several important components, such as specifying the behaviors to be monitored, rating the behaviors on a set schedule, sharing the information with people other than the rater, and using the chart either to monitor an intervention or as the intervention itself (Chafouleas, Riley-Tillman & McDougal, 2002). However, behavior charts may vary depending on the behavior to be rated, the type of rating system, the rating frequency, the rater, the consequences used (reinforcers vs. punishment), and the setting and schedule of consequence delivery.

Behavior charts are useful because they are a simple and flexible way to provide feedback to both the individual being monitored as well as others involved with this person (Chafouleas et al., 2002). Behavior charts can be easily modified to meet the specific needs of an individual. Also, behavior charts are time efficient, taking as little as 10 seconds to 1 minute to complete each day.

HOW TO IMPLEMENT THE BEHAVIOR CHART TECHNIQUE

Behavior charts are simple to create. First, define the target behaviors in positive and specific terms (Chafoulas et al., 2002). Next, decide upon the frequency and type of rating system to be used. Then, design the behavior chart stating clearly both the behavior desired and when it will be monitored (Henington & Doggett, 2004). Once the chart has been created, decide how the individual will earn consequences (positive or negative) and what these consequences will be (Chafoulas et al.).

EXAMPLES OF THE BEHAVIOR CHART TECHNIQUE

EXAMPLE 1:

Freddie is a right wiggly and distractible youngster whose second grade teacher is constantly redirecting and refocusing so that he will complete his class work. The professional school counselor consulted with Mrs. Lear to construct a behavior chart to address the time on task and redirection issue. Figure 23.1

Freddie's Plan

Goal: Freddie will sit quietly during class time, attend to class activities, and complete work.

   The check sheet will be monitored daily and marked by Freddie's classroom teacher every 15 minutes. It will be scored at lunch and 3:00 p.m. Freddie will carry this check sheet with him to each class on a clipboard. He will be responsible for handing it to the teacher in charge and getting it back at the end of each period. Rewards will be started after Freddie has carried the check sheet and has proven he can be responsible for giving it and getting it back from each teacher.

Scores*	AM rewards/consequences	PM rewards/consequences
54-60	Coupon	Coupon
42-53	Prize Box or pink ticket	Prize Box or pink ticket
0-41	No coupon	No coupon

   * Scores reflect: 90% compliance = Coupon; 70% compliance = Prize box or pink ticket for school store; and <70% compliance = No coupon

Progressive Discipline Plan

After 4 zeros in a row, Freddie must come to the office. Freddie will see Mrs. Johnson (assistant principal), who will then determine a course of action.

Bonus: If Freddie obtains the 90% criterion each day for the entire week, he will also earn one food coupon.

Freddie   Week of:_____

Key:

+ (5 points) = Used time appropriately. Freddie is quiet, stays on task, and completes work.

√(3 points) = Was redirected to use time appropriately or stay on task 1 or 2 times.

0 (0 points) = Not using time appropriately. Did not complete work. Was redirected 3 or more times.

 # 1 Report to office to pick up clip board.

	Time	Monday	Tuesday	Wednesday	Thursday	Friday
Morning Work	8:45 9:00					
Carpet Time	9:15 9:30					
Reading—Mrs. Lear	9:45 10:00 10:15 10:30 10:45					
Special	11:00 11:15 11:30					
Office—Morning Total						
Writing—Mrs. Lear	11:45 12:00 12:15 12:30					

	Time	Monday	Tuesday	Wednesday	Thursday	Friday
Lunch Recess Math—Mrs. Lear	→ → 1:30 1:45 2:00 2:15 2:30 2:45					
Office— Afternoon Total						

Rewards for each of the morning and afternoon sessions:
54–60 points=Coupon
42–53 points=Prize Box/Pink Ticket
41 points or less=No coupon

FIGURE 23.1 Freddie's behavior plan.

shows the chart constructed for Freddie. Note that it integrates a point system and rating scale, as well as a reward plan.

EXAMPLE 2:

Justin is an aggressive fifth grader who often calls out without raising his hand and invades others' personal space (e.g., hits or touches others). Miss Jug chose to implement a sticker-based chart monitoring system. The professional school counselor consulted with Miss Jug to construct a behavior chart to address the calling out and touching/hitting issues. Figure 23.2 shows the chart constructed for Justin. Note that it integrates a sticker-based monitoring system broken down according to class activities and a reward plan. As Justin meets success with the 9 of 16 criteria, the number of criteria will be raised until the target behavior is eliminated.

USEFULNESS AND EVALUATION OF THE BEHAVIOR CHART TECHNIQUE

Behavior charts can be used for a wide variety of interventions that involve shaping specific behaviors. Target behaviors may include following directions, keeping hands to self, or using appropriate language (Henington & Doggett, 2004). Behavior charts have been found to be effective in a number of empirical studies. In one study, behavior charts monitoring students' obedience of classroom rules produced significant decreases in misbehavior and increases in the amount of work students completed (Bailey et al., as cited in Chafouleas et al., 2002).

Of course, behavior charts are not always effective, primarily because clients are not always motivated to buy into the system. In such cases, counselors should revisit the reward system to find something more motivating for the client to work for. Sometimes clients do not understand the chart system, or the client or adult responsible for overseeing the monitoring system does not follow through with his responsibilities. These difficulties are common in behavior therapy, and counselors need to make large and small adjustments to any behavioral system to maximize success.

Justin's Plan

Goal 1: Justin will control his verbal actions (e.g., raise hand before calling out, maintain appropriate speaking volume).
Goal 2: Justin will keep his hands to himself (e.g., will not hit or touch others).

   A sticker chart will be used to monitor Justin's behavior. Justin will have the chance to earn two stickers for each "section" of the day (i.e., including morning meeting, whole group instruction, word study, centers, lunch, math, special, and kid writing).

   Justin will earn one sticker for controlling his verbal actions (e.g., raising his hand before speaking, not calling out, not saying inappropriate or silly things during lessons) and another for keeping his hands to himself during that time period (e.g., not hitting, not touching others).

   There are 8 sections in the day, so Justin has the chance to earn a total of 16 stickers. Justin will earn a prize at the end of the day if he earns 9 out of 16 stickers during the day. This number will be increased once Justin has earned a prize every day of 1 entire week. Prizes will include visits to Mrs. Bryant (professional school counselor) or Mrs. Martin (assistant principal) to share his daily progress and receive a sticker.

   Miss Jug (Justin's teacher) will communicate Justin's progress with Mrs. Jackson (Justin's mother). Miss Jug will send home a note daily with the number of stickers Justin earned for the day, and at the end of the week, she will send home a copy of the sticker chart. These daily notes will take the place of the papers that had been coming home with a report of how many bones (i.e., inappropriate behavior warnings) Justin received during the day. Miss Jug will try to focus on rewarding Justin's good behavior rather than punishing his bad behavior (although, Justin will still receive bones for hurting other students or continually failing to follow Miss Jug's directions).

	Monday		Tuesday		Wednesday		Thursday		Friday	
	Control Voice	Hands to self	Control Voice	Hands to self	Control Voice	Hands to self	Control Voice	Hands to self	Control Voice	Hands to self
Morning Meeting										
Whole Group										
Word Study										
Centers										
Lunch										
Math										
Special										
Kid Writing										

Justin will receive a prize at the end of the day for having 9 out of 16 stickers

FIGURE 23.2   Justin's behavior plan.

CHAPTER 24

Token Economy

ORIGINS OF THE TOKEN ECONOMY TECHNIQUE

The token economy is a technique stemming from the work of the operant behavior theorist, B. F. Skinner (Liberman, 2000). Skinner held the view that "behavior is maintained by its consequences" (Murdock, 2004, p. 147); reinforcers are those consequences that increase the likelihood of the occurrence of a behavior. Token economies are a form of positive reinforcement in which clients receive a token when they display the desired behavior. After the participant has accumulated a certain number of tokens, he can turn them in for one of the reinforcers. The tokens serve to reinforce participants' appropriate behavior by rewarding them with tokens for selected behaviors. The receipt of the token is contingent upon the display of appropriate behavior (Comaty, Stasio, & Advokat, 2001).

Ayllon and Azrin (1968) suggested that when using tokens one needs to consider the "conditioned reinforcement rule" in which one provides "a distinctive and tangible stimulus event to bridge any delay between the desired response and the delivery of the reinforcers" (p. 77). Thus rather than receiving some tangible reinforcement immediately, tokens are issued that can be exchanged later for tangible rewards. Pioneered by Azrin, Paul, Krasner, and Ayllon, the earliest token economies existed in closed-ward psychiatric hospitals (Liberman, 2000; Stolz, Wienckowski & Brown, 1975). However, token economies are considered to be successful across a wide variety of populations and target behaviors.

HOW TO IMPLEMENT THE TOKEN ECONOMY TECHNIQUE

Reid (1999) provided the following steps for implementing a token economy. Because one of the main goals of a token economy is to modify behavior, the first step should be to identify the behaviors that warrant change. Reid suggested naming specific behaviors and describing the standards for satisfactory performance. For example, instead of saying that a participant should have better hygiene, one should say that the participants should shower or brush their teeth. Likewise, instead of saying a child should "calm down," the professional counselor should specify the child will "remain in the seat" or will "raise his hand and wait to be called upon by the teacher before calling out."

The second step is creating and displaying the rules. It is very important to make sure that all participants understand the rules, which include "when tokens will be dispensed, how many tokens are to be awarded for a behavior, and the times when participants can play with tokens" (Reid, 1999, p. 19).

Next, the professional counselor needs to select what will be used as tokens. Tokens should be safe, sturdy, easy to dispense, and hard to replicate (i.e., forge). The professional counselor then needs to determine the back-up reinforcer, the reward items that the participants can receive when they exchange their tokens. It is important that the back-up reinforcer have some significance or appeal to the client. If the client enjoys watching television or loves candy, these reinforcers can be offered in exchange for tokens (Reid, 1999). Importantly, to discourage materialistic consumption and encourage social interaction, the reward menu should include a number of activities the client may engage in with others (e.g., lunch with teacher, 15 minutes of play time with a friend, 15 minutes playing a game board with mother).

The next step is to set up prices by selecting how many tokens a participant must have before exchanging them for a back-up reinforcer. Before implementing the system, the persons in charge should field test the system, ensuring that prices are accurate; if the students are not able to earn enough tokens to make a purchase, they will lose the motivation to engage in the desired behaviors (Reid, 1999). It is good practice to construct a reward menu with wide-ranging values of tokens required for the reward options. This encourages clients to save tokens for "big ticket items" (e.g., family pizza night, baseball mitt, sleepover at a friend's house), rather than immediately spend the tokens on quick consumable items (e.g., candy, toy).

VARIATIONS OF THE TOKEN ECONOMY TECHNIQUE

A variation of the token economy is the addition of a response cost system (see chapter 28), a strategy based upon punishment. In this approach, not only does the client earn tokens for displaying positive behaviors, but when an individual misbehaves (i.e., violates a target behavior or rule), one of the tokens is surrendered in an attempt to decrease the future likelihood of an undesirable

behavior and increase the future likelihood of the desired behavior (Murdock, 2004). Goals are set for participants to retain a certain number of tokens in order to be rewarded at the end of a determined time period (McGoey & DuPaul, 2000; Truchlicka, McLaughlin, & Swain, 1998).

Another variation to the basic token economy is called the mystery motivator. In this variation, instead of telling the participants what the back-up reinforcer is, the reward is placed in an envelope and remains a mystery. In some cases, this motivates the participants to earn tokens in order to discover what is in the envelope. In a study of children with acquired brain injury, Mottram and Berger-Gross (2004) placed mystery motivators based on the children's interests in envelopes and marked them with question marks. If the child earned the required number of tokens, she was given the envelope and rewarded with the contents. As the study went on, the number of tokens needed to receive the mystery motivator increased. The mystery motivator variation improved behavioral compliance over the standard token economy procedure.

In another variation of the token economy, self-monitoring is included in an effort to extend the behavioral changes after the rewards are phased out. Along with the basic token economy procedures, the participant is asked to record instances in which he behaves inappropriately. The rules are posted and specific, so participants should be able to easily tell when the rules are broken. In a classroom study of self-monitoring (Zlomke & Zlomke, 2003), several disruptive students were given an index card to record each instance of his inappropriate behavior. At the end of the class, the teacher and the student compared cards and if they had the same number of incidents written down, the student earned an extra token. Self-monitoring plus the token economy procedure resulted in significantly fewer problematic behaviors than use of the token economy alone.

Yet another variation of the token economy is group versus individual implementation. Using the token economy with the whole group, whether it is a class, a school, or a prison, takes considerably more time, planning, and patience on the part of the implementer. Filcheck, McNeil, Greco, and Bernard (2004) performed a classroom study using the whole-class method. A level system was also used in which the students received a shape with their name on it and every day it was placed on the center of the ladder chart. The shape was moved up the ladder if the child demonstrated appropriate behavior or down the ladder if the child violated classroom rules (i.e., the token economy with the response cost variation). The children were rewarded according to the level their shape had attained at given times throughout the day. At these times, all of the shapes were moved back to the center to give the participants a fresh start.

EXAMPLE OF TOKEN ECONOMY TECHNIQUE

The following occurred during a counseling session with a student with Attention-Deficit/Hyperactivity Disorder (AD/HD), named Charlie—an 8-year-old, third grade student. Charlie's mother and teacher were also present so that the token economy system could be created and understood by all primary participants. The target behaviors identified by Charlie's teacher for the classroom were:

1. Stays in seat.
2. Raises hand and waits to be called on.
3. Keeps hands to self.
4. Makes comments relevant to the topic.
5. Follows teacher directions the first time asked.

The target behaviors identified by Charlie's mother were:

1. Keeps room tidy.
2. Follows parent directions the first time.

Note that the target behaviors are written to specify behaviors that can be increased. Thus, a strategy based on positive reinforcement, such as a token economy, can be used. The school day lasts about 6 hours so Charlie's teacher chose to award six points per target behavior. Each target behavior was deemed of equivalent importance. Thus, she could award up to one point (i.e., 0, 1/2;, or 1 point increments) for each 1-hour time period during the school day for each of the five target behaviors—a possible total of 30 token points during each school day. Charlie's mother decided that following her directions at home was twice as important as keeping a tidy room and decided to award up to three points to Charlie each day for keeping his room tidy. She also decided that Charlie could earn up to one point for following her directions for the hour preceding school in the morning and for each of the 5 hours after he arrives home in the afternoon and evening. This made it possible for Charlie to earn an additional nine token points at home on a school night. To extend the token economy to non-school days (i.e., weekends, holidays), Charlie's mother could award up to three points for a tidy room and up to 36 points on these days for compliance with her instructions. In summary, Charlie could earn a total of 39 points on any given day, or a total of 273 points per week. A daily chart was constructed to monitor Charlie's progress and allow daily home-school communication (see Figure 24.1).

Next, a reward menu was constructed and points attached to each reinforcer to be purchased. It is essential to align the points needed for reinforcers with the total number of points that can be

Day: _____   Date:_____   Name: Charlie

School	1 2 3 4 5 6	Total
1. Stays in seat.		
2. Raises hand and waits to be called on.		
3. Keeps hands to self.		
4. Makes comments relevant to the topic.		
5. Follows teacher directions the first time.		

Home		
1. Keeps room tidy.	0 1 2 3	
2. Follows parent directions the first time.	0 1 2 3 4 5 6	Total for the day:_____

FIGURE 24.1

earned daily. For example, it is unlikely that Charlie will be properly motivated if the system requires that 30 points are needed for 15 minutes of playtime with a friend. Likewise, if the same activity requires only one point, Charlie will soon learn that he can fail to meet most of the target behaviors most of the time and still receive a good deal of reward for minimal effort. Figure 24.2 contains the reward menu collaboratively agreed upon by the group. Importantly, Charlie had to agree to place each reward on the menu, even though his mother, teacher, and professional counselor could suggest ideas. There is no need to put a reward on the menu that the client does not find motivating.

The group then discussed how the token economy system would be monitored and reinforcements managed. It was determined that Charlie, under supervision of his mother at home, would keep a checkbook style accounting of his token points. At the end of each day Charlie will make a "deposit" to his token account of the points he earned for that day. When he chooses reinforcers from his reward menu, he will enter these transactions as "withdrawals."

Finally, the group decided on follow-up and evaluation procedures. Charlie's mother and teacher will use the daily checklist to communicate back and

forth as necessary and will inform the professional counselor every Friday of the daily number of points earned, rewards chosen, and any difficulties encountered over the week. The group will modify the system as needed, including deleting target behaviors that are consistently met and adding new target behaviors of interest. The group will begin to thin and fade the token economy system after 1 month of consistently appropriate behavior on all target behaviors.

USEFULNESS AND EVALUATION OF THE TOKEN ECONOMY TECHNIQUE

Of all of the techniques presented in this book, the token economy is arguably the procedure that received the most detailed coverage in the outcome literature. Token economies have been used to change the behavior of groups or individuals in a variety of different settings. It is likely that a token economy could be implemented, with some success, for any population whose behavior warrants modification.

When a token economy is implemented in an educational setting, it is likely that teachers have noticed behavior problems in individual student or in their classes as a whole. A token economy can be used to improve classroom management, specifically with students who have behavior problems including, but not limited to, disruptive behavior, attention-deficit/hyperactivity disorder (AD/HD), and serious emotional problems (Filcheck et al., 2004; McGoey & DuPaul, 2000; Musser, Bray, Kehle, & Jenson, 2001). A token economy can also be used to increase classroom participation (Boniecki & Moore, 2003) or increase positive behaviors that are incompatible with "school phobia, tantrums, thumb-sucking, encopresis, fighting, and so forth" (Wadsworth, 1970, p. 63).

Mental health professionals have had good success using token economies to treat problem behaviors related to many psychological disorders, including autism (Charlop-Christy & Haymes, 1998; Reinecke, Newman, & Meinberg, 1999), eating disorders (Kahng, Boscoe, & Byrne, 2003; Okamoto et al., 2002), schizophrenia (Elliot, Barlow, Hooper, & Kingerlee, 1979), and addictions (Boggs, Rozynko, &

Item	# Points
15 minutes playtime with friend	7
15 minutes game with mother/father	7
Family pizza party	125
First baseman's mitt	1,000
Family movie	75
Sleepover with a friend	250
15 minutes bike riding time	7
15 minutes computer/Playstation	10
Choose what to have for a meal	10
15 minutes of TV time	10
Stay up an extra 30 minutes	12
A one-half day outing (park, zoo, etc.)	200

FIGURE 24.2   Charlie's reward menu.

Flint, 1976; Silverman, Chutape, Bigelow, & Stitzer, 1999). Behavior management specialists at prisons have also successfully implemented the token economy to help the prisoners learn the skills and behaviors necessary to adapt to society when they return to the outside world (Stolz et al., 1975).

A major criticism of the token economy is that the "use of tokens will decrease the intrinsic satisfaction of activities" (Ford & Foster, 1976, p. 87). Intrinsic motivation is the drive that comes from within the individual to complete a task or set of tasks. Critics of the token economy fear that because the participants are rewarded extrinsically through the use of tokens, the motivation to act or behave in a certain way will dissipate once the tokens cease to be rewarded. Of course, the counterargument to this criticism is that if clients possessed the intrinsic motivation to successfully and consistently perform a task, there would be no need for external reinforcers. As such, the purpose of a token economy and other positive reinforcement strategies is to create motivation to perform using extrinsic rewards so that the client will experience success, then fade the reinforcement system so that intrinsic desires for continued success will maintain and expand behavioral gains. For example, in a study conducted in an educational setting, McGinnis, Friman, and Carlyon (1999) examined the outcome of using a token economy to enhance students' intrinsic motivation to do math. The study showed continued gains in math even after the treatment stopped, indicating that successes prompted by token economies may actually help create and bolster, not hinder or supplant, intrinsic motivation.

Token economies have been criticized for their use in educational settings because they lead students to develop performance goals rather than learning goals. Self-Brown and Mathews (2003), in a controlled study, found the students in the token economy group developed goals related to their performance and behavior in class rather than goals that had to do with increasing their knowledge and academic understanding. De Martini-Scully, Bray, and Kehle (2000) had previously responded to criticisms of this type by stating that student compliance is necessary in order for learning to occur and their study suggested that academics do improve following improved behavior changes. A final criticism of the token economy is that it often fails to generalize to real world situations after clients are released from an institutional setting (Liberman, 2000).

Despite the criticism surrounding the technique of the token economy, the research provides overwhelming support of its efficacy when employed with various groups or individuals (Boggs et al., 1976; Boniecki & Moore, 2003; Elliott et al., 1979; Filcheck et al., 2004; Kahng et al., 2003; Reinecke et al., 1999).

CHAPTER 25

Behavioral Contract

ORIGINS OF THE BEHAVIORAL CONTRACT TECHNIQUE

Behavioral contracts, or contingency contracts, are based upon the operant conditioning (Mikulas, 1978) principle of positive reinforcement (or punishment). Behavioral contracts are written agreements between two or more individuals in which one or both persons agree to engage in a specific target behavior (Miltenberger, 1997). In addition, behavioral contracts involve the administration of positive (or negative) consequences contingent on the occurrence or nonoccurrence of the target behavior. Behavioral contracts specify all the details of the target behavior, including where the behavior will occur, how the behavior will be carried out, and when the behavior must be completed (Hackney & Cormier, 2005). All persons involved in the contract must negotiate the terms so that the contract is acceptable to everyone (Miltenberger).

The term "contingency contract" was first used by L. P. Homme in 1966 when he reported using contracts with high school drop outs in order to reinforce academic performance (Cantrell, Cantrell, Huddleston, & Woolridge, 1969). Although they were made popular by behavioral and reality therapists, behavioral contracts are now integrated into many different theoretical approaches (Hackney & Cormier, 2005).

A major strength of behavioral contracts is that they require people to be consistent (Mikulas, 1978). Therefore, contracts tend to be popular with children since they can hold their parents or teachers responsible to an agreement. Children no longer feel at the mercy of the person in power. Instead, they learn to accept responsibility for their own actions (Gallagher, 1995). Behavioral contracts establish a level of reciprocity between the involved parties, whether it be a married couple, parents and child, or a teacher and student (Mikulas). Contracts can be altered or renegotiated over time and eventually phased out once the target behaviors become routine.

HOW TO IMPLEMENT THE BEHAVIORAL CONTRACT TECHNIQUE

Behavioral contracts should be used when simpler and less intrusive techniques, such as praise and reinforcement, have failed, and a more powerful procedure is required (Downing, 1990). When possible, behavioral contracts should be individualized rather than using group contracts (Gallagher, 1995). Before writing up a behavioral contract, the target behaviors should be identified. Target behaviors may include undesired behaviors to be decreased or desired behaviors to be increased (Miltenberger, 1997). If possible, the target behavior should be phrased in a positive manner (Gallagher); for instance, "staying on task during seat work time" rather than "not distracting others during seat work time." All concerned parties should meet together as a team to decide which behavior, usually the most disruptive or pervasive, will be addressed first (Downing). Baseline data should be gathered to determine where, under what conditions, and how frequently the behavior currently occurs. This information will be used later in determining the starting goal.

A behavioral contract has a number of essential components (see Table 25.1). Once the target behavior is identified, there are three more steps to complete before writing the behavioral contract. First, decide how the target behaviors will be measured (Miltenberger, 1997). The behaviors may be directly observed or measured by outcomes. Choose where the contract will be used and who will be involved in measuring the target behavior

TABLE 25.1 Components of a Behavioral Contract

1. Identify the behavior to be modified.
2. Introduce and discuss the idea of a behavioral contract.
3. Develop the contract and present it to all involved. Include:
   a. The client's name.
   b. The specific behavior to be changed (start small).
   c. How you will know when successful.
   d. The reinforcement for successful performance.
   e. (Optional) A natural consequence for noncompliance.
   f. (Optional) A bonus clause.
   g. Follow up by (time and date).
   h. Signatures.
4. Outline the follow-up procedures.
5. Initiate the program.
6. Record progress and evaluate outcomes.
7. Modify as necessary (start small and expand).

(Downing, 1990). Next, using the baseline data of behavior frequency, identify realistic behavioral expectations and goals. Specify how often the target behavior must be performed in order to be considered a success. The contract should be flexible and allow for successive approximations toward to goal, namely expectations should be increased slowly in order to allow progress toward the target frequency (Gilliland, James, & Bowman, 1994). In order to change behavior, the client must be observed behaving appropriately and receive reinforcement (Carns & Carns, 1994). Therefore, it is important that the client experience success in the first week. Finally, once the behavioral goal is set, identify the reinforcements and/or punishments that will be used contingent on success (Miltenberger). Whenever possible, allow the client to help create a menu of reinforcements especially when working with children, but remember to keep the reinforcements small and manageable (Downing). Decide if negative consequences will be used for failure to meet the goal. Also, decide who will implement the contingency plan and determine what schedule the reinforcement will follow. Fixed ratio or fixed interval schedules are often best at the beginning, but moving to a variable ratio or variable interval schedule once the target behavior has been mastered can assist in maintenance of this behavior. A bonus clause may also be included to reward the client for sustained or exceptional progress (Gilliland et al., 1994)

After solidifying the details of the behavior plan, the contract can be written. Be sure to include the beginning date, the target behavior, the criteria and deadline for task completion, and the reinforcement that will be used (Gallagher, 1995). Discuss the contract with the client and all other parties involved (Downing, 1990). The contract should be clear to every person included, and the behavioral goals should be specific (Gilliland et al., 1994). Everyone involved should sign the contract and receive a copy (Downing). Finally, set up an evaluation meeting after a week or two in order to monitor the progress of the contract. A progress chart, log, or other visible means should be used to show improvement toward goal attainment (Gilliland et al.).

When monitoring progress, every aspect of the contract should be examined. Be sure that the target behavior was appropriate, attainable, and understood by the client (Downing, 1990). Decide whether suitable time was allotted to complete the task. Evaluate if the reinforcements were fitting, effective, and delivered in a timely manner. Also, decide whether the expectations of the contract were realistic, clear, and stated as small approximations to the desired goal (Gilliland et al., 1994).

VARIATIONS OF THE BEHAVIORAL CONTRACT TECHNIQUE

There are several types of behavioral contracts. In one-party contracts, also referred to as unilateral contracts, one individual desires to change a target behavior (Miltenberger, 1997). He makes arrangements for a contract manager to implement reinforcement or punishment contingencies. One-party contracts may be used to increase desirable behaviors, such as exercise, studying, good eating habits, or school/work-related behaviors, or to decrease undesirable behaviors, such as overeating, nail-biting, excessive TV watching, or tardiness. On the other hand, two-party contracts, or bilateral contracts, allow both parties to identify target behaviors and contingencies that they will implement for each other. Two-party contracts are usually written between people who have a significant relationship with each other (e.g., spouses, parents and children, siblings, friends, co-workers). *Quid pro quo* contracts involve a relationship between both target behaviors; one thing will be given in return for something else. However, parallel contracts allow each individual to work on his own target behavior without relying on the performance of the other.

Another type of behavioral contract, self-contracts, may be designed in order to help an individual meet a goal (Hackney & Cormier, 2005). Self-contracts are identical to other behavioral contracts, except that the rewards are administered by the client himself. These contracts can be very helpful when working with children or adolescents. The required behaviors should be clearly identified and

broken into smaller subtasks that can be rewarded separately. Often traditional behavioral contracts can be transitioned into self-contracts as the client becomes more successful at performing the target behavior (Gallagher, 1995). The contract manager slowly relinquishes control over the contract beginning with the reinforcements, then the task identification, and finally the time or frequency requirements.

EXAMPLE OF THE BEHAVIORAL CONTRACT TECHNIQUE

Patrick is a 16-year-old high school sophomore who was brought to the attention of the professional school counselor for truancy. Patrick has no history of reported behavior problems and has maintained above average grades throughout his school career. However, during the current spring semester, his teachers have become increasingly concerned about his potential to successfully pass through to the 11th grade due to skipping classes.

Counselor (C): So you aren't skipping entire days of school? You are here . . . at school . . . you just aren't showing up to particular classes?

Patrick (P): I guess so.

C: Help me understand your reasons for this; I bet you have good reasons . . .

P: Not really. I don't know why really. I mean . . . it just kind of started in the beginning as a once or twice kind of thing because my friends are bad about just hanging out in the parking lot or behind the football field instead of going to class. And I just started sitting around with them. Then I'd feel bad about missing and I'd avoid that teacher 'cause I figured she'd be steamed at me. Or maybe I'd miss that class again cause you know, once you miss, you get behind or whatever. I might miss an assignment or material I needed to study with or something. It just kind of snowballed, I guess. You know what I mean?

C: Yes, I believe I do, Patrick. Seems to make a lot of sense to me.

P: Really?

C: Sure. And I really appreciate how you're sitting here being so honest with me. It takes a lot to just lay it out there like that. And it does, it does make sense how it started out just as this thing to do, and then it just kind of got out of control.

P: Yeah, exactly.

C: So does it bother you that you might not pass through to the 11th grade if you keep skipping?

P: Nah, not really. I guess it should. But I don't see what the big deal is. My parents are freaking out that I might have to go to summer school. But, I mean, that wouldn't be that big of a deal either. Most of my friends will probably be going. So, I mean, yeah, whatever. Umm, no, I guess it doesn't bother me too much.

The professional school counselor now understands the motivation for Patrick's behavior. She also understands that the natural consequence of grade retention is not enough of a motivator for Patrick to improve his class attendance. Finally, the professional school counselor has taken notice of Patrick's respectfulness and honesty within the counseling session and feels both he and his situation could benefit from a behavioral contract. Step 1, identify the behavior to be modified, has been accomplished and the professional school counselor moves onto step 2, introduce the idea of the behavioral contract. In doing so, she tries to collect information she needs to eventually construct the written contract.

C: And your "parents freaking out" doesn't bother you either?

P: I mean . . . yeah . . . it does. But then I get here and I'm like, "Man, I don't feel like going to English class today" or whatever class it is, and it's just easier to skip because I'm not thinking about my parents freaking or about passing 10th grade. Those things just seem too far off and my parents chill out pretty easy anyway, and like I already said, summer school's no big deal.

C: Patrick, do you want to do better about attending classes . . . if there was a reason that was more important to you, would you commit to attending classes more regularly?

P: Sure, I guess. I mean, sure I would want to do better if there was a reason.

C: Okay, so what I'd like to do is to find out what is important to a 16-year-old like you. What are some things that you find yourself trying to negotiate for from time to time, either with your parents, yourself, or your teachers?

The counselor tries to discern a possible positive reinforcement.

P: Sleeping in late on Saturday! Man, it drives me crazy that my parents will *not* let me sleep past 8:30 or 9:00 a.m. on a Saturday morning . . . never have . . . drives me nuts! I would *love* to sleep until like lunch time or something. But they are both freaks about that and it's like the dang golden rule around my house or something.

C: Lunch time, huh? That would be pretty nice. Good. Anything else?

P: I negotiate all the time for a new car. Is that what you mean?

C: Well, let me tell you what I have in mind here and then you'll see how your two suggestions fit in. Your parents and your teachers really want you to do well in school. And they know that can't happen if you continue to skip classes. And now I know that you don't really care all that much about what I call the natural consequences . . . those being failing the 10th grade or your parents freaking out as you say . . . at least you don't care at the time that it matters most . . . like when you are sitting in the parking lot or behind the football field with your friends. In fact, some of the natural consequences, like missing assignments and your teacher's perceptions, actually increase your likelihood to skip again. (Pauses for a moment to let this all sink in with Patrick) This presents a dilemma.

P: When you put it that way, yeah, (pauses while nodding head and reflecting) I guess it does.

C: What would be great is if we could come up with some mutual agreement between you, your teachers, myself, your parents . . . all of us, that would make you more likely to go to class.

P: I don't see that happening.

C: Well, your parents want you to stop cutting class. Cutting class doesn't really bother you all that much. You want to sleep in on Saturday mornings. Your parents don't allow that. See where I'm going?

P: I think so.

C: With that sort of tit for tat in mind, can you think of any other examples or points of negotiation between you and your parents. The sleeping in on Saturdays fits nicely into a possible proposal to your parents. That is something we might actually get them to consider. The new car is probably not, although we can check if you want.

P: Nah—they already told me no way. Curfew is always a big deal. I'm always asking for a later curfew, and they're always turning me down.

C: Okay, good. That gives us a couple of options. What I'd like to do then is sit down with you and your parents and flesh out a contract that will give you a little more incentive to attend class. This contract would be very specific about what is expected of you, and what happens if you follow through, as well as what happens if you don't.

P: What do you mean by what happens if I don't follow through?

The counselor is trying to discern the natural consequence for noncompliance.

C: Well, something you said earlier got my attention. You said you assumed your teachers were steamed when you cut their classes and that you knew you fell behind when you cut. Right? And that these two things actually made you more likely to cut that class again. Right?

P: Yep.

C: Well, we don't know yet what the positive will be for you if you improve your attendance . . . we still have to negotiate that with your parents . . . but I would like for the negative consequence to be something along the lines of reporting to your teachers at the end of the day, if you skipped their classes, and

obtaining the material you missed and any homework assignments. That way, knowing you have to face your teacher that same day will hopefully be a deterrent to you skipping to begin with. If you skip anyway, obtaining the missed material and assignments will make you less likely to skip the same class the next day. What do you think?

P: Wow, that'd be hard. But . . . I think I like the idea anyway . . . I mean, it'd be good for me to have to do that . . . I'll get to see all this and know the specifics before I definitely agree, right?

C: Yes. We'll actually put it in writing, and you'll see it all before I ask you to sign the contract. I tell you what, let's set up another appointment for later this week with you and your parents. And in the meantime, I'll discuss our options with your teachers. How does that sound?

P: Cool.

Later that week, the following session takes place with Patrick and both his parents.

C: So, Patrick, your teachers are all on board with giving you your missed material and assignments that same day when you come to them and ask them for it. They are also going to each keep a separate attendance sheet for you each day that I will pick up every afternoon after your last class period. That way, I will be keeping a daily record of your attendance in each class and will report that directly to mom and dad. Sound okay?

P: Sounds fine. So, if I do skip a class, I have to go to that teacher that same day and ask her for my homework and missed material?

C: Yep.

P: So she'll know I'm really here that day.

C: They know anyway, Patrick. You may as well be brave and just go do what you have to do to keep from falling behind . . . keeps it from snowballing like you said.

P: Yeah, you're right.

C: Okay, so Mom and Dad, what we want to discuss with you today are some ideas that

Patrick and I have already mulled over, that may serve to encourage his class attendance, and I know you guys want that!

Mom (M): Okay, we're listening.

C: Patrick, why don't you start . . . tell them the two ideas we are considering.

P: Well, the two things that I could come up with that would really help make me more likely to diss the guys in between classes would be if I knew I could sleep in on Saturday or if I could stay out later on Friday or Saturday night.

Dad (D): Really? Sleeping in or later curfew is more important than passing 10th grade? Remarkable.

C: Sometimes, Dad, what seems obviously important to us is not at all what makes a teenager tick.

D: I guess so. (Toward Mom) What do you think?

M: So, we could consider one or the other as a reward for his class attendance?

C: Yes. As I explained on the phone, I would like to use a behavioral contract between all of us that will outline a specific positive that Patrick will gain for attending a set number of classes, and a negative that Patrick will have to face each time he skips a class. Here's what we've got so far. Whenever he skips a class, he knows and is agreeing to go to that teacher in person before the school day is up, first showing that he was in fact present that day, and second, requesting any missed information and assignments. We know this is something that Patrick wants to avoid, and we also know that doing so will help prevent him from skipping this class the very next day as an avoidance measure.

M: Okay. I like that.

C: Now, what I'd like to do is state in the contract that for every 5 days, not 5 days in a row, but a culmination of 5 total days where each and every class was attended, he gets a certain something, he gets your word that

you will follow through with whatever it is we decide today . . . something related to curfew or sleeping in preferably. Those are the privileges that mean the most to him.

M: I see, I see. Well, I am willing to budge on the sleeping in on Saturday mornings more so than on the curfew.

D: I prefer extending his curfew.

M: Extending his curfew could lead to potential dangers. What harm will come from him sleeping in late?

D: True. I see your point. I'm not against sleeping in then.

P: You have *no* idea how much I am going to go to class!!!

C: All right, let's get this all down on paper, with all the specifics, and get everyone's signatures. And remember, we are all giving our word here. We all have an agreement.

The professional school counselor outlines all agreed upon terms in the contract, complete with the expected behavior phrased in positive language, the means for the counselor to keep track of his attendance, the positive and negative consequences for attendance or truancy, a starting date and an ending date. Finally, an appointment is made for 2 weeks to assess Patrick's compliance with the terms of the contract. The actual contract designed for Patrick follows in Figure 25.1.

USEFULNESS AND EVALUATION OF THE BEHAVIORAL CONTRACT TECHNIQUE

The successfulness of behavioral contracts have been well documented in the literature for 40 years. Behavioral contracts may be used to teach new behaviors, to decrease unwanted behaviors, or to increase desirable behaviors (Downing, 1990). Contracts are very helpful to teachers for use with academic and social skills. Contracts have been successful with students in regular classrooms as well as those in special education. Allen, Howard, Sweeney, and McLaughlin (1993) demonstrated

Behavioral Contract

Student Name: Patrick Daniels   Date: March 2

Terms of Agreement

Patrick agrees to attend each class for which he is enrolled Monday through Friday at Payne High School. Patrick understands that exceptions to class attendance include serious illness or family emergency, which would require leaving campus for the remainder of the day to attend to these matters. Classes scheduled include: American History, Anatomy & Physiology, English Literature I, Sociology, and Excel Applications.

When all five classes have been attended for 5 cumulative days, Patrick's parents, Eileen and Davis Daniels, agree to reward Patrick by allowing him to sleep until noon on the upcoming Saturday morning. This reward will continue throughout the remainder of this contract.

When Patrick skips a class, he agrees to meet with the teacher of that course, that same day, in person, to request missed material and assignments. This course of action will be expected for the duration of this contract.

The professional school counselor, Monica Reed, will keep a record of Patrick's class attendance, reporting his progress to Mr. and Mrs. Daniels. This system of tracking attendance will remain in place for the duration of this contract.

The terms of this contract will begin Monday, March 5, and will continue through the spring semester, ending on Friday, May 18.

We agree to the terms of this behavior contract as written.

Patrick Daniels	Date	Eileen Daniels	Date
Monica Reed	Date	Davis Daniels	Date

FIGURE 25.1 Patrick's behavioral contract.

that behavioral contracts were able to immediately and significantly increase on-task behavior in second and third grade students. In addition, Kelley and Stokes (1982) reported that behavioral contracts using money as a reward for completing workbook pages in a vocational training program were able to increase the productivity of disadvantaged students. Parent-designed behavioral contracts have also achieved increases in the homework performance of their children (Miltenberger, 1997). Miller and Kelley (1994) reported that when parents and elementary school-aged children negotiated weekly behavioral contracts, three out of four students improved their homework accuracy and two out of four students significantly improved their on-task behavior.

In addition to the school environment, contracts have been used in prisons, mental hospitals, and halfway houses (Mikulas, 1978). Contracts are also frequently used in marital or couples therapy (Miltenberger, 1997). Moreover, behavioral contracts have been used for weight management, drug and alcohol treatment, reduction in cigarette smoking, and monitoring physical fitness (Gilliland et al., 1994).

Techniques Based Upon Behavioral Approaches Using Punishment

Recall from the figure in Section 6 that punishment is defined as anything, either applied or removed, that decreases or suppresses the display of an undesirable behavior. When a client's goal is to do less of something, punishment procedures are very effective in helping clients meet that goal. However, professional counselors should realize that, very frequently, punishment does not totally eliminate the undesirable behavior. More often, punishment reduces the display of an undesirable behavior within the environment that the punishment occurred (e.g., punishing a teen for smoking in the house will probably reduce smoking in the house but will not necessarily reduce smoking outside of the house). It is essential to understand that in order to totally extinguish a behavior, a combination of punishing the undesirable behavior and reinforcing the incompatible desirable behavior is suggested.

Punishment can either involve adding a stimulus to the situation or removing a reinforcer from the situation. Examples of punishment with stimulus added would include corporal punishment, assigning extra chores or homework, or requiring additional practice attempts. Examples of punishment while removing a reinforcer would include grounding or restricting a child from going out of the house to play, not allowing use of something ordinarily allowed (e.g., car, bike, video gaming system), or any other restriction of privileges ordinarily granted.

While punishment can be quite effective in reducing undesirable behaviors, its success depends upon many factors. When designing a punishment program, one must consider the type of behavior being punished, the type of punishment that will be used, the schedule of punishment, whether warnings will be given before punishment is delivered, and whether other techniques, such as positive reinforcement, should be used in conjunction with the punishment procedures (Vought, 1984). In addition, those using punishment techniques should ensure that the consequences are delivered immediately, the intensity of the consequences is appropriate, and the punishment procedure is consistently applied.

Punishment is a controversial technique. On the one hand, punishment procedures have been used effectively with a variety of situations and populations. Punishment has been used with person with mental retardation, clients with autism, children with schizophrenia, psychiatric patients, self-abusive or physically aggressive persons, and children presenting with noncompliant behavior

(Matson & DiLorenzo, 1983). Applications of punishment, such as response cost, have been successful at reducing excessive crying, hyperactivity, noncompliance in children, and alcoholic drinking (Groden & Cautela, 1981). Likewise, time out has been used effectively to diminish disruptive behaviors in children.

Yet, on the other hand, some people argue that punishment procedures should only be used in extreme cases and that positive reinforcement procedures should be used exclusively whenever possible (Matson & DiLorenzo, 1983). But, since punishment procedures often work more rapidly than reinforcement procedures, punishment may be useful with life-threatening behaviors, such as rumination or self-injury.

Regardless, it is important to note that the effects of punishment procedures may be temporary. When punitive consequences are removed, the punished behavior often reappears (Vought, 1984). Because of this temporary effect, punishment is often called a suppressor of behavior. Punishment may also have a few other negative side effects. Punishment sometimes leads to escape, avoidance, or aggression (Doyle, 1998). It can also be a poor social learning model, teaching children to use punishment on others. Finally, some aversive stimuli can have negative physiological side effects and end up doing more harm than good.

A number of techniques based upon punishment are presented to help clients decrease display of the target behavior, including extinction, time out, response cost, and overcorrection (positive practice). Extinction is a classic procedure that basically deprives the client of any positive reinforcer that helps to continue an undesirable behavior. For example, when a child's acting out behavior in class is reinforced by a teacher's attention, the teacher tries to extinguish the behavior by paying absolutely no attention to the child during the acting out episodes. When the child is not acting out, the teacher attends to and rewards the child for desirable behavior.

Time out is a technique that removes the client from a reward rich environment and places the client in a reward deprived area. In classic time out, a child is placed in a time out chair for a certain amount of time. Time out is a punishment technique that serves to deter future misbehavior. Response cost is pretty much the opposite of positive reinforcement. In response cost, a client starts with a certain number of tokens and display of the target behavior results in the loss of one token. At the end of the time period, if the client has any tokens remaining the client gets the agreed upon reward. Overcorrection, sometimes called positive practice, is an effective punishment technique that requires the client to repeatedly perform the correct action—usually 10 times—in order to: (1) teach the client the proper way to perform the behavior, and (2) serve as a deterrent to future misbehavior. So if a child slams the door when he enters the house, the child would practice entering and exiting the house silently 10 times. In the future, the child will likely remember to close the door quietly. It is important for professional counselors to remember that the effectiveness of punishment interventions is enhanced when the punishment procedure is coupled with a positive reinforcement strategy. See Section 6 for a review of multicultural implications when using techniques based on behavioral approaches.

CHAPTER 26

Extinction

ORIGINS OF THE EXTINCTION TECHNIQUE

Extinction is a behavioral technique based on punishment that involves withholding reinforcements in order to reduce the frequency of a specific behavior (Groden & Cautela, 1981). It is commonly used in parent training and classroom management and was developed and validated more than 50 years ago. Extinction can be used to eliminate behaviors that were previously reinforced unknowingly in the environment. For instance, if a student in class is constantly calling out to gain teacher attention, the teacher should ignore that student rather than acknowledging the student's responses (George & Christiani, 1995). Acknowledgment of the student constitutes a positive reinforcement of the calling out behavior. Once this reinforcement is withdrawn, the calling out behavior should cease.

As with other forms of punishment, extinction is often more effective when combined with positive reinforcement of an alternate behavior (Groden & Cautela, 1981). The strategy of substituting a more desirable behavior for the undesirable one is sometimes referred to as counter-conditioning (George & Christiani, 1995). It is essential to note that extinction often results in a temporary increase in the target behavior before its decline. This increase in negative behavior is called an *extinction burst*. In addition, when used alone, extinction produces a gradual rather than immediate reduction in the behavior. However, combining extinction with consistent positive reinforcement of an alternate (i.e., competing) behavior can lead to more permanent and rapid results.

HOW TO IMPLEMENT THE EXTINCTION TECHNIQUE

Before deciding to use an extinction procedure, the professional counselor must consider the nature of the behavior to be terminated. If the target behavior is extremely disruptive to the point that an increase in the behavior would not be tolerable or if the behavior is likely to be imitated by others when ignored, extinction is not an appropriate technique (Benoit & Mayer, 1974).

The first step in designing an extinction procedure is to recognize all possible reinforcers of the target behavior (Benoit & Mayer, 1974). Common reinforcers for disruptive behaviors are adult attention, adult comments, attention of peers, or escape from an activity. In order to determine the reinforcers of a behavior, a contingency analysis may be conducted. This analysis requires studying the events and conditions that occur before the undesired and desired behaviors and the consequences of each behavior. Once all reinforcers have been identified, a method of withholding these reinforcements must be designed. If all reinforcers cannot be withheld, then extinction will not be successful. The last step before implementing the extinction procedure is to choose an alternative behavior to be positively reinforced along with the extinction procedure.

When applying extinction, the professional counselor should be prepared for an increase in the target behavior (i.e., extinction burst). The professional counselor should withhold all reinforcement when the target behavior occurs and present positive reinforcement whenever the alternate (competing) behavior takes place. The professional counselor can also monitor or graph the client's behavior to determine the success of the extinction and positive reinforcement procedures.

VARIATIONS OF THE EXTINCTION TECHNIQUE

Covert extinction is identical to extinction except that it occurs in the client's imagination (Ascher & Cautela, 1974). Once the target behavior and consequences maintaining that behavior are identified, the client is instructed to imagine a scene in which the reinforcement does not occur (Cautela, 1971). The client imagines this scene over and over until the behavior is eliminated in reality. Covert extinction can be especially useful when the reinforcers are hard to control in the real environment. It can also be used in conjunction with traditional extinction or covert reinforcement. In a laboratory study, Ascher and Cautela (1974) found that covert extinction was successful in eliminating a previously reinforced overt response regardless of whether or not external conditions supported the extinction procedure.

EXAMPLE OF THE EXTINCTION TECHNIQUE

Craig is a 5-year-old boy with a recent history of frequent tantrum behavior. It began suddenly, following a weekend trip to grandma's house, where Craig's 3-year-old cousin, quite adept at tantrum behavior, was also visiting. Craig's parents were so taken aback at their son's new reaction to disappointment that they've yet to devise a consistent plan for how to handle it.

Counselor (C):   Okay, Mom and Dad, tell me in a little bit more detail about this new skill your son has developed.

Mom (M):   (With Craig in her lap) Well, it has been happening daily for some time now, usually several times in one day. He begins to cry very loudly and buries his face in the floor. He seems more distraught than angry, unless you don't give in immediately and then it becomes more of an angry fit. Umm, the crying will turn more to yelling or screaming . . . not directly at me or my husband, just in general. It's so nerve-wracking. I can feel my blood pressure rise. I just want it to stop.

C: So it really gets to you, huh?

M: Yeah, I mean it's so hard to see him in the floor crying, like he's really devastated. I'm his mother. I don't want him to feel so upset. And then I think to myself, "Is it really worth all this?" You know? Is it that big of a deal for him to go to bed right now, or to put his toys away, or brush his teeth right at this moment? It just doesn't seem worth it. So usually I just give in.

C: So you might let him stay up a little later, or leave his toys out or avoid brushing his teeth?

M: Yes.

C: And how does he respond when you give in?

M: Oh, he returns to normal very quickly, sometimes even happier than before the tantrum began.

C: Which reinforces you to keep giving in! Okay, I'm getting the idea. And does he ever do anything to hurt himself or others during these tantrums?

M: No, never. Even though it really gets to me, part of me knows it's very contrived.

Sometimes he even stops long enough to look up to see if we're paying attention.

C: Oh, I see. Okay. Well, Dad, can you tell me your take on all this?

Dad (D): I just feel like maybe it's a phase he's going through. Or I thought it was at first. But it seems to be getting worse lately and that bothers me. I feel like we've tried everything and its getting worse instead of better.

C: Right. Right. Can you tell me how you respond to these tantrums?

D: Umm, well, usually I just let my wife deal with it but if she's not around then I usually try to talk to him to calm him down. I've tried being very soothing and I've tried being very stern. Neither seems to work really.

C: Okay. Let me make sure I've got this right. (Craig gets down from Mom's lap and goes to the paper and crayons in the bookcase. He sits down at the other end of the office and begins coloring.) Craig probably picked this new behavior up from his cousin. He saw this cousin use tantrums when he didn't get his way, and then probably saw him get his way as a result of the tantrum. At the very least, he probably saw his cousin receive an awful lot of attention from all the commotion. So Craig decided this seemed to be a very effective behavior and he should try it out himself. So, he gets home from Grandma's and the first time he doesn't get what he wants he gives it a try. The pair of you were probably so surprised that you thought something was terribly wrong. Imagine his delight when you rushed to him, gave in to his demands, and soothed him.

M: (Laughs) Kids are so smart, aren't they?

C: They do learn quickly—which will work to our advantage. Okay, so Craig continues this behavior, it is working more and more effectively and he is fine-tuning his emotional displays. Dad may not always give in to him, but does give him attention, which is nice, and Mom almost always gives in, which is even

better. I'd say you have a pretty smart kid on your hands!

D: He takes after me.

M: That's true!

C: (Laughs) All right. So let me ask just one or two more questions to make certain I have a clear idea of the situation. It seems to me so far that Craig uses tantrums to get attention and to get his way, either by avoiding something he does not want to do, or getting something he does want. Thinking on the most recent instances, can you see anything that occurs before the tantrum or after that would indicate any other reason for the tantrums?

Both parents think for several moments.

M: Every example I'm coming up with in my mind is exactly for those reasons. Exactly those.

D: Yeah, me too. I agree. (Nods head in agreement.)

The counselor is now going to introduce the concept of extinction, also called planned ignoring.

C: What I'd like to suggest is the use of a technique known as extinction. The general rule behind this principle is that if you want a behavior to continue and increase, you attend to it. If you don't want to see it anymore, you do not attend to it. Now, the more the child wants the reinforcer, which in Craig's case is the attention and getting his way, the more he will resist your attempts at extinction.

D: Oh boy.

C: Yeah. It is very important for you to know this going in, though, so that you'll be prepared. In fact, you should know that he may actually tantrum more in the beginning.

Recall that this is known as an extinction burst.

C: Do either of you watch television?

D: I do when I get home from work and on Saturdays during football season.

C: Okay. Umm, imagine that you settle into your seat with a drink and a snack to watch a football game one Saturday afternoon. You make yourself comfortable, prop your feet up perhaps, have your drink in your hand, and reach for the remote control. You push the power button to turn the television on and nothing happens. What do you do?

D: Push it again!

C: And probably again, and again, and again. Anytime you've pushed this button on the remote in the past, the television set has come on. You know that if you only keep pushing it, maybe a little more forcefully, maybe holding it up and at a different angle, it will work. Why not just put the remote down and walk to the television set and turn it on manually?

D: Because I know that remote will eventually work!

C: Exactly my point. This is exactly what Craig will be thinking when you first begin to extinguish his tantrums. He'll try even harder, because he is certain it will eventually work as it has in the past. Now, will you eventually give up on the remote?

D: Yes.

C: And so will Craig. There are a few things though that you can do to speed up that process. First, be consistent. If sometimes you use extinction and sometimes you don't, you will actually increase his tantrums. Second, giving in later is worse than giving him what he wants to begin with. So decide up front that if you are going to refuse a request of Craig's that you are certain you are going to stick with it and see it through. If you know you are going to eventually give in to it, just give in before the tantrum behavior ever begins. The last thing is to immediately, as soon as he begins to calm down and displays appropriate behavior, immediately give him attention and praise. You want there to be a marked difference between your reactions to him while in a tantrum and your reactions to him while calm. Remember, <u>ignore behavior you do not want to continue and attend to behavior you want to see more of.</u>

M: This is going to be hard, isn't it?

C: It will not be easy. But it will be worth it. And it will work if we are right in assuming the reasons for the tantrums and if you are consistent and don't give up. (Pause) I tell you what, why don't we give it a try now? (Up to this point, Craig has been sitting in the floor coloring off to the side in the counselor's office.)

D: You mean right now? Here? How?

M: All we'd have to do is take the crayons away.

C: Good idea, Mom. We could ask him to put them up and come join us. What do you think?

M: And then what will we do?

C: We will do exactly what you will be doing when you leave here today. We will carry on as if nothing is happening. We will not look at him, raise our eyebrows, or address him in any way. And when he calms himself, we will be overjoyed at how good he is being.

M: This could really help. Okay. Let's do it.

C: Dad?

D: Sure, why not?

C: Mom, why don't you do the honors?

M: Okay. (Turns towards Craig) Craig, I would like for you to put the crayons back in the bookcase and come sit with us for a moment.

Craig: I'm not done yet.

M: You may finish after we talk to you. I would like for you to place the crayons back in the bookcase and come sit with us for a moment.

Craig: *Mom!!!* I'm not done yet!!!

(There is a pause.)

Craig: Nooooooo!!! (Wailing begins) I don't want tooooo! (Craig's wailing gets louder and he places his face in his hands, bends at the knees, and buries his face in his hands in the floor. Craig's mother becomes visibly nervous.)

C: Okay, Mom, look at me and talk to me about anything as normally as possible. Nothing is happening. We are still three adults having a conversation. Everything is fine. Why don't you talk to me about how anxious you seem right now. Tell me how this is for you. (There is a long pause as Mom looks at the floor, possibly to prevent herself from looking over at Craig.)

M: He seems so disappointed. (Looks over to Craig, who is still wailing)

C: Look this way. Remember, no eye contact, no body language, no reaction at all.

M: Okay. (Deep breath) Part of me just wants to go hand him the c-r-a-y-o-n-s so he won't be upset.

C: (Looks out of the corner of an eye to see that Craig has looked up to see if he is being attended to. Then the crying gets louder and, just as his parents stated, begins to sound less devastated and more angry.) Wow, you predicted that exactly. So part of you wants to just make it all better for him. Keep talking. It will help you get through this.

M: (Looks at Craig's dad, who then takes her hand) Yeah, but you know it's funny . . . the fact that right now was so predictable is actually helping me feel better. If it's that routine, then surely it can't be that real. Don't you think? (Craig has just taken the intensity level up another notch.) Do you think the people in the hall can hear?

(Before the counselor has a chance to respond Craig very suddenly stops and becomes quiet.)

C: Oh, Craig. I like the way you just calmed right down. That was very good. We'd like for you to join us now. (Crying and yelling begins again, with even more enthusiasm.)

C: It's okay. Don't attend to it. Remember? It isn't happening.

M: But why did it happen again? Usually once he stops he's done.

C: That's because in the past, he stops because he gets what he wants. This time was different. I actually made the same request as the one that initially set him off. This is the extinction burst we discussed. (This time, after

a more intense, though shorter lived tantrum, Craig stops again.) Mom, you go ahead this time.

M: Very good, Craig! We'd like you to come over here now. (Craig complies, gets in Mom's lap, and Mom gives him a big hug. Dad pats him on the back.)

C: Mom, Dad, Craig, you all did great. Notice how our reactions did not change no matter how loud or upset he became, nor when he stopped and began again. Notice that he still does not have the c-r-a-y-o-n-s, yet he is fine. Also notice the difference in our reactions to him while having a tantrum, we ignored him, and after calming himself, we praised and hugged him.

M: He does seem just fine now.

C: Yes, he certainly does.

D: I think we can do this. It really helped to try it out here. We would have been stuck with the second wave of it and wouldn't have known how to react.

C: Good. I'm glad it helped. Do you have any questions before you venture out on your own?

M: It's okay to give in to some things, right? Just make sure I do it to begin with?

C: Of course. But once you make a choice, stand your ground.

M: Okay.

C: Okay? It would help for you to keep a record each day of how frequent the tantrums are and how long they last. This will help you gauge the effectiveness of the extinction.

M: All right. Just write down when they occur and when they stop?

C: Yes, that should do it. You can be more detailed if you like. The important thing though is that you get an idea over the next few weeks of the progress that is being made. Oh, and one other thing . . . if anyone else is going to be at your home or with you, explain to them ahead of time that you are working on eliminating Craig's tantrum behavior. Stress to them the importance of following your lead and ignoring Craig's behavior.

D: Wish us luck!

USEFULNESS AND EVALUATION OF THE EXTINCTION TECHNIQUE

Much of the outcomes research on the extinction technique was conducted almost 50 years ago and is considered "classic." Extinction can be used in a variety of situations, as long as the target behavior is not too disruptive or prone to imitation by others (Benoit & Mayer, 1974). Likewise, it is important that the professional counselor have control over all possible reinforcers of the target behavior before using extinction. When combined with positive reinforcement of an alternate behavior, extinction has been used successfully with child noncompliance and aggression (Groden & Cautela, 1981). Likewise, Williams (1959) found that extinction was effective in eliminating tantrum behavior in a child. When the parents no longer reinforced the child's tantrums by re-entering the child's bedroom after putting him to sleep, the tantrum behavior was completely eliminated within 10 occasions.

CHAPTER 27

Time Out

ORIGINS OF THE TIME OUT TECHNIQUE

The widely used time out technique is a form of behavioral treatment based upon the operant conditioning principle of punishment. Those who espouse behavioral therapy hold that all behavior, maladaptive and adaptive, is learned through operant processes and modeling. Negative punishment involves removing a stimulus to reduce the probability that a behavior will reoccur. Time out is a type of negative punishment in which any form of positive reinforcement is removed from the child after a display of maladaptive behavior. This is done with the hope that the child will not continue to engage in the maladaptive behaviors in the future because the child wants to keep the positive reinforcers. Thus, time out serves as punishment for current misbehavior and a deterrent to future misbehavior. It is commonly used by parents and teachers of young children.

HOW TO IMPLEMENT THE TIME OUT TECHNIQUE

Time out is used most frequently with children. Before implementing time out, professional counselors should be familiar with the three different types. *Seclusionary time out* occurs when a child is sent to a different room, referred to as a time out room. *Exclusionary time out* occurs when the child is removed from the environment where the activity is happening. She is sent to another location such as the steps or the hallway. *Non-seclusionary time out* occurs when a child remains in the environment but is not allowed to participate in the reinforcing activity.

When implementing time out the adult needs to make sure to tell the client, in a clear and concise manner, why he is being sent to time out. Time out should be used only after redirection and a warning have been given to the child. Depending on the type of maladaptive behavior displayed, the adult should choose which type of time out to use. The adult should attempt to have the client go to time out without having to physically constrain the client, but at times may need to use some force to get the client to comply. Physical restraint requires specialized training and should be used only if the client is endangering himself or another person. The amount of time the client stays in time out varies, but typically 5 minutes is effective. With younger children, less time may be needed, and with older children, more time may be necessary (Harris, 1985). The adult can make the decision of the duration of time out after taking into consideration personal characteristics of the client (Cuenin & Harris, 1986). When a client comes back from time out, the adult should make sure to treat the client with respect and update the client on what to do to rejoin the activity in progress. The client should not be reprimanded or forced to apologize (Bacon, 1990). It is important for the adult to monitor the client when in time out, and when his time is up, he needs to rejoin the activity (Betz, 1994).

When one chooses to implement the time out technique, it is a good idea to gather baseline data to support its use. The record should include a description of the client's behavior before implementing time out, the time of day the behavior occurred, the duration of time out, the type of time out used, and a description of how the client behaved while in time out. After a 2-week period of time, the adult can examine the data to evaluate whether or not time out appears to be effective. Typically, this technique can be used with clients as young as 2 or 3 years old (Spencer, 2000) or as old as the early teenage years. Time out has even been used effectively with adults with mental retardation.

When a client is in time out, Erford (1999, p. 208) suggested having the client follow these seven rules to enhance behavioral compliance: (1) feet on the floor; (2) chair legs on the floor; (3) hands in lap; (4) bottom on chair; (5) eyes open and on the wall; (6) not a sound; and (7) sit up straight.

VARIATIONS OF THE TIME OUT TECHNIQUE

Erford (1999) described a contingent delay variation of time out. After the client is sent to time out and understands the seven rules described above, he is expected to follow the rules for the entire time spent in time out. The client is informed that any time he violates one of the rules, 1 minute will be added to the amount of time he needs to spend in time out (e.g., 5 minutes plus any penalty minutes). It is important that whoever is implementing the technique with the child is strict about adding the extra minute, or the child will not view the time out as a punishment.

The "Sit and Watch" variation of this technique is for use in the classroom setting. If the student is sent to "Sit and Watch," she picks up an hourglass (filled with enough sand to last 3 minutes), moves to an area away from the class, and sits down and watches the timer. Once the sand flows through the timer, the student can rejoin the activity. Teachers may find it useful to develop contingencies when using "Sit and Watch." Examples include:

> Go to Sit and Watch once, lose daily computer time. Go to Sit and Watch more than once, lose a free play period every 2 weeks. Engage in disruptive behavior while in Sit and Watch, lose free play time later in the day. Talk to someone in Sit and watch or tattle on others, go to Sit and Watch. (White & Bailey, 1990, p. 356)

EXAMPLE OF THE TIME OUT TECHNIQUE

The following transcript illustrates the teaching and use of contingent delay time out with 8-year-old Kevin and his mother. After properly assessing Kevin's behavior and determining time out to be an appropriate intervention for his mother to use to reduce problematic behavior, the professional counselor works with Kevin's mother to teach and train her in the use of time out. During the session below, the professional counselor first role-plays the time out procedure briefly with Kevin and then assists the mother as she does the same.

Counselor (C):   Okay, Mom, Kevin, what I'd like for us to do now is go ahead and go through all the steps and specifics of the time out procedure with contingent delay. So, Mom, you can watch as I role-play and we will keep it short, just long enough to give you and Kevin the general feel for it, and then I will ask you to do the same. Sound okay?

Mom (M):   Okay.

Kevin (K):   Yeah, all right.

C: Here we go then. "Kevin, it's time to turn off the television and come get dressed for bed."

Now, Kevin, just for the sake of role-playing, it's okay not to follow through with my directions. Remember, Mom, he gets 5 seconds to comply. If he says "no" or chooses not to comply by the end of that time, you give a warning.

K: Okay, then . . . No! I ain't gonna!

C: "Kevin, you may choose to come get dressed for bed or go to time out. You decide." This way, Mom, you are letting Kevin make the choice—to either get dressed for bed or punish himself. It is *his* decision!

M: Yes, I like that it feels like it's of his own making.

K: (Kevin sticks out his tongue at the counselor and crosses his arms.)

C: Right, and again, he has 5 seconds. "Okay, Kevin. Go and sit in the time out chair until I say you can get up." (Kevin complies.) Remember, Mom, once he is in the chair, you should remind him of the seven rules of time out. Or, you can post them on the wall at home in front of the chair as a reminder for him.

M: Yes, the seven rules.

C: "Kevin, remember to follow the seven rules: keep your feet on the floor, the chair legs on the floor, your hands stay in your lap, all of your bottom is on the chair, your back is against the back of the chair, do not make any sounds, and look at the wall in front of you with your eyes open. If you break a rule, 1 minute will be added to your stay in time out."

M: Is it okay if he breaks a rule now so I can see how you handle it?

C: Sure, Kevin, just so we can demonstrate for Mom, go ahead and break one of the time out rules just this once.

K: Okay. (Kevin begins swinging and tapping his feet loudly on the floor.)

C: (In a firm but calm voice) "I said to keep your feet on the floor. One minute has been added, Kevin." (Pauses for a few moments)

Now, Mom, ordinarily Kevin would need to stay in the time out chair for the minimum 5 minutes plus any penalty minutes for violating any of the seven rules. Okay, Kevin, we have completed our role-play of time out. You did a very good job, and I appreciate your help.

K: Sure. Is that what it will be like?

C: Yes, but it will feel different when it is the real thing because you probably won't like it and you'll want to do other things instead. Okay, Mom, your turn. Kevin, Mom is now going to role-play with you.

Thus far, the professional counselor has assessed Kevin's problem behaviors, educated the mother about the contingent delay time out procedure, and modeled the procedure for Mom. It is only at this point that Mom tries it with Kevin, first through role-play in the professional counselor's office, and then realistically at home.

K: I'll be in the chair.

M: Okay, why don't you come sit in the chair then? Can he do that?

C: That's okay. Now go over the seven rules of the time out chair.

M: "Now remember, feet on the floor, sit back, eyes on the wall, no talking, no sounds or anything for 5 minutes."

C: "Also, chair legs on the floor, hands in lap, and your entire bottom on the chair, Kevin." Once you feel he has gotten to know the rules, you won't have to repeat them each time. And also, as I mentioned earlier, some parents have actually written the rules down and placed them on the wall in front of the chair so that they're up there in writing, kind of as your contract . . . So, Mom, how's he doing sitting for his 5 minutes?

M: He has his eyes closed.

C: Go ahead and attend to that.

M: "Kevin, keep your eyes open."

C: Remember that if he is violating one of the rules, then go ahead and put an extra minute on his contingency.

M: "You eyes are closed Kevin, I'll have to add a minute, okay?"

C: One of the things that I notice in the way you give your directives, and I don't know if this is what you notice at home also, but I notice that when you gave the directive, you seem to put it like it is a question. Don't ask it as a question. Don't add an "okay" at the end of it.

M: Okay.

C: It's not important that he agree with your directive, it's important that he do it. So that questioning tone at the end often times leads to, leads the kid to think, "Well I might have a choice here." Or another thought it could lead to, it could lead to kind of thinking in response, "No, actually, Mom, it's not okay." You asking "okay" can lead him to think he is allowed to actually disagree or even argue with you, and that is not okay. You want a directive to be a directive, so to help with that, it's a good idea to always take your voice down at the end of that as opposed to up.

M: Okay, that makes sense. I am bad about that. Gosh, if I could just improve that, it would probably help tremendously.

C: I agree with you. It will be interesting to see. So, he's been doing pretty good and it looks like his time is up . . .

M: "Kevin, can you come here please?"

C: (Modeling for mom) "Kevin, come here please."

M: Okay, "Kevin, come here please. Now, you are going to go with me now and create no problems when you go to Grandma's, correct?" I can say correct, right?

C: That's okay, or "do you understand" would work well also.

M: "Do you understand that you have to come with me when we go to Grandma's and behave? And no whining or complaining."

K: "I guess so."

C: I wouldn't accept "I guess so."

M: Okay.

C: Okay, I would accept "yes" or I would accept "no".

M: What do you do then?

C: Well, I would say to him, at that point, I would say, "Kevin, I need for you to answer me yes or no. I guess so is not an acceptable answer."

K: "No."

C: "You can either go with me to Grandma's, or you can go and sit in the time out chair for another 5 minutes. You decide."

K: "I'll go with you."

C: The chair is, at this point, not something that he wants. Okay. Mom, how do you feel about using this at home? Do you feel ready?

M: I believe so.

C: Good. And remember to continue to use the noncompliance chart I gave you last time we met and continue to chart Kevin's behavior over this coming week, so that when we meet next, we can look at this chart together, and we will have a good idea of how well the time out is working.

Kevin and his mom return approximately 1 week later to evaluate the effectiveness of the time out procedure and discuss any areas that may need elaboration. Now that Mom has had the opportunity to use the method at home in real situations with Kevin, complete with his reactions and her emotions, there will surely be some questions or areas that need fine-tuning. It is imperative that the professional counselor be available for this type of consultation, as all too often the reason time out procedures are not effective is because they are not implemented consistently or as intended. Below is a short excerpt from this session.

C: All right, this is what I call a trouble-shooting session so we can monitor changes in Kevin's behaviors and talk about how the time out has been going for you.

M: Well, I charted Kevin's behavior over the course of the last week and compared it to the week before. He has certainly improved and we had fewer problems, but not as much as . . . .

C: Not as much as you thought, or would like?

M: Well, yes. And maybe it will just be this way . . .

C: You believe the time out method should be working more than it is?

M: I thought that it would, yes. I also find it more difficult to do than I thought I would.

C: Okay. Well, what we know is that time out is very effective for reducing noncompliant behaviors like those that Kevin displays. What we also know is that when it is not as effective as it could be that it's usually simply a matter of tweaking a few things. So, let me hear more about any specific difficulties you've had implementing it. You said it's harder than you thought it would be?

M: Yes . . . well, first let me start with what I don't find difficult and then I can tell you the other.

C: Good idea. Yes, let me hear the parts that are going well for you first.

M: I remember you stressing that it should be very boring and not stimulating . . . and I feel I do a good job of making certain that there is a big difference between when he's in time out and when he's not. Umm, I mean, I make sure that as soon as he comes from time out and he complies with my original request, I make sure that I praise him immediately for his appropriate behavior, and I make certain that there is no positive reinforcement while he is in time out.

C: Okay, great. Sounds like you really are intentional about that.

M: I try. And I also feel like I've been able to stress that he is making a choice to enter time out and therefore is choosing to punish himself, so I don't feel badly about it.

C: Very important, yes. Good.

M: What I seem to have trouble with though, is not getting irritated while he's in time out and not following all of the rules.

C: So when Kevin doesn't sit still or quietly you find your emotions getting involved.

M: Yes. And then I feel like we end up in this power struggle while he's in time out.

C: What do you mean? Tell me more.

M: Well, say he won't keep his feet on the floor and quiet. I'll remind him to, and then he doesn't, and then I tell him I'm going to have to add another minute, and he still doesn't follow the rule, and then I say, "Okay, that's another minute you've added, Kevin, for not keeping your feet still," and then he begins to argue with me and whine. Then I get more irritated and add another minute, and then I feel like I've added too many too quickly and so I try to explain it to him and its just this cycle . . . I feel like time out lasts too long because of it and it feels like too much work.

C: Yes, I think I understand. Let me see . . . well, what I see as the biggest issue here is that as long as you are engaging Kevin, and emotionally at that, time out isn't nearly as boring as it should or could be. In fact, Kevin is being entertained quite nicely. Many parents actually have this same trouble when using contingent delay time out, so know that you are in good company with many parents. I know it is so difficult to do, but it is very important that you do your very best to keep your dialogue with him to a minimum. Could you and Kevin demonstrate for me what a typical dialogue has been like for you this week during time out? Kevin?

K: Okay. Can this be the time out chair that I'm in now?

C: Sure.

M: Okay. So he's in time out and it isn't long before he begins tapping his toes or squirming around, sometimes even closing his eyes on purpose.

C: Okay, Kevin, go ahead and do one of those things. (Kevin closes his eyes tightly with a grin on his face.)

M: Kevin, you should have your eyes open and on the wall. Kevin, open your eyes or I'll have to add a minute . . . .okay, Kevin, you have another minute in time out now because you didn't open your eyes.

C: Okay, I see. And then Kevin might begin to argue or whine, you say? And then you try to explain?

M: Yes.

C: All right, thank you, Kevin. (Turning back to Mom) Again, let me say that what seems to be happening is that you are engaging him in conversation in a way that is both stimulating to him and leads him to believe he has choices while in time out. Let me offer you a few options to remedy this and see which one you might be most comfortable with.

M: All right.

C: If you'll recall from last week, when I modeled adding 1 minute, I simply stated, "I said to keep your feet on the floor. One minute has been added, Kevin." Stating it very firmly and precisely like this does not encourage him to bargain or negotiate back. It also does not issue a warning, as I heard you do. There are no warnings while in time out. A warning is used before going to time out, but once he is there, he knows the seven rules and there is no need for a warning. If he breaks a rule, he gets an extra minute added to his time. If he breaks another rule, he gets yet another minute added.

M: Would it be okay if I talked even less than you just did and simply state that he has a minute added?

C: Why do you ask?

M: Well, because he probably already knows why the 1 minute was added because like you said, he knows what the rules are.

C: That's very true. And if he is confused about why, this can be discussed when he is released from time out. Well, because it is difficult for you to refrain from a full-blown conversation with Kevin while he is in time out, thus reducing its effectiveness, perhaps another suggestion will be helpful. One way to bypass any talking whatsoever while Kevin is in time

out, which could make a very big difference for you two, is to simply use an egg timer or some other timing device that Kevin can clearly see. When he breaks a time out rule, you simply, without saying a word, add 1 minute to the timer. He sees this and he knows what has happened and why. The other option is called a "finger method." All this means is that each time a rule is broken during time out, you simply, and again without saying a word, hold up a finger to let him know 1 minute has been added to his time. This way, there is no conversation, no explanation, and no warning while in time out.

M: Okay. I like the idea of just holding up one finger each time a minute is added.

C: I believe this will also help prevent any power struggles and will reduce your feelings of frustration. Why don't we role-play this one more time?

Kevin and his mom return in 2 weeks once again for the professional counselor to assess their progress and offer any additional assistance that may be needed.

C: It's been about 2 weeks since I've seen you last and we sent you home with the time out procedure, but this time having tweaked it a bit to make it easier on you, Mom, and more effective for Kevin. How did that go?

M: Kevin, you want to tell or do you want me to talk first?

K: I've been good!

M: He has been.

C: Tell me what good means Kevin.

K: I only went to time out two times!

C: In 2 weeks? You've only been in time out two times in the last 2 weeks? You're kidding me. You went twice in 2 weeks? Really?

M: It's incredible. It was incredible.

C: Tell me about it.

M: Well, the first thing is that it is no longer this emotional battle with us. I give a directive, and he has a choice to follow through with it or not. Once in time out, he follows the rules. If he does not, I hold up one finger to show him that I have added one minute because he has broken a rule. I'm not upset. He understands the procedure. And when his time is up, it's like everything is back to normal and he then complies with the original request. You can really tell that he wants to avoid being in time out now. It really is boring for him, and he prefers to just comply.

C: So it's kind of become this deterrent that we talked about?

M: Yes. The only two times we've used it, in both cases he was extremely tired and there was a lot going on. He was more irritable than anything, and he is more stubborn and defiant when he's irritable and tired. But you know, we used it and it worked.

C: So, Kevin, you would say that time out is something that you would not want to do? Tell me, specifically, what's not so good about it that you want to stay away from time out.

K: You have to sit still and then when it's over you still have to do whatever it was she asks you to do in the first place.

C: Kevin, do you feel proud of yourself for behaving so well these past 2 weeks?

K: It's been a lot more fun not staying in trouble so much.

M: Things have been running so much more smoothly, and it is just much more peaceful than before. I've got to say, too, that as a parent, it feels nice to feel in control.

USEFULNESS AND EVALUATION OF THE TIME OUT TECHNIQUE

Time out is a technique often recommended for use "when a student is so totally unable to cope with his present situation that the positive reinforcers which are normally effective are no longer working because of the student's emotional state" (Hayes, 1986, p. 458). This method has been used to reduce a variety of different behaviors including tantrums, alcoholic consumption, thumb sucking, and aggression. Time out has also been used with a number of different populations including children with mental retardation who had disruptive behaviors (Foxx & Shapiro, 1978), children in special education classrooms (Cuenin & Harris, 1986), adults with mental retardation who had undesirable behavior during meals (Spindler Barton, Guess, Garcia, & Baer, 1970), or were self-injurious and aggressive (Matson & Keyes, 1990), children with AD/HD (Reid, 1999), children who are noncompliant (Erford, 1999; Reitman & Drabman, 1999), and children who are violent and aggressive (Sherburne, Utley, McConnell, & Gannon, 1988).

There are a number of aspects that influence the efficacy of this technique. Many of the factors that contribute toward the success of this technique fall to the person implementing the time out procedures. In addition, Erford (1999) discerned that nearly all children dislike being bored and will go to great lengths to avoid this deterrent. Thus, the time out environment needs to be devoid of visual and auditory stimulation so that the child is not receiving any sort of positive reinforcement for being sent to time out (Erford, 1999).

There is a significant amount of empirical research that lends support to the effectiveness of time out for children with self-control issues. One researcher found that using time out as part of a treatment plan for students with emotional disturbance positively affected the students' behavior and work effort (Ruth, 1994). Barton, Brulle & Repp (1987) found time out effective in helping students with mental retardation to develop more self control. Another study found time out to be effective in reducing the amount of inappropriate, noncompliant, behavior of a 4-year-old child (Olmi, Sevier, & Nastasi, 1997). Time out has also been used effectively in reducing the amount of aggression between siblings (Olson & Roberts, 1987). Tingstrom (1990) investigated behaviors teachers found time out procedures useful toward and discovered that time out was more acceptable for severe problem behaviors. To increase the usefulness of time out, Erford (1999) suggested using it along with positive reinforcement to teach children desirable behaviors.

One of the major problems of the time out technique is that it is often misused (Betz, 1994). Betz suggested using time out for serious matters and as a last resort. Others who do not support time out criticized that "it is not an appropriate way to deal with misbehavior . . . it may create subsequent childhood problems that can affect a child's well-being and severely strain the parent-child relationship" (Haimann, 2005, p. 1). When using time out appears to be ineffective, the implementer should check to make sure the placement of the time out chair or space is not more interesting than the environment from which the child was removed. If it is, some children may act out to get sent to time out (Bacon, 1990).

Time out is often unsuccessful for low-functioning children with Autistic Disorder, who, by definition, do not mind reduced social contact. Factors that decrease the likelihood that time out will be effective include overusing it for every rule broken, postponing the time out, not following through, and yelling at the child. It is important for those implementing time out to be realistic and remember that this technique is not a cure-all; it is most effective when it is not used frequently (Spencer, 2000); time out is meant to serve as a deterrent to future misbehavior.

When using time out, it is important for one to know that there could be legal and ethical implications. Yell (1994, p. 295) provided the following guidelines for use by those in schools who choose to employ this technique: be aware of local or state policies regarding time out; have written procedures on the use of time out; obtain permission prior to using time out; the IEP team should be involved in making decisions concerning the behavior reduction procedures, such as time out, with children in special education services; time out must serve a legitimate educational function; time out must be used in a reasonable manner; and when using time out, keep thorough records.

CHAPTER 28

Response Cost

ORIGINS OF THE RESPONSE COST TECHNIQUE

Response cost is a method of operant conditioning based upon punishment principles that involves removing a positive stimulus in order to decrease a specific behavior (Huitt & Hummel, 1997). Response cost, also called cost contingency, is the basis for fines, traffic tickets, and yardage penalties in football (Walker, Colvin, & Ramsey, 1995). Response cost often takes the form of a point or token system where the individual loses points or tokens for performing some undesired behavior. Response cost may be externally or internally managed (Salend & Allen, 1985). In externally managed programs, teachers, parents, or some other trained individual is responsible for removing the positive stimulus. In self-managed programs, the individual is responsible for removing the stimulus.

Response cost can be extremely effective in reducing unwanted behaviors, especially when used in combination with praise, a point (token) system, and time out as a back up procedure (Walker et al., 1995). Response cost can be used at home in the classroom, or on the playground, and is easy to implement (Keeney, Fisher, Adelinis, & Wilder, 2000). Response cost can be monitored by a single person and requires little extra time or money (Proctor & Morgan, 1991).

HOW TO IMPLEMENT THE RESPONSE COST TECHNIQUE

Response cost is typically used with school-aged students. Before implementing response cost, three important steps must be completed (Help for Families, 2005a, 2005b). First, identify the specific behaviors that will be targeted and try to focus only on one or two behaviors at a time. Next, decide what the penalty or cost will be for each of the above mentioned behaviors. If possible, costs should be natural or logical consequences, although tokens are frequently used to represent chances or reminders. Sometimes clients may be able to help determine the costs. Finally, inform the client of the costs before beginning the program. Reminder lists or behavior contracts may be used.

There are many ways to construct a response cost program. The important component is that the individual is losing a specified positive stimulus for performing the behavior targeted for extinction. To begin, a baseline count of the target behavior should be observed. The professional counselor should then decide whether the individual will start with a set number of points at the beginning of the day, whether tokens must be earned through a positive reinforcement procedure, or whether the system will rely on some other form of stimulus removal, such as minutes taken off recess time. Next, implement the response cost program by removing the stimulus, whatever it may be, every time the individual performs the target behavior. Finally, a reward should be built in at the end of the time period, day, or week if the program is based on a point or token system. Importantly, if the client has any tokens left at the end of the time period the reward is given. If all of the tokens have been removed, the reward is not given.

Several guidelines will help make the response cost program more effective (Walker et al., 1995). Response cost systems should be linked to a reinforcement system in order to strengthen desired behaviors. The individual's positive behavior should be praised frequently. Also, the response cost must be employed immediately after the target behavior occurs, every time it occurs. Individuals should not be able to accumulate negative points, and the ratio of points earned to those lost should be controlled.

The number of remaining tokens should be monitored. After 3 to 5 consecutive days of the client receiving the reward, the criterion can be lowered. For example, if 15 tokens per day comprise the beginning level, and the client has five left on day 1, seven on day 2, and eight on day 3, the professional counselor should begin the next day by presenting the client with only six or seven tokens. And the process repeats in this manner until only one token remains. This represents a modified fading procedure and serves as an outcome measure to determine the effectiveness of the response cost procedure. Once the client goes 1 week without losing the sole token (i.e., no display of the inappropriate target behavior), the system may end.

EXAMPLE OF THE RESPONSE COST TECHNIQUE

Nine-year-old Samantha has already made much improvement in her behavior with the help of her parents and professional counselor. Thus far, Samantha's mom and dad have incorporated a strong and consistent system of positive reinforcement through praise and rewards for behaviors such as making up the bed, completing homework, and displaying good table manners. They have also successfully implemented the use of contingent delay time out as a punishment technique for Samantha's inappropriate behaviors, usually related to refusal to follow Mom or Dad's directives and rules. During the session below, Samantha and her parents discuss a behavior that does not seem as easily suited to either of the behavior modification plans already in place.

Counselor (C): So when you called to set up the appointment, Mom, you said there was a specific behavior that Samantha was displaying that you really wanted to work on with her, but that didn't really fit well with time out or positive reinforcement?

Mom (M): Yes. And I just knew you'd have a suggestion for us. I hope you do.

C: I bet we can come up with something helpful if we put our heads together!

M: I was hoping you would say that! So, Samantha has done really well. I just want to start with that. But there is this little issue of . . . whining . . . that's really hard to overlook.

C: Ahh . . . the whining . . . yes, whining is hard to overlook. And we shouldn't necessarily overlook it. Whining doesn't go over well in life outside of the home, so I agree that it is important to attend to or we wouldn't be doing Samantha here any favors . . . .

Samantha (S): And the screaming.

M: You don't really scream like you whine. You're not a real screamer, screamer.

S: (In a whining voice) But I want to work on the screaming . . . .

M: See what I mean?

C: I do, I do. Yep, that's whining. Dad? What about you? Is the whining a difficulty that you'd like to have her work on?

S: Yeah, ask Dad.

C: Dad?

Dad (D):   I would say whining or talking back.

C: Okay. Now we can treat those as one, but it's often times better if we, or better to . . .

M: Separate.

C: Separate them, yes. It's probably best to just start simple, work on one behavior at a time, the one you're most interested in. So, Mom, Dad . . . the whining or the talking back?

D: Is the whining really more of a response to requests or is it whining in general? I mean I'm trying to figure it out.

M: To requests. She whines when we make requests, yeah.

D: It's a reaction to requests. So that makes it a form of talking back, right?

C: Now you can choose to specify only when she's given a directive or a request is made of her. You can say that that is specifically what we will work on and that is the definition of the behavior we want to eliminate. But, what that does is it limits you to only use this new behavior modification plan when she whines in response to a request, making all other whining fair game . . . and I don't know that you want that. It might be more effective and less confusing for us to include whining in general, any whining, whining that is in response to a request or any other form of whining. What do you think?

M: Why specify it to just whining about requests? As soon as she whines for some other reason, we'll wish we had defined it more globally.

C: Dad? Don't feel pressured to agree. Give us your thoughts on this.

D: I'm sorting it out in my mind and trying to think back on specific examples with Samantha . . . it seems that all talking back is whining, but not all whining is talking back, so, yeah, I'm on board. Whining in general is the way to go.

C: Great! Now, the next very important thing we must do is to define what we mean by whining.

Of course, it seems obvious in some ways, but it is important to specify it out loud, because what we don't want is for you, Mom, to have one definition of whining in your mind and Dad to have another image and Samantha to have yet another. We want everyone to be on the same page with their idea of what constitutes whining.

M: Right.

C: So what we'll do right now is just have Mom give us an example of what Samantha sounds like whenever she whines. Now pay close attention to this everyone. All right, let's hear it Mom.

M: Okay. I might say, "Samantha, we're all going on a trip" . . . just for an example. "You're going to go with us, we're going to take a trip." And she would immediately start with, "I don't wanna go, I'm not gonna go, I don't wanna, I don't want you to take meeeeee!" Her facial expressions change, her voice changes, even the way she is standing or sitting . . . it's an all-out production.

D: (Laughing) You did pretty good there. You even got the little high-pitch thing right.

C: That really was pretty good, Mom. And Dad, based on your comment, I assume that was a good example of how you define the whining also?

D: Definitely.

C: Okay, then, Samantha? I'd like you to demonstrate responding to Mom's request to go on a trip in a way that defines whining for you. I want to hear you whining, Samantha.

S: That's easy. "*Mom!!!!* But, but, but, I don't wanna go on a trip . . . I don't like trips . . . (Pokes lip out, slumps over, even fakes a crying sound)

C: Wow. Mom was right on the facial expressions and body language changing too. (Mom is shaking her head in agreement.) Okay. Now then, Samantha, I would like to hear you give me an example of a response to your mom, still protesting the trip, but without whining.

S: I don't know how to do that.

C: Umm, okay, well, how about pretend you are me. Pretend you are me when you respond to Mom saying you are all going on a trip. If you were all grown-up, how might you sound?

S: (Giggles. Sits straight up in her chair and places her hands in her lap. Giggles again. Clears throat.) "I prefer for you to take the trip without me. I prefer not to go."

D: Cute, Samantha. Now could you do that all the time?

C: That tells me, Samantha, that you do have a clear idea of what whining is and what whining is not . . . and that you know how to respond to Mom and Dad's requests without whining after all.

S: Oops.

C: Okay, so it seems we all agree that whining involves a pleading, pouting type of dialogue with a different tone of voice than regular conversation. The words also get drawn out when whining. Everybody have a clear definition of what is and is not whining?

M: You know, Samantha, if you would actually respond like you did just now to our requests that you don't like, we might actually talk about it.

D: Or if you had an alternative suggestion, and you approached it in a less childish way, instead of whining about it . . .

S: (Takes a deep breath, groans, and bounces the back of her head against the back of her chair) I am, I'm not, I will, I won't, I do, I don't . . .

C: Okay, Samantha, are you understanding this? You just demonstrated that you do understand when you were able to respond to Mom in a responsible and respectful way and then the other way with the little whining, bratty, immature way.

S: (Making whining noises)

C: Exactly. You made my point. Okay? So what we're trying to do is, to get you from being

disrespectful and whiny to being more respectful and mature.

The professional counselor has now assisted Samantha's parents in selecting one specific behavior to target. They have also worked together to define this behavior in a very specific fashion that everyone agrees upon.

C: We are all in agreement that whining is the focus and we all agree on what whining is and is not. The method I want to talk to you about today, that I believe will be very appropriate for eliminating the whining, is response cost, and response cost is simply the opposite of positive reinforcement. As you know, positive reinforcement is giving a positive stimulus every time you get a specific good or appropriate behavior from Samantha. Now, the good news is I am going to provide you with the information and tools you will need to begin using the response cost method. However, although you will leave here today with a plan to implement, before beginning, you will first need to document her episodes of whining for a few days. This is very important for reasons I will explain in a few moments.

M: You mean document her whining like we have when we charted other behavior in the past?

C: I mean exactly that. You will want to mainly get a frequency count of how many episodes of whining there are a day and at what times they are occurring.

M: Okay, okay. Got it.

C: All right. So, umm, let's see . . . where to start. Okay, so response cost is akin to the teacher who on the first day of class tells her new students, "You all start out with an A+ in my class. Now you have to work to keep it."

S: I like that teacher!

C: Exactly. This is very motivating for students. It makes them feel good to have such a positive start, and this motivates them to work extra hard to keep that average as high as possible.

M: So I start Samantha with an A+?

C: Well, not exactly. But it's a similar idea. Let's say after you keep a tally of Samantha's whining episodes for a couple of days, you discover that on average, she has about . . . well, off the top of your head, Mom and Dad, how many episodes would you say she has a day?

D: 20!

S: Do not!

M: Around three to five.

D: Yeah, okay, probably more like around five. It just seems like more.

C: Okay, so we'll know for sure after you write it down for a few days, but let's just assume for now that it is around three to five. Okay then. The response cost system means that instead of giving a positive for a positive, or giving a negative for a negative, you take away a positive for every time there is a negative. Now the negative is going to be the whining. Every time there is a whining episode, a positive will be taken away. Now, just for now, let's call the positive a marker. We'll decide what that will be specifically in a moment. But for now, the markers are the positive that you will be taking away each time Samantha whines. Make sense so far?

M: I'm with you.

C: Dad?

D: I'm good.

C: Okay. Now the reason determining the average number of whining episodes is important prior to implementing response cost is because you sort of want to rig the system in favor of the child in the beginning so that Samantha has a good chance of being successful. You also do not want to have more negative occurrences than you have markers or a child will have no incentive to refrain from the negative behavior and will give up . . . perhaps even get worse. Makes sense, right? Oh, and one other thing . . . you do not want to have too many markers left over each day either or the feeling of really

having to work hard to earn that reward will lessen and she may not try as hard. I mean, if it's too easy to get, then what's the big deal, right? You want there to be a good fit between markers and occurrences throughout the process.

M: Throughout the process?

C: Yes, you'll actually decrease the number of markers she begins with each day as her behavior improves. So if she goes, oh, say, 3 to 5 days without losing all her markers, you'll want to decrease the number of markers accordingly.

M: Oh . . . okay.

C: Okay, so assuming Samantha has an average of three to five episodes of whining a day, you'll want to begin your first day of response cost with, oh, say six or seven markers. That morning, remind Samantha that she has six or seven markers, and that the fewer whining episodes she has throughout the day, the more markers she'll get to keep for herself at the end of the evening. So her goal, her incentive for the day, is to retain as many markers as possible. So she starts with this clean slate each morning, but each time she whines, she loses a marker . . . you simply remove one of the markers.

M: And we'll decide what those are in a bit?

C: Yep. Or now if you'd like. We can . . .

M: I've actually been thinking about it and already have an idea. But first, could you give us a few examples of what others usually use as markers?

C: Certainly. Markers can themselves be rewards, or they can stand for a reward. What I mean is, you can use quarters for example. And you might start the day off with, what did we say? Oh, yes, six or seven . . . let's just say six to make the point. And say Samantha had four episodes of whining that day, so that by the end of the day, she has two quarters left over. The quarters themselves are the prize or reward, and the incentive is to whine less to keep more quarters. Some parents use a snack or candy item, like jelly beans or sticks of gum. Either way, in these examples, the marker is, in and of itself, a prize. The other way you can go about it is to use markers that are representative of some other prize . . . like a token economy. You could use pennies, or tokens, or popsicle sticks . . . and these items don't hold much value to Samantha by themselves, but we decide what X number of tokens means, and we build that reward into the system. Am I making sense?

D: It always sounds a little complicated at first, and then it seems perfectly sensible . . .

M: It's making sense to me.

C: All right, so, Mom, you said you had an idea for a marker?

M: Yes. I was thinking about stickers.

C: Oh, yes, stickers could make very appropriate markers. It's important that markers are both safe to use and impossible for Samantha to reproduce or counterfeit, and I believe stickers meet both of these standards!

M: Well, Samantha does keep a sticker collection, so we could use them as the rewards themselves, like in the first example you gave. Only, they would need to be the really nice stickers that she enjoys collecting, not just stars or smiley face stickers.

C: All right.

M: Or, they could just be the little star stickers and we could use them as tokens for a reward . . . (Pauses and is thinking) . . . Samantha, do you have a preference?

S: Sometimes you don't get the stickers I like.

M: That's true. I can just hear it now . . . her whining that the stickers I have for the reward are not the good ones. Yes, let's use simple stickers as tokens. I could even set up a chart for her to put them on at the end of each day and she can trade that sheet in for a reward when she has enough. Isn't that how it works?

C: Exactly. So let's talk about the reward we want to build in.

D: I prefer not having to buy something every time she turns in a full sticker sheet.

M: I agree.

C: What about activities or special privileges?

M: Yes, that could work! We could make a list to choose from . . . like maybe a picnic in the park, or a slumber party, or a popcorn and movie rental of your choice . . . what do you think Samantha?

S: (Excitedly) Yeah! And a spa night!

C: What's a spa night?

S: It's when me and Mom do our toe nails and finger nails, and we give each other facials and stuff. It's my favorite!

C: These all sound wonderful, and Samantha looks motivated to stop whining already . . . and that is the most important point . . . that the positive reinforcer that is being taken away each time she whines is something she values and wants to work hard to keep. So you'll make an official activity list, and each time Samantha collects a certain amount of stickers on her sticker sheet, she can trade it in for an activity.

M: I think we're set!

C: One more important component of response cost that I want us to cover is the specifics of taking away the token or sticker. Earlier I said to remind Samantha each morning, "Samantha, remember you start today with five new stickers, and each time you whine, you lose a sticker. I want you to work very hard today to keep as many of them as you can!" And so whenever you hear her voice do the whining thing, you would immediately remove a sticker and say, "Samantha, you just violated the whining rule. You just lost one of your stickers. You have four left," and you take a sticker off of the shelf and place it back with your supply. Remember to keep this brief, without emotion, and without a discussion. Continue to chart her whining episodes and how many stickers she has left over each day, and remember that as she becomes successful in keeping more and more stickers, the trick then is to calibrate the system back down. So then the next time she only gets four of them, and the next time she only gets three of them, until eventually she only gets one sticker a day, which means she only has one shot at the misbehavior. Once you have an entire week without losing that one and only sticker each day, meaning no whining episodes have occurred for an entire week, the system can end. Then you can use it with another behavior if you'd like, and you would start from the beginning with first charting and defining the behavior specifically. Remember though to rig it for success in the beginning. A lot of people make the mistake with behavior modification of making the system so difficult that from the very beginning the child doesn't experience the success, he never gets the rewards, so he thinks that it's hopeless. This child is thinking, "Why should I even try because I'm never going to get it anyway?" So, if you think even five episodes or less of whining is going to be impossible for her, then just do five times in the morning, between the time that she gets up and the time that she has lunch and if she's good there then you have another five in the afternoon. And then the next day just make it four until eventually she's able to be successful without even having to have the system, because the goal of any behavior modification is to not need it. We all want our children to be successful every day with just the minimum amount of supervision. We want them to see that they can behave appropriately without intervention, and to eventually have that personal responsibility for themselves. That's the goal.

USEFULNESS AND EVALUATION OF THE RESPONSE COST TECHNIQUE

Response cost has been used successfully to manage classroom behavior. Proctor and Morgan (1991) studied the use of a response cost raffle on the disruptive behavior of adolescent students. Students were given five tickets at the beginning of class, and the students lost tickets for performing disruptive behaviors. All tickets remaining at the end of class were placed in a raffle for a prize. This procedure was effective in increasing appropriate behaviors and decreasing disruptive behaviors. Likewise, Salend and Allen (1985) found that externally managed and self-managed response cost systems were equally effective in reducing the inappropriate classroom behavior of learning disabled students. Both response cost programs greatly reduced the number of out of seat behaviors and inappropriate verbalizations from the students.

Response cost has also been used with children with hyperactive and antisocial behaviors. Carlson, Mann, and Alexander (2000) tested the effectiveness of rewards and response cost on the arithmetic performance of children with AD/HD. Although they found that children with AD/HD completed fewer problems correctly than control children regardless of whether they were in the reward, response cost, or control condition, they also observed that response cost was more effective than reward in improving the performance of children with AD/HD. In the same way, Walker et al. (1995) compared the effectiveness of praise, token reinforcement, and response cost in reducing aggression among elementary school-aged antisocial boys. Neither praise alone nor praise combined with token reinforcement was able to control negative-aggressive behavior or increase positive social interactions among these boys. However, once negative-aggressive behavior was countered with a response cost procedure, the boys' social interactive behavior began to increase substantially.

Finally, response cost has been used with persons with mental retardation. Keeney et al. (2000) studied the effects of a response cost procedure on the aggressive outbursts of a woman with mental retardation, comparing noncontingent reinforcement, removal of attention, and removal of music against baseline behaviors. They found that the response cost removal of music was extremely effective in reducing the destructive behavior.

CHAPTER 29

Overcorrection

ORIGINS OF THE OVERCORRECTION TECHNIQUE

Overcorrection was originally developed by Foxx and Azrin in the early 1970s as a technique to eliminate maladaptive behaviors while also re-educating the individual (Luiselli, 1980), and so much of the classic literature on the technique is quite old. Overcorrection involves two components: restitution and positive practice. Restitution requires the individual to restore the situation that was disrupted to the same or an even better condition than existed previously, and positive practice entails repeated practice of an appropriate behavior for that same situation (Clements & Dewey, 1979). For example, if a child slams a door, the parent may be encouraged to have the child apologize and then practice silently opening and closing the door while entering and exiting ten times, or for 5 minutes. Such repeated positive practice has the effect of making the punishment "worse than the crime," and leads frequently to "one-trial learning," in which the child remembers to never slam the door again!

Overcorrection is a form of punishment, but does not follow a single theory, rather incorporating aspects of many different techniques including feedback, time out, compliance training, extinction, and punishment (Clements & Dewey, 1979). However, unlike other forms of punishment, overcorrection is not arbitrary; instead, it teaches individuals to take responsibility for their actions and recognize the impact their actions have on others (Luiselli, 1980). Restitution is designed to teach natural consequences of misbehavior, and positive practice teaches appropriate behavior, thus acting as a preventative measure (Matson, Horne, Ollendick, & Ollendick, 1979).

HOW TO IMPLEMENT THE OVERCORRECTION TECHNIQUE

Before using overcorrection, positive reinforcement methods should be tried in an attempt to shape the individual's behavior (Luiselli, 1980). However, if positive reinforcement is unsuccessful, overcorrection may be implemented. There are four steps to using overcorrection. First, the professional counselor must identify the target behavior as well as the alternate behavior to be taught through positive practice. When the target behavior is performed, the professional counselor should immediately tell the individual that the behavior is inappropriate and instruct him to stop (Smith & Misra, 1992). Then the professional counselor should verbally guide the individual through the overcorrection procedure, instructing him to complete restitution and then to undergo positive practice for a set time or number of repetitions. If necessary, the professional counselor may manually guide the individual through the overcorrection procedure using the minimum force necessary (Luiselli). Finally the individual is allowed to return to his previous activity.

Foxx and Azrin (1972) made several recommendations for the effective use of overcorrection. Restitution should be directly related to the misbehavior. In addition, restitution should be performed immediately after the misbehavior in order to achieve two outcomes. First, the misbehavior should eventually reach extinction since the individual will have no time to enjoy the effects of the misbehavior. And second, future acts of misbehavior should be discouraged because immediate negative consequences are more effective than nonimmediate consequences. Also, restitution should be extended in duration. Finally, the individual should be actively involved in performing restitution and should not pause during the restitution process.

However, Foxx and Azrin's recommendations are not set in stone as later research suggested that successful overcorrection results may be achieved without following some of their recommendations. Overcorrection has been accomplished even when the overcorrection behaviors are unrelated to the target misbehavior (Luiselli, 1980). Likewise, similar results can be achieved with immediate and delayed positive practice overcorrection. In addition, overcorrection has been successful in short, intermediate, and long durations.

VARIATIONS OF THE OVERCORRECTION TECHNIQUE

Although most overcorrection procedures involved both restitution and positive practice, there has been some research to suggest that these two procedures are effective when used alone, and it may not be necessary to use both (Matson et al., 1979). In a study of school-aged children, Matson et al. found that restitution reduced target behavior by 89% and positive practice reduced these behaviors by 84%, suggesting that the two procedures are equally effective in treating childhood classroom misbehaviors. Indeed, some situations may involve a simple apology, and one can never really insure that an apology is heartfelt

restitution leading to positive behavior change. In such instances the repeated positive practice becomes the active intervention.

EXAMPLE OF THE OVERCORRECTION TECHNIQUE

Ken is an 8-year-old boy consistently displaying moderate oppositional behavior toward his parents. This session was attended by Ken, his mother, and his father with the goal of decreasing noncompliant episodes and increasing his compliance with parental requests. One request Ken consistently chooses not to comply with is to clean up after himself: his coat, shoes, clothing, school books, dishes, etc. As his father stated at the outset of counseling, "Ken has taken the 'stop, drop, and roll' technique to heart—he *never* cleans up after himself!" Note also that this example uses positive practice without restitution.

Counselor (C):   This procedure is called overcorrection, which is the one that will help to get him to stop leaving his towel lying on the floor, his coat, shoes and everything else as he comes into the house, strips down, and goes on his merry way . . . Sometimes we call it positive practice because it is a punishment procedure, and positive practice sounds so much nicer than talking about punishment . . . Overcorrection has him do what he should have done the first time, but repeating it a great number of times so that in the future, he realizes before it happens that he was punished for not just doing it the first time. So basically I use, under most circumstances, the 10 practice rule. If he comes in and drops his coat, then what he needs to do is go over, pick up his coat, put it on the hanger, and hang it in the closet. That's one practice. Then he takes it out, throws it on the floor, and starts over. You have him do that 10 times. Okay? So what can we do in here today to practice? Of course you've got your shoes with you, and that has been a problem in the past . . . (Parents nod yes, Ken nods no) . . . So, Ken, take your shoes off . . .

Ken (K): My socks, too.

C: Those are cute little socks.

K: They're too small.

C: Leave the socks on. All right, now where are you supposed to put your shoes whenever you come into the house?

K: In the shoe basket, which I always do. (Ken gives a big smile and a chuckle. Mother and Father both grunt and roll their eyes.)

C: Okay, so you're pretty good about your shoes, but let's pretend that you're not (everyone laughs) so that Mom and Dad can practice the overcorrection procedure. So you're supposed to come in the house, take your shoes off, and put them under . . .

K: The shoe thing. In the basket.

C: The little shoe basket. Now let's pretend that you just came home and you tossed your shoes on to the side. (Ken does this with some flair.) Mom, you role-play with Ken about what it is that he should do.

Mom (M): Ken, you didn't put your shoes away where they belong the first time so you have to practice doing it the right way 10 times. So please go put your shoes back where they belong 10 times.

C: Okay. Now you have to pick them up and put them back on your feet . . . (Ken does this as the counselor directs his actions.) . . . tie them . . . take them back off . . . and put them in the basket. That's one.

M: Okay. Let's do the second practice—put them back on.

K: 10 times??!!!

M: Yeah.

K: Arrghhhh!! (Ken begins again.)

C: Yep, practicing is hard; makes you realize that it is just easier to do it right the first time. (To parents) As we've already discussed, that's what a deterrent is.

M: (Mom encourages) That's a good one, Ken.

C: Now I usually have them count while they're doing it. Now, how many times is that?

K: Five.

M: No, it's two.

K: Okay, two. (Ken continues to do 10 practices.)

C: Very good. Now you can see how this can be kind of annoying to a young lad . . .

M: (Ken finishes his final practice.) OK, that's 10.

K: That was hard—and boring!

Father (F): It can't be that hard, Ken. I've seen you play outside a lot harder than that.

C: Beautiful, okay. Now, Ken, how does that make you feel whenever you have to do that 10 times?

K: Tired.

C: Is it something you would like to repeat?

K: No way!!

C: Now this can be used with just about any kind of annoying behavior that he does that involves an action or behavior that he did not perform correctly, but could and should; particularly one that involves responsible behavior, any kind of clothing, you know if he leaves a towel on the floor, dropping the coat, slamming the door. It has a very powerful effect on kids, sometimes even what we call one-trial learning; that is, he does it the first time and he remembers from then on whenever he comes into the house where his shoes are supposed to go.

F: If you want some exercise, you can drop your clothes on the floor, then pick them up and put your clothes down the laundry chute and fetch them 10 times. That would be a real exercise.

K: (Ken offers his patented "death stare.")

USEFULNESS AND EVALUATION OF THE OVERCORRECTION TECHNIQUE

Overcorrection began as a procedure used to help persons with mental retardation reduce property destruction, physical attacks, and self-stimulating behaviors, as well as to teach toileting and correct eating behaviors (Axelrod, Brantner, & Meddock, 1978). There is extensive research attesting to the success of overcorrection procedures with persons with mental retardation. For instance, Foxx and Azrin (1972) found that restitution training was effective in eliminating disruptive-aggressive behaviors, such as throwing objects, attacking others, and screaming fits. The results were immediate and endured over several months. Likewise, Azrin and Wesolowski (1974) found that overcorrection reduced thefts among institutionalized persons with mental retardation by 90% in 3 days.

However, overcorrection has since been used with a variety of populations ranging from non-handicapped to the severely handicapped, including persons with schizophrenia (Axelrod et al., 1978). Overcorrection has been used to treat nervous habits and out of seat behaviors. Likewise it has

been used by teachers as a classroom management technique (Smith & Misra, 1992). Overcorrection is a procedure that can easily be used by those without formal counseling training.

Unfortunately, overcorrection has several drawbacks. Overcorrection requires considerable time on the part of both the professional counselor and the client (Clements & Dewey, 1979; Smith & Misra, 1992). Finally, the results of overcorrection do not tend to generalize to other behaviors in the individual or to other individuals observing the procedure (Luiselli, 1980). Instead the results tend to be specific to the behaviors treated, the setting in which they were treated, and the person who experienced the treatment. Therefore, some generalization can be encouraged by varying the setting in which the treatment occurs and person who administers the treatment.

Techniques Based Upon Cognitive-Behavioral Approaches

As discussed in Section 5, cognitive therapy emerged in reaction to behavioral approaches that minimized or even denied the importance of thoughts in promoting changes within counseling. Over the past several decades, the passions that created both the behavioral and cognitive approaches to counseling have abated and more and more counselors have recognized that, although thoughts alone and behaviors alone can lead to helpful changes, the integration of these two approaches may be even more effective. Thus, the integrated practice of cognitive-behavior approaches to counseling emerged. Pioneers such as Albert Ellis, William Glasser, and Donald Meichenbaum all developed theories of counseling based upon cognitive-behavior approaches. An additional force behind the emergence of cognitive-behavioral approaches was the prominence of managed care programs, which promoted cognitive-behavioral therapy as a time- and cost-effective treatment.

The first two chapters within this final section involve rational-emotive behavior therapy (REBT) and bibliotherapy. True enough, Albert Ellis would roll in his grave if he knew his REBT was referred to as a technique. It is not a technique, but it is a process that can be taught and implemented using a step-by-step procedure. REBT is a well-known cognitive-behavior therapy that helps clients alter distorted thinking, ordinarily accomplished using rational-emotive imagery, an imagery-based procedure discussed below. Bibliotherapy is a technique claimed by several theoretical approaches, but is included in this section on cognitive-behavioral approaches because of its cognitive component. Bibliotherapy is a literacy-based approach to counseling in which the counselor and/or client reads a story or passage and engages in discussion about the book or story's content, meaning, and implications for the client.

Research has shown a number of cognitive-behavioral techniques are particularly effective in reducing stress and addressing simple phobias. As discussed in Section 5 (Techniques Based Upon Cognitive Approaches), several of these techniques are based on Wolpe's principle of reciprocal inhibition; e.g., a client cannot breathe quickly and slowly at the same time or have a muscle group that is tense and relaxed at the same time. Often these techniques are used in concert to maximize effectiveness. For example, clients can be taught the techniques of self-talk, visual or guided imagery, deep breathing, and progressive muscle relaxation training in sequence, and encouraged to use them simultaneously as homework in order to reduce stress by blocking out negative self-talk, negative visualizations, shallow breathing, and muscle tension. Self-talk and visual or guided imagery were covered in Section 5. Deep breathing and progressive muscle relaxation training (PMRT) are both cognitive and physiologically based interventions that have been shown to be very effective in reducing stress and anxiety after the stressor has occurred.

These four techniques (i.e., self-talk, visual imagery, deep breathing, and PMRT) can also be taught to clients preparing for systematic desensitization, a very effective counseling technique for addressing simple phobias. Systematic desensitization, also based upon reciprocal inhibition, incorporates the subjective units of distress scale (SUDS; a modified scaling technique) and a fear hierarchy into a procedure that allows clients to experience a fear-producing event during a relaxed state. Doing so breaks the classically conditioned phobic cycle. The final technique covered in this section is stress inoculation training. Stress inoculation training, originally developed by Donald Meichenbaum, helps clients systematically process and resolve cognitively-based stressors.

MULTICULTURAL CONSIDERATIONS

The multicultural considerations for counselors using techniques based on a cognitive-behavioral approach are in many ways similar to the multicultural considerations for the cognitive and behavioral approaches addressed earlier. Cognitive-behavioral approaches allow clients and counselors to collaboratively modify beliefs, cognitions, and actions while still stressing the importance of the therapeutic relationship. An approach like REBT does not question cultural values or practices; instead, it challenges the inflexible application of the "shoulds" and "musts"

that stem from a client's views of cultural rules. These approaches allow clients to decide whether to adhere to, give up, or modify the perceived rules, giving clients more freedom and flexibility related to their own thoughts, feelings, and behaviors.

Professional counselors must be careful not to challenge client beliefs before understanding the cultural context within which those beliefs developed because many clients hesitate or resist questioning their own basic cultural values. For example, some Arab American clients adhere to very strict customs and beliefs related to religion, family, and child-rearing. Disputing or even questioning motives or behaviors related to these customs could create additional dilemmas for these clients.

The cognitive-behavioral approach is quite directive, and the counselor is frequently perceived to be an expert by the client. Clients from some cultures (e.g., Middle Eastern, Hispanic, Asian) may be very comfortable with the expert perception, while others (e.g., men) may be less comfortable. It is essential that counselors not facilitate a dependency relationship with clients, a possibility when clients perceive the counselor as an expert with all of the answers. Ordinarily, clients from diverse racial, religious, and ethnic backgrounds appreciate the straight-forward, even no-nonsense cognitive-behavioral approach because it focuses on the client's thinking and subsequent behavior, rather than a person's nature, sociocultural background, or cultural beliefs.

Finally, techniques such as bibliotherapy may be particularly accepted by cultures with storytelling traditions. For example, Native Americans have a very strong oral storytelling tradition and *cuento* therapy was designed for use with Latinos/as and uses historical and cultural stories to underscore important lessons to help ground clients in an understanding and adapt to life situations.

CHAPTER | **30**

Rational-Emotive
Behavior Therapy (REBT)

ORIGINS OF THE REBT TECHNIQUE

Rational-emotive behavior therapy (REBT) was created by Albert Ellis in 1955 after he determined that Rogerian therapy and psychoanalysis were ineffective methods of treatment because they failed to focus on a client's current thoughts and beliefs. REBT has undergone several transformations, from rational therapy to rational emotive therapy to its current name, REBT, in an attempt to encompass thinking, feeling, and behaving (Epstein, 2001). When Ellis changed the name to REBT, his actions pointed out that "although thoughts are emphasized, emotions, behaviors, and thoughts are intertwined and inseparable" (Seligman, 2001, p. 360). In REBT, emotions are important; however, a person's cognitions are the source of psychological issues. The professional counselor needs to help the client understand that feelings are not caused by events, other people, or the past, but by the thoughts the person has developed surrounding the situation (Walen, DiGuiseppe, & Dryden, 1992).

HOW TO IMPLEMENT THE REBT TECHNIQUE

What follows is a somewhat simplified or deconstructed version of REBT. In REBT, the professional counselor takes a directive approach in helping the client, and treatment is brief (Seligman, 2001). The professional counselor needs to remain somewhat detached from the client in order to have an objective view of the client's irrational beliefs. In this approach, the therapeutic alliance is desirable but not a necessary aspect of treatment. There are three goals of REBT: (a) to help clients gain insight into their self-talk, (b) to help clients assess their thoughts, feelings, and behaviors, and (c) to train clients in the principles of REBT so that they will function more effectively in the future without the aid of a professional counselor (Ellis & Wilde, 2002).

A core concept of Ellis' REBT is the ABCDE model. The activating event (A) is the situation that triggers a client's beliefs; it can be an event that happened or is inferred, is external or internal, or may refer to the past, present, or future (Dryden, 1999). It is important for the professional counselor to understand what actually happened during the event as well as the client's perceptions of what happened. The professional counselor needs to help the client give the right amount of details about A; some clients will want to give more details than necessary and others will be too vague. If the client describes many As, the professional counselor needs to help the client choose one upon which to begin working.

169

According to REBT, there are two types of beliefs (B), rational and irrational (Hackney & Cormier, 2005). A person's beliefs affect both thoughts and actions (Dryden, 1995). Rational beliefs are realistic and can be supported by evidence (Hackney & Cormier, 2005). They are flexible, logical, and help the client reach goals (Dryden, 1999). Irrational beliefs are not realistic and are often based on "absolutistic musts" (Ellis, 1999). They are rigid, illogical, and do not help the client reach goals (Dryden, 1999). To identify a client's irrational belief system, a professional counselor needs to examine the client's shoulds and musts, awfulizings, can't-stand-its, feelings of worthlessness, and overgeneralizations (Ellis, 1996). Usually, a client's irrational beliefs will be related to self-denigration or a blaming/condemning of others' intolerance of frustration. Typically, irrational beliefs fall under one of the following 11 statements (Hackney & Cormier, 2005, p. 82):

1. I believe I must be loved or approved of by virtually everyone with whom I come in contact.
2. I believe I should be perfectly competent, adequate, and achieving to be considered worthwhile.
3. Some people are bad, wicked, and villainous, and therefore should be blamed and punished.
4. It is a terrible catastrophe when things are not as I would want them to be.
5. Unhappiness is caused by circumstances that are out of my control.
6. Dangerous or fearsome things are sources of great concern and their possibility for harm should be a constant concern for me.
7. It is easier to avoid certain difficulties and responsibilities than it is to face them.
8. I should be dependent to some extent on other persons and should have some person on whom I can rely to take care of me.
9. Past experiences and events are what determine my present behavior; the influence of the past cannot ever be erased.
10. I should be quite upset over other peoples' problems and disturbances.
11. There is always a right or perfect solution to every problem, and it must be found or the results will be catastrophic.

The consequence (C) should be assessed after A, but before B. C is the client's "emotional and/or behavioral response to the beliefs that he holds about the event in question" (Dryden, 1995, p. 33). This is usually what sparks the client to initially seek counseling. Negative emotions such as concern, sadness, remorse, and sorrow are healthy responses, whereas anxiety, depression, guilt, and hurt are unhealthy responses (Dryden, 1999).

After A, B, and C are identified and assessed, the professional counselor facilitates a dispute (D) of the client's irrational belief "by asking questions that encourage the person to question the empirical, logical, and pragmatic status of" the irrational belief (Dryden, 1995, p. 34). There are three steps to D: debating, discriminating, and defining (Gilliland & James, 1998). The professional counselor debates the client's belief system surrounding A, helps the client discriminate between rational and irrational reactions, and helps the client define statements in a more rational way. When debating, the professional counselor can use some of the following questions: "Is that good logic?, If a friend held that idea, would you accept it?, Why does it have to be so?, Where's the evidence?" (Hackney & Cormier, 2005), What would happen if . . . ?, Why must . . . ?, or Can you be happy even if you don't get what you want?

D can be achieved through cognitive, emotive, and behavioral techniques (Gilliland & James, 1998). Professional counselors can choose to use logical disputes in which they attack the accuracy of the client's argument, empirical disputes in which they center on the truth of the client's irrational beliefs, or functional disputes in which they focus on changing the belief to reduce the amount of discomfort experienced at C. Rational self analysis can also be used for disputing. In rational self analysis, the client examines A, B, C, and D, and describes an alternate reaction (Walsh, 2002).

After disputing, the professional counselor and client evaluate the effects (E) of D. If D is successful, the client will alter "feelings and actions at C because he or she has changed his or her thinking at B" (Dryden, 1995, p. 34). When A occurs, the client will be able to make more rational conclusions. Corey and Corey (2006) expanded upon the ABCDE model by adding F. F stands for the new feeling that a client has if disputing was in fact effective.

Dryden (1995) outlined a fairly specific 13-step process for implementing REBT:

1. Ask the client what brought them to counseling.
2. Agree on a target problem to discuss and goals for counseling.
3. Assess the activating event (A). It is important to determine the action that triggered an irrational belief (alternatively, step 4 may precede step 3).
4. Assess the consequence (C) of the issue that resulted in seeking counseling. The consequence may be behavioral, emotional, or cognitive.
5. Identify and assess a client's secondary emotional problems, if any.
6. Teach the client that beliefs behind A were directly related to C.
7. Assess B, distinguishing between absolutist (traditional) thinking and more rational thoughts.
8. Make the connection between the irrational B and C.
9. Help the client dispute (D) the irrational belief and facilitate a deeper understanding of the irrational B.
10. Help the client deepen his confidence in the new rational belief.
11. Assign homework allowing the client to put into practice what has been learned.
12. Check the client's progress on the homework during the next session.
13. Help the client work through any difficulties with the issue or homework, and generalize use of the process to other issues.

Practically speaking, the primary author (Erford) observed Ellis in action both in person and on video on numerous occasions consistently using the following 7-step process with clients.

1. *Accessing the client's self-talk:* The client is encouraged to talk about a presenting issue in order to assess the A and C. Particular attention is given to what self-messages the client is thinking, making these messages explicit.
2. *Determining the client's underlying belief:* From the explicit self-talk messages, the client's B is determined. If this belief is irrational, consensus is gained to alter the belief in order to reach a more desirable feeling and consequence.
3. *Agreeing on a more rational belief:* Together, the client and professional counselor can reach agreement on a more rational and appropriate belief to obtain the more desirable feeling and consequence.
4. *Performing rational emotive imagery (REI):* Refer to the REI section below for a discussion on these procedures. REI is practiced in the session at least once to be sure the client understands how to implement the technique properly.
5. *Assigning homework:* The client is required to practice REI using the presenting issue three to five times every day until the next session in order to develop the more rational belief.
6. *Positive consequence:* The client self-rewards for complying with the homework each day.
7. *Negative consequence:* The client self-punishes for not complying with the homework each day.

Ordinarily, processing a client issue using REBT procedures requires 20 to 50 minutes.

Rational Emotive Imagery

Often subsumed within the REBT process, the technique of rational emotive imagery (REI) was developed by Maultsby in 1974 and is "a form of intense mental practice designed to establish new emotional patterns" (Corey, 2007, p. 307). With the help of the professional counselor, the client visualizes herself thinking, feeling, and behaving just as she would like to be able to do in everyday life. This is one of the techniques that emerged from Albert Ellis' REBT. The primary goal is for the client to change her emotions from unhealthy to healthy with the help of the professional counselor (Seligman, 2001).

Before implementing this technique, it is important for the professional counselor to help the client perform a rational self-analysis to ensure that the client understands his irrational beliefs surrounding the distressing situation (Maultsby, 1984). It is also necessary for the professional counselor to understand the ABCDEs of REBT. Once the client has identified his irrational beliefs, the professional counselor and client can begin the following 7-step process (Seligman, 2001):

1. *Visualize an unpleasant activating event:* The professional counselor should tell the client to vividly imagine the details of the event.
2. *Experience the unhealthy negative emotions:* The client needs to let himself get in touch with the emotions that surface during the activating event and then spend several minutes facing the emotions. Imagining these inappropriate emotions is called negative imagery. It is important for the client to picture himself "as vividly as possible back in the situation" (Maultsby, 1984, p. 203).
3. *Changing the emotions:* Once the client has experienced the unhealthy emotions, he needs to spend time changing them into appropriate responses by visualizing himself responding with healthy emotions to the activating event. When the client imagines the healthy response, it is called positive imagery.
4. *Examine the process:* In this step, the professional counselor needs to help the client understand how changing his belief system (B) affected the activating event (A) and the resulting emotional consequence (C). It is essential that the client understand how his self-talk changed from the old belief to bring about the more rational, new belief.
5. *Repetition and practice:* The client needs to repeat steps one to three for at least 10 minutes every day until he no longer experiences unhealthy emotions in response to the activating event.

6. *Reinforcing the goal:* After several weeks, the client should be able to experience healthy, appropriate emotions while experiencing little if any of the previously experienced inappropriate emotions when he encounters the activating event.
7. *Generalization of skills:* Once the client has learned this technique, he can use it for other activating events that also trigger inappropriate emotional responses.

VARIATIONS OF THE REBT TECHNIQUE

While general REBT is used with clients who have a wide range of concerns, elegant REBT is used with clients who "seek deep philosophical changes" (Seligman, 2001, p. 360). When using elegant REBT, the professional counselor frequently engages the client in "rational, positive, coping statements" (Gilliland & James, 1998, p. 256). The client writes down irrational beliefs, disputes, and effective rational beliefs. The professional counselor can videotape the client reciting the effective rational beliefs so that the client can view the tape at home so that work from the sessions will be reinforced.

EXAMPLE OF THE REBT TECHNIQUE

Barb is an adult female teacher and mother of two teenagers who has struggled with perfectionism since childhood. The following case exemplifies use of REBT and rational emotive imagery (REI). Importantly, Barb initially presented with Panic Disorder and that condition was successfully treated first. Her struggle with perfectionism is being addressed as a secondary issue during the fourth session. The activating event (A) (perfectionism-related occurrences) has already been identified, and Barb has given several examples of how the events affect her (C). The counselor starts by accessing Barb's self-talk (Step 1).

Counselor (C):   . . . How do you know that the perfectionism is there, what kinds of things do you notice about your life and actions?

Barb (B):   Well, first of all, I don't handle it very well when things don't go according to my plan. If everything isn't just right, I get very upset and I get very, I'm very much, umm, very much afraid, that umm, if everything isn't just right, that nothing's going to be right, and if it's not just right, that it's my fault that it's not just right. I get very stressed.

C: And the stress comes. What effect does it have on your life, and the general way that you live your life?

The counselor is helping Barb explore the C.

B: Umm, I can be neurotic sometimes about planning things and making things just right, and you know my expectations have gotten very high. I think I've gotten better over time. When I was younger it used to be really bad, if I couldn't accomplish something immediately, then I assumed that I couldn't do it and it was probably my fault that I couldn't do it and I wasn't even going to try any more. Some things I probably could have done and now, it's just, you know I've gotten better, but it's made me afraid to try things because if I don't accomplish them successfully I'm afraid what other people will think, that there's something wrong.

C: All right. That's interesting because I hear you imply that your perfectionism keeps you from trying new things because you may get kind of frustrated and take your hands off of things. Other people sometimes decide that they will get even more controlling, sort of "I'm gonna master this no matter what."

B: I'm more of the former. If I don't think I can do it, I avoid it, more afraid to fail—or least others seeing that I fail.

C: And you go back from it. Okay, so that's where we're at today. We want to deal with this issue of perfectionism and I'd like to use this process with a big, fancy name called rational-emotive behavior therapy, which has about all the components of someone's psychological being wrapped up in there somewhere: the rational thinking self, the

emotive feeling self and of course the behaving, or acting, self. We're going to try to do something to counteract your thoughts of perfectionism and the accompanying feelings and actions. So I hear you say a number of things about the perfectionism. One thing that I heard you say is that everything has to be just right and whenever everything has to be just right, you're saying these things to yourself, some kind of conversation going on inside your brain. And I heard some of that self-talk conversation in the first minute or two, "If everything isn't just right, nothing is going to be right, and it's all my fault," and that makes you behave in a stressed out, worried, and perfectionistic manner.

B: Right.

Counselor begins Step 2: Determining the client's underlying belief; or determine the B.

C: So what I want you to focus on now is, what do you think the values and beliefs are that underlie those thoughts going on in your brain?

B: Oh, umm, well, that if it's worth doing, if something's worth doing, it's worth doing right! Umm, so I feel like, I feel like I've got to do everything I do well. Because if I'm doing something, then I have to do it well. That failure isn't really something that you're allowed to do, you know. I can't really mess up. Umm.

C: Okay.

B: I'm trying to think of . . .

C: I'm even hearing that it's more than just, if I'm going to do something, then I have to do it well, it's almost as if, I *must* do it well, I *should* do it well and if I *don't* do it well, then . . . (Pause)

B: I fail, then something's wrong with me!

C: I have failed, I have failed (writes this down), something is wrong with me, now we're getting somewhere. Something is wrong with you and what is wrong with you, because I know you've been thinking about this for a long time.

B: Umm, oh, I'm not perfect and I'm not a good person and people will think that I'm not a good person and you know people will judge me to be inferior. You know, I will be inferior to them, inferior to co-workers, or inferior to friends.

C: So what kind of emotional reaction do you get, when you think, oh, I am not perfect, I am inferior to all of my friends and neighbors and colleagues?

B: Oh, it's like this big welling up like of, that your heart fills up and you're crushed and you know, you get overwhelmed sometimes with it, like you don't know what to do next and you don't know how to fix it, and oh my gosh, I've gotta do, I've gotta do something to fix it. So with me it's always been, well, I just won't do it at all because if I can't do it well, I'll just make up some reason that I'm not doing it anymore, instead of just soldiering on and trying to just do the best I can at something. I'm not doing it right, so I shouldn't be doing it at all.

C: Okay, so you get this visceral reaction, you can feel it inside your body and get all tensed up. I can see from your hands, that you get kind of edgy and fidgety about this.

B: Definitely.

C: Okay, good.

B: Good?

C: I mean it's good that you're able to describe all those things because that's what we're trying to do something about here, so that really helps.

Introduce scaling procedure—see chapter 1.

C: Now on a scale of 1 to 10, with 1 being calm, cool, relaxed, no problems at all and 10 being on the edge of that panic attack, emotionally upset, and the stomach turning and all that. Whenever you're saying these things to yourself, like I'm not perfect or I'm inferior to all

my colleagues, friends, and neighbors, where are you on that scale?

B: Oh, I'm probably 9 or 10.

C: 9 or 10, so you're way right up there, on the verge of something really negative happening

B: Mmmhmm.

C: Okay, so I'm not perfect, I'm inferior to all these other folks. What's so horrible about realizing that you're not perfect that would lead everybody else to think that you're inferior or no good, or is that just what you're saying to yourself?

B: Well, I'm saying that to myself, you know, it's like this little thing that goes on in your head. Like if they knew that I wasn't perfect, if they knew I couldn't do this well, they wouldn't like me, or hire me, or live near me, or be my friend. They wouldn't talk to me or sit by me at sporting events or whatever. If people think I'm not perfect they're not gonna like me . . . If I'm not perfect, they're not going to accept me.

C: Okay. That's a pretty powerful belief. Now, what's the emotional consequence of these thoughts, if you could label these feelings, what do they lead you to? Okay, I have to be perfect, I have to be superior, I have to be as good as everyone else or even better than everyone else. And if I'm not, then it's awful and horrible.

B: Yeah.

C: But, where does it lead in the way of your emotional reaction. I mean, if you could label it, what would you call it?

B: Umm, it depends, sometimes it makes me put on this front of, appearance, it makes me, I don't know, superficiality.

C: Right, now that's how you *cope* with the emotional reaction . . . I'm hearing you say something more like you get extraordinarily anxious, worried and . . .

B: Hurt, like emotionally hurt, like someone has done something to you. You've already accepted the judgment, you don't know, I don't know if anyone is really making it, but a little voice in the back of my head is telling me, yes they are and they're judging you and they're judging you negatively.

C: Everyone's looking at you and judging you. Okay, so we get this worriedness and this hurtness and this real anxiety, this kind of visceral anxiousness happening every time. We think about how I'm not perfect and it's horrible and awful and if I can only be perfect, my life would be so much better.

B: Mmmhmm.

C: Has your life ever been perfect?

B: Oh, no.

C: No, has anyone's life ever been perfect?

B: No.

C: Okay, so we're aware of this on the cognitive level. We're thinking okay, I know that this is kind of irrational, that this is not the way I should be thinking but I just can't help it. You know, I just have this way of thinking and it leads me to this almost panic reaction, this worrisomeness and this anxiety. Is this rational?

B: No way.

The counselor begins Step 3: Agreeing on a more rational belief and emotional consequence.

C: Rather than intense anxiety, worrying, or panic when you are not perfect, what would be a more rational response to these situations?

B: I dunno. Maybe, maybe others would just be disappointed, or just suck it up and go on. I dunno.

C: Okay, disappointed (writes this down). And so what we need to do now is do something about it . . . so you're about a 9 or a 10 out here on the scale when these types of things happen and you're saying them to yourself, you're kind of realizing, hey, I'm bringing a lot of these things on myself. In fact probably just about all of it, I'm bring it on myself. And now what we need to do, is get you a little bit closer to what a normal reaction might

be. You see, it's normal to make mistakes sometime. You kind of feel, wow, you know I should have done better, because I'm a bright, articulate, capable woman and I should be able to get things done in a fairly efficient manner. Not necessarily perfectly, but fairly efficiently. We want to get you back closer to more of a normal reaction. So what I want to do with you right now is a technique called rational emotive imagery.

Begin Step 4—REI.

C: So I want you to go ahead and close your eyes and I want you to imagine that something is happening, and you are basically failing at it, that it's not going well. And you're saying to yourself things like "I can't believe this, I'm not perfect. What would the neighbors think? What would my colleagues think? They're going to think that I'm inferior." And I really want you to feel it inside your stomach and inside your body that you're up there about that 9 or 10 on the scale and that this is just a horrible, awful thing that happened to you. Can you feel that?

B: (Barb laughs and shakes her head in an obvious "yes" gesture.) Oh, yeah . . .

C: Yeah, that's pretty easy to do. I want you to sit there with that feeling for a bit and just really feel all that churning going on inside of you.

(Pause for about a minute.)

C: And now Barb I want you to change that emotion or that feeling from this horrible, awful 10. I want you to just be, instead anxious and churning, and really worried and upset, I want you to be somewhat disappointed in yourself. Just slightly disappointed. Not *really* disappointed, way out there at the end of the scale. I just want you to be somewhat disappointed. That yeah, you probably could've, if you had had more time, put a little bit more effort into it, maybe things would have gone better. But hey, everything is going to be all right. Just be slightly disappointed that I didn't do everything perfectly. And then give me a little sign that you're able to do that. You might even want to do some of your deep breathing to calm yourself down. So go ahead and bring yourself down to just slightly disappointed. Disappointed, but not worried and upset and angry about everything.

(Pause for a half-minute until Barb gives a nod)

C: Are you there?

B: Yeah.

REI helps transition to the (D) Disputation phase by creating a new internal dialogue.

C: Okay. Now, what did you do to get from the 9 or 10, you can open your eyes now and look again. What did you do to get from the 9 or the 10 down to just slightly disappointed? What kinds of things did you say to yourself? What kinds of things went on in your brain?

B: Umm, I don't have to be perfect.

C: Okay.

B: I'm not perfect. Nobody's perfect. The other person's not perfect. Umm, nobody's, uh, you know, the worst consequences, we've talked about this. Nobody's going to, uh, take you out back and shoot you or bludgeon you to death. Nobody's going to fire you or tell you to get lost. They'll give you a chance to explain yourself. Even if not, well, you know, don't worry about it, 'cause the worst consequence is not gonna be as bad as all that.

C: Okay. Has it ever been as bad as you thought it was going to be?

B: Maybe once in my entire life.

C: Yeah. Okay, so maybe once in a great while it might be a very negative, nasty consequence. But what you're saying is that it's hardly ever that way. It is very rarely the worse consequence. And so a lot of that worrying is just basically having an effect on you and on your body and on your mind, but it's not really having an effect on your life. As far as other people can see.

B: Yeah.

C: Just making you a nervous wreck and everything.

B: (Laughs out loud)

The counselor is ready to move to Step 5: Assigning homework, but completes Step 6: Positive consequence, and Step 7: Negative consequence, before making the homework assignment.

C: Okay, good. What I want you to do now, is to tell me, something that you really like to do. Something that you find rewarding or kind of fun and something you would do just to kind of reward yourself.

B: Shopping.

C: Go shopping, all right.

B: Or read for pleasure.

C: All right, go shopping, read for pleasure. I'm certain that your husband would prefer if you read for pleasure . . .

B: Yeah, definitely . . .

C: Okay, now tell me something that you don't like to do, something that you'd rather avoid. . . .

B: Ironing!!! . . .

C: OK. For your homework, I want you to practice your rational emotive imagery 5 times a day, every day until I see you next week. Spread them out, a couple in the morning, afternoon and evening. When you practice your rational emotive imagery 5 times during the day, I want you to reward yourself with 30 minutes of pleasure reading, and if you do not practice 5 times I want you to do 30 minutes of ironing. Start with the clothes that need to be ironed in your house, then pull clothes out of your closet and iron them again, even call your relatives and neighbors to ask if they have any ironing for you to do.

B: (Laughing at seeing the humor in the situation). Gee. Should I do what I'm supposed to do and get something I like, or not do it and iron all night?!! Hmm, which should I choose. . . ?

C: Reward or punish yourself this way each day until I see you next week . . .

The counselor goes to (E) Evaluation by exploring with Barb how the process worked for her today.

USEFULNESS AND EVALUATION OF THE REBT TECHNIQUE

Professional counselors can use REBT with clients who have a variety of different presenting problems including high levels of stress (Abrams & Ellis, 1994), relationship problems, and coping with disabilities (Ellis, 1997b). Yankura and Dryden (1997, p. 1) described using REBT with "children and adolescents, culturally diverse clients, clients with disabilities, families, and ongoing therapy groups" and provided models for professional counselors to use when working with these populations. REBT is useful when working with women, couples, and adults (Seligman, 2001). Dryden and Walker (as cited in Dryden & Ellis, 1997) created a self-help worksheet that professional counselors may find helpful to use with their clients to teach them how to use REBT.

REBT is praised as being effective and leading, "to rapid reduction in symptoms as well as philosophical change" (Seligman, 2001, p. 378). It has been effective in reducing disruptive behaviors of children and adolescents (Gonzalez et al., 2004), anxiety, and feelings of regret (Weinrach et al., 2001). It is an effective way to "help people to think more rationally, to feel less anxious, depressed, and enraged when they fail and get rejected" (Ellis, Shaughnessy, & Mahan, 2002, p. 356). REBT is also an effective technique to use with clients from different cultural backgrounds (Lega & Ellis, 2001) and people experiencing emotional problems after bereavement (Boelen, Kip, Voorsluijs, & van den Bout, 2004).

While REBT is effective, it also has its limitations. It is criticized for overlooking the client's past and having too fast of a pace (Seligman, 2001). In addition, the efficacy of REBT is limited when working with clients who have severe personality disorders (Ellis et al., 2002) and impulse control disorders (e.g., alcohol abuse, burglary, pedophilia, voyeurism) unless the client is truly motivated to change.

CHAPTER 31

Bibliotherapy

ORIGINS OF THE BIBLIOTHERAPY TECHNIQUE

Bibliotherapy is a term coined by Samuel Crothers in 1916 to describe the use of books as a part of the counseling process (Jackson, 2001). While several theoretical counseling approaches integrate or use bibliotherapy, we have chosen to include it in the cognitive behavioral section. The popularity of bibliotherapy was advanced during the 1930s by librarians and professional counselors who put together lists of books that aided in altering the readers' thoughts, feelings, or behaviors (Abdullah, 2002). Bibliotherapy is a technique that is frequently used by professional counselors today whose clients need to modify their ways of thinking (Seligman, 2001). One of the major propositions underlying this technique is that the client needs to be able to identify with one of the characters who is experiencing a problem similar to the client's issue. By reading a book and being able to identify with a character, clients can, "learn vicariously how to solve their problems" and "release emotions, gain new directions in life, and explore new ways of interacting" (Abdullah, 2002, p. 2). Films, videos, and movies can also be used during bibliotherapy; it is not limited to books (Vernon, 1993). There are five goals of bibliotherapy (Vernon, 1993, p. 93): "1. Teaching constructive and positive thinking. 2. Encouraging free expression of problems. 3. Assisting the client in analyzing his or her attitudes and behaviors. 4. Fostering the search for alternative solutions to problems. 5. Allowing the client to discover that his or her problem is similar to others' problems."

HOW TO IMPLEMENT THE BIBLIOTHERAPY TECHNIQUE

There are four "stages" involved in implementing bibliotherapy: identification, selection, presentation, and follow-up (Abdullah, 2002). In the first stage, it is necessary for the professional counselor to identify the client's needs. Next, the professional counselor needs to select books that will be appropriate for the client's situation. Books need to be written at a level that the client will be able to understand and the characters in the story need to be believable (Jackson, 2001). The professional counselor should recommend only books that she has read and that are in line with the client's values and goals (Young, 1998). In the presentation stage, the client reads the book, usually on his own outside of session time, and, during counseling sessions, discusses important aspects of the book with the counselor. The professional counselor can request that the client underline key points in the book or keep a journal if she feels that it would help the client.

Jackson (2001) described how to help the client identify with a character in the story. The professional counselor needs to have the client retell the story and the client can choose how he would like to do so (orally, artistically, etc.). During this process, it is important to have the client concentrate on the feelings experienced by the character in the story. The next step is to help the client point out transformations in the character's feelings, relationships, or behaviors. The professional counselor then assists the client in making comparisons between himself and the character from the story. One essential part of this stage is for the client to identify alternative solutions for the character's problems and to discuss the consequences of each (Jackson, 2001).

In the final stage of bibliotherapy, follow-up, the professional counselor and the client discuss what the client has learned about himself as well as what he has gained from being able to identify with the character (Abdullah, 2002). The client can express his experience through discussion, role-play, artistic medium, or a variety of other creative ways (Jackson, 2001). Throughout the implementation of this technique, <u>it is important that the professional counselor keep the reality of the client in mind</u> (Vernon, 1993).

VARIATIONS OF THE BIBLIOTHERAPY TECHNIQUE

There are many variations of bibliotherapy. Traditional bibliotherapy as described above tends to be reactive in nature; that is, the client has a problem and the professional counselor selects a book for the client to read that will help her resolve the problem. Interactive bibliotherapy involves clients participating in ways that will allow them to reflect on their readings. The ways in which professional counselors have the clients participate vary, but can include group discussion or journaling. Clinical bibliotherapy is used only by trained professional counselors to help clients who are undergoing severe emotional problems (Abdullah, 2002), and may use journal writing, role-playing, or drawing. Cognitive bibliotherapy is used to teach cognitive behavioral therapy to clients who

suffer from depression with the intention that depression levels will be reduced (Gregory, Canning, Lee, & Wise, 2004). Teachers typically use developmental bibliotherapy with their students during group guidance or literacy based educational experiences, helping to promote normal health (Abdullah, 2002).

When using bibliotherapy with students, teachers should make sure to capture student interest at the beginning of the lesson. One idea is to have students make puppets to use as the characters in the story. The teacher should also engage the students in a follow-up discussion requiring higher-level thinking (Johnson, Wan, Templeton, Graham, & Sattler, 2000). Johnson et al. outlined a 5-step process for implementing bibliotherapy in the classroom: (1) motivate students with introductory activities, (2) allow reading time, (3) allow incubation time, (4) engage in follow-up discussion time, and (5) closure and evaluation.

EXAMPLE OF THE BIBLIOTHERAPY TECHNIQUE

Following is an excellent example of use of bibliotherapy with children who have experienced the loss of a father. The story is excerpted from *When My Daddy Died* by J. M. Hammond (Cranbrook Publishing, 1981):

> An awful thing happened when my Daddy died. When my mom told me she started to cry. I felt kind of sick and started to cry too. I didn't think I would ever stop crying . . . but I did.
>
> I went with my mother to the funeral. There were a lot of flowers and a lot of people. Some of the people were crying. Mother and I looked in the casket together. I said it looked like my dad was sleeping and might wake up. Mom explained that when people die they can never be alive again. They don't sleep, they don't think, they don't feel, they don't eat and they don't sleep.
>
> Being dead is not like sleeping at all . . .

Sometimes I worry about who will take care of me, make money for us, and play with me the way my dad use to do. Mom says that she will see that I am always taken care of. My mom used to be home when I came home from school. Now she is at work. At first I was mad about that, but now I understand that she needs to make money for us. We still have time to play too.

Sometimes I worry that Mom feels so sad she might die. Sometimes I think about me dying too. Mom says that most people live for long, long, long time until they are very old. She thinks we will live to be very old grandmas and grandpas. Sometimes I get angry at my dad for dying and leaving me. Sometimes I just want to scream, "I want my daddy back". . .

When dad died I was afraid I made it happen. I know now that nothing I did made Dad die. It wasn't my fault. . . .

One night Mom and I talked about a funny thing we remembered Dad did once. We both started laughing so hard that I fell off the couch. Afterwards I asked Mom if it was wrong for us to laugh when Dad was dead. She said, "No, it is good for us to talk about the thing we remember. I think your father would be glad we talked about how funny he could be and laughed." That made me feel better. It is good for us to be happy again . . . (B)est of all I have my mother. We talk a lot and help each other even more now. I love her and I know she loves me so much too.

Good bibliotherapy goes beyond the simple reading of stories. Following are some guided questions that accompany *When My Daddy Died*.

When my dad died I felt _____

Sometimes I worry about _____

These are some things I remember about my dad _____

Some things I enjoy are _____

Now I'm feeling _____

Now that I've finished the book, here are some things that I learned _____

USEFULNESS AND EVALUATION OF THE BIBLIOTHERAPY TECHNIQUE

Professional counselors choose to use bibliotherapy with their clients for a variety of different issues including illness, death, self-destructive behaviors, family relationships, identity, violence and abuse, race and prejudice, sex and sexuality, and gender issues (Christenbury & Beale, 1996). Other populations who may benefit from this technique include students with math anxiety (Hebert & Furner, 1997), females with body image issues (Corey, 2007), people with depression (Mahalik & Kivlighan, 1988), gay and lesbian youth (Vare & Norton, 2004), and children of divorce (Yauman, 1991). Bibliotherapy helps to reinforce rational thoughts (Gilliland & James, 1998), promote other viewpoints, instill social interest, and can be used at any point during the therapeutic process (Jackson, 2001). Books can allow clients to have insight into a part of themselves that they otherwise may not have recognized. Bibliotherapy is used to "stimulate discussion about problems, communicate new values and attitudes, and provide realistic solutions to problems" (Abdullah, 2002, p. 3). This technique can be used to promote therapeutic goals (Schumacher & Wantz, 1995) or can be assigned as homework (Young, 2006). Professional school counselors can use bibliotherapy in classroom guidance lessons, small group sessions, and individual counseling (Gladding & Gladding, 1991).

Many practicing professional counselors use this technique because of their belief in its efficacy (Jackson, 2001). Studies showed that bibliotherapy was effective in reducing aggressive behavior among adolescents with behavior problems (Shechtman, 2000), reducing depression levels for people who have a high internal locus of control (Mahalik & Kivlighan, 1988), and promoting developmental growth in elementary school children (Borders & Paisley, 1992). The efficacy of this technique increases when the counselor implements it well (Abdullah, 2002).

Riordan & Wilson (1989) reviewed the research surrounding bibliotherapy and found mixed results, especially in its efficacy in changing attitudes, views of self-concept, and behavior. Professional counselors also must be aware that clients may "project their own motives onto characters and thus reinforce their own perspectives and solutions" (Gladding & Gladding, 1991, p. 8). Bibliotherapy may be ineffective when participants have the following limitations: "lack of social and emotional experiences, failure, flights into fantasy, and defensiveness" (Gladding & Gladding, p. 9). Clients may not be ready to change or they may not be willing to use this technique. Another limitation of bibliotherapy may be that material on a given subject is not available (Abdullah, 2002). For lists of books that can be used during bibliotherapy, professional counselors are directed to Thompson and Rudolph (1996), Christenbury and Beale (1996), Dreyer (1997), and Pardeck (1984, 1986).

CHAPTER 32

Deep Breathing

ORIGINS OF THE DEEP BREATHING TECHNIQUE

While breathing exercises are a relatively new technique in Western culture, they have been highly regarded by Eastern cultures for a long time. The early roots of deep breathing can be traced back to the Hindu yoga traditions. Hindu philosophers' belief in yoga centers on the concept of pranayama. Prana means life energy as well as breath, and by being able to control one's breathing, it is thought that a person is able to control her life energy. An ancient metaphor used to describe breath is the string which controls the kite; the kite represents the mind and the string represents breath. In Western culture, this same concept is described as a "physiological relationship between the centers that control respiration and the centers that control our general nervousness" (Girdano, Everly, & Dusek, 1990, p. 162). To calm the body, many professional counselors now recommend using breathing techniques. By learning to breathe more deeply and efficiently, clients can learn to manage their stress (Powell & George-Warren, 1994).

HOW TO IMPLEMENT THE DEEP BREATHING TECHNIQUE

Powell and George-Warren (1994) provided some basic guidelines to follow when implementing the breathing techniques.

1. One should breathe through the nose on the inhale and either exhale through the nose or mouth.
2. In between the deep breaths, one should be sure to breathe normally to avoid dizziness.
3. One should first practice the exercises lying on the back, and can sit or stand during the exercise after learning the basic techniques.
4. One may yawn frequently so that the body can establish equilibrium and begin to relax.
5. One should note what one's breathing is like before starting the exercises.

It is also important to know that a person's exhale should take about twice as long as the inhale. For example, if a person inhaled for 3 seconds, the same breath should be exhaled over a 6-second period of time (Nuernberger, 1981).

A person at rest is typically using only one third of lung capacity. A professional counselor can use sessions with clients to teach how to breathe more effectively. Before learning the deep breathing technique, it is important for the person to know how to do diaphragmatic or abdominal breathing. To begin, the clients should lie on their backs and notice how they are breathing. They can use their hands to get an understanding of how they are breathing. By putting one hand on the stomach and one hand on the chest, clients can feel how they are breathing. If the hand on the stomach rises, the client is breathing from the abdomen. If the hand on the chest rises, the client is breathing from the chest. The professional counselor can instruct the client to shift from chest to abdominal breathing to help him become more aware of the difference (Davis, Robbins-Eshelman, & McKay, 1995).

Once the client is able to breathe from the abdomen, the professional counselor can teach the client the deep breathing technique. Davis et al. (1995, p. 27) provide the following procedures for implementing the deep breathing technique.

1. Lie down on a blanket or rug on the floor. Bend your knees and move your feet about 8 inches apart, with your toes turned slightly outward. Make sure that your spine is straight.
2. Scan your body for tension.
3. Place one hand on your abdomen and one hand on your chest.
4. Inhale slowly and deeply through your nose into your abdomen to push up your hand as much as feels comfortable. Your chest should move only a little and only with your abdomen.
5. When you feel at ease with step 4, smile slightly and inhale through your nose and exhale through your mouth, making a quiet, relaxing whooshing sound like the wind as you blow out gently. Your mouth, tongue, and jaw will be relaxed. Take long, slow deep breaths that raise and lower your abdomen. Focus on the sound and feeling of breathing as you become more and more relaxed.
6. Continue deep breathing for about 5 or 10 minutes at a time, once or twice a day, for a couple of weeks. Then, if you like, extend this period to 20 minutes.
7. At the end of each deep breathing session, take a little time to once more scan your body for tension. Compare the tension you feel at the conclusion of the exercise with that which you experienced when you began.
8. When you become at ease with breathing into your abdomen, practice it any time during the day when you feel like it and you are sitting down or standing still. Concentrate on your abdomen moving up and down, the air moving in and out of your lungs, and the feeling of relaxation that deep breathing gives you.
9. When you have learned to relax yourself using deep breathing, practice it whenever you feel yourself getting tense.

VARIATIONS OF THE DEEP BREATHING TECHNIQUE

While there are over two dozen variations of the deep breathing technique, the ones thought to be most useful to professional counselors are highlighted below. When a person is in a situation that causes her to have feelings of anxiety, a variation of the deep breathing technique called "breathing down" can be used. In this exercise, the person sits in a comfortable position and places both hands over the bellybutton, with the right hand on top. The client imagines that there is a pouch at the point where the hands meet the stomach. As the person takes in a breath, she imagines the pouch is filling with air and continues the breathing exercise to fill the pouch to the top. When the pouch is full, the person holds her breath, keeping the air in the pouch, and repeats, "My body is calm." As the person exhales, emptying the pouch, she says, "My body is quiet." After repeating this exercise four times in a row, 10 times a day for a couple of weeks, one will be better able to relax.

Another variation of this technique is described by Vernon (1993). In this alternative, the clients are instructed to toss their concerns away as they exhale. As they inhale, they are instructed to imagine a calmness filling their bodies. Similar to this variation is another one called "the waiting in line peacefully breath." Faelton and Diamond (1990) suggested that people waiting in traffic jams or similar situations can use deep breathing to help their impatience dissipate. While waiting, it is important for the person to remind himself that being impatient makes the time pass slower. People also should think of the others waiting as "fellow human beings working to the best of their ability" (p. 61).

Another variation of the deep breathing technique can be used with a group. A professional counselor who is leading a group whose members can benefit from this technique can teach deep breathing to the members. After every member knows the technique, it can be used to open a session.

The rolling breath is another variation of the deep breathing technique. It involves working with a partner to complete the exercise. In this variation, one person lies on the floor; the partner puts one hand on the person's stomach and one hand on the person's chest. The person inhales in two steps, first filling the abdomen and then the chest, watching his partner's hands move rhythmically. The person exhales the air in his chest and abdomen at the same time. After the first person has practiced this exercise and attained a rolling effect for several minutes, the partners switch places (Sam Houston State University, 2006).

The three-breath release is yet another variation of this technique. This alternative should be used at least once a day. The client needs to close her eyes if she is able to do so. When the client exhales, she needs to loosen her whole body and go limp. The client needs to make sure that while she is doing this exercise, she has something to balance on so she does not fall. This exercise should be done three times (Schafer, 1998).

"Controlling pain with imagery breath" is another variation described by Faelton and Diamond (1990). In this variation, the person does diaphragmatic breathing with his eyes closed. When inhaling, the person imagines the breath filling the painful spot with calmness. On the exhale, the person imagines the pain leaving his body. After 10 minutes, the person opens his eyes and stretches his body.

EXAMPLE OF THE DEEP BREATHING TECHNIQUE

Counselor (C):   Okay, Sam. Lie down on your mat and close your eyes. Bend your knees a bit and keep your feet apart . . . great. Now I want you to place one hand on your abdomen and one hand on your chest . . .

Inhale slowly and deeply through your nose into your abdomen. You will notice that your hand over your abdomen will rise with your abdomen. The hand on your chest should move only a little. Now exhale very slowly through your mouth. Just purse your lips slightly and allow the air to escape slowly . . . slowly, barely enough to make a candle flame flicker. Good. Continue to take long, slow deep breaths that raise and lower your abdomen. Focus on the sound and feeling of your breathing . . . (pause) . . . Become more and more relaxed.

Sam continues to breathe with periodic encouragement and comments from the counselor for between 5 and 10 minutes. The counselor then assigns homework: deep breathing for 5 to 10 minutes, three times per day until the next appointment.

USEFULNESS AND EVALUATION OF THE DEEP BREATHING TECHNIQUE

Breathing techniques are used for a variety of different reasons. Most commonly, a professional counselor suggests this technique to a person who is working on controlling anxiety or managing stress. This technique is also used to reduce "generalized anxiety disorders, panic attacks and agoraphobia, depression, irritability, muscle tension, headaches, fatigue . . . breathholding, hyperventilation, shallow breathing, and cold hands and feet" (Davis et al., 1995, p. 25).

A version of this technique is incorporated into a popular method of childbirth, Lamaze. The theory behind the Lamaze breathing techniques is that if the deep breathing exercises are performed, a part of the cortex will not respond to the pain.

Nuernberger (1981) described how breathing techniques can be used when people have difficulty sleeping. Not only will this technique allow a person to get to sleep, but the sleep will be more restful. The deep breathing exercise should be completed in the following way: "8 breaths lying on your back, 16 breaths lying on your right side, and 32 breaths lying on your left side" (p. 197). Most people fall asleep before they finish this exercise.

Kabat-Zinn, in an interview with Moyers (1993), described how deep breathing techniques can be used to help manage pain. During the time when a person is performing a deep breathing technique, she should attempt to go into the part of the body causing the pain, "breathe with it, and try to penetrate the pain" (p. 39). By being aware of the pain and their breathing, people can penetrate the affected area and reduce stress.

Deep breathing exercises can also be used to help smokers quit. Some people smoke to relax and when smoking, they take the time to slowly inhale and exhale. This habit has some of the same relaxing effects as the deep breathing exercises. By learning how to relax by breathing deeply without the cigarette, a person may be more successful in quitting smoking (Faelton & Diamond, 1990).

Deep breathing techniques can also be used to help manage one's anger. While anger is a normal response, it can cause problems if it is not handled well. One cool-down strategy recommended by Arenofsky (2001) is a deep breathing exercise. People can be taught to use deep breathing exercises before attempting to resolve their conflicts so that the chance of a peaceful outcome increases.

While a survey conducted by Laselle and Russell (1993) indicated that professional counselors were not commonly incorporating breathing techniques in their work with students, it is a technique that could be valuable to many young people. By teaching students relaxation techniques, including deep breathing, professional counselors could help to reduce the number of behavior problems and conflicts in school.

Brown and Uehara (1999) described how deep breathing techniques can be used in workplace settings where stress exists. In particular, these authors focus on teacher stress and teacher burnout. Many times, stress is a factor when a teacher chooses to leave a school or the entire profession. Stress also contributes to higher rates of absenteeism among staff members. After becoming aware of stress, Brown and Uehara recommend that teachers become involved in physiological training. In this process, teachers learn coping strategies, including deep breathing techniques, that are a part of an effective stress management plan.

Van Dixhorn (1988) performed a randomized trial of relaxation therapy where the main techniques taught were breathing awareness and diaphragmatic breathing. When compared to exercise alone, relaxation therapy was more effective in reducing the risk of abnormalities that suggest the heart condition myocardial ischemia. At the 2-year follow-up study, participants who learned the relaxation technique did not experience as many cardiac problems as the other participants.

Deep breathing exercises are commonly used by professional counselors with their clients for a variety of different purposes. Perhaps one of the reasons why this technique is popular is because of how quick and easy it is to perform. A person can engage in this exercise almost anywhere, as it is not noticeable to others when one is performing it. The deep breathing technique is a valuable relaxation exercise that is simple for nearly any person to learn.

CHAPTER 33

Progressive Muscle Relaxation Training (PMRT)

ORIGINS OF THE PMRT TECHNIQUE

Edmund Jacobson developed the technique of progressive relaxation years after noticing how anxious his father, a calm and quiet natured man, became after living through a house fire. Jacobson performed many studies examining human skeletal muscles and, in particular, what made the muscles tense up and what helped them to relax. Through some of his studies, Jacobson showed that mental activity takes place in the neuromusculature as well as in the brain. By measuring the activity taking place in the neuromusculature when a person was tense and when a person was calm, Jacobson used data to help create the progressive relaxation technique (Jacobson, 1977). A person learns to relax striated muscles through this process. Muscles are relaxed when a person does not have to use any energy.

The belief that underlies the technique of progressive muscle relaxation training (PMRT) is that a muscle cannot be both relaxed and tensed at the same point in time—a fact based upon the principle of reciprocal inhibition. By learning to identify the ways muscles feel when they are tensed and when they are relaxed, a person can learn to relax (Kiselica & Baker, 1992). When a person is able to identify a tense muscle, he will realize that it needs to be relaxed. PMRT is commonly used to manage stress. Some of the benefits of PMRT include "positive and beneficial immune system responses, greater resistance to psychosocial stressors, a more internal locus of control, positive mental health, and greater physical health" (Myers, Sweeney, & Witmer, 2000, p. 256).

HOW TO IMPLEMENT THE PMRT TECHNIQUE

When training a client in PMRT, the professional counselor should make sure that the space is free from any distractions. The client needs to find a place, such as couch or a mat on the floor, where she can lie comfortably with her eyes closed (Hackney & Cormier, 2005). Progressive relaxation sessions typically last about 30 minutes and are performed in a dimly lit area. More often than not, six or seven sessions of progressive relaxation are enough to have a positive effect on the stress level of a client (Jacobson, 1977). Clients need to make sure to wear loose clothing and should take their shoes off before the session starts. Beginning with the toes and proceeding up the body, clients tighten each muscle group, and after noting the feeling, they quickly relax the given muscle group. It is important to repeat the muscle contraction exercises many times so that the client becomes aware of the difference that exists between a tense and a relaxed muscle. The professional counselor teaches the client to relax all of the different muscle groups in the body (Jacobson, 1987).

Although Jacobson initially suggested 30 muscle groups (implemented over 40 individual sessions!) most professional counselors currently use some or all of the following muscle groups implemented in a single session: right foot, right lower leg, right thigh, left foot, left lower leg, left thigh, buttocks, abdomen, right hand, right arm, left hand, left arm, lower back, shoulders, neck, lower face, upper face (see Table 33.1).

Ordinarily, the client is instructed to take in a deep breathe, hold the breath for 5 seconds while tensing each muscle group, then release the tension in the muscle while slowly exhaling. The pairing of the tension release and exhale leads to deeper relaxation and a potential classically conditioned association.

Once the client knows how to relax each muscle group, the professional counselor can lead the client in a full session of progressive muscle relaxation training, going through each of the groups. After practicing this technique, clients should be able to keep their muscle groups relaxed at the same time (Jacobson, 1987). At the end of each session, the clients lie in silence for several minutes to allow progressive relaxation to have the greatest impact (Carroll et al., 1997).

TABLE 33.1 Instructions for Tensing and Relaxing Major Muscle Groups and Areas of Tension

- Right arm—Take a deep breath and hold it for about 5 seconds as you make a fist, curl your wrist, flex your forearm, and flex your bicep. Then relax these muscles and release the tension as you exhale.
- Left arm—Take a deep breath and hold it for about 5 seconds as you make a fist, curl your wrist, flex your forearm, and flex your bicep. Then relax these muscles and release the tension as you exhale.
- Right leg—Take a deep breath and hold it for about 5 seconds as you curl your toes under, lift the ball of your foot to flex your shin, and flex your thigh muscle. Then relax these muscles and release the tension as you exhale.
- Left leg—Take a deep breath and hold it for about 5 seconds as you curl your toes under, lift the ball of your foot to flex your shin, and flex your thigh muscle. Then relax these muscles and release the tension as you exhale.
- Abdomen—Take a deep breath and hold it for about 5 seconds as you pull in your stomach and bend your waist to lean your shoulders forward about 6 inches. Then relax these muscles and release the tension as you exhale.
- Lower back and shoulders—Take a deep breath and hold it for about 5 seconds as you arch your back and push your elbows back while keeping your forearms parallel with the ground, effectively pushing your shoulder blades together. Then relax these muscles and release the tension as you exhale.
- Neck—Take a deep breath and hold it for about 5 seconds as you turn your head to the right and look out over your right shoulder. Then relax these muscles and release the tension as you exhale. Next, take a deep breath and hold it for about 5 seconds as you turn your head to the left and look out over your left shoulder. Then relax these muscles and release the tension as you exhale. Take a deep breath and hold it for about 5 seconds as you lean your head to the right and try to touch your right ear to your right shoulder. Then relax these muscles and release the tension as you exhale. Next, take a deep breath and hold it for about seconds as you lean your head to the left and try to touch your left ear to your left shoulder. Then relax these muscles and release the tension as you exhale.
- Lower face (jaw, lips, and tongue)—Take a deep breath and hold it for about 5 seconds as you clench your teeth, press your lips together, and push your tongue up to the roof of your mouth. Then relax these muscles and release the tension as you exhale.
- Upper face (forehead, eyes, and nose)—Take a deep breath and hold it for about 5 seconds as you close your eyes tightly, wrinkle your nose, and knit your brows in a frown. Then relax these muscles and release the tension as you exhale.

VARIATIONS OF THE PMRT TECHNIQUE

According to Jacobson (1987), there are three different types of progressive relaxation: general, relative, and specific relaxation. Clients relax every muscle group in their bodies when they are practicing general relaxation. Relative relaxation occurs when a person is doing something but relaxes as much as possible. For example, while sitting at his desk at work, a person could practice relative relaxation; he is not able to relax completely, but relaxes as much as he can. A person is practicing specific relaxation when he relaxes and tenses only certain muscle groups. Lazarus called the general relaxation procedure total relaxation and the relative relaxation procedure differential relaxation.

Carroll et al. (1997) used PMRT in small group work following a deep breathing exercise. They suggested using relative relaxation after completing the breathing exercise. The professional counselor should have the clients sit in chairs and relax the muscles that they do not need to use.

Another variation of progressive relaxation is tape recorded training. In this alternative, the professional counselor audio tapes a session of PMRT with the client and then gives the client a copy of the tape to listen to at home. This tape takes the place of the professional counselor's training, and the client practices the technique repeatedly in the comfort of her own home. There is some debate over this version, as the professional counselor is not with the client throughout the learning process and cannot correct any mistakes made by the client (Lehrer, 1982). Still using PMRT tapes as homework assignments may make treatment progress faster for many clients.

EXAMPLE OF THE PMRT TECHNIQUE

In this session, Sam is being instructed in how to use PMRT to enhance relaxation.

Counselor (C):   I want you to get in a comfortable position for this activity. Sit up in your chair with your back supported. Take a few long deep slow breaths, and begin to feel yourself relax as your breathing slows . . . (Pause for a minute or two as Sam does his deep breathing) Now, Sam, you are going to learn a relaxation technique called progressive muscle relaxation training. Progressive means step by step, so you are going to learn a step by step process to help you to relax the major muscle groups in your body. Begin by taking a couple of long, deep, slow breaths, just like we practiced over the past week.

Sam (S):   (Closes his eyes and breathes deeply and slowly for about 6 breathing cycles.)

C: PMRT is based on the fact that the same muscle groups cannot be tense and relaxed at the same time. So by relaxing the muscle groups one at a time, we can achieve total body relaxation. The basic process is to take in a deep breath, hold it for about 5 to 7 seconds while you tense the specific group of muscles, then release the tension in the muscles as you exhale. The relaxation of the exhale gets coupled with the relaxing of the muscle tension so that, after you practice this long enough, you may be able to just exhale and feel the tension leave your muscles.

S: That would be great! And save some time.

C: Right, so it is important that we become very good at this procedure and practice hard so that in the future, you're right, you can save a lot of time. By the way, this whole procedure works similarly to a physics concept known as resting potential. You see, you can estimate the tension in your muscle on a scale of 1 to 10 or 1 to 100 just like we have done with other concepts. If the resting potential, the present state of tension in your muscle, is, say, a 7, then when you tense the muscle group, the tension will raise to, say, a 9 or 10. Then when you release the tension, the muscle will relax to, say, a 5 or 6, more relaxed than it was before we started.

S: Oh, I see. So by tensing and relaxing a muscle you can actually get it to relax.

C: Right. Now let's start by with the first muscle group, your right arm. But first take in a couple more long, deep slow breaths. (Pause for 3 breathing cycles.) Okay, take a deep breath and hold it for about 5 seconds as you take your right arm and make a fist, curl your wrist, flex your forearm, and flex your bicep. But keep your shoulder and the rest of your body relaxed. Just tense your right arm. Then, after about 5 seconds, relax these muscles and release the tension as you slowly exhale. Also, concentrate on the feeling of relaxation in your arm as you release the tension. Great. Do you understand the process now? Deep breath in, hold for 5 to 7 seconds as you tense the muscle group, then relax the muscles as you exhale . . . Now take a breath in and exhale it before we go on to the next muscle group . . .

S: Got it—sounds pretty simple.

Because Sam caught on quickly, the counselor now proceeds through the remaining muscle groups.

C: Okay. Let's try the left arm. Take a deep breath and hold it for about 5 seconds as you make a fist, curl your wrist, flex your forearm, and flex your bicep. Then relax these muscles and release the tension as you exhale . . .

Now your right leg. Take a deep breath and hold it for about 5 seconds as you curl your toes under, lift the ball of your foot to flex your shin, and flex your thigh muscle. Then relax these muscles and release the tension as you exhale . . .

Left leg. Take a deep breath and hold it for about 5nseconds as you curl your toes under, lift the ball of your foot to flex your shin, and flex your thigh muscle. Then relax these muscles and release the tension as you exhale . . .

Your abdomen. Take a deep breath and hold it for about 5 seconds as you pull in your stomach and bend your waist to lean your shoulders forward about 6 inches. Then relax these muscles and release the tension as you exhale . . .

Your lower back and shoulders. Take a deep breath and hold it for about 5 seconds as you arch your back and push your elbows back while keeping your forearms parallel with the ground, effectively pushing your shoulder blades together. Then relax these muscles and release the tension as you exhale . . .

The neck is a little more complex because it includes several sets of complementary muscles. Take a deep breath and hold it for about 5 seconds as you turn your head to the right and look out over your right shoulder. Then relax these muscles and release the tension as you exhale. Next, take a deep breath and hold it for about 5 seconds as you turn your head to the left and look out over your left shoulder. Then relax these muscles and release the tension as you exhale. Take a deep breath and hold it for about 5 seconds as you lean your head to the right and try to touch your right ear to your right shoulder. Then relax these muscles and release the tension as you exhale. Next, take a deep breath and hold it for about 5 seconds as you lean your head to the left and try to touch your left ear to your left shoulder. Then relax these muscles and release the tension as you exhale . . .

Now let's do your lower face, that is your jaw lips and tongue. Take a deep breath and hold it for about 5 seconds as you clench your teeth, press your lips together, and push your tongue up to the roof of your mouth. Then relax these muscles and release the tension as you exhale . . .

Finally, your upper face, which includes your forehead, eyes and nose. Take a deep breath and hold it for about 5 seconds as you close your eyes tightly, wrinkle your nose, and knit your brows in a frown. Then relax these muscles and release the tension as you exhale . . .

Okay. We have relaxed all of the major muscle groups in your body. Scan your whole body again and search for any muscles that are still tense. Tense and relax them as we did before.

S: (Sam tenses and relaxes the muscles in his lower back and shoulders one more time.)

C: Now take a few more long deep slow breaths to end the exercise and concentrate on the feeling of relaxation in your muscles, allowing them to become even more relaxed as you continue to breathe.

S: (Sam completes another 3 or so breathing cycles).

C: Okay. Open your eyes and guess what your homework is.

S: 3 times a day, every day until I see you next time . . .

USEFULNESS AND EVALUATION OF THE PMRT TECHNIQUE

PMRT is effective in addressing a wide array of physical and psychological complaints (Harris, 2003). While PMRT is a technique frequently used by itself, it is often combined with techniques such as systematic desensitization, assertion training, self-management programs, biofeedback induced relaxation, hypnosis, meditation, and autogenic training (Corey, 2007). Progressive relaxation is also used to alleviate an array of clinical problems including anxiety, stress, high blood pressure and other cardiovascular problems, migraine headaches, asthma, and insomnia (Corey, 2007). When people experience stress due to the pressures they feel from work or their lifestyles, PMRT can often be beneficial. PMRT has also been used effectively as a method of reducing anxiety in gifted children (Roome & Romney, 1985), as well as facilitate coping in the workplace, and to treat chronic low back pain (Carlson & Hoyle, 1993).

Kiselica and Baker (1992) provided further cautions for professional counselors who intend to use progressive relaxation. They warn counselors that for some clients, the relaxation procedures can actually induce anxiety. To help clients who have anxiety about relaxing, professional counselors should inform their clients that they may feel some uncommon sensations during the procedure. Professional counselors can also talk to their clients about how progressive relaxation can increase, rather than decrease, their control over themselves. For some anxious clients, keeping the lights on may ease their concerns. Other clients may recall vivid memories that can be disturbing or pleasant. In either case, the counselor needs to help the client process the memory. When completing the progressive relaxation procedure, there may be some clients who fall asleep. To help prevent this from happening, a counselor can tell the client to stay awake, make the room brighter, or change the client's position (Kiselica & Baker, 1992). The professional counselor can also develop a signal for the client to use to let the counselor know that he is relaxed but awake.

34

Systematic Desensitization

ORIGINS OF THE SYSTEMATIC DESENSITIZATION TECHNIQUE

In the late 1950s, Joseph Wolpe developed systematic desensitization, one of the most common techniques used to treat anxiety and phobias (Corey, 2007). This technique, originally considered to be strictly behavioral, is now considered to include cognitive components as well, thus creating the rationale for including it in this section on techniques based on cognitive-behavioral approaches. Systematic desensitization is a procedure in which clients repeatedly recall, imagine, or experience anxiety-provoking events and then use relaxation techniques to suppress the anxiety caused by the event (Richmond, 1998).

The basis for systematic desensitization stems from classical conditioning, counterconditioning, and, in particular, a concept reviewed earlier called reciprocal inhibition (Seligman, 2001); that is two competing responses cannot occur simultaneously. It is not possible to be fearful and calm at the same time. The key is strengthening the desirable response (calm) so as to block out the undesirable response (fear). In the case of systematic desensitization, the relaxation technique learned and used by the client decreases the likelihood that the event will trigger an anxious response in the client. Anxiety and relaxation are incompatible responses, so the client, with gradual exposure to the feared event and relaxation training, becomes less sensitive to the event (Young, 1992). Examples of phobias for which systematic desensitization can be used include a fear of an animal or insect (e.g., dog, bee, spider), heights, or closed spaces (e.g., elevator).

Systematic desensitization can be conducted either covertly, through visualization in the professional counselor's office (e.g., visually imagine the bee or heights), or *in vivo*, translated as "real life" exposure to the fear producing stimulus (e.g., actually exposing the client to bees or heights). We advocate for use of covert imagery because it gives the professional counselor greater control over the environment and counseling process. Both are equally effective.

HOW TO IMPLEMENT THE SYSTEMATIC DESENSITIZATION TECHNIQUE

There are three general components involved in the process of systematic desensitization. First, the client is taught a relaxation technique (e.g., PMRT) in which he or she needs to become proficient. Second, an anxiety hierarchy scale is created. The third component is "counterposing relaxation and anxiety-provoking stimuli" (Young, 1992, p. 138). Before the client and counselor get to the point where they are ready to begin the actual desensitization process, the first two components must be accomplished to a satisfactory level.

After the counseling relationship is formed between the client and the counselor, the first step in systematic desensitization is to discover the behavior upon which to focus the intervention. To do this, the professional counselor needs to gather a complete history of the client. By extensively questioning the client, the counselor can analyze the client's problem and connect it with other events occurring in the client's life (Young, 1992). One reason for this in-depth review of the client's background is that "it reveals a variety of situations to which he reacts with undue disturbance" (Wolpe, 1958, p. 139). In addition to learning general information about the client, the counselor also learns which situations and circumstances bring out the client's anxiety, which will help with the second step of the process (Corey, 2007).

In step two, the professional counselor works with the client to discover any factors that are linked to the client's anxiety. It is important for the client to give accounts filled with details of the anxiety-provoking situations. For systematic desensitization to be most effective, the counselor needs to know all of the situations that cause the client distress. This information is learned via discussion, although the *Fear Survey Schedule*, *Willoughby Questionnaire*, or *Bernsenter Self-Sufficiency Inventory* are also methods for the counselor to find out the client's fears (Young, 1992).

Next, the professional counselor assists the client in constructing an anxiety hierarchy. It is important that the hierarchies are "as real and concrete as possible" (Young, 1992, p. 138). The *Willoughby Questionnaire* provides some of the raw data needed. The professional counselor should also assign the client homework of creating "a list of everything he can think of that is capable of frightening, disturbing, distressing, or embarrassing him in any way, excepting of course, situations that would frighten anybody" (Wolpe, 1958, p. 139). If needed, the counselor should help the client come up with at least 10 items; typically the list should not have more than 100. The counselor then reviews the list and groups items related to a specific

fear together. The client views the divided list and ranks the themed items using the subjective units of distress scale (SUDS) (see below). The hierarchy/hierarchies is/are then constructed by placing the situations that cause the most anxiety at the top of the list and those situations that cause the least anxiety at the bottom of the list, in descending order (see Table 34.1 in the example below).

Once the hierarchy is created, the client is ready to learn a relaxation technique (Young, 1992). Although Wolpe (1958) suggests hypnosis, the technique most commonly taught to clients is progressive muscle relaxation training (PMRT; see chapter 33). Clients learn how to relax all of the different muscles in their bodies. In order for systematic desensitization to be most effective, the client needs to be able to completely relax. To become proficient in relaxation techniques, the client should practice them at home (Young).

The professional counselor next needs to create a plan to present the scenarios from the hierarchy to the client (Young, 1992). Typically, there is a slow progression "from covert scenes having little intensity to overt and more realistic situations" (Young, 1992, p. 139). The professional counselor and client need to agree upon a signal that the client will give to the counselor if he or she becomes distressed; a slight raise of the hand usually works just fine (Wolpe, 1958).

When the client and counselor are ready to begin the desensitization process, the client needs to reach the state of deep relaxation learned earlier. The client's eyes should be closed. The counselor begins by introducing a neutral scene not found on the client's hierarchy. If the client can imagine this scene without experiencing anxiety, the counselor asks the client to imagine the situation at the bottom of the hierarchy (Corey, 2007). After three seconds, the counselor asks the client to imagine the situation that is next on the gradual progression of the hierarchy. If the client feels any anxiety during this process, the client is to raise a hand to let the counselor know (Wolpe, 1958). When the client experiences anxiety, he is to stop imagining the scene and return to a state of deep relaxation. Once the client is relaxed, the professional counselor can continue presenting scenes from the hierarchy. The content of the second session is determined by how far along the client progressed through the hierarchy during the first session. Scenes to which the client had no adverse reaction are taken out of the hierarchy. If the client had significant anxiety to the weakest situation, it must be replaced with a weaker one. If a stimulus that is too strong is presented, harm may be done; a counselor should always err on the side of presenting a stimulus that is weak, since no harm comes out of it. Following sessions should be conducted in a similar way. Wolpe (1958) indicated that, typically, treatment will take 10 to 25 sessions of systematic desensitization. When a client is able to imagine the situation at the top of the hierarchy while remaining in a relaxed state, treatment is complete.

The last step is for the counselor and client to develop a follow-up plan. This plan should involve having the client practice the technique at home once the sessions have ended. The counselor should also schedule follow-up visits with the client as reinforcement may be necessary to ensure the success of the treatment (Young, 1992).

Subjective Units of Distress Scale (SUDS)

In order to measure shifts in levels of client anxiety, Joseph Wolpe created the Subjective Units of Distress Scale (SUDS). SUDS is a more specific example of the general procedure known as scaling, which was presented in chapter 1. The SUDS was originally designed for use with clients during systematic desensitization procedures (Kaplan & Smith, 1995). The SUDS is used so that the professional counselor can assess and understand which situations cause the most anxiety for the client (Kaplan & Smith). To introduce the SUDS to the client, Wolpe (1990, p. 91) suggested posing the following scenario to the client:

> Think of the worst anxiety you can imagine and assign to it the number 100. Then think of being absolutely calm—that is, no anxiety at all—and call this number 0. Now you have a scale of anxiety. At every moment of your waking life, you must be somewhere between 0 and 100. How do you rate yourself at this moment?

Usually the 0-100 scale is used because of the flexibility of range it provides. However, a scale of 0-10 can also be used, making the SUDS similar to the scaling technique discussed previously. The client's self report on the SUDS establishes a baseline in terms of the client's anxiety level (Wolpe, 1990). When a client is experiencing anxiety about several different things, the professional counselor can have the client use the SUDS to figure out which situation is the most anxiety provoking. With this knowledge, the professional counselor can help focus the session on just one situation (Shapiro, 2001).

Wolpe (1990, p. 160) described how the SUDS can be used to create an anxiety hierarchy that is "a thematically related list of anxiety-evoking stimuli, ranked according to the amount of anxiety they evoke." The subject of the hierarchy can be internal to the client, but most commonly is something external. To create the hierarchy, the professional counselor and client make a list consisting of the scope of the client's thoughts about the anxiety-provoking stimuli. Then, the client rates each of the items using the SUDS. Finally, the professional counselor creates the hierarchy by arranging the statements from the least anxiety provoking to the most anxiety provoking according to the magnitude of the SUDS score (Thorpe & Olson, 1997). This provides the framework for the professional counselor to implement systematic desensitization with the client.

VARIATIONS OF THE SYSTEMATIC DESENSITIZATION TECHNIQUE

Corey (2007) described a common variation of systematic desensitization, *in vivo* desensitization. While the procedure described above calls for the client to solely imagine the scenarios, in vivo desensitization includes exposing the clients to the real feared situation. When appropriate, the client can self-manage *in vivo* desensitization. If necessary, the counselor can go with the client to face the anxiety-provoking situation. Supporters of this alternative advocate that the results of treatment are more effective because the client is better able to generalize the learning experience.

Young (1992) suggested another variation of systematic desensitization with a focus on "learning to reduce anxiety rather than to reduce fear of a particular stimulus" (p. 206). Instead of subdividing the client's list and having several hierarchies to work through with the client, only one hierarchy is constructed. The treatment plan consists of only six sessions; relaxation is still taught and a hierarchy is still constructed. Each situation from the list is written on its own index card. The session begins with the client becoming relaxed and imagining a neutral scene. Then, the counselor begins by reading the description on the lowest anxiety-provoking situation card. If the client is able to stay relaxed, the counselor can go on to the next situation card. On each card, the counselor records the ranking number, the original SUDS score, a description of the anxiety-provoking situation, the trial number, for how long the client was able to stay relaxed, and the SUDS level associated with each trial number. Young recommends introducing *in vivo* desensitization to the client when appropriate.

Another variation, self-administered systematic desensitization, is described by Richmond (1998). It contains the same three components of the original version of systematic desensitization. The client first needs to become familiar with a relaxation technique and then needs to create an anxiety hierarchy, including detailed descriptions of the situations. Richmond suggests having 10 to 15 situations, writing each on a separate card, and using the SUDS to rate each situation. After sorting the cards, the person should order them from lowest to highest anxiety provoking. The next day, the person can start "pairing relaxation with situations from the anxiety hierarchy" (p. 7). Each session should last 30 minutes and the person should attempt to work on three situations per session. A deep state of relaxation should be attained at the end of each session for several minutes. Richmond (p. 8) provides the following steps for the self-administered version:

Step 1: Induce relaxation.

Step 2: Read the appropriate item from your hierarchy. (In the first session, this will be the first item in the hierarchy. In all other sessions, this will be the last item from the previous session.)

Step 3: Imagine yourself in the situation for a tolerable time, which will vary with each situation. Aim to imagine each situation for 30 seconds on subsequent presentations.

Step 4: Stop imagining the situation and determine the level of anxiety that you are experiencing. Re-establish your relaxation again and relax for 30 seconds.

Step 5: Re-read the description of the situation. Imagine yourself in the scene for a tolerable time.

Step 6: Stop and again determine your level of anxiety. If you are experiencing any anxiety, return to Step 2. If you feel no anxiety, go on to Step 7.

Step 7: Move on to the next item of your hierarchy. Repeat the above procedure beginning with Step 1.

Importantly, clients should be prohibited from trying systematic desensitization on their own between sessions. However, it is a good practice for the professional counselor to assign homework between sessions, including practicing and strengthening client skills in deep breathing, progressive muscle relaxation training, visual imagery, and self-talk.

EXAMPLE OF THE SYSTEMATIC DESENSITIZATION TECHNIQUE

Systematic desensitization is composed of three facets: (a) teaching relaxation, (b) constructing an anxiety hierarchy and scaling it using the subjective units of distress scale, and (c) systematically applying the relaxation to the hierarchy to accomplish desensitization. Earlier in this session, Nicole was taught the techniques of positive self-talk, visualization, deep breathing, and progressive muscle relaxation training. She is now ready to begin the process known as systematic desensitization to treat her test phobia. Nicole's treatment was conducted using an imagery implementation strategy in the counseling office rather than in real life (*in vivo*). The imagery-based method gives the counselor more control over the anxiety-producing stimulus (it is easier to handle panic reactions related to fear of heights when the client is sitting in a chair in your office imagining they are in an elevator, than when they are actually on the elevator) and is generally as effective as *in vivo* desensitization. The following transcript demonstrates creation of an anxiety hierarchy, implementation of the subjective units of distress scale (SUDS), and the imagery-based systematic desensitization procedure.

Counselor (C):   All right, let's see. So we've learned about positive self-talk and visual imagery. We've done some deep breathing and some progressive muscle relaxation. We are now ready to deal with your presenting concern, a test phobia, using what is called systematic desensitization. That's a big fancy term, but it basically means that we are going to help you to get used to a testing situation step by step and replace your anxiety with relaxation. We are going to do this by accomplishing two more things. We're going to construct what's called an anxiety hierarchy, with some things that have to do with testing that aren't very anxiety producing at all and then proceeding all the way up to the things about a testing situation that make you incredibly anxious, like where you're actually sitting there taking your SAT test, and shaking and "it's end of the world" and you're getting up to that 9 or that 10 on the panic scale, frightening and anxiety producing things.

Nicole (N):   Okay.

C: And then we're also going to use the progressive relaxation training, which we've already learned how to do. So these two parts, fear hierarchy and the progressive relaxation training, will be used in the third part, systematic desensitization, okay?

N: Let's do it.

C: Let's talk for a second about the fear hierarchy. We want to get somewhere between 10 and 15 steps on this hierarchy. So what are some anxiety-producing things that you've experienced in the way of testing, from minor stuff

to the times that you've been the most frightened or fearful?

N: Just involving tests?

C: Yes, the test anxiety?

N: You mean like, when I like, when I get like stressed out the most?

C: Okay, sure. Something that would be real close to a 9 or a 10 on that scale.

N: Probably when I'm stuck, something really bad. Like I'm actually in the test, I'm taking it and there's a question or a part that I don't understand whatsoever. It's probably the worst I think.

C: Okay, so you're in the test and you're stuck on a question you don't understand?

(Counselor writes this and subsequent contributions down.)

N: Yeah.

C: Okay, well, what else? What other kinds of things do you run into?

N: I'm watching and I see all kinds of people are done and I see everyone else is done and I'm still frantically working. That's pretty bad.

C: So they . . .

N: They have their pencils down or sitting there.

C: What else?

N: If I'm running out of time, that's a big one, and I'm not anywhere near finished or I still have a lot left in a short period of time to do.

C: Okay. What else?

N: In the beginning I guess or if I see that the test is a lot. Like a lot of pages or a lot of questions, I may panic because I may feel like I'm never going to finish it all.

C: Okay. You've got some things at that high end of the scale, we need some things kind of in the middle, maybe even things down at the bottom that aren't really so anxiety producing but they are still things that kind of get you a little bit churned up. What's some, what might some of those things be? . . .

N: Well, maybe when the teacher announces that we are going to have a test soon. In the middle somewhere would probably be more the fact that I know that the test is coming up soon and I need to prepare more.

C: You need to prepare more?

N: Yeah.

C: That would be even more stressful than the teacher announcing the test?

N: Yes.

C: (Counselor helps to fill in some low and medium range responses.) And then we could probably even say things like, well, you know, some on the morning of the test?

N: Yes.

C: Okay, and the night before the test?

N: (Nods head yes)

C: Maybe even the day before if you're in class?

N: (Nods head yes)

C: And how much time do they usually give you from the time they say, that the teacher says oh there's going to be a test? Is it usually like a week ahead or a couple of days?

N: A week, sometimes a couple of days.

C: A couple of days?

N: A week. Usually they'll give us.

C: Okay, I'm writing like 2 days ahead, 3 days, 4 days ahead.

N: Okay.

C: Anything else that you can think of?

N: That's pretty much everything that I can think of.

C: There's probably a lot that happens between when you wake on the morning of the test and when the test occurs, as you are getting closer and closer to when the test starts.

N: I guess when I wake up and I'm going through the information again. Reviewing it all.

C: So you're reviewing on the morning of?

N: Mmmhmm.

C: What else? How about on your way to school?

N: Yeah, it does. Really nervous.

C: How about when you arrive?

N: Yes, when I get there. Basically all the way up until the test.

C: So, is there anything that happens from the time that you arrive at school to the time that you actually, that the teacher passes the test out?

N: I'm more anxious and more nervous. When it's getting closer and closer and time is getting less and less before the test.

C: Okay. And that would kind of be the waiting time?

N: Yeah.

C: And then there's the waiting time in between it and then there's the time that the teacher actually passes the tests out, okay, and then you see that there's a lot of pages or questions on the test. You're running out of time and you have a lot left to do, you see other people already have their pencils down and so forth and then you're stuck on a question that you don't understand.

N: Yeah.

C: Okay? So by my count we've got 2, 4, 6, 8, 10, 12, 14, 16. Okay, we can add or scratch a few because we're coming up on the close of our session right now. The next thing we're going to do is what's called the subjective units of distress scale, or SUDS, where you actually get to rank each of these on a scale of 1 to 100.

N: Okay.

C: On how much anxiety you feel whenever these things happen. Some of them might be close to 90 or 100 and some of them might be down close to, you know, a 10 or a 15 or a 20.

N: Right.

C: And so what will happen, we will have all these ranked in order of how much anxiety they produce in you and we will go ahead and do the systematic desensitization. I will have you close your eyes and we'll imagine each one of these things is happening, we'll start at the really easy ones and you will relax yourself while you are imagining these things. While imagining these scenes, you will be relaxing using your deep breathing. And you'll have your progressive muscle relaxation training . . . positive self-talk . . . and you'll be able to switch your image to the beach to calm yourself down if you need to, okay?

N: Okay.

C: As we kind of move our way up this hierarchy—and we'll probably get through four or five of them in each of the next few sessions—from now on our sessions will be a lot quicker because we'll only do four or five of these things and then we'll stop, and then do four or five the next time, and so on until we get to the top of the scale without having you feel like you're really upset and anxious about things . . .

Begin session 2.

C: All right, Nicole, another week until school starts, huh?

N: Yep.

C: Whoa, you think they are going to give you any tests this year?

N: Yes, a lot.

C: All right, you think so? A lot of tests. You're expecting, a ton of tests.

N: Yep.

Counselor reviews activities from previous session and checks to make sure all homework assignments were completed before continuing with systematic desensitization. Note: Nicole's anxiety hierarchy prepared during this session can be located in Table 34.1.

C: Since last session, I took the anxiety hierarchy listing and put the events in what seems to me a reasonable starting order and I have them listed on my paper here. So the first thing that we want to do today is to apply the subjective units of distress scales, its acronym is SUDS, to this fear hierarchy list. And what that does is helps us to rate each of these events that you imagine would happen or do happen in real life. You need to rate each one so we can put them in order from lowest, or the least stress producing, up to the highest,

TABLE 34.1   Nicole's Anxiety Hierarchy

SUDS	Event
015	The teacher is announcing there will be a test in a week.
025	It is 4 days before the test will be administered.
032	It is 3 days before the test will be administered.
040	It is 2 days before the test will be administered.
055	The test is coming up and you need to prepare.
068	It is the day before the test.
078	It is the night before the test.
084	It is the morning of the test.
086	You are on your way to school on the morning of the test.
087	You arrive at school on the morning of the test.
089	The teacher passes out the test and is ready to begin.
091	You see a lot of pages and questions on the test.
094	You get stuck on a question.
096	Other people are finishing and have their pencils down on the deck.
097	You are running out of time but still have a lot to do.

or the most stress producing things to do with test anxiety. When we are finished with the list, we will be able to start at the bottom of that list and work our way up to the highest things, using our relaxation, using our visual imagery, using our self-talk and deep breathing, so that we'll be able to relax while we're imagining the nasty stuff happening. What will eventually happen then is you'll become desensitized to the nasty stuff because you're relaxed while you're thinking about it, imagining it. And then when you go into real life you'll be relaxed because you've taken care of this in the office here. All right?

N: Okay.

C: So the first thing we need to do is the subjective units of distress scale. Have you ever seen an alarm clock with an LCD readout? It's the numbers that show up, the background is dark and red or some other colored numbers flash up? (Nicole nods.) I want you to imagine an LCD panel with three digit spots on it, where three numbers can come up and the numbers can go anywhere from 000 to 100. So 000 means I'm not stressed out at all, I'm totally relaxed, this doesn't bother me at all, and 100 is whenever you are stressed out you're like ready to have a panic attack and everything, because you're just so upset and stressed out. Okay?

N: Okay.

C: So what we want to do is on that scale from 0 to 100 we want you to read each one of these little comments that we have, each one of these activities or events that'll happen so we can put them in order. I'm just going to read some of them off. Close your eyes. I'm going to say one of them, and I want you to go ahead and imagine it happening in your mind. That's why I want you to close your eyes. I want you to visually imagine that this is happening to you, and I want you to put that little LCD panel up in the top right hand corner of your mind's eye.

N: Okay.

C: Does that make sense?

N: Sure, that makes sense.

C: Nicole, I want you to imagine yourself in the classroom and in whatever subject you like to imagine yourself being in. I want you to imagine that the teacher is announcing that there will be a test a week from now in the subject. On that scale from 0 to 100, with 0 being absolutely stress-free and 100 being totally stressed out, where would you be on that scale?

N: 015.

C: 015. So that's pretty close to stress-free, right?

N: Yeah.

C: Now I want you to imagine that you're now 4 days away, 4 days from the test being administered. Where are you on that scale?

N: 025.

C: 025? Okay, so we're getting a little bit higher there.

N: Yep.

C: How about 3 days away?

N: 040.

C: 040?

N: Yeah.

C: A test is coming up and you need to prepare.

N: 055.

C: 055?

N: Yeah.

C: Okay, how about 2 days away?

N: 050.

C: Okay. How about a day before the test?

N: It's going up more. About 068.

C: 068. So really that last day before the test, that day before the test is where you start really getting stressed out.

N: Yes.

C: Okay. How about the night before the test? You are at 068 on the day, knowing it's the next day?

N: 078.

C: 078. Okay, how about the morning of the test?

N: 087. Oh, no, actually 084.

C: 084. Okay. And you're reviewing. You just woke up, and you're reviewing for that test in the morning.

N: 086.

C: Okay, and now you're on your way to school.

N: Probably about the same, 086, it usually doesn't change really.

C: How about right when you arrive at school?

N: Probably like 087.

C: Okay, just a little tiny bit higher.

N: Yeah.

C: The teacher passes out the test, and you're waiting to begin.

N: That's bad. 089.

C: 089. Okay, you're stuck on a question, you're taking the test and you're stuck on a question that you don't understand.

N: That's pretty high because I usually panic at that point so that would probably be 094. Yeah.

C: 094?

N: Yeah.

C: Okay, other people have their pencils down.

N: Oh, gosh. So high, 096.

C: And you're running out of time and you have a lot left to do.

N: That's probably the highest I think. That would probably be like 097.

C: 097?

N: Yeah.

C: Okay, so you're really close to a 100.

N: Yeah.

C: What would a 100 be, by the way? Is there something that would put you at a 100?

N: I don't think I'd ever really get to 100 but probably get really close, but I'm sure I'd lose it.

C: We'd be carrying you out of the room or something?

N: Yeah.

C: All right, so you've got some down here, the teacher announces that the test will be a week ahead, that was about a 015, and as the test gets closer you're starting to feel more stress until the morning of the test. And on your way to school, you arrive at school, you're getting real close to 090 and then as the teacher is passing it out you're right at 089. And you see there are a lot of pages, you get stuck on a question that you are not understanding. Other people seem to be finishing and you're running out of time and you have a lot of questions left.

N: Yeah, that's the worst.

C: Was there anything as you were kind of running your way through that list, is there anything that you want to add at this point? Anything that you think is something particularly problematic for you that we've forgotten?

N: I think that pretty much covers everything. I think that's everything I need.

C: All right and because you gave two of them the same rating, on the way to school and review the morning of, I'm just going to scratch the one and that will leave us 15 steps on the anxiety hierarchy. Is there anything else that I need to know about before we begin?

N: Nope.

The professional counselor now begins the actual systematic desensitization procedure.

C: Okay, well, let's go ahead then and we'll start at the bottom of the list and we'll work through about three or four or maybe five today and see how you do.

N: Okay.

C: Now I want you to just kind of get comfortable, even use some deep breathing and progressive muscle relaxation training to work out any kinks you might have in your body. I want you to take a couple of deep breaths. Okay.

N: You want me to start now.

C: Yep. Take a couple of deep breaths, close you eyes, you might even want to take yourself to the beach right now or use some positive self-talk to reach a deep state of relaxation . . . (Pause for a couple of minutes or so)

C: Okay. Now for this next step, we're going to take the nice calming, deep, slow breath and then I'm going to have you imagine what's on the list here, what we were just talking about. I'm going to start at the lowest one and I want you to imagine that scene in your mind's eye. And then, I want you to, while you're imagining it, keep taking deep slow breaths. If you become very anxious or stressed, I want you to block out the testing image and replace it with your beach scene. Okay?

N: Okay.

C: Also, I want you to give me a little sign that you are relaxed and ready to move on to the next step. When you have visualized the scene in your mind and have regained a state of calm and relaxation, just twitch your finger to let me know you are ready to move on.

N: Like this. (Lifts her finger as a signal)

C: Exactly, great. Let's start with the first one. I want you to imagine, visually imagine, that your teacher has announced that there will be a test about a week from now. So picture that and keep breathing and relaxing, and then give me another little finger sign when you're ready to go on, when you are able to imagine the scene while remaining calm and relaxed. (Pause)

N: Okay, now open your eyes for a second and come back to me. How do you feel right now on that scale from 0 to 100?

N: Probably about a 003, maybe. I'm really relaxed right now.

C: Originally that one was a 015. And now it is a 003, pretty calm and relaxed, not really stressed out at all.

N: No.

C: Okay, go ahead and close your eyes and take another couple of deep breaths and give me a finger sign and we'll go on to the next one and we'll probably go through the next three or four. (Pause until finger twitch.)

C: Okay, now I want you to imagine that it's now 4 days away from the test, 4 days. Imagine it, keep breathing, and keep relaxing. (Pause until finger twitch)

C: All right, now I want you to imagine that there are 3 days until the test. (Pause until finger twitch)

C: Good, now I want you to imagine there are only 2 days until the test is going to be administered. Try to stay calm with good breathing. (Pause until finger twitch)

C: Good, now I want you to imagine that the test is coming up very soon and you need to prepare for the test. Imagine yourself needing to prepare. (Pause until finger twitch) . . . Okay, Nicole, now come back to me slowly and, when you are ready, open your eyes . . . Where on that scale of 1 to 100 are you now?

N: (Nicole yawns and stretches) 010.

C: 010?

N: Or maybe a 008.

C: That's good, that's great, that's fantastic . . . You are doing a great job. You made it a third of the way up your hierarchy, okay, so you're already at the 055 point and you're understanding now what I mean. That you're going to get up there, here you were imagining something that was about a 055 and you're now able to visualize that scene and keep yourself all the way back down to about a 010 on your scale. This is basically what we are going to do over the next three to five sessions. We're going to do a few more next time and try to keep you calm and relaxed while imagining those things, so that whenever you take tests in real life the stress won't be so bad. You'll be able to be calm and relaxed and use your deep breathing when you're in real life situations and able to control your thoughts and the pictures in your mind so that you'll be able to cope with all those stresses, all right?

N: All right.

C: Now—and this is very important—do *not* try to do this on your own outside of our sessions. Got it—it is only for inside our sessions when I am here to make sure you are doing it correctly and safely.

N: No problem . . .

Begin session 5. During session 3, Nicole backed up and began with step 4 on her anxiety hierarchy then completed steps 5 through 10 without incident. During session 4, Nicole backed up and began with step 9 on her anxiety hierarchy then completed steps 10 through 14 without incident. At this point the treatment was nearly completed. Had she experienced any adverse reaction during these steps, the counselor would have used reciprocal inhibition to block the stressful visualization and deep breathing, self-talk and PMRT to return her to a relaxed state, ending the session for the day. As fate would have it, Nicole missed a session between sessions 4 and 5 and had several tests in school during the week before the final session.

C: Missed you last week. Bring me up to date on what is happening in school.

N: Well . . . I had a couple of tests.

C: Really? How did they go? Any tough ones?

N: Oh, yeah. Precalc and chem were tough. But the weird thing was I didn't panic, or feel sick or anything. I just took deep breaths when things got hard and kept the nasty stuff out of my mind . . .

At this point the treatment was obviously having the desired effect. The counselor finished the session by beginning with step 13 and proceeding through step 15, completing the hierarchy, then using the "flagging the minefield" technique. Interestingly, Nicole finished her senior year with no adverse testing reactions, raised her SAT score by 150 points (math and verbal combined score), and got into her first choice university and desired major.

USEFULNESS AND EVALUATION OF THE SYSTEMATIC DESENSITIZATION TECHNIQUE

Systematic desensitization is commonly used to treat specific phobias and in some cases using *in vivo* desensitization can be achieved in a single session (Ost, 1989; Zinbarg, Barlow, Brown & Hertz, 1992). A specific phobia occurs when a person's anxiety is related to a specific situation, such as test taking or a fear of heights (George & Christiani, 1995). The use of systematic desensitization is most appropriate when the client possesses the necessary coping skills, but avoids situations because of her high level of anxiety.

Austin and Partridge (1995) suggested use of systematic desensitization with students to alleviate stressful situations like test anxiety. Crawford (1998) described using systematic desensitization with preservice teachers who had reading anxiety.

Most professional counselors are in agreement that systematic desensitization is successful in treating phobias, however, there is disagreement over whether imaginal or *in vivo* exposure is more effective (Zinbarg et al., 1992). Graziano, DeGiovanni, and Garcia (1979) conducted a review of the literature focused on behavioral treatments

of children's phobias and found that systematic desensitization, whether applied individually or in groups, whether actually experienced or vicariously experienced, is more effective in reducing certain phobias and anxiety related to situations than are other types of treatments. Such findings make the discussion of superior effectiveness between imagery-based and *in vivo* approaches moot.

Some supporters claim that this technique works because of reciprocal inhibition (Wolpe, 1958). Others claim that systematic desensitization is successful because the clients learn through repeated exposure that the stimulus will not harm them (Young, 1992). Another explanation is that clients gain insight during the time it takes to complete the desensitization process (Young, 1992). Meichenbaum (as cited in Young, 1992) suggested that actual cognitive changes occur during the process and clients change their expectations about the anxiety-provoking situations. Yet another explanation of the efficacy of this technique is that the client learns a new, more effective coping skill (relaxation) to help deal with anxiety.

Importantly, systematic desensitization is not always the appropriate technique to use with a client experiencing anxiety. In order for this technique to be effective, the client must become proficient with progressive muscle relaxation or another relaxation technique; if the client cannot learn to relax, another technique should be chosen. Also, some clients cannot imagine the situations vividly enough, which generally causes systematic desensitization to be ineffective (Young, 1992). If a client continues to experience high levels of anxiety even after numerous exposures to the items on the hierarchy, Richmond (1998) suggested that the professional counselor consider several things. First, the ranking which the client gave the item may be too low. Second, the item may be described in so much detail that it contains aspects of scenes further along in the hierarchy. The professional counselor should also be sure that the client is not focusing too long on a scene without giving the professional counselor the signal she is in distress (Richmond).

CHAPTER 35

Stress Inoculation Training

ORIGINS OF THE STRESS INOCULATION TRAINING TECHNIQUE

Stress inoculation training (SIT), a technique developed by Donald Meichenbaum, is based on the idea that helping clients cope with mild stressors will allow them to develop a tolerance for more severe forms of distress (Corey, 2007). Meichenbaum believed that clients could increase their ability to cope by modifying their beliefs about their own performance in stressful situations. Stress inoculation training seeks to enhance the client's coping skill set as well as encourage the client to use the coping skills he already possesses (Meichenbaum, 1993). SIT combines elements of Socratic and didactic teaching, client self-monitoring, cognitive restructuring, problem solving, relaxation training, behavior rehearsal, and environmental change. However, stress inoculation training is not a formula treatment that can be applied blindly to all distressed clients; instead, SIT is composed of general principles and clinical procedures that must be tailored to fit each individual client.

Stress inoculation training was introduced by Meichenbaum in the early 1970s. The first clients were individuals who experienced multiple fears, who had difficulty controlling their anger, and who had problems coping with physical pain (Meichenbaum, 1993). Meichenbaum stressed cognitive behavior modification, which concentrated on changing the client's self-talk (Corey, 2007). SIT involves a cognitive component which focuses on helping clients modify their self-instructions in order to cope more effectively with the problems they encounter. SIT assists clients in conceptualizing and reframing stress, allowing them to rescript their lives or develop a new narrative about their ability to cope (Meichenbaum).

Stress inoculation training is based on a transactional view of stress, which states that stress occurs whenever the perceived demands of a situation outweigh the perceived ability of the system to meet the demands (Meichenbaum, 1993). Stress is therefore defined as a relationship between the person and the environment in which the person sees the current demands as exceeding his coping resources. SIT seeks to boost the client's coping skills and increase the client's confidence in his coping abilities, thus enabling him to deal more effectively with life stressors.

Stress inoculation training has several goals. First, clients learn to see their stress as a normal, adaptive reaction (Meichenbaum, 1993). Clients also discover the course of their disorder, the transactional nature of stress, and their own role in maintaining their stress level. In addition, clients learn to manage stress by changing their conceptualization of it and by understanding the difference between changeable and unchangeable aspects of stressful situations. Finally, clients work on breaking down large stressors into specific short-term, intermediate, and long-term coping goals.

HOW TO IMPLEMENT THE STRESS INOCULATION TRAINING TECHNIQUE

Stress inoculation training can be conducted with individuals, couples, small groups, or large groups (Meichenbaum, 1993). Typically SIT consists of 8 to 15 sessions, plus booster or follow-up sessions that extend for between 3 and 12 months. Stress inoculation training involves three phases: (1) conceptualization, (2) skill acquisition and rehearsal, and (3) application and follow-through.

The first phase of stress inoculation training, the conceptualization phase, teaches the client the nature of stress as well as his own role in creating stress (Corey, 2007). The client and professional counselor work together to identify the presenting problem (Meichenbaum, 1993). Once global stressors have been identified, the professional counselor can help the client break down these stressors into specific stressful situations and evaluate his present coping efforts. The client then develops short-term, intermediate, and long-term behaviorally specific goals with the understanding that some aspects of stress are changeable and some are unchangeable. The client also self-monitors the internal dialogue, feelings, and behaviors that occur during stressful situations. The professional counselor can then use the client's self-reports to help him develop a re-conceptualization of the distress.

During the second phase, the skill acquisition and rehearsal phase, clients learn a variety of behavioral and cognitive coping techniques to use in stressful situations (Corey, 2007). These coping skills may include collecting information about the stressful situation, planning for resources and escape routes, cognitive restructuring of negative self-statements, task oriented self-instruction, problem solving, and behavioral techniques such as relaxation, assertiveness, or self-rewarding for coping (Meichenbaum & Deffenbacher, 1988). Other important coping skills are social skills, time-management, developing support systems, and re-evaluating priorities (Corey). Once the client has been taught a number of coping strategies, skills can be reinforced through behavioral and imagery rehearsal, coping modeling, and self-instruction training (Meichenbaum, 1993). The professional counselor should also discuss with the client possible barriers and obstacles to using the coping techniques.

The third phase, the application and follow-through phase, allows for transfer of skills from the therapeutic setting to the real world (Corey, 2007). In this stage, skills are rehearsed in role plays, simulations, imagery, and graduated *in vivo* practice (Meichenbaum & Deffenbacher, 1988). As skills are mastered, they are integrated into the external world through graded homework assignments. Another important aspect of this last phase is relapse prevention (Meichenbaum, 1993). To prevent relapses, the client and professional counselor work together to identify high-risk situations, anticipate stressful reactions, and rehearse coping responses. Also, stress inoculation training frequently includes follow-up or booster sessions and may involve significant others in the training to assist the client.

VARIATIONS OF THE STRESS INOCULATION TRAINING TECHNIQUE

Only one variation of the SIT technique has been reported. A five-step process to help children learn to deal with stress has been developed by Dr. Archibald Hart (Shapiro, 1994). Dr. Hart suggested that children be gradually exposed to problems. Children should be told age-appropriate information about family problems and not be overprotected. Parents should resist the urge to rescue children but rather should allow children to solve their own problems. Parents should also teach their children to use healthy self-talk, saying encouraging, rational things to themselves. Children should be allowed adequate time for recovery after a stressful period and should be taught to give themselves this time. Lastly, children need to learn to filter stressors in order to determine what events are worthy of a stressful reaction.

EXAMPLE OF THE STRESS INOCULATION TRAINING TECHNIQUE

Sarah is a 21-year-old college student seeking counseling due to feeling overwhelmed and unable to cope with the ramifications of a previous rape. Approximately 10 months ago, at the end of the spring semester, Sarah was raped at an off-campus party. At the insistence of her mother, she immediately entered into counseling with a professional counselor located in her home town and withdrew from summer classes as well as fall courses. After 4 months of counseling, she terminated counseling as she felt she had made significant improvements in her emotional state and re-enrolled for spring semester courses. Upon her return to campus, she has had much difficulty coping with the past trauma. The following excerpt is from the second session.

Sarah (S):   I just feel I should be over it by now. It is so frustrating to me that it is still affecting my life this way. I had no idea it would be this difficult to come back. I feel like maybe I should go back home again.

Counselor (C):   You felt safe there.

S: Exactly. And I don't feel safe at all here. There are all these reminders, and I'm so afraid I will run into him at any moment.

C: I can see where that would be very difficult for you.

S: It's so unfair. And there is nobody that would even begin to understand. I don't even keep in touch with any of the friends I had last year. They probably think I'm some moron for leaving so quickly and running home to my mom.

C: Or they might think you are brave for coming back.

S: Maybe. I don't know.

C: You did make the choice to come back. You felt strong enough.

S: I did. But then it felt a lot different when I got here. Now I feel like I am going to fall apart at any moment. I feel just like I did almost a year ago when it happened. I really don't think I can deal with this. I mean, what if I see him? What if everyone knows and thinks I deserved it? What if they are all siding with him and still think he is just this incredibly great guy? And I can't even begin to think about the court dates coming up. I wish I had never told my mom. She made me press charges and it was just awful. And I think all of that is about to come up and I am going to have to face him again. I can't do it. I just want to go home and forget it ever happened.

C: You know I would love to tell you that all of these things you worry about are nothing to worry about at all. But instead, I have to say that everything you've mentioned . . . well, they are possibilities. You may run into him on campus or when you're out. There may be some people that don't understand what that is like and they may inaccurately judge you. There may be people who still think he is a wonderful person. And court hearings will eventually take place and you will see him. These are all possibilities, if not certainties. And they are all situations that you can cope with.

S: I just don't see how.

C: Well, first what I'd like to do is determine what things we can change and what things we cannot change.

S: What do you mean? I can't change any of it. It is all out of my hands. That's the worst part.

C: Well, some things, like if you run into him, we cannot change. But we can change how that affects us and how you respond to it when it happens. He raped you—that we cannot change either. But you've already seen how much control you were able to have over how that affected you. You coped with that terrible tragedy and you will cope with these problems as well. They are problems to be solved.

The professional counselor is working to build a relationship and an alliance. He is also looking for problems in thinking such as avoidance, rumination, and catastrophizing. The professional counselor attempts to reframe threats that feel overwhelming to problems to be solved, that are neither overwhelming nor debilitating. Finally, the professional counselor wants to begin laying the groundwork for the client to see that she always has control—if not direct control to change the facts of the situation, then emotional control to direct her response to the facts.

The following excerpt is from the fourth session.

The professional counselor wants to create small stressors and successes prior to and in order to prepare her for the court date, which will surely be a large stressor requiring much resiliency.

C: So, I'm curious, what might it be like for you to run into him, into Tray I mean?

S: Hmm. (Begins to fidget with the bottom of her t-shirt.) Do I have to think about that?

C: Seems to me you probably already think about it. I would guess you think about it often.

S: True enough. I imagine it in my mind.

C: Tell me about what you imagine it to be like.

S: Well, for some reason I always think it's going to be right outside the library when it happens. Like I'd be walking in and he'd be walking out or something like that. I can see him coming long before I get to where he is. And I panic. I stop in my tracks and just stare. I start to shake and I want to scream really loud for someone to help me. I want someone to jump in between me and him to protect me . . . to guard me. But no one does. And I can't scream. My voice seems to be completely gone. And then I start to feel sick . . . really sick . . . like I'm going to throw up.

C: Then what?

S: Then I start to focus on my stomach and the image goes away.

C: Wow, Sarah. (Takes a deep breath) That sounds like a pretty terrible feeling you are imagining.

S: It scares me to death.

C: Remember how I said before about how all these things that upset you are problems to be solved, and that at least one aspect of each of them is within our control?

S: Yes, I remember. And I like that. It's comforting . . . even though I don't understand how just yet.

C: Okay. Well, taking this situation for example, the eventual encounter with Tray, what can we control about this problem?

S: Well, I remember you said if we can't change the facts of a situation, we can control how we react to the facts, or how they affect us.

C: That's right. And do you suppose that this image you've created for yourself, the one where you freeze and your voice is gone and you want to scream but you can't, and then you feel sick enough to throw up, is this image making it more likely for you to actually respond this way to your eventual encounter, or less likely?

S: I would say thinking about that scenario over and over, playing it through my mind, that probably makes me more likely to actually react that way.

C: That's what I would say too. But let me ask you . . . is that how you want to react? If you could decide right now how that situation might play out, is that what you would choose?

S: No! No, not at all. That's how I'm afraid it will play out.

C: And you thinking it may in fact be making it more likely.

S: Yes.

C: So, tell me how you would want it to happen, just *if* you could choose? *If* you could control it?

S: Well, I would definitely want to appear strong and unfazed.

C: And how would strong and unfazed look exactly on a typical campus sidewalk outside the library?

S: Well, let's see . . . I would stand up straight and I would look straight ahead with my head held high. And I would not have an expression on my face.

C: Can you show me? Can you stand up and go to the door and walk across the office just like you've described?

S: That's silly.

C: But this situation, that will eventually happen, is not silly. We have to get prepared.

S: (Nods head in agreement and changes demeanor from embarrassed to serious. Stands up and walks across the office in the strong and unfazed manner she described.) I want to do it again.

C: Of course. (Sarah walks back across the office and back to the door with her head held even higher.) That was very good, Sarah. Now I'd like you to do it a couple more times and I want you to repeat out loud, "I am strong. I am in control." (Sarah rehearses this several times, walking strong, looking unfazed, and repeating her statements out loud.) Great, Sarah! You certainly look strong and unfazed to me.

S: I do? C: You do. But this is just in my office. Do you think you can practice this week?

S: What do you mean? C: Five times a day, I want you to pick some random guy on campus who is walking your way, and pretend that he is Tray. Would that be too frightening for you?

The professional counselor is careful to assess the degree of emotional risk with this exercise as he wants to create positive and strengthening experiences for practice, experiences that will arouse her defenses but not overwhelm her so that she has a negative outcome.

S: No, I can do that. Because I would know it wasn't really him.

C: Very well. So five times a day, I want you to choose some random guy and as he is walking towards you, I want you to say, "Okay, this is it. I have to be strong and unfazed."

And I want you to immediately assume the posture and stance you've just displayed in here and walk past him with your head held high and your face expressionless. Got it?

S: I'm going to enjoy this.

Sarah is already making the shift from viewing this potential occurrence as scaring her to death to enjoyable.

The following is an excerpt from the fifth session.

C: So you feel fairly certain that the comment was directed towards you?

S: Yeah, it seemed pretty obvious. I didn't know how to react or what to say, so I just left and went home.

C: What about your friends that were there with you?

S: I told them I didn't feel well and I just left some cash to pay for my meal.

C: I see. So it ruined your whole evening. And next time, you would want to address comments like these?

S: Yes, because otherwise I just feel helpless again. But I wouldn't know what to say.

C: All right. What do you say I pretend to be you for a moment, and you pretend to be one of these guys in the restaurant?

S: Okay.

C: Okay. So were you standing up or sitting down? What was going on when this was said?

S: I had just ordered my food and had to use the restroom. I was walking out of the restroom when I passed their table and heard it.

C: Okay. So go right ahead and say what it is you heard them say to you.

S: Okay. "Oh, look, there's Tray's girlfriend." And then another said, "Hey, isn't she the one that . . . "

C: And I might respond with "Yes, as a matter of fact I am. And I would prefer that you not refer to me as his girlfriend." How's that?

S: That would have been good. It was strong and unashamed and unemotional.

C: What do you say we role-play a few other possible remarks and situations you might encounter?

The following is an excerpt from the sixth session.

C: So this is something that you really want to do?

S: I really do. I feel like as long as I avoid it, it has power over me. And I've been a lot of things this past year—mostly fearful and anxious. But now I think I'm actually ready to grieve like we talked about last time. I lost something back there. Something I may never have again. And I need to grieve that. I owe myself that. And with the 1-year mark coming up, I think this would be an excellent way for me to stop avoiding the place, to grieve what happened, and to move past another hurdle as a way to commemorate the 1-year anniversary. I'm ready. It's time. I know it's a huge step but I feel more confident. I mean, I know it won't be easy at all. But I'm ready for this next step.

C: Okay. You've decided to do this, so I want to help equip you with everything necessary to ensure a healthy outcome. You've already spoken to your mom?

S: Yes, and she's fine with coming up to support me. She definitely wants to be there for me if I need her.

C: Okay. So what we'll do is learn and practice muscle relaxation and deep breathing today. And if we feel comfortable with it after today, you'll take these tools we've practiced home with you and practice no less than three times a day. Then, at the end of the week, if you are ready, you will revisit the place that this happened . . . the place where Tray raped you. And mom will be there waiting to offer support.

S: Yes.

C: Okay, sit comfortably in your chair and close your eyes. And feel the weight of your body in the chair . . . and now you are very aware of how the chair feels on your back . . . and the back of your legs . . . and you want to squeeze you toes together . . . as tight as you can . . . and hold them like that for a moment . . . and release . . . and you want to now tense the arch of both your feet . . . and hold them very tightly now . . . hold them just like that . . . and now release and feel all that energy leaving your body . . . and squeeze your calf muscles . . . and really focus on your calves and your lower leg and how tense it feels now as you squeeze it . . . and now let all of that go . . .

The professional counselor continues to help Sarah tense and relax each part of her body (i.e., upper thighs, buttocks, stomach, lower back, chest, upper back, fingers, hands, arms, shoulders, neck, and face).

S: I can't believe how good that feels.

C: And imagine you can do that and feel that good three times a day now. Here (hands a compact disc to Sarah), I have it all on CD for you to listen to and do each time. You will find that by the end of the week you've become so good at it that your body has learned to relax much sooner and more easily. That's why it's so important to practice plenty before the moment comes when you really need it.

USEFULNESS AND EVALUATION OF THE STRESS INOCULATION TRAINING TECHNIQUE

Stress inoculation training can be used for both remediation and prevention. It has been applied to a variety of issues, such as speech anxiety, test anxiety, phobias, anger, assertion training, social incompetence, depression, and social withdrawal in children (Corey, 2007). This training has also been used with persons coping with stress due to life transitions, medical patients, athletes, teachers, military personnel, and police officers (Meichenbaum, 1993).

Studies show the effectiveness of stress inoculation training. Sheely and Horan (2004) studied stress among law students and discovered that students receiving SIT exhibited a decline in stress and irrational beliefs which endured throughout a follow-up period. In addition, Schuler, Gilner, Austrin, and Davenport (1982) examined the effectiveness of stress inoculation training with and without the education phase as a treatment for public speaking anxiety. Those receiving full SIT including the education phase reduced anxiety significantly more that those who experienced only the rehearsal and application phases of the training. Those receiving full SIT reported higher levels of confidence as a speaker and lower levels of communication apprehension. No studies were located that indicated any adverse effects of SIT.

CONCLUDING REMARKS

Successful counseling involves moving clients from problem identification to successful attainment of their goals and objectives. The operational word in the previous sentence is "moving." All professional counselors know how to establish counseling objectives and how to tell when those objectives have been met. All professional counselors are skilled in implementation of a counseling process, whether it stems from a single theoretical orientation, or from an integrative approach. But what happens when the counseling process stagnates, the client becomes frustrated with little or no progress, and the counseling relationship is in danger of premature termination?

In this book, we have advocated for a flexible approach to counseling that allows professional counselors to choose techniques shown in the outcome literature to effectively address specific counseling objectives and create the movement in counseling that is vital to success. We have *not* advocated for the nonjudicious or haphazard application of the techniques contained herein; such an approach is unprofessional and unethical. But when you are in session with a client whose progress has halted, we hope you will recall enough of the knowledge and procedures contained within this book to help move that client forward in the counseling process and ever closer to the counseling objective that both you and the client committed to reaching. Counseling is indeed an art, but a little technical know-how can at times allow the artist to create an exceptional work.

REFERENCES

Abdullah, M. (2002). *Bibliotherapy* (Report No. EDO-CS-02-08). Washington, D.C.: Office of Educational Research and Improvement. (ERIC Document Reproduction Service No. ED00036)

Abrams, M., & Ellis, A. (1994). Rational emotive behavior therapy in the treatment of stress. *British Journal of Guidance and Counseling, 22*(1), 39–51.

Adler, A., & Brett, C. (1998). *What life could mean to you.* Center City, MN: Hazelden Publishing.

Akerblad, A., Bengtsson, F., von Knorring, L., & Ekselius, L. (2006). Response, remission and relapse in relation to adherence in primary care treatment of depression: A 2-year study. *International Clinical Psychopharmacology, 21*, 117–124.

Allanson, S. (2002). Jeffrey the dog: A search for shared meaning. In A. Cattanach (Ed.), *The story so far: Play therapy narratives* (pp. 59–81). Philadelphia: Jessica Kingsley Publishers.

Allen, L. J., Howard, V. F., Sweeney, W. J., & McLaughlin, T. F. (1993). Use of contingency contracting to increase on-task behavior with primary students. *Psychological Reports, 72*, 905–906.

Ansbacher, H. L., & Ansbacher, R. R.. (1956). *The individual psychology of Alfred Adler: A systematic presentation in selections from his writings.* New York: Basic Books.

Arad, D. (2004). If your mother were an animal, what animal would she be? Creating play stories in family therapy: The animal attribution story-telling technique (AASTT). *Family Process, 43*, 249–263.

Arbuthnott, K. D., Arbuthnott, D. W., & Rossiter, L. (2001). Guided imagery and memory: Implications for psychotherapists. *Journal of Counseling Psychology, 48*, 123–132.

Arenofsky, J. (2001). Control your anger before it controls you! *Current Health 1, 24*(7), 6.

Ascher, L. M., & Cautela, J. R. (1974). An experimental study of covert extinction. *Journal of Behavior Therapy and Experimental Psychiatry, 5*, 233–238.

Austin, S. J., & Partridge, E. (1995). Prevent school failure: Treat test anxiety. *Preventing School Failure, 40*, 10–14.

Atkinson, C. (2007). Using solution-focused approaches in motivational interviewing with young people. *Pastoral Care in Education, 25*(2), 31–37.

Axelrod, S., Brantner, J. P., & Meddock, T. D. (1978). Overcorrection: A review and critical analysis. *The Journal of Special Education, 12*, 367–391.

Ayllon, T., & Azrin, N. (1968). *The token economy: A motivational system for therapy and rehabilitation.* Englewood Cliffs, NJ: Prentice-Hall.

Azrin, N. H., & Wesolowski, M. D. (1974). Theft reversal: An overcorrection procedure for eliminating stealing by retarded persons. *Journal of Applied Behavior Analysis, 7*, 577–581.

Bacon, E. H. (1990). Using negative consequences effectively. *Academic Therapy, 25*, 599–610.

Bandura, A. (1971). *Psychological modeling: Conflicting theories.* Chicago: Aldine-Atherton.

Barber, J., Liese, B., & Abrams, M. (2003). Development of cognitive therapy adherence and competence scale. *Psychotherapy Research, 13*, 205–221.

Barton, L. E., Brulle, A. R., & Repp, A. C. (1987). Effects of differential scheduling of timeout to reduce maladaptive responding. *Exceptional Children, 53*, 351–356.

Beamish, P. M., Granello, D. H., & Belcastro, A. L. (2002). Treatment of Panic Disorder: Practical guidelines. *Journal of Mental Health Counseling, 24*, 224–246.

Beck, A., Berchick, R., Clark, D., Solkol, L., & Wright, F. (1992). A cross over study of focused cognitive therapy for Panic Disorder. *The American Journal of Psychiatry, 149*, 778–783.

Beck, A. T., & Weishaar, M. (1995). Cognitive therapy. In R. J. Corsini & D. Weddings (Eds.), *Current psychotherapies* (5th ed.) (pp. 21–36). Itasca, IL: F. E. Peacock.

Benoit, R. B., & Mayer, G. R. (1974). Extinction: Guidelines for its selection and use. *The Personnel and Guidance Journal, 52*, 290–295.

Berg, I. K., & Miller, S. (1992). *Working with the problem drinker.* New York: Norton.

Betz, C. (1994). Beyond time-out. *Young Children, 49*(3), 10–14.

Boelen, P., Kip, H., Voorsluijs, J., & van den Bout, J. (2004). Irrational beliefs and basic assumptions in bereaved students: A comparison study. *Journal of Rational-Emotive & Cognitive-Behavior Therapy, 22*, 111–129.

Boggs, L. J., Rozynko, V., & Flint, G. A. (1976). Some effects of reduction in reinforcement magnitude in a monetary economy with hospitalized alcoholics. *Behaviour Research and Therapy, 14*, 455–461.

Boniecki, K. A., & Moore, S. (2003). Breaking the silence: Using a token economy to reinforce classroom participation. *Teaching of Psychology, 30*, 224–227.

Bootzin, R. R. (1975). *Behavior modification and therapy: An introduction.* Cambridge, MA: Winthrop Publishers, Inc.

Borders, S., & Paisley, P. (1992). Children's literature as a resource for classroom guidance. *Elementary School Guidance and Counseling, 27*, 131–139.

Borton, J., Markowitz, L., & Dieterich, J. (2005). Effects of suppressing negative self-referent thoughts on mood and self-esteem. *Journal of Social and Clinical Psychology, 24*, 172–190.

Bowles, N., Mackintosh, C., & Torn, A. (2001). Nurses' communication skills: An evaluation of the impact of solution-focused communication training. *Journal of Advanced Nursing. 36*, 347–354.

Brown, J. F., Spencer, K., & Swift, S. (2002). A parent training programme for chronic food refusal: A case study. *British Journal of Learning Disabilities, 30*, 118–121.

Brown, Z. A., & Uehara, D. L. (1999, November). Coping with teacher stress: A research synthesis for Pacific educators. *Pacific Resources for Education and Learning*, 2–22.

Bucknell, D. (2000). Practice teaching: Problem to solution. *Social Work Education, 19*, 125–144.

Budman, S. H., & Gurman, A. S. (1988). *Theory and practice of brief therapy*. New York: Guilford Press.

Burnett, P., & McCrindle, A. (1999). The relationship between significant others' positive and negative statements, self talk, and self-esteem. *Child Study Journal, 29*, 39–44.

Burr, W. R. (1990). Beyond I-statements in family communication. *Family Relations, 39*, 266–273.

Burwell, R., & Chen, C. P. (2006). Applying the principles and techniques of solution-focused therapy to career counseling. *Counseling Psychology Quarterly, 19*, 189–203.

Byrne, N., Regan, C., & Livingston, G. (2006). Adherence to treatment in mood disorders. *Current Opinion in Psychiatry, 19*, 44–49.

Cantrell, R. P., Cantrell, M. L., Huddleston, C. M., & Woolridge, R. L. (1969). Contingency contracting with school problems. *Journal of Applied Behavior Analysis, 2*, 215–220.

Carlson, C., & Hoyle, R. (1993). Efficacy of abbreviated progressive muscle relaxation training: A quantitative review of behavioral medicine research. *Journal of Consulting and Clinical Psychology, 61*, 1059–1067.

Carlson, C. L., Mann, M., & Alexander, D. K. (2000). Effects of reward and response cost on the performance and motivation of children with ADHD. *Cognitive Therapy and Research, 24*, 87–98.

Carlson, J., Watts, R. E., & Maniacci, M. (2005). *Adlerian theory and practice*. Washington, DC: American Psychological Association.

Carns, A. W., & Carns, M. R. (1994). Making behavioral contracts successful. *School Counselor, 42*, 155–160.

Carroll, M., Bates, M., & Johnson, C. (1997). *Group leadership: Strategies for group counseling leaders* (3rd ed.). Denver: Love Publishing.

Cautela, J. R. (1971). Covert extinction. *Behavior Therapy, 2*, 192–200.

Chafouleas, S. M., Riley-Tillman, T. C., & McDougal, J. L. (2002). Good, bad, or in-between: How does the daily behavior report card rate? *Psychology in the Schools, 39*, 157–169.

Charlop-Christy, M. H., & Haymes, L. K. (1998). Using objects of obsession as token reinforcers for children with autism. *Journal of Autism and Developmental Disorders, 28*, 189–199.

Chaves, J. (1994). Recent advances in the application of hypnosis to pain management. *American Journal of Clinical Hypnosis, 37*, 117–129.

Cheung, S., & Kwok, S. Y. C. (2003). How do Hong Kong children react to maternal I-messages and inductive reasoning? *The Hong Kong Journal of Social Work, 37*, 3–14.

Christenbury, L., & Beale, A. (1996). Interactive bibliocounseling: Recent fiction and nonfiction for adolescents and their counselors. *School Counselor, 44*, 133–145.

Clance, P. R., Thompson, M. B., Simerly, D. E., & Weiss, A. (1993). The effects of the Gestalt approach on body image. *The Gestalt Journal, 17*, 95–114.

Clements, J., & Dewey, M. (1979). The effects of overcorrection: A case study. *Behaviour Research & Therapy, 17*, 515–518.

Cohen, J. J., & Fish, M. C. (1993). *Handbook of school-based interventions: Resolving student problems and promoting healthy educational environments*. San Francisco: Jossey-Bass.

Coker, J. K. (2004). Using Gestalt counseling in a school setting. In B. T. Erford (Ed.), *Professional school counseling: A handbook of theories, programs, and practices* (pp. 123–130). Austin, TX: pro-ed.

Comaty, J. E., Stasio, M., & Advokat, C. (2001). Analysis of outcome variables of a token economy system in a state psychiatric hospital: A program evaluation. *Research in Developmental Disabilities, 22*, 233–253.

Corcoran, J. (1997). A solution-oriented approach to working with juvenile offenders. *Child and Adolescent Social Work Journal, 14*, 277–288.

Corcoran, J. (1998). Solution-focused practice with middle and high school at-risk youths. *Social Work in Education, 20*, 232–244

Corcoran, J. (1999). Solution-focused interviewing with child protective services clients. *Child Welfare, 78*, 461–479.

Corey, G. (2007). *Theory and practice of counseling and psychotherapy* (7th ed.). Belmont, CA: Thomas Brooks/Cole.

Corey, M. S., & Corey, G. (2006). *Groups: Process and practice* (7th ed.). Belmont, CA: Thomson Brooks/Cole.

Corsini, R. J. (1982). The relapse technique in counseling and psychotherapy. *Individual Psychology, 38*, 380–386.

Crawford, R. M. (1998). Facilitating a reading anxiety treatment program for preservice teachers. *Reading Improvement, 35*, 11–14.

Croll, W. L. (1974). Some limitations of the Premack principle. *Bulletin of the Psychonomic Society, 3*, 375–376.

Crose, R. (1990). Reviewing the past in the here and now: Using Gestalt therapy techniques with life review. *Journal of Mental Health Counseling, 12*, 279–287.

Cuenin, L. H., & Harris, K. R. (1986). Planning, implementing, and evaluating timeout interventions with exceptional students. *Teaching Exceptional Children, 17–18*, 272–276.

Cupal, D., & Brewer, B. (2001). Effects of relaxation and guided imagery on knee strength, re-injury anxiety, and pain following anterior cruciate ligament reconstruction. *Rehabilitation Psychology, 46*, 28–43.

Dattilio, F. M. (1987). The use of paradoxical intention in the treatment of panic attacks. *Journal of Counseling and Development, 66*, 102–103.

Dattilio, F. M. (2001). Crisis intervention techniques for Panic Disorder. *American Journal of Psychotherapy, 55*, 388–405.

Davidson, A., & Horvath, O. (1997). Three sessions of brief couples therapy: A clinical trial. *Journal of Family Psychology, 11*, 435–442.

Davidson, K., & Fristad, M. (2006). The *Treatment Beliefs Questionnaire* (TBQ): An instrument to assess beliefs about children's mood disorders and concomitant treatment needs. *Psychological Services, 31,* 1–15.

Davis, M., Robbins-Eshelman, E., & McKay, M. (1995). *The relaxation and stress reduction workbook* (4th ed.). Oakland, CA: New Harbinger Publications.

DeBord, J. B. (1989). Paradoxical interventions: A review of the literature. *Journal of Counseling and Development, 67,* 394–398.

De Jong, P., & Miller, S. D. (1995). How to interview for client strengths. *Social Work, 40,* 729–736.

De Martini-Scully, D., Bray, M. A., & Kehle, T. J. (2000). A packaged intervention to reduce disruptive behaviors in general education students. *Psychology in the Schools, 37,* 149–156.

deShazer, S. (1988). *Clues: Investigating solutions in brief therapy.* New York: W. W. Norton.

deShazer, S. (1991). *Putting difference to work.* New York: W. W. Norton

Dinkmeyer, D., McKay, G. D., & Dinkmeyer, Jr., D. (1997). *The parent's handbook: Systematic training for effective parenting.* Circle Pines, MN: American Guidance Services.

Dolliver, R. H., Williams, E. L., & Gold, D. C. (1980). The art of Gestalt therapy or: What are you doing with your feet now? *Psychotherapy: Theory, Research and Practice, 17,* 136–142.

Douglas, A. R. (1989). The limits of cognitive-behavior therapy: Can it be integrated with psychodynamic therapy? *British Journal of Psychotherapy, 5,* 390–401.

Downing, J. A. (1990). Contingency contracts: A step-by-step format. *Intervention in School & Clinic, 26,* 111–113.

Doyle, J. S., & Bauer, S. K. (1989). Post-traumatic Stress Disorder in children: Its identification and treatment in a residential setting for emotionally disturbed youth. *Journal of Traumatic Stress, 2,* 275–288.

Doyle, R. E. (1998). *Essential skills and strategies in the helping process* (2nd ed.). Pacific Grove, CA: Brooks/Cole.

Dreyer, S. S. (1997). *The book finder.* Circle Pines, MN: American Guidance Services.

Dryden, W. (1995). *Brief rational emotive behaviour therapy.* New York: John Wiley & Sons.

Dryden, W. (1999). *Rational emotive behavior therapy: A training manual.* New York: Springer Publishing Company.

Dryden, W., & Ellis, A. (1997). *The practice of rational emotive behavior therapy* (2nd ed.). New York: Springer Publishing Company.

Eckstein, D. (1997). Reframing as a specific interpretive counseling technique. *Individual Psychology, 53,* 418–428.

Egan, G. (1998). *The skilled helper* (6th ed.). Pacific Grove, CA: Brooks/Cole.

Elias, M. J. (1983). Improving coping skills of emotionally disturbed boys through television-based social problem solving. *American Journal of Orthopsychiatry, 53,* 61–71.

Elliot, P. A., Barlow, F., Hooper, A., & Kingerlee, P. E. (1979). Maintaining patients' improvements in a token economy. *Behaviour Research & Therapy, 17,* 355–367.

Ellis, A. (1993). Reflections on rational-emotive therapy. *Journal of Consulting and Clinical Psychology, 61,* 199–201.

Ellis, A. (1996). *Better, deeper, and more enduring brief therapy: The rational emotive behavior therapy approach.* New York: Brunner/Mazel Inc.

Ellis, A. (1997a). Must musterbation and demandingness lead to emotional disorders? *Psychotherapy: Theory, Research, Practice, Training, 34,* 95–98.

Ellis, A. (1997b). Using rational emotive behavior therapy techniques to cope with disability. *Professional Psychology: Research and Practice, 28,* 17–22.

Ellis, A. (1999). Why rational-emotive therapy to rational emotive behavior therapy? *Psychotherapy: Theory, Research, Practice, Training, 36,* 154–159.

Ellis, A., Shaughnessy, M., & Mahan, V. (2002). An interview with Albert Ellis about rational emotive behavior therapy. *North American Journal of Psychology, 4,* 355–362.

Ellis, A., & Wilde, J. (2002). *Case studies in rational emotive behavior therapy with children and adolescents.* Upper Saddle River NJ: Merrill Prentice Hall.

Emlyn-Jones R. (2007). Think about it till it hurts: Targeting intensive services to facilitate behavior change – two examples from the field of substance misuse. *Criminal Behavior & Mental Health, 17,* 234–241.

Epstein, R. (2001). The prince of reason. *Psychology Today, 34,* 66–76.

Erford, B. T. (1999). A modified time-out procedure for children with noncompliant or defiant behaviors. *Professional School Counseling, 2,* 205–210.

Erford, B. T. (2000). *The mutual storytelling game CD-rom.* Alexandria, VA: American Counseling Association.

Erford, B. T. (2001). *Stressbuster relaxation exercises* (Vol. 1). Alexandria, VA: American Counseling Association.

Erford, B. T. (Ed.)(2007). *Transforming the school counseling profession* (2nd ed.). Columbus, OH: Pearson Merrill Prentice Hall.

Erford, B. T. (Ed.)(2008a). *Research and evaluation in Counseling.* Boston: Houghton Mifflin/Lahaska Press.

Erford, B. T. (2008b). How to write learning objectives. In B. T. Erford (Ed.), *Professional school counseling: A handbook of theories, programs, and practices* (2nd ed.)(pp. 273–278). Austin, TX: pro-ed.

Evans, J. R., Velsor, P. V., & Schumacher, J. E. (2002). Addressing adolescent depression: A role for school counselors. *Professional School Counseling, 5,* 211–219.

Faelton, S., & Diamond, D. (1990). *Tension turnaround.* Emmaus, PA: Rodale Press.

Filcheck, H. A., McNeil, C. B., Greco, L. A., & Bernard, R. S. (2004). Using a whole-class token economy and coaching of teacher skills in a preschool classroom to manage disruptive behavior. *Psychology in the Schools, 41,* 351–361.

Flowers, J. V. (1991). A behavioural method of increasing self-confidence in elementary school children: Treatment and modeling results. *British Journal of Educational Psychology, 61,* 13–18.

Ford, J. D., & Foster, S. L. (1976, January). Extrinsic incentives and token-based programs: A reevaluation. *American Psychologist, 31,* 87–90.

Foxx, R. M., & Azrin, N. H. (1972). Restitution: A method of eliminating aggressive-disruptive behavior of retarded and brain damaged patients. *Behaviour Research & Therapy, 10,* 15–27.

Foxx, R. M., & Shapiro, S. T. (1978). The timeout ribbon: A nonexclusionary timeout procedure. *Journal of Applied Behavior Analysis, 11,* 125–136.

Frankl, V. E. (1946). *Man's search for meaning.* London: Hodder & Stoughton.

Franklin, C., Streeter, C. L., Kim, J. S., & Tripodi, S. J., (2007). The effectiveness of a solution-focused, public alternative school for dropout prevention and retrieval. *Children & Schools, 29,* 133–144.

Frew, J. (1992). From the perspective of the environment. *The Gestalt Journal, 15,* 39–60.

Frey, A. J., & Doyle, H. D. (2001). Classroom meetings: A program model. *Children & Schools, 23,* 212–223.

Gallagher, P. A. (1995). *Teaching students with behavior disorders: Techniques and activities for classroom instruction* (2nd ed.). Denver: Love.

Gardner, R. A. (1974). The mutual storytelling technique in the treatment of psychogenic problems secondary to minimal brain dysfunction. *Journal of Learning Disabilities, 7,* 135–143.

Gardner, R. A. (1986). *The psychotherapeutic techniques of Richard A. Gardner.* Cresskill, NJ: Creative Therapeutics.

George, E., Iveson, C., & Ratner, H. (1990). *Problem to solution.* London: BT Press.

George, R. L., & Christiani, T. S. (1995). *Counseling: Theory and practice* (4th ed.). Boston: Allyn & Bacon.

Gilliland, B. E., & James, R. K. (1998). *Theories and strategies in counseling and psychotherapy.* Boston: Allyn & Bacon.

Gilliland, B. E., James, R. K., & Bowman, J. T. (1994). *Theories and strategies in counseling and psychotherapy* (3rd ed.). Boston: Allyn & Bacon.

Girdano, D. A., Everly, G. S., & Dusek, D. E. (1990). *Controlling stress and tension: A holistic approach* (3rd ed.). Englewood Cliffs, NJ: Prentice Hall.

Gitlin-Weiner, K., Sandgrund, A., & Schaefer, C. (Eds.) (2000). *Play diagnosis and assessment* (2nd ed.). New York: John Wiley & Sons.

Gladding, S., & Gladding, C. (1991). The ABCs of bibliotherapy for school counselors. *School Counselor, 39,* 7–11.

Gonsalkorale, W. (1996). The use of hypnosis in medicine: The possible pathways involved. *European Journal of Gastroenterology & Hepatology, 8,* 520–524.

Gonzalez, J., Nelson, J., Gutkin, T., Saunders, A., Galloway, A., & Shwery, C. (2004). Rational emotive therapy with children and adolescents: A meta-analysis. *Journal of Emotional and Behavioral Disorders, 12,* 222–235.

Gordon, T. (1970). *P.E.T., Parent effectiveness training: The tested new way to raise responsible children.* New York: Peter H. Wyden, Inc.

Gordon, T. (1974). *T.E.T., Teacher effectiveness training.* New York: Peter H. Wyden, Inc.

Grainger, R. (1991). The use and abuse of negative thinking. *American Journal of Nursing, 8,* 13–14.

Graziano, A. M., Degiovanni, I. S., & Garcia, K. A. (1979). Behavioral treatment of children's fears: A review. *Psychological Bulletin, 86,* 804–830.

Greenberg, L. S., & Higgins, H. M. (1980). Effects of two-chair dialogue and focusing on conflict resolution. *Journal of Counseling Psychology, 27,* 221–224.

Greenberg, R. P., & Pies, R. (1983). Is paradoxical intention risk free? A review and case report. *Journal of Clinical Psychiatry, 44,* 66–69.

Greer, M. (2004). Positive reinforcement helps children avoid junk food. *Monitor on Psychology, 35*(11), 10.

Gregory, R., Canning, S., Lee, T., & Wise, J. (2004). Cognitive bibliotherapy for depression: A meta-analysis. *Professional Psychology: Research and Practice, 35,* 275–280.

Groden, G., & Cautela, J. R. (1981). Behavior therapy: A survey of procedures for counselors. *The Personnel and Guidance Journal, 60,* 175–180.

Guterman, J. T. (1992). Disputation and reframing: Contrasting cognitive-change methods. *Journal of Mental Health Counseling, 14,* 440–456.

Hackney, H., & Cormier, L. (2005). *The professional counselor: A process guide to helping* (5th ed.). Needman Heights, MA: Pearson Education Company.

Haiman, P. E. (2005). Time out to correct misbehavior may aggravate it instead. *Brown University Child & Adolescent Behavior, 14,* 1–5.

Hains, A. A., & Szyjakowski, M. (1990). A cognitive stress-reduction intervention program for adolescents. *Journal of Counseling Psychology, 37,* 79–84.

Hallenbeck, B. A., & Kauffman, J. M. (1995). How does observational learning affect the behavior of students with emotional or behavioral disorders? A review of research. *Journal of Special Education, 29,* 45–71.

Hansen, J. C., Warner, R. W., & Smith, E. J. (1980). *Group counseling: Theory and process* (2nd ed.). Chicago: Rand McNally College Publishers.

Harman, R. L. (1974). Techniques of Gestalt therapy. *Professional Psychology, 12,* 257–263.

Harris, G. E. (2003). Progressive muscle relaxation: Highly effective but often neglected. *Guidance and Counseling, 18,* 142–148.

Harris, K. (1985). Definitional, parametric, and procedural conditions in timeout interventions and research. *Exceptional Children, 51,* 279–288.

Harrison, R., (2001). Application of Adlerian principles in counseling survivors of sexual abuse. *The Journal of Individual Psychology, 57*(1), 91–101.

Hayes, M. L. (1986). Resource room: Space and concepts. *Academic Therapy, 21,* 453–464.

Hays, D. G., & Erford, B. T. (Eds.) (in press). *Developing multicultural counseling competency: A systems approach.* Columbus, OH: Pearson Merrill Prentice Hall.

Hebert, T., & Furner, J. (1997). Helping high ability students overcome math anxiety through bibliotherapy. *Journal of Secondary Gifted Education, 8,* 164–178.

Help for Families. (2005a). *Response cost.* Retrieved on November 16, 2005, from http://www.helpforfamilies.com/ help/parents/response1.htm

Help for Families. (2005b). *Response cost lesson.* Retrieved on November 16, 2005, from http://www.helpforfamilies.com/ help/parents/response3.htm

Henington, C., & Doggett, R. A. (2004). Setting up and managing a classroom. In B. T. Erford (Ed.), *Professional school counseling: A handbook of theories, programs, & practices* (pp. 287–301). Austin, TX: pro-ed.

Herring, R. D., & Runion, K. B. (1994). Counseling ethnic children and youth from an Adlerian perspective. *Journal of Multicultural Counseling & Development, 22,* 215–226.

Hewes, D. D. (1975). On effective assertive behavior: A brief note. *Behavior Therapy, 6,* 269–271.

Hogg, V., & Wheeler, J. (2004). Miracles R them: Solution-focused practice in a social services duty team. *Practice, 16,* 299–314.

Hollandsworth, J. G., Jr. (1977). Differentiating assertion and aggression: Some behavioral guidelines. *Behavior Therapy, 8,* 347–352.

Hopp, M. A., Horn, C. L., McGraw, K., & Meyer, J. (2000). *Improving students' ability to problem solve through social skills instruction.* Chicago: St. Xavier University.

Horan, J. J. (1996). Effects of computer-based cognitive restructuring on rationally mediated self-esteem. *Journal of Counseling Psychology, 43,* 371–375.

Horton, A. M., Jr., & Johnson, C. H. (1977). The treatment of homicidal obsessional ruminations by thought-stopping and covert assertion. *Journal of Behavioral Therapy & Experimental Psychiatry, 8,* 339–340.

Howard, K. I., Kopta, S. M., Krause, M. S., & Orlinsky, D. E. (1986). The dose-effect relationship in psychotherapy [Special issue: Psychotherapy research]. *American Psychologist, 41,* 159–164.

Huitt, W., & Hummel, J. (1997). An introduction to operant (instrumental) conditioning. *Educational Psychology Interactive.* Valdosta, GA: Valdosta State University. Retrieved November 16, 2005, from http:// chiron.valdosta.edu/ whuitt/col/behsys/operant.html

Ivey, A. E., & Ivey, M. B. (2007). *Intentional interviewing and counseling: Facilitating client development in a multicultural society.* Belmont, CA: Brooks/Cole-Thomson Learning.

Jackson, S. (2001). Using bibliotherapy with clients. *Journal of Individual Psychology, 57,* 289–297.

Jacobson, E. (1977). The origins and development of progressive relaxation. *Journal of Behavior Therapy & Experimental Psychiatry, 8,* 119–123.

Jacobson, E. (1987). Progressive relaxation. *American Journal of Psychology, 100,* 522–537.

Johns, K. (1992). Lowering beginning teacher anxiety about parent-teacher conferences through role-playing. *School Counselor, 40,* 146–153.

Johnson, C., Wan, G., Templeton, R., Graham, L., & Sattler, J. (2000). *"Booking it" to peace: Bibliotherapy guidelines for teachers.* (ERIC Document Reproduction Service No. ED451622)

Kahng, S. W., Boscoe, J. H., & Byrne, S. (2003, Fall). The use of an escape contingency and a token economy to increase food acceptance. *Journal of Applied Behavior Analysis, 36,* 249–353.

Kammerer, A. (1998). *Conflict management: Action research.* Greensboro, NC: ERIC-CASS (ERIC Document Reproduction Services No. ED422100).

Kantor, L., & Shomer, H. (1997). Lifestyle changes following a stress management programme: An evaluation. *South African Journal of Psychology, 27,* 81–246.

Kaplan, D. M., & Smith, T. (1995). A validity study of Subjective Unit of Discomfort (SUD) score. *Measurement & Evaluation in Counseling & Development, 27,* 195–199.

Keeney, K. M., Fisher, W. W., Adelinis, J. D., & Wilder, D. A. (2000). The effects of response cost in the treatment of aberrant behavior maintained by negative reinforcement. *Journal of Applied Behavior Analysis, 33,* 255–258.

Kelley, M. L., & Stokes, T. F. (1982). Contingency contracting with disadvantaged youths: Improving classroom performance. *Journal of Applied Behavior Analysis, 15,* 447–454.

Kiselica, M., & Baker, S. (1992). Progressive muscle relaxation and cognitive restructuring: Potential problems and proposed solutions. *Journal of Mental Health Counseling, 14,* 149–165.

Knell, S. M. (1993). *Cognitive-behavioral play therapy.* Northvale, NJ: Jason Aronson Inc.

Kolko, D. J., & Milan, M. A. (1983). Reframing and paradoxical instruction to overcome "resistance" in the treatment of delinquent youth: A multiple baseline analysis. *Journal of Consulting and Clinical Psychology, 51,* 655–660.

Konarski, E. A., Jr., Johnson, M. R., Crowell, C. R., & Whitman, T. L. (1981). An alternative approach to reinforcement for applied researchers: Response deprivation. *Behavior Therapy, 12,* 653–666.

Kopp, R. R., & Kivel, C., (1990). Traps and escapes: An Adlerian approach to understanding resistance and resolving impasses in psychotherapy. *Individual Psychology, 46,* 139–147.

Kottman, T. (1990). Counseling middle school students: Techniques that work. *Elementary School Guidance & Counseling, 25,* 216–224.

Kottman, T. (1999). Integrating the crucial C's into Adlerian play therapy. *The Journal of Individual Psychology, 55,* 288–297.

Kottman, T., & Stiles, K. (1990). The mutual storytelling technique: An Adlerian application in child therapy. *Individual Psychology, 46,* 148–156.

Koziey, P. W., & Andersen, T. (1990). Phenomenal patterning and guided imagery in counseling: A methodological pilot. *Journal of Counseling & Development, 68,* 664–667.

Kraft, R. G., Claiborn, C. D., & Dowd, T. E. (1985). Effects of positive reframing and paradoxical directives in counseling for negative emotions. *Journal of Counseling Psychology, 32,* 617–621.

Kubany, E. S., & Richard, D. C. (1992). Verbalized anger and accusatory "you" messages as cues for anger and antagonism among adolescents. *Adolescence, 27,* 505–516.

Kubany, E. S., Richard, D. C., Bauer, G. B., & Muraoka, M. Y. (1992). Impact of assertive and accusatory communication of distress and anger: A verbal component analysis. *Aggressive Behavior, 18,* 337–347.

Lamb, C. S. (1980). The use of paradoxical intention: Self-management through laughter. *The Personnel and Guidance Journal, 59,* 217–219.

Laselle, K. M., & Russell, T. T. (1993). To what extent are school counselors using mediation and relaxation techniques? *School Counselor, 40,* 178–184.

Lega, L., & Ellis, A. (2001). Rational emotive behavior therapy in the new millennium: A cross-cultural approach. *Journal of Rational-Emotive & Cognitive-Behavior Therapy, 19,* 201–222.

Leger, L. A. (1979). An outcome measure for thought-stopping examined in three case studies. *Journal of Behavior Therapy & Experimental Psychiatry, 10,* 115–120.

Lehrer, P. (1982). How to relax and how not to relax: A re-evaluation of the work of Edmund Jacobson: I. *Behaviour Research & Therapy, 20,* 417–420.

Lethem, J. (2002). Brief solution focused therapy. *Child and Adolescent Mental Heath, 7,* 189–192.

Liberman, R. P. (2000, September). Images in psychiatry: The token economy. *The American Journal of Psychiatry, 157,* 1398.

Lowe, R. (2004). *Family therapy: A constructive framework.* Thousand Oaks, CA: Sage Publications.

Luiselli, J. K. (1980). Programming overcorrection with children: What do the data indicate? *Journal of Clinical Child Psychology, 9,* 224–228.

Lynch, R. (2006). Coercion and social exclusion: The case of motivating change in drug-using offenders. *British Journal of Community Justice, 4*(1), 33–48.

Macht, J. (1990). *Managing classroom behavior: An ecological approach to academic and social learning.* New York: Longman.

Macrae, C. N., Bodenhasen, G. V., Milne, A. B., & Jetten, J. (1994). Out of mind but back in sight: Stereotypes on the rebound. *Journal of Personality and Social Psychology, 67,* 808–817.

Mahalik, J., & Kivlighan, D. (1988). Self-help treatment for depression: Who succeeds? *Journal of Counseling Psychology, 35,* 237–242.

Martinez, C. R. (1986). Classroom observations of three behavior management programs. Greensboro, NC: ERIC-CASS. (EDRS No. ED269164)

Matson, J. L., & DiLorenzo, T. M. (1983). *Punishment and it's alternatives: A new perspective for behavior modification.* New York: Springer Publishing Company.

Matson, J. L., Horne, A. M., Ollendick, D. G., & Ollendick, T. H. (1979). Overcorrection: A further evaluation of restitution and positive practice. *Journal of Behavior Therapy & Experimental Psychiatry, 10,* 295–298.

Matson, J. L., & Keyes, J. B. (1990). A comparison of DRO to movement suppression time-out and DRO with two self injurious and aggressive mentally retarded adults. *Research in Developmental Disabilities, 11,* 111–120.

Maultsby, Jr., M. (1984). *Rational behavior therapy.* Englewood Cliffs, NJ: Prentice-Hall, Inc.

McGinnis, J. C., Friman, P. C., & Carlyon, W. D. (1999, Fall). The effect of token rewards on "intrinsic" motivation for doing math. *Journal of Applied Behavior Analysis, 32,* 375–379.

McGoey, K. E., & DuPaul, G. J. (2000, Fall). Token reinforcement and response cost procedures: Reducing the disruptive behavior of preschool children with Attention-Deficit/Hyperactivity Disorder. *School Psychology Quarterly, 15,* 330–343.

Meeks, L., & Heit, P. (1999). *Totally awesome health.* Chicago: Everyday Learning Corporation.

Meichenbaum, D. (1993). Stress inoculation training: A 20-year update. In P. M. Lehrer & R. L. Woolfolk (Eds.), *Principles and practices of stress management* (pp. 373–398). New York: The Guilford Press.

Meichenbaum, D. (1994). *A clinical handbook/practical therapist manual for assessing and treating adults with Post-traumatic Stress Disorder.* Ontario, Canada: Institute Press.

Meichenbaum, D. H., & Deffenbacher, J. L. (1988). Stress inoculation training. *The Counseling Psychologist, 16,* 69–90.

Mikulas, W. L. (1978). *Behavior modification.* New York: Harper & Row.

Miller, D. L., & Kelley, M. L. (1994). The use of goal setting and contingency contracting for improving children's homework performance. *Journal of Applied Behavior Analysis, 27,* 73–84.

Miller, M., Kelly, W., Tobacyk, J., Thomas, A., & Cowger, E. (2001). A review of client compliancy with suggestions for counselors. *College Student Journal, 35,* 504–513.

Miller, N. E., & Dollard, J. (1941). *Social learning and imitation.* London: Oxford University Press.

Miltenberger, R. G. (1997). *Behavior modification: Principles and procedures.* Pacific Grove, CA: Brooks/ Cole Publishing Company.

Mottram, L., & Berger-Gross, P. (2004). An intervention to reduce disruptive behaviours in children with brain injury. *Pediatric Rehabilitation, 7,* 133–143.

Moyers, B. (1993). Meditate! For stress reduction, inner peace, or whatever! *Psychology Today, 26,* 36–43.

Murdock, N. L. (2004). *Theories of counseling and psychotherapy.* Upper Saddle River, NJ: Pearson Education.

Murphy, J. J. (1997). *Solution-focused counseling in middle and high schools.* Alexandria, VA: American Counseling Association.

Musser, E. H., Bray, M. A., Kehle, T. J., & Jenson, W. R. (2001). Reducing disruptive behaviors in students with serious emotional disturbance. *School Psychology Review, 30,* 294–305.

Myers, J., Sweeney, T., & Witmer, J. (2000). The wheel of wellness counseling for wellness: A holistic model for treatment planning. *Journal of Counseling and Development, 78,* 251–267.

Myrick, R. D., & Myrick, L. S. (1993). Guided imagery: From mystical to practical. *Elementary School Guidance & Counseling, 28,* 62–70.

Naugle, A. E., & Maher, S. (2003). Modeling and behavioral rehearsal. In W. O'Donohue, J. E. Fisher, & S. C. Hayes (Eds.), *Cognitive behavior therapy: Applying empirically supported techniques in your practice.* New York: John Wiley & Sons.

Nock, M., & Kazdin, A. (2005). Randomized control trial of a brief intervention for increasing participation in parent management training. *Journal of Consulting and Clinical Psychology, 73,* 872–879.

Nuernberger, P. (1981). *Freedom from stress: A holistic approach.* Honesdale, PA: The Himalayan International Institute of Yoga Science and Philosophy.

Nystul, M. S., & Muszynska, E. (1976). Adlerian treatment of a classical case of stuttering. *Journal of Individual Psychology, 32,* 194–202.

Oberst, E., & Stewart, A. E., (2003). *Adlerian Psychotherapy: An advanced approach to Individual Psychology.* New York: Brunner-Routledge.

O'Brien, J. D. (1992). Children with ADHD and their parents. In J. D. O'Brien, D. J. Pilowsky, & O. W. Lewis (Eds.), *Psychotherapies with children and adolescents: Adapting the psychodynamic process* (pp. 109–124). Washington, DC: American Psychiatric Press.

Ockene, J. (2001). Strategies to increase adherence to treatment. *Compliance in Healthcare and Research,* 43–55.

O'Hanlon, W. H., & Weiner-Davis, M. (1989). *In search of solutions: A new direction in psychotherapy.* New York: Norton.

Okamoto, A., Yamashita, T., Nagohshi, Y., Masui, Y., Wada, Y., Kashima, A., et al. (2002). A behavior therapy program combined with liquid nutrition designed for Anorexia Nervosa. *Psychiatry and Clinical Neurosciences, 56,* 515–520.

Olmi, D. J., Sevier, R. C., & Nastasi, D. F. (1997). Time in/time-out as a response to noncompliance and inappropriate behavior with children with developmental disabilities: Two case studies. *Psychology in the Schools, 34,* 31–39.

Olson, R. L., & Roberts, M. W. (1987). Alternative treatments for sibling aggression. *Behavior Therapy, 18,* 243–250.

Orr, J. (in press). Counseling theories: Traditional and alternative approaches. In D. G. Hays & B. T. Erford (Eds.), *Developing multicultural counseling competency: A systems approach.* Columbus, OH: Pearson Merrill Prentice Hall.

Ost, L-G. (1989). One-session treatment for specific phobias. *Behavior Research and Therapy, 27,* 1–7.

Overholser, J. (2000). Cognitive-behavioral treatment of Panic Disorder. *Psychotherapy: Theory, Research, Practice & Training, 37,* 247–256.

Oxman, E. B., & Chambliss, C. (2003). Reducing psychiatric in-patient violence through solution-focused group therapy (ERIC Doc No. ED475586). Retrieved on July 3, 2008 from http://www.eric.ed.gov/ ERICDocs/data/ericdocs2sql/content_storage_01/0000019b/80/1a/f9/e3.pdf

Paivio, S. C., & Greenberg, L. S. (1995). Resolving "unfinished business": Efficacy of experimental therapy using empty chair dialogue. *Journal of Consulting and Clinical Psychology, 63,* 419–425.

Pardeck, J. A. (1984). *Young people with problems: A guide to bibliotherapy.* Westport, CT: Greenwood Press.

Pardeck, J. A. (1986). *Books for early children: A developmental perspective.* New York: Greenwood Press.

Parrott, L., III (1997). *Counseling and psychotherapy.* New York: McGraw-Hill.

Patton, M., & Kivlighan, D. (1997). Relevance of the supervisory alliance to the counseling alliance and to treatment adherence in counselor training. *Journal of Counseling Psychology, 44,* 108–115.

Pearson, J. (2000). Develop the habit of health self-talk. Retrieved September 28, 2005, from http://www.healthyhabits.com/selftalk.asp

Pearson, Q. M. (1994). Treatment techniques for adult female survivors of childhood sexual abuse. *Journal of Counseling & Development, 73,* 32–37.

Peck, H. L., Bray, M. A., & Kehle, T. J. (2003). Relaxation and guided imagery: A school-based intervention for children with asthma. *Psychology in the Schools, 40,* 657–675.

Peden, A. R., Rayens, M. K., Hall, L. A., & Beebe, L. H. (2001). Preventing depression in high-risk college women: A report of an 18-month follow-up. *Journal of American College Health, 49,* 299–306.

Penzien, D., & Holroyd, K. (1994). Psychological interventions in the management of recurrent headache disorders 2: Description of treatment techniques. *Behavioral Medicine, 20,* 64–74.

Peterson, R. F., Loveless, S. E., Knapp, T. J., Loveless, B. W., Basta, S. M., & Anderson, S. (1979). The effects of teacher use of I-messages on student disruptive and study behavior. *Psychological Record, 29,* 187–199.

Phillips-Hershey, E., & Kanagy, B. (1996). Teaching students to manage personal anger constructively. *Elementary School Guidance & Counseling, 30,* 229–234.

Piccinin, S. (1992). Impact of treatment adherence intervention on a social skills program targeting criticism behaviours. *Canadian Journal of Counseling, 26,* 107–121.

Powell, J. R., & George-Warren, H. (1994). *The working woman's guide to managing stress.* Englewood Cliffs, NJ: Prentice Hall.

Premack, D. (1962). Reversibility of the reinforcement relation. *Science, 136,* 255–257.

Presbury, J. H., Echterling, L. G., & McKee, J. E. (2002). *Ideas and tools for brief counseling.* Upper Saddle River, NJ: Pearson Education.

Prins, P., & Hanewald, G. (1999). Coping self-talk and cognitive interference in anxious children. *Journal of Consulting and Clinical Psychology, 67,* 435–439.

Proctor, M. A., & Morgan, D. (1991). Effectiveness of a response cost raffle procedure on the disruptive classroom behavior of adolescents with behavior problems. *School Psychology Review, 20,* 97–109.

Prout, H. T., & Brown, D. T. (1999). *Counseling and psychotherapy with children and adolescents* (3rd ed). New York: John Wiley & Sons.

Purdon, C., & Clark, D. A. (2001). Suppression of obsession-like thoughts in nonclinical individuals: Impact on thought frequency, appraisal and mood state. *Behaviour Research and Therapy, 39,* 1163–1181.

Quigney, T. A., & Studer, J. R., (1999). Using solution-focused intervention for behavioral problems in an inclusive classroom. *American Secondary Education, 28*(1), 10–18.

Rabinowitz, F. (1997). Teaching counseling through a semester long role play. *Counselor Education & Supervision, 36,* 216–224.

Rasmussen, P. R. (2002). Resistance: The fear behind it and tactics for reducing it. *The Journal of Individual Psychology, 58,* 148–159.

Rasmussen, P. R., & Dover, G. J., (2006). The purposefulness of anxiety and depression: Adlerian and evolutionary views. *The Journal of Individual Psychology, 62,* 366–396.

Reid, R. (1999). Attention Deficit Hyperactivity Disorder: Effective methods for the classroom. *Focus on Exceptional Children, 32(4),* 1–20.

Reinecke, D. R., Newman, B., & Meinberg, D. L. (1999, Spring). Self-management of sharing in three pre-schoolers with autism. *Education and Training in Mental Retardation and Developmental Disabilities, 34,* 312–317.

Reiter, M. D. (2004). The surprise task: A solution-focused formula task for families. *Journal of Family Psychotherapy, 14(3),* 37–45.

Reitman, D., & Drabman, R. S. (1999). Multifaceted uses of a simple timeout record in the treatment of a noncompliant 8-year-old boy. *Education & Treatment of Children, 22,* 136–146.

Remer, R. (1984). The effects of interpersonal confrontation on males. *American Mental Health Counselors Association Journal, 6,* 56–70.

Rhones, J., & Ajmal, Y. (1995). *Solution focused thinking in schools: Behaviour, reading and organisation.* London: BT Press.

Richmond, R. L. (1998). Systematic desensitization. Retrieved on September 21, 2005, from http://wwww.guidetopsychology.com/sysden.htm

Ridley, C. R. (1995). *Overcoming unintentional racism in counseling and therapy: A practitioner's guide to intentional intervention.* Thousand Oaks, CA: Sage.

Riordan, R., & Wilson, L. (1989). Bibliotherapy: Does it work? *Journal of Counseling & Development, 67,* 506–508.

Robbins, M. S., Alexander, J. F., & Turner C. W. (2000). Disrupting defensive family interactions in family therapy with delinquent youth. *Journal of Family Psychology, 14,* 688–701.

Roemer, L., & Burkovec, T. D. (1994). Effect of suppressing thoughts about emotional material. *Journal of Abnormal Psychology, 103,* 467–474.

Roome, J., & Romney, D. (1985). Reducing anxiety in gifted children by inducing relaxation. *Roeper Review, 7,* 177–179.

Ross, M., & Berger, R. (1996). Effects of stress inoculation training on athletes' post-surgical pain and rehabilitation after orthopedic injury. *Journal of Consulting and Clinical Psychology, 64,* 406–410.

Ruth, W. J. (1994). Goal setting, responsibility training, and fixed ratio reinforcement: Ten-month application to students with emotional disturbance in a public school setting. *Psychology in the Schools, 31,* 146–154.

Rutledge, P. C. (1998). Obsessionality and the attempted suppression of unpleasant personal intrusive thoughts. *Behaviour Research and Therapy, 36,* 403–416.

Salend, S. J., & Allen, E. M. (1985). Comparative effects of externally managed and self-managed response-cost systems on inappropriate classroom behavior. *Journal of School Psychology, 23,* 59–67.

Saltzberg, J., & Dattilio, F. (1996). Cognitive techniques in clinical practice. *Guidance & Counseling, 11,* 27–31.

Sam Houston State University Counseling Center. (2006). Breathing techniques. Retrieved on September 5, 2005, from http://www.shsu.edu/~counsel/hs/breathtech.html

Samaan, M. (1975). Thought-stopping and flooding in a case of hallucinations, obessions, and homicidal-suicidal behavior. *Journal of Behavioral Therapy & Experimental Psychiatry, 6,* 65–67.

Schaeffer, C. E., & O'Connor, K. J. (Eds.)(1983). *Handbook of play therapy.* New York: John Wiley & Sons.

Schafer, W. (1998). *Stress management for wellness* (4th ed.). Fort Worth, TX: Harcourt Brace Jovanovich College Publishers.

Schoettle, U. C. (1980). Guided imagery: A tool in child psychotherapy. *American Journal of Psychotherapy, 34,* 220–227.

Schuler, K., Gilner, F., Austrin, H., & Davenport, G. (1982). Contribution of the education phase to stress-inoculation training. *Psychological Reports, 51,* 611–617.

Schumacher, R., & Wantz, R. (1995). Constructing and using interactive workbooks to promote therapeutic goals. *Elementary School Guidance and Counseling, 29,* 303–310.

Scorzelli, J. F., & Gold, J. (1999). The mutual storytelling writing game. *Journal of Mental Health Counseling, 21, 113–123.*

Self-Brown, S. R., & Mathews, S. (2003, November/December). Effects of classroom structure on student achievement goal orientation. *The Journal of Educational Research, 97,* 106–111.

Seligman, L. (2001). *Systems, strategies, and skills of counseling and psychotherapy.* Upper Saddle River, NJ: Merrill Prentice Hall.

Shapiro, F. (2001). *Eye movement desensitization and reprocessing: Basic principles, protocols, and procedures* (2nd ed.). New York: Guilford Press.

Shapiro, L. (1994). 101 *Tricks of the trade.* Plainview, NY: Childswork Childsplay.

Sharry, J. (2004). *Counseling children, adolescents and families. A strengths-based approach.* Thousand Oaks, CA: Sage Publications.

Shechtman, Z. (2000). An innovative intervention for treatment of child and adolescent aggression: An outcome study. *Psychology in the Schools, 37,* 157–167.

Sheely, R., & Horan, J. J. (2004). Effects of stress inoculation training for 1st-year law students. *International Journal of Stress Management, 11,* 41–55.

Shepard, D. (1992). Using screenwriting techniques to create realistic and ethical role plays. *Counselor Education & Supervision, 42,* 145–158.

Sherburne, S., Utley, B., McConnell, S., & Gannon, J. (1988). Decreasing violent or aggressive theme play among preschool children with behavior disorders. *Exceptional Children,55,* 166–173.

Silverman, K., Chutuape, M. A., Bigelow, G. E., & Stitzer, M. L. (1999). Voucher-based reinforcement of cocaine abstinence in treatment-resistant methadone patients: Effects of reinforcement magnitude. *Psychopharmacology, 146,* 128–138.

Sklare, G. B. (2005). *Brief counseling that works: A solution-focused approach for school counselors* (2nd ed.). Thousand Oaks, CA: Corwin Press.

Smead, R. (1995). *Skills and techniques for group work with children and adolescents.* Champaign, IL: Research Press.

Smith, G., & Celano, M. (2000). Revenge of the mutant cockroach: Culturally adapted storytelling in the treatment of a low-income African-American boy. *Cultural Diversity and Ethnic Minority Psychology, 6,* 220–227.

Smith, I. C. (2005). Solution-focused brief therapy with people with learning disabilities: A case study. *British Journal of Learning Disabilities, 33,* 102–105.

Smith, M. A., & Misra, A. (1992). A comprehensive management system for students in regular classrooms. *The Elementary School Journal, 92,* 353–371.

Smith, S. (2002). *Applying cognitive-behavioral techniques to social skills instruction* (Report No. EDO-EC-02-08). Arlington, VA: ERIC Clearinghouse on Disabilities and Gifted Education. (ERIC Document Reproduction Service No. ED469279).

Smokowski, P. R. (2003). Beyond role-playing: Using technology to enhance modeling and behavioral rehearsal in group work practice. *Journal for Specialists in Group Work, 28,* 9–22.

Southam-Gerow, M. A., & Kendall, P. C. (2000). Cognitive behavior therapy with youth: Advances, challenges, and future directions. *Clinical Psychology and Psychotherapy, 7,* 343–366.

Spencer, P. (2000). The truth about time-outs. *Parenting, 14*(8), 116–121.

Spiegler, M. D., & Guevremont, D. C. (2003). *Contemporary behavior therapy* (4th ed.). Pacific Grove, CA: Brooks/Cole.

Spindler Barton, E., Guess, D., Garcia, E., & Baer, D. (1970). Improvement of retardates' mealtime behaviors by timeout procedures using multiple baseline techniques. *Journal of Applied Behavior Analysis, 3,* 77–84.

Stiles, K., & Kottman, T. (1990). Mutual storytelling: An intervention for depressed and suicidal children. *School Counselor, 37,* 337–342.

Stolz, S. B., Wienckowski, L. A., & Brown, B. S. (1975, November). Behavior modification: A perspective on critical issues. *American Psychologist, 30,* 1027–1048.

Strohmetz, D., & Skleder, A. (1992). The use of role-play in teaching research ethics: A validation study. *Teaching of Psychology, 19,* 106–108.

Strumpfel, U., & Goldman, R. (2002). Contacting Gestalt therapy. In D. J. Cain & J. Seeman (Eds.), *Humanistic psychotherapies: Handbook of research and practice* (pp. 189–219). Washington, DC: American Psychological Association.

Swoboda, J. S., Dowd, E. T., & Wise, S. L. (1990). Reframing and restraining directives in the treatment of clinical depression. *Journal of Counseling Psychology, 37,* 254–260.

Tanaka-Matsumi, J., Higginbotham, H. N., & Chang, R. (2002). Cognitive-behavioral approaches to counseling across cultures: A functional analytic approach for clinical applications. In P. B. Pedersen, J. G. Draguns, W. J. Lonner, & J. E. Trimble (Eds.), *Counseling across cultures* (5th ed., pp. 337–379). Thousand Oaks, CA: Sage.

Thomas, M. B. (1992). *An introduction to marital and family therapy.* New York: Macmillan.

Thompson, C. L., & Rudolph, L. B. (1996). *Counseling children* (4th ed.). Pacific Grove, CA: Brooks/Cole.

Thompson, K., & Bundy, K. (1996). Social skill training for young adolescents: Cognitive and performance components. *Adolescence, 31,* 505–521.

Thompson, S., Sobolew-Shubin, A., Galbraith, M., Schwankovsky, L., & Cruzen, D. (1993). Maintaining perceptions of control: Finding perceived control in low-control circumstances, *Journal of Personality and Social Psychology, 64,* 293–304.

Thorpe, G. L., & Olson, S. L. (1997). *Behavior therapy: Concepts, procedures, and applications* (2nd ed.). Boston: Allyn & Bacon.

Tingstrom, D. H. (1990). Acceptability of time-out: The influence of problem behavior severity, interventionist, and reported effectiveness. *Journal of School Psychology, 28,* 165–169.

Tracey, T. J. (1986). The stages of influence in counseling and psychotherapy. In F. Dorn (Ed.), The social influence process in counseling and psychotherapy (pp. 107–116). Springfield, IL: Charles C. Thomas.

Treadwell, K., & Kendall, P. (1996). Self-talk in youth with anxiety disorders: States of mind, content specificity, and treatment outcome. *Journal of Consulting and Clinical Psychology, 64,* 941–950.

Treyger, S., Ehlers, N., Zajicek, L., & Trepper, T., (2008). Helping spouses cope with partners coming out: A solution-focused approach. *American Journal of Family Therapy, 36*(3), 30–47.

Truchlicka, M., McLaughlin, T. F., & Swain, J. C. (1998). Effects of token reinforcement and response cost on the accuracy of spelling performance with middle-school special education students with behavior disorders. *Behavioral Interventions, 13,* 1–10.

Turner, S. M., Calhoun, K. S., & Adams, H. E. (1981). *Handbook of clinical behavior therapy.* New York: John Wiley & Sons.

Upright, R. (2002). To tell a tale: Use of moral dilemmas to increase empathy in the elementary school child. *Early Childhood Education Journal, 30,* 15–20.

Van Dixhorn, J. (1988). Breathing awareness as a relaxation method in cardiac rehabilitation. In F. J. McGuigan, W. E. Sime, & J. M. Wallace (Eds.), *Stress and tension control 3: Stress management* (pp. 19–36). New York: Plenum Press.

Vare, J., & Norton, T. (2004). Bibliotherapy for gay and lesbian youth overcoming the structure of silence. *Clearing House, 77,* 190–194.

Velting, O. N., Setzer, N. J., & Albano, A. M. (2004). Update on advances in assessment and cognitive-behavioral treatment of anxiety disorders in children and adolescents. *Professional Psychology: Research and Practice, 35,* 42–54.

Vernon, A. (1993). *Developmental assessment and intervention with children and adolescents.* Alexandria, VA: American Counseling Association.

Vought, J. J. (1984). Punishment and alternative strategies for decreasing a behavior. *Personnel & Guidance Journal, 62,* 588–591.

Wadsworth, H. G. (1970, July). Initiating a preventive-corrective approach in an elementary school system. *Social Work, 15*(3), 54–59.

Walen, S., DiGiuseppe, R., & Dryden, W. (1992). *A practitioner's guide to rational-emotive therapy* (2nd ed.). New York: Oxford University Press.

Walker, H. M., Colvin, G., & Ramsey, E. (1995). *Antisocial behavior in school: Strategies and best practices.* Pacific Grove, CA: Brooks/Cole Publishing Company.

Walsh, J. (2002). Shyness and social phobia. *Health & Social Work, 27,* 137–144.

Walter, J. L., & Peller, J. E. (1992). *Becoming solution-focused in brief therapy.* New York: Brunner/Mazel.

Warnemuende, C. (2000). The art of working with parents. *Montessori Life, 12,* 20–21.

Watzlawick, P., Weakland, J. & Fisch, R. (1974). *Change: Principles of problem formation and problem resolution.* New York: W. W. Norton & Company.

Webb, N. B. (Ed.)(1999). *Play therapy with children in crisis: A casebook for practitioners* (2nd ed). New York: Guilford Press.

Wegner, D. M., Schneider, D. J., Carter, S. R., & White, T. L. (1987). Paradoxical effects of thought suppression. *Journal of Personality and Social Psychology, 53,* 5–13.

Weikle, J. (1993). *Self-talk and Self-Health* (Report No. EDO CS-93-07). Bloomington, IN: ERIC Clearinghouse on Reading, English, and Communication. (ERIC Document Reproduction Service No. ED361814).

Weinrach, S., Ellis, A., Maclaren, C., DiGiuseppe, R., Vernon, A., Wolfe, J., Malkinson, R., & Backx, W. (2001). Rational emotive behavior therapy successes and failures: Eight personal perspectives. *Journal of Counseling & Development, 79,* 259–269.

Wenzlaff, R. M., Wegner, D. M., & Roper, D. W. (1988). Depression and mental control: The resurgence of unwanted negative thoughts. *Journal of Personality and Social Psychology, 55,* 882–892.

White, A. G., & Bailey, J. S. (1990). Reducing disruptive behaviors of elementary physical education students with sit and watch. *Journal of Applied Behavior Analysis, 23,* 353–359.

Williams, C. D. (1959). Case report: The elimination of tantrum behavior by extinction procedures. *Journal of Abnormal & Social Psychology, 59,* 269.

Wolfert, R. & Cook, C. A. (1999). Gestalt therapy in action. In D. J. Wener (Ed.), *Beyond talk therapy: Using movement and expressive techniques in clinical practices* (pp. 3–27). Washington, DC: American Psychological Association.

Wolpe, J. (1958). *Psychotherapy by reciprocal inhibition.* Stanford, CA: Stanford University Press.

Wolpe, J. (1990). *The practice of behavior therapy* (4th ed.). New York: Pergamon Press.

Wolters, C. (1999). The relation between high school students' motivational regulation and their use of learning strategies, effort, and classroom performance. *Journal of Learning & Individual Differences, 11,* 281–293.

Wubbolding, R., & Brickell, J. (2004). Role play and the art of teaching choice theory, reality therapy, and lead management. *International Journal of Reality Therapy, 23,* 41–43.

Yankura, J., & Dryden, W. (Ed.)(1997). *Special applications of REBT: A therapist's casebook.* New York: Springer Publishing Company, Inc.

Yauman, B. (1991). School-based group counseling for children of divorce: A review of the literature. *Elementary School Guidance and Counseling, 26,*130–138.

Yell, M. L. (1994). Timeout and students with behavior disorders: A legal analysis. *Education and Treatment of Children, 17,* 257–271.

Young, M. E. (1992). *Counseling methods and techniques: An eclectic approach.* Upper Saddle River, NJ: Merrill.

Young, M. E. (2006). *Learning the art of helping: Building blocks and techniques* (3rd ed.). Columbus, OH: Merrill-Prentice Hall.

Zinbarg, R. E., Barlow, D. H., Brown, T. A., & Hertz, R. M. (1992). Cognitive-behavioral approaches to the nature and treatment of anxiety disorders. *Annual Review of Psychology, 43,* 235–267.

Zlomke, K., & Zlomke, L. (2003). Token economy plus self-monitoring to reduce disruptive classroom behaviors. *The Behavior Analyst Today, 4,* 177–182.

INDEX